# Lecture Notes in Computer Science 6758

Zhigeng Pan Adrian David Cheok
Wolfgang Müller (Eds.)

# Transactions on Edutainment VI

Springer

Editors-in-Chief

Zhigeng Pan
Zhejiang University, Hangzhou, China,
E-mail: zhigengpan@gmail.com

Adrian David Cheok
National University of Singapore, Singapore
E-mail: adriancheok@mixedrealitylab.org

Wolfgang Müller
University of Education, Weingarten, Germany
E-mail: mueller@md-phw.de

ISSN 0302-9743 (LNCS)
e-ISSN 1611-3349 (LNCS)
ISSN 1867-7207 (TEDUTAIN)
e-ISSN 1867-7754 (TEDUTAIN)
ISBN 978-3-642-22638-0
ISBN 978-3-642-22639-7 (eBook)
DOI 10.1007/978-3-642-22639-7
Springer Heidelberg Dordrecht London New York

Library of Congress Control Number: 2011934678

CR Subject Classification (1998): K.3.1-2, I.2.1, H.5, H.3, I.3-5



*Typesetting:* Camera-ready by author, data conversion by Scientific Publishing Services, Chennai, India

Printed on acid-free paper

Springer is part of Springer Science+Business Media (www.springer.com)

# Preface

In this issue, we have 25 papers, which are from two main sources. The first seven papers are from the DMDCM 2010 conference, which was held during December 18–20, 2010 in Chongqing, China. The main topics of this conference are: digital media and processing; digital content management; digital media transmissions; digital right management; digital museum; geometry modeling; image-based rendering; real-time rendering; computer animation; 3D reconstruction; geographic information systems (GIS); virtual reality / augmented reality; image/model/video watermarking; image segmentation; multimedia technology; image/model retrieval; cultural relics protection; ancient literature digitization; cultural relic restoration; modeling and rendering for heritage; interactive technology and equipment; media art and digital art; game design and development; digital entertainment. The seven papers cover the following aspects: pen-based interface, urban heat island simulation, VR-based on-line expo, physically based tree animation, 3D face texture stitching, chessboard corner extraction, and textured-based tracking.

The other source of this issue is CASA 2011, which was held during May 26-28, 2011 in Chengdu, China. The themes are varied, covering the following: motion control, motion capture and retargeting; path planning; physics-based animation; image-based animation; behavioral animation; artificial life; deformation; facial animation; multi-resolution and multi-scale models; knowledge-based animation; motion synthesis; social agents and avatars; emotion and personality; virtual humans; autonomous actors; AI-based animation; social and conversational agents; inter-agent communication; social behavior; gesture generation; crowd simulation; animation compression and transmission; semantics and ontologies for virtual humans and virtual environments; animation analysis and structuring; anthropometric virtual human models; acquisition and reconstruction of animation data; level of details; semantic representation of motion and animation; medical simulation; cultural heritage; interaction for virtual humans; augmented reality and virtual reality; computer games and online virtual worlds. Eighteen papers were selected from this conference; the topics have a good match to the main theme of this journal.

This issue contains a nice spectrum of current research on edutainment and we hope it will contribute to and attract more research interest in this area. We would like to thank all reviewers of the papers and all IPC members of DMDCM 2010 and CASA 2011.

May 2011 Zhigeng Pan

# Transactions on Edutainment

This journal subline serves as a forum for stimulating and disseminating innovative research ideas, theories, emerging technologies, empirical investigations, state-of-the-art methods, and tools in all different genres of edutainment, such as game-based learning and serious games, interactive storytelling, virtual learning environments, VR-based education, and related fields. It covers aspects from educational and game theories, human–computer interaction, computer graphics, artificial intelligence, and systems design.

## EDITORIAL OFFICE


Address: Ninghai Road 122, Edu-Game Research Center, School of Education Science, Nanjing Normal University, Nanjing, 210097, China
E-mail: njnu.edutainment@gmail.com; edutainment@njnu.edu.cn
Tel/Fax: 86-25-83598921

# Table of Contents

## Digital Media and Digital Content Management (Papers from DMDCM 2010)



## Computer Animation and Social Agents (Papers from CASA 2011)

# Prediction and Visualization for Urban Heat Island Simulation

Bin Shao[1,2], Mingmin Zhang[2,*], Qingfeng Mi[2], and Nan Xiang[2]

[1] School of Information and Engineering,Huzhou Teachers College, Huzhou,313000, China
[2] State Key Laboratory of CAD&CG, Zhejiang University, Hangzhou,310027,China
zmm@cad.zju.edu.cn

**Abstract.** The simulation and forecast of urban heat island effect was studied. Since the reason for the formation of urban heat island is complex, the current model cannot take all the influence factors into consideration. When a new influence factor is introduced, it will lead to a comprehensive change of the model. In order to solve these problems, the paper provides an urban heat island effect analysis and forecast model based on artificial neural network. The experiment shows the efficiency of this forecast model. Furthermore, the heat island effect information visualization has been carried on in this paper. This prediction model for urban heat island has raised a new idea for the latest achievements of computer technology applications in related fields.

**Keywords:** urban heat island; urban air temperature simulation; neural network; genetic algorithm; information visual.

## 1 Introduction

The earliest study of heat island effect has begun since 1818. Lake Howard of UK mentioned that in his book "London Climate", compared meteorological records of the city and suburbs of London, and found the temperature of London city center was higher than the temperature around the suburbs. It is urban heat island effect. More simply, the development of urbanization makes the city's land surface structure have undergone great changes; at the same time, the energy consumption and emissions in the cities make the temperature higher than the outer suburbs. In meteorology, on the temperature charts of the atmosphere near the ground, temperature change of vast areas outside air is very small, like a calm sea, while the city is an obvious high temperature zone, as the highlighting Sea Islands. The island represents urban areas of high temperature, so vividly called the urban heat island. It compared the image of "urban heat island floating in the village over the cold ocean".

For the urban heat island studies, people at home and abroad have done a lot of work. Jonsson, etc [1] proposed that concentration of particulate matter in Dares Salaam urban areas was higher than rural areas at night; concentration and nocturnal urban heat island intensity was positively correlated. Kevin, etc [2-3] also believed that urban heat islands can affect mixed layer height, thereby affect the concentration

[*] Corresponding author.

Z. Pan et al. (Eds.): Transactions on Edutainment VI, LNCS 6758, pp. 1–11, 2011.

of the surface pollutants. Miao Manqian [4] of China simulated concentration distribution of pollutant with a two-dimensional unsteady diffusion model. The pollutant is generated by a continuous line source, different effective height (20m, 72m, 110m) in the nocturnal urban boundary layer.

In recent years, many scholars began to study the urban heat island simulation. For example, TAS and Envi-met model [5-6] were used to simulate energy consumption patterns of the typical commercial building in the large green space surrounding, and compare thermal environment between with vegetation cover and no vegetation cover. Using computational fluid dynamics model (CFD) Priyadarsini [7] calculated the building geometry, building facade materials and location of the outdoor air conditioning condenser how to impact on the outdoor temperature. Using the city one-dimensional heat balance equation, combing with atmospheric surface layer Monin-Obukhov similarity theory [9], Tian Zhe[8] designed mathematical model of the city hourly temperature calculating, and compiled simulation program of hourly temperature in different underlying surface case.

However, the reasons for the formation of urban heat island are very complex. A variety of factors on the heat island effect is not yet clear. The existing simulation model TAS, Envi-met, CFD and one-dimensional heat balance equation can not cover all factors. Whenever new factors appear in the research results, it is necessary for Model adjustment; and sometimes this adjustment may be disruptive, and need comprehensive changes.

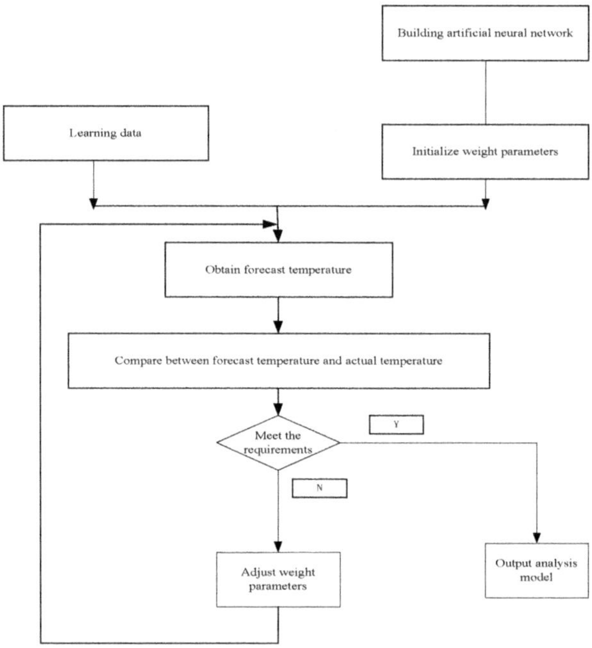


**Fig. 1.** Analysis and forecast model of urban heat island based on artificial neural network

Combing with the latest research results of artificial neural networks and artificial intelligence, the paper presented analysis and forecast model based on artificial neural networks, and made a visual analysis in order to analysis impaction factor at a glance. Analysis and forecast model is shown in figure 1.

### 1.1 Artificial Neural Network

Artificial neural network (ANN) is an extremely simplified model to structure and function of the real nervous system. It has features that a massive parallel, distributed storage and processing, self-organizing, adaptive, self-learning and fault tolerance. It is particularly suitable for treatment of the problems that need taking into account of multi-factors, multi-conditions, or unclear interaction mechanism among factors [10].

Mathematically people have proven multi-layer feedforward neural network has a strong function mapping. Network consists of several layers of nonlinear neurons (also called nodes). A layer of source node composes of input layer; one or more layers compute hidden layer of nodes, and a layer computes output layer of nodes. Input vector enters into each node of the first hidden layer; output nodes of the first hidden layer are sent to the second hidden layer neurons, and so on, until output.

The parameters learning of artificial neural network commonly used BP algorithm, which is a simpler method calculating single weight change that causes change value of the network performance. But the BP algorithm is very sensitive to initial weights, easily converges to the local minimum; often arrests at the flat surface area error gradient, slow convergence or even not convergence. So this paper adopts genetic algorithm to learn parameters of artificial neural network.

### 1.2 Basic Idea of Genetic Algorithm

Genetic algorithm [11] is an optimization method that imitation natural selection and genetic mechanism. It regards each possible solution for problems as an individual of group. According to a predetermined objective function, make evaluation for each individual. At the beginning of the algorithm, randomly select a number of possible solutions to form the initial population; according to the fitness value of each individual, using genetic operators (selection, crossover and variation), manipulate individuals of group to get a new group. Crossover and variation may produce a better individual. Repeated selection, crossover and variation result in continuous evolution; on average, individuals in groups showed a better and better performance.

Generally, solving genetic algorithms of a specific issue includes the following four steps: 1 Specify the parameters, variables and termination conditions of control algorithm; 2 Create initial populations; 3 Determine the fitness function; 4 Genetic operations.

### 1.3 Information Visualization

Information visualization is an interactive visual representation of non-spatial, non-numerical high-dimensional information, with computer and network communication technology support, for the purpose of cognitive. The main purpose is to interact efficiently with large data sets and find hidden internal information characteristics and laws. It is an important part of human-computer interaction technology; it can convert data, information and knowledge into visual form for human perception, or lay the foundation for the further processing information [12].

## 2 Simulation of Heat Island Effect

### 2.1 Building Artificial Neural Networks

For this study, set an input layer, which is considered as factors of the urban heat island. Because of limited data sources in the paper, five factors are set: solar radiation, precipitation, sunshine duration, the average wind speed, underlying surface. Among those, underlying surface has four parameters: evaporation rate, thermal conductivity (unit: $w/m^2.C$), reflectivity, heat capacity (unit: $kj/m^3.C$). Although not many factors are considered, it does not affect research of the overall effect. There are 8 nodes ($x_1,x_2,x_3,x_4,x_5,x_6,x_7,x_8$) in input layer. Set one output layer, which includes one output node as forecast temperature. Considering the model convergence curve and computing time-consuming, set one hidden layer. Mathematically people have proven single hidden layer can implement nonlinear mapping from m dimensions to n dimensions. But determination of hidden nodes number has not any theoretical guidance. Although there are some empirical formulas, they are only for reference. In this paper, set 10 hidden nodes($m_1,m_2,m_3,m_4,m_5,m_6,m_7,m_8,m_9,m_{10}$), which are slightly more than nodes of input layer. Parameters of needing adjust learning are as follows: weight $wxm_{ij}$ from $x_i$ of input layer to $m_i$ of hidden layer, threshold $t_j$ of hidden layer, and weight $wmy_j$ from mi of hidden layer to the node of output layer.

Output of node $m_i$ of hidden layer:

$$y_i = \sum_i x_i \bullet wxm_{ij}$$

$$y_i = \begin{cases} y_i, y_i > t_i \\ 0, y_i \le t_i \end{cases} \quad (1)$$

Formula of output layer node:

$$temp = \sum_j y_j \bullet wmy_j \quad (2)$$

Model of artificial neural networks is shown as follows.

### 2.2 Neural Learning of Genetic Algorithm

#### 2.2.1 Control Parameters

Selected individuals make the crossover and variation operation at a certain probability. Generally, crossover probability is several orders of magnitude higher than variation in program design. Crossover probability takes a value between 0.6 to 0.95; the paper takes 0.7. Variation probability takes a value between 0. 001 to 0. 01; the paper takes 0.005. The total number of population is called population size, which has significant impact on the efficiency of algorithms. Too small is not conducive to

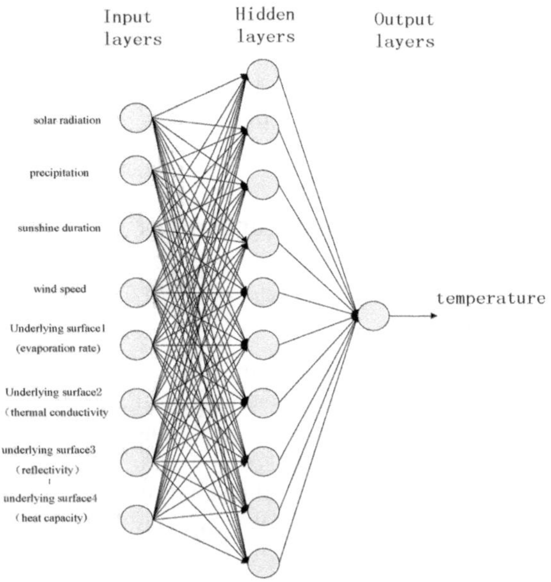


**Fig. 2.** Model structure of artificial neural networks

the evolution, but too large will cause the program to run for too long. For different issues there are own appropriate population size. Population size is usually 30 to 150; this takes 100. Termination conditions are usually taken to be a continuous generation of new solutions which are not accepted.

### 2.2.2 Creat Initial Population

Initial population is randomly generated 100 group weight $wxm_{ij}$ from $x_i$ of input layer to $m_j$ of hidden layer, threshold $t_j$ of hidden layer, and weight $wmy_j$ from mi of hidden layer to the node of output layer. They store using vector. That is 100 group weight $wxm_{pij}$ , 100 group threshold $t_{pj}$ and weight $wmy_{pj}$ ($1<=p<=100$).

### 2.2.3 Determine the Fitness Function

Determination of fitness function should combine with specific applications. Application of this paper is simulation and prediction of heat island effect. So fitness function is defined as differences of learning data forecast temperature and actual temperature. The differences value is smaller and fitness function is larger.

### 2.2.4 Genetic Manipulation

There are three basic genetic operators: crossover, variation, selection.

1) Crossover: In 100 group $wxm_{ij}$, $t_j$, $wmy_{j,}$ two random numbers ($p_1$,$p_2$) first generated. They make crossover operation with $wxm[p_1]$ and $wxm[p_2]$ as parent. Generate a random number k again. Prior k data of $wxm[p_1]$ and latter data of $wxm[p_2]$ compose one new individual. Prior k data of $wxm[p_2]$ and latter data of $wxm[p_1]$ also compose one new individual. $t_{pj}$ and $wmy_{pj}$ also do the same operation.

2) Variation: In 100 group $wxm_{ij}, t_j, wmy_j$, select randomly one data to be replaced by a random number.

3) Selection: Genetic algorithm is the survival of the fittest in the choice of operation. With new parameters generated by crossover and variation, calculate the forecast temperature. If it is smaller than the actual temperature, accept new solution and eliminate the original individual.

# 3 Simulation and Prediction Algorithm of the Urban Heat Island Effect

## 3.1 Algorithm Explanation

In the model, there are two sample sets: one is the training sample set named Source, the length of set is SourceNum; the other is the test sample set named Check, the length of the set is CheckNum. The number of the input layer nodes is N, the hidden layer nodes is M, the genetic population size is P; the weights from input layer node to the hidden layer is wxm[P][N][M]; the threshold of the hidden layer is t[P][M]; the weights from hidden layer to output layer node is wmy[P][M]; training data is Source[SourceNum][N+1]; the test sample data is Check[CheckNum][N+1].

## 3.2 Algorithm Description

Step 1: Read the Source, and randomly generate 100 groups of wxm, t, wmy;

Step 2:

1) Crossover: Select the subset randomly for cross from wxm, t, wmy, using a certain percentage of the $P_c$, uses it to cross-breed.

2) Variation: In addition to mating, select the subset from the wxm, t, wmy, using a smaller proportion of the $P_k$ for variation.

3) Selection: The program generated by Crossover and variation called the new program. After calculating the fitness of the old and new programs (variation or Crossover before and after) using the formula 2, the algorithm can determine the fate of the two programs.

Step 3: According to the formula 2, calculate the predicted temperature of the every sample with a training data set and wxm, t, wmy, and the difference between the predicted temperature and actual temperature.

Step 4: If the difference between the predicted temperature and actual temperature is a certain error, or the better new program is generated after several continuous generations, the algorithm is over. Or the algorithm switches to Setp2.

Step 5: Read Check and forecast the temperature with the wxm, t, wmy received by training.

# 4 Experiment and Correlation Analysis

## 4.1 Experiment Analysis

In order to verify the effectiveness of this algorithm, the paper analyses meteorological data of a total of 36 months from 1995 to 1997 in Hangzhou Xihu

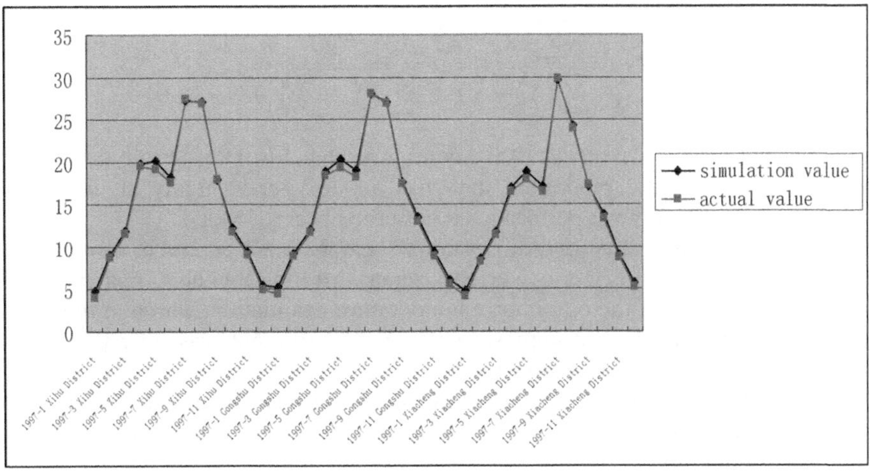


**Fig. 3.** Curves Comparison of forecast and actual temperature

District, Gongshu District, Xiacheng District. Experimental environment use PC of the Intel C2D E4600 (Core 2 Duo core, clocked at 2.2GHz, 2M shared secondary cache). Meteorological data comes from man-land system theme database of Institute of Geographic Sciences and Natural Resources Research of Chinese Academy of Sciences (the original database of natural resources, http://www.data.ac.cn). A total of 72 samples from three districts in 1995 and 1996 24 months uses as the training sample set. A total of 36 samples from three districts in 1997 uses as testing sample set. The weights iterate about 2,000 times to make learning adjust using genetic algorithm. Length SourceNum of various parameters training sample set takes 72; length CheckNum of testing sample set takes 36. Input layer nodes set N = 8, M of hidden layer taking 10, the genetic population size P taking 100.

Comparison of forecast temperature and actual temperature of 36 testing sample set is shown as figure 3

Preliminary observations from the figure we can see, data curve of simulation almost accords with the actual temperature curve. It shows that simulated data can reflect changes of heat island intensity to a certain extent.

## 4.2 Correlation Analysis

Correlation analysis can reveal the relationship of the two variables or between the two sets of data. If correlation is strong, it shows that correlation between these two variables or data is more closely. Or one of the variables or data has a strong following another variable or data trend. Therefore, through the correlation analysis between temperature simulation data and observed data, it can verify following performance between simulation results of simulation program and observed values.

Using Pearson correlation coefficient [13], make correlation analysis; the formula is as follows:

$$\gamma = \frac{\sum (x_i - \overline{x}) * (y_i - \overline{y})}{\sqrt{(\sum (x_i - \overline{x})^2 * \sum (y_i - \overline{y})^2)}} \quad (3)$$

Using the formula (3), results of the confidence level is 0.953. From the calculation results, the simulated temperature data has a very good (highly significant, 95% confidence level) following performance with the observed value.

Literature [8] used city one-dimensional heat balance equation, combined with similarity theory atmospheric surface layer Monin-Obukhov and designed a mathematical model of the city hourly temperature calculation. Through the deviation and correlation analysis, the highest correlation coefficient was only 0.901 and the lowest was 0.812 in the simulation results.

Through the correlation analysis between simulation data and observed data, it is thought that simulation results of simulation program can better accord with actual observation situation.

## 5 Visual Analyses

Taking the block scale as an example, we visually simulate the weather of a district of Hangzhou, Zhejiang Province, shown in figure 4.

The system can adjust property values of the district to directly reflect the various attributes how to affect the urban heat island, shown in figure 5. Figure 6 and figure7 are the simulated maps of December and July.

The parameters of the middle block in figure 7 are set as follows: the solar radiation is 36543, the precipitation is 114, the hours of sunshine is 279, the average wind speed is 2.2, the evaporation rate of the underlying surface is 0.001, the thermal

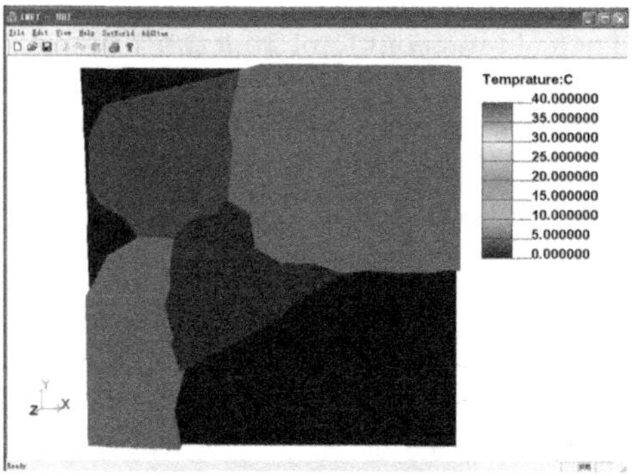


**Fig. 4.** Urban Heat Island Simulation System (UHIS)

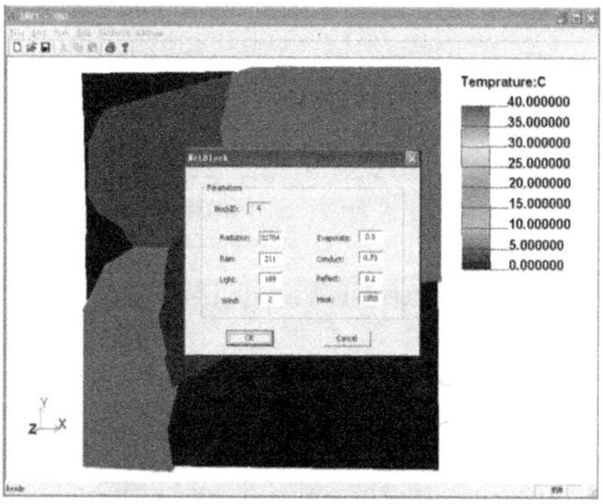


**Fig. 5.** UHIS attributes adjustment

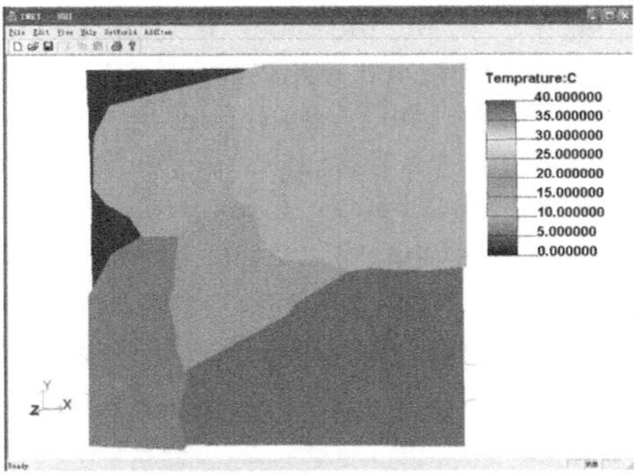


**Fig. 6.** The simulation map for December

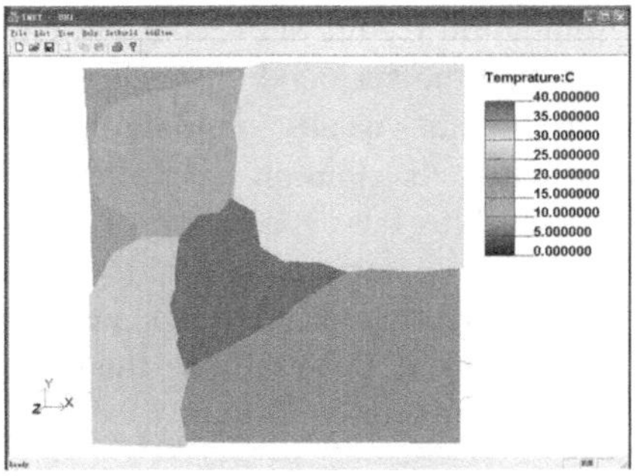


**Fig. 7.** The simulation map for July

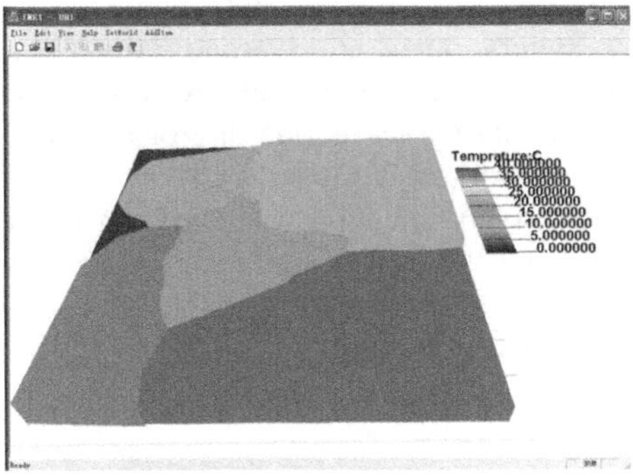

**Fig. 8.** The 3D simulation map for December

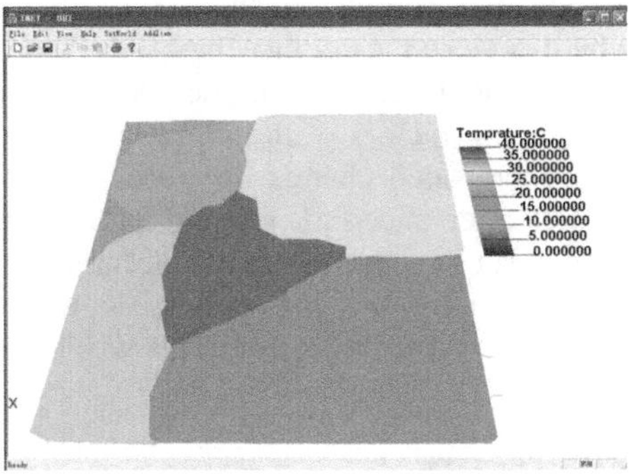


**Fig. 9.** The 3D simulation map for June

conductivity of underlying surface is 1.95, the reflection rate of the underlying surface is 0.3, the heat capacity of the underlying surface is 1760; the different between the upper left block and the middle block is the value of the underlying surface parameters, set as follows: the solar radiation is 36543, the precipitation is 114, the hours of sunshine is 279, the average wind speed is 2.2, the evaporation rate of the underlying surface is 0.5, the thermal conductivity of underlying surface is 0.71, the reflection rate of the underlying surface is 0.1, the heat capacity of the underlying surface is 2500.

The prototype system simulates the generation of he urban heat island and displays the distribution of the temperature through three-dimensional visualization techniques shown in figure 8 and figure 9.

The figure 8 and figure 9 are 3D simulation maps for the December and June basing on figure 6 and figure 7. The 3D maps describe the distribution of the temperature through the three-dimensional visualization techniques. The 3D maps are more intensity and authenticity of immersion, higher quality of the picture and more perfect in the details than the 2D maps, making you have feeling of exposure to the scene.

Simulation results show that the temperature of the middle block is significantly higher than the surrounding neighborhood. The experimental results well reflect that the system can visually simulate the urban heat island, intuitively reflect the various entity types, distribution, and attributes of the entity on the impact of urban heat island. Such as the distribution of water and vegetation, greatly improve the thermal environment of surface space, playing a significant cooling effect. The impact of the material properties of buildings and roads on the thermal environment has also been well represented. For example, the temperature of the buildings with the cooling-type material significantly decreases.

## 6 Conclusion

This paper has analyzed the prediction of urban heat island effect simulation. Due to limited data sources, in this model, the input layer has only five impact factors, of which underlying surface has only four parameters. They are average data of one month, the large size of the data, but it does not affect the study results. When influencing factors of the input layer or data granularity set as one day or one hour, we do not need change the model. As long as the data is input, it can be used to predict after a certain amount of learning. Relatively speaking, the larger training sample set to learn, the more accurate forecast, but the longer study, this time is all spent learning the parameters. If using GPU parallel computing, it can greatly enhance the learning speed. This will be our next research work.

## References

1. Jonsson, B.C., Eliassoni, et al.: Suspended particulate matter and its relation to the urban climate in Dares Salaam. Tanzania Atmospheric Environment 38, 4175–4181 (2004)
2. Kevin, C., Christian, H., Barryl: Estimating the effects of increased urbanization on surface meteorology and ozone concentrations in the New York City metropolitan region. Atmospheric Environment 41, 1803–1819 (2007)
3. Kim, S.W., Yoon, S.C., Won, G., et al.: Ground-based remote sensing measurements of aerosol and ozone in an urban area: A case study of mixing height evolution and its effects on Ground-level ozone concentrations. Atmospheric Environment 41, 7069–7081 (2007)
4. Miao, M.: Numerical simulation of the urban heat island over pollutant dispersion. Journal of Atmospheric Science 14(2), 207–214 (1990)
5. Huang, H., Ooka, R., Kato, S.: Urban thermal environment measurements and numerical simulation for an actual complex urban area covering a large district heating and cooling system in summer. Atmospheric Environment 39(34), 6362–6375 (2005)
6. Chen, X.-L., Zhao, H.-M., Li, P.-X., Yin, Z.-Y.: Remote sensing image-based analysis of relationship between urban heat island and land use/cover changes. Remote Sensing of Environment 104(2), 133–146 (2006)
7. Priyadarsini, R., Hien, W.N., David, C.K.W.: Microclimatic modeling of the urban thermal environment of Singapore to mitigate urban heat island. Solar Energy 82(8), 727–745 (2008)
8. Tian, Z.: Analysis of Urban Heat Island and Study on Impact of UHI on Building HAVC Energy Consumption. Tianjin University, PhD thesis 6, 39–69 (2005)

9. Moriyama, M.: Making method of Klimatope map based on normalized vegetation index and one dimensional heat budget model. Journal of Wind Engineering and Industrial Aerodynamics 220 (1999)
10. Mi, X.C., Ma, K.P., Zou, Y.B.: Artificial neural network and its application in agricultural and ecological research. Acta Phytoecologica Sinica 29(5), 863–870 (2005)
11. Holland, J.H.: Adaptation in natural and artificial system, pp. 23–140. University of Michigan Press, Ann Ardor (1975)
12. Zhou, N., Zhang, L.: Method of Information Resources Visualization Model, 8th edn. pp. 37–58. Science Press, Beijing (2008)
13. Zhao, X., et al.: Mathematical Statistics, vol. 9, pp. 70–96. Science Press, Beijing (2002)
14. Man-land system theme database of Institute of Geographic Sciences and Natural Resources Research of Chinese Academy of Sciences (the original database of natural resources) [DB/OL], http://www.data.ac.cn
15. Mi, Q., Zhang, M., Pan, Z.: 3D visualization of adaptive multi-scale UHI simulation based on a computer aided modeling method. Journal of Information & Computational Science 6(5), 2061–2066 (2009)
16. Yang, H., Zhang, H., You, S.: CFD simulation and study on office thermal environment of Airpark. Journal of Shandong Institute of Architecture and Engineering 19(4), 41–52 (2004)
17. Danny, H.W.L., Wont, S.L., Lam, J.C.: Climate effect on cooling load determination in subtropical regions. Energy Conversion & Management 1, 831–843 (2003)
18. Gugliermetti, F., Passerini, G., Bisegna, F.: Climate models for the assessment of office buildings energy performance. Building and Environment 39, 39–50 (2004)

# Architecture Design and Avatar Customization of On-Line Expo*

Zheng Li[1], Nan Xiang[2], Ruiying Jiang[2], and Cailiang Shen[3,**]

[1] Ministry of Shanghai Expo Affairs, Shanghai,200125, China
[2] Sate Key Lab of CAD&CG, Zhejiang University, Hangzhou, 310027,China
[3] School of Computer, Zhejiang Industry Polytechnic College , Shaoxing, China
lizheng@expo2010.gov.cn, Xiangn-1984@163.com, penancee@126.com, scly1996@163.com

**Abstract.** The On-line Expo is one of the highlights of Shanghai Expo in 2010. It presents the content of real Expo in 3D forms with the help of Internet, multimedia and virtual reality, constructing a virtual environment or platform between visitors and Expo, allowing people to access the on-line Expo in anytime anywhere. In this paper, we first discuss the architecture of the on-line Expo, and then describe the design and implementation of avatar customization. With this method, the system can create the 3D face for avatars based on the input of one front picture of the user without any interaction..

**Keywords:** virtual reality internet, virtual museum, virtual human, avatar.

## 1 Introduction

This Virtual reality is an active research field in recent years. It brings together computer graphics, multimedia, artificial intelligence, human-computer interface, sensors, highly parallel computation and human behavior analyze. It gives the user a more immersive experience and provides a great convenience for the people to explore the macro and micro world where, for various reasons, the changes of the thing's movement are not easy to observe directly.

In the real world, some immersive environments are difficult to achieve because the conditions is hard to reach and the cost is too large. But, virtual reality can transcend time and space, reality and abstraction which put the unreachable environment in front of people. It provides a new way for human development. Virtual reality has been widely used in military, education, medicine, product design, scientific visualization, training, construction, entertainment, art and other aspects.

Traditional museums include galleries and Science and Technology Museum mainly adopt entity presentation to meet the users' curiosity for the distant past and scientific knowledge. The relevant historical knowledge or scientific knowledge is introduced to the visitors in the forms of pictures and characters. This kind of presentation has great limits in display time, space, objects and user observation.

* Project supported by the National Key Technology R&D Program (No. 2009BAK43B07).
** Corresponding author.

Z. Pan et al. (Eds.): Transactions on Edutainment VI, LNCS 6758, pp. 12–19, 2011.

Using online computer technology and network technology, the digital museum can virtualize the display objects to extend these objects in time and space. Online Expo is a special case of digital museum and covers a wider range.

Online Expo can display the exhibit without limitation of time and space. More important, it can show visitors the rarities easily. Utilizing 3D photography, panoramic photography, visitors can observe the rarities from different angles. It provides more choices to visitors and satisfies the individual needs maximally that the visitors can observe what they want. Furthermore, it can realize the collection share on the net.

Online digital museum has been widely applied both at home and abroad. So far, the American museum most joined Internet, 100 of Japanese museum have their own home page on the Internet. In 2001, China launched a project named "digital museum construction engineering", 18 university museums are built, which greatly promote the share of museum information. The museum's online display are mainly static images, some of them adopt panorama, flash animation, virtual reality technology.

About research on technology of Digital Museum on internet, many research institutes in the United States, Japan, and Europe have carried out relevant work which refers to the structure of digital museum, digital methods and retrieval. The major domestic institutes related to digital museum technology are Peking University, Nanjing University, Shandong University, Beijing University of Aeronautics, Fudan University, Zhongshan University, Northwestern University, Zhejiang University and other units.

The analysis above display a digital and network trend on Museum realization. But on technical level, the Internet World Expo, in addition to deal with plenty of static content, there are very abundant needs of dynamic content .So there should be many special processing technology for better on-line display and transmission.

Combining with virtual human technology, we can set a virtual human as a guide in virtual museum; artificial intelligence and data mining technology make the guide be capable of analyzing the historical roaming behavior of the users in virtual environment and provide them efficient tour guide, In addition, each user has an avatar here; the wizard (on behalf of the system) and virtual avatar (on behalf of users) need to interact. On customization problem of avatar, domestic research on facial modeling is relatively late. The first modeling of the human face began in the late 90s [4].

In the past ten years, face modeling and animation have attracted great interest in the domestic. Many different research institutions have done a lot of research work in this field and achieved a number of face modeling and animation systems. Typical researches of face modeling are mainly from Harbin Institute of Technology [4], [5], CAS Institute of Computing [6], Zhejiang University [7], China University of Technology [8] and some other research institutions.

From analysis above we can see in currently online digital museum/virtual environment, researchers at home and abroad have carried out fruitful research and development work. According to our research, there were no special system operations in Expo held in previous period. But Existing online digital museum/virtual environment system has its own drawbacks and limitations. Currently there is a lot static/two-dimensional display, but recent research doesn't make full use of existing virtual reality technology. There is also no effective three-dimensional modeling tool or a platform for virtual display environment. There is no enough interaction between systems which reduce users' accessing interest. Few Interface based on virtual human is provided. There exists great shortness in real-time plotting and network three-dimensional geometric model transmission, the network runs slowly.

There are still shortages in merging of virtual scene and real-time data. The previous network virtual system is mainly on scene simulation. The distribution, position and motion status of the model in the virtual scene are assigned manually. There are no direct relationship between the running states of the virtual scene and the real scene.

Therefore, it is necessary to combine the specific application of online Expo with further studying the key technologies systematically. In order to solve the problem occurred in 2010 Shanghai Expo and build the online Expo successfully, furthermore to improve the technology level and expand its influence in the world, supported by Shanghai local government, a special funs named "key technology and application of online Expo" are founded.

## 2 Architecture Design of Online Expo

Online Expo is a highlight and challenge of 2010 Shanghai Expo for solving global tourists' problems. As a result, the key target of this project is how to set up a large virtual environment with entertainment, interactivity and make it support construction, implement and convenient information service of online Expo.

According to the large capacity, high concurrent service and continued rapid user experience of Shanghai Expo, online Expo utilize technologies such as intelligent content management, hierarchical content distribution, on-demand service deployment, 3D virtual scene construction and roaming and avatar based intelligent navigation. The technology and the function design can be divided into: construction system architecture of on-demand service deployment, research and development service oriented distributed diversified information management and coordination system, network cache based hierarchical intelligent content distribution system, 3D scene modeling and virtual display, efficient resource management and business cooperative technology and avatar based intelligent interaction. Its architecture is shown in figure 1.

(1) Mass-level 3D information automatically and quickly production and hierarchical display
Because there are a lot of countries and regions participating in online Expo, design scheme, material and the scale and parameters they provide are various. So, online Expo involves large scene rapid production and publishing. The needs of terminals and network environment are not the same. The 3d visualization of display application service, digital content production tools and services on middleware need special design.

(2) Strategy based coordinated management and content distribution
Online Expo involves large amount of data storage, scheduling, management. It needs to establish cluster virtual system which cluster the super nodes and make cache service go to peripherization by establishing

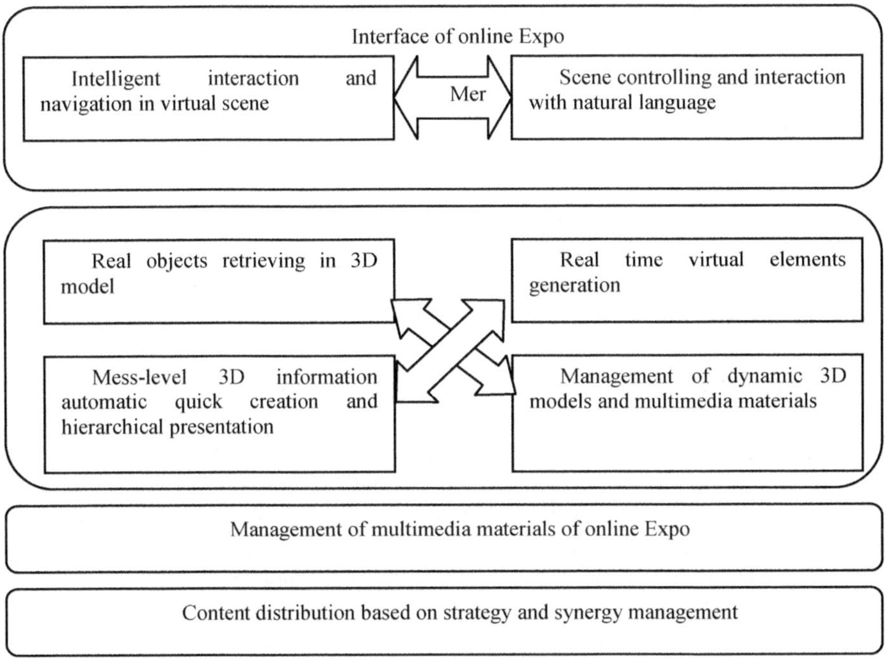


**Fig. 1.** Architecture of online Expo

distributed oriented service architecture. It can reduce the stress of content source server and transmission of core network. Using object-oriented program design framework, the Agent based SOA process collaborative technology to realize business management and coordination. Thus, an effective network structure and management mechanism is established and can provide the user effective information service.

(3) Dynamic 3d models and multimedia data management

For large virtual system, adopt 3d modeling method is very difficult. On the other hand, for the user's involvement, using mobile phone, camera, etc. low-end imaging device to integrate into a virtual system is an important demand. This requires research on dynamic 3d models and multimedia data integration technology. The system Loads dynamic model into 3D image data and integrate multimedia elements to realize interaction between user to scene and scene to scene. It will be a platform for 3D video online production.

(4) Online expo service continuity and information security

For large network service, it must ensure the stable and reliable of server. Furthermore, the virus prevention and the security of the information publishing should be maintained, too.

(5) 3D data search technology

It can handle all kinds of 3D contents created by all kinds of 3D tools cross platforms. And can formulate corresponding special online Expo metadata standard and XML universal description and efficient index system.

(6) Avatar based intelligent interaction in virtual environment
Online Expo needs to build interaction among visitors, volunteers, navigation, celebrities. These involve face modeling, face animation, avatar animation and interaction technologies. This paper will discuss the avatar modeling later.
(7) Natural languages(Chinese) based role behavior control and multidimensional decision model
It makes the avatar in the virtual scene obey the user's oral command.
(8) User input supported personalized virtual scene and characters building

It can realize personalized construction of virtual human from both client terminal and show room construction terminal in WEB 3D model.

## 3 3D Face Modeling with Frontal Face Photo

Every user can control an avatar in the virtual environment. Consider of the 3D scene, the avatar should be 3D, too. Thus, the avatar should support the personalization.

This system modeling can be divided into two parts, the face detection and personalization of the standard face model. The basic process is fist capturing a face photo from camera and then detecting the 65 feature points of the human face by utilizing Active Shape Model (ASM). After this, choose a common face network model as a standard face model and label the corresponding 65 feature points for the network adapter. The detected points can generate points of personalized model by projection operation. The value of the depth equals the experience value of the standard model. Move the labeled 3D feature points to the projection position. The other net points are set by Radial Basis Function. Then a standard model is translated to a personalized face model. The face texture can draw from the face photo correspondingly. The whole process is shown in figure 2. This framework can generate a realistic personalized face model quickly and automatically.

(1) feature points detection

Automatic extraction and mutual extraction are two kinds of face feature extraction methods. The former method using computer vision and image reorganization first locates the face position from the image and then distinguishes the specific position of every feature. Consider of the existing technology, this paper adopts Active Shape

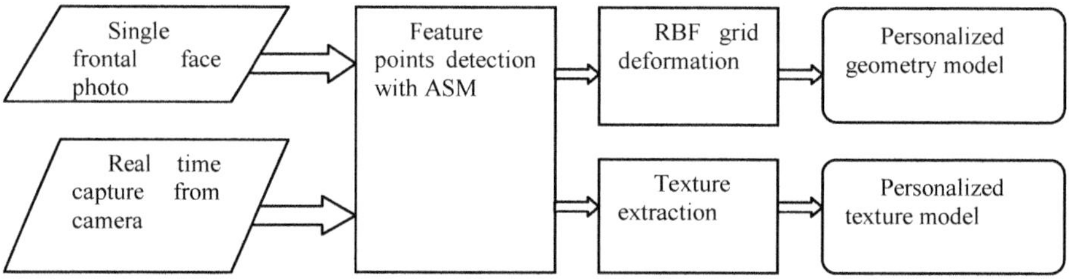


**Fig. 2.** Face modeling framework

Model to implement feature points detection of human face. ASM utilizes a statistic active appearance model. Its basic principle is first choosing a group of frontal face photos for labeling the shape of face with n points and then aligning them to generate a common face model, at last iteration searching feature points along the direction of shape normals with local gray model. Adapt the programs while searching the feature points to make the model fit the target shape and keep it reasonable.

(2) personalization of standard model

The standard model is generated by FaceGen which is professional face modeling software. The vertexes of the face grids generated by FaceGen are no uniform. Vertexes are dense in the part like eyes and corners of the mouth while in forehead and the top of head are few and scatter. The purpose of adaption is to make the position of feature points of the model corresponding to that of images by specifying the some grid vertexes of the model.

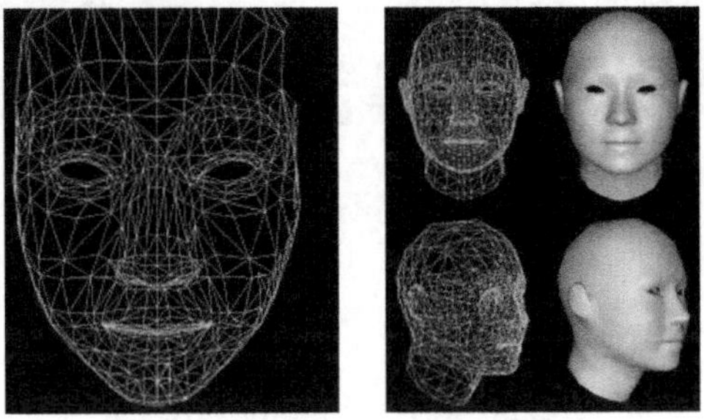

**Fig. 3.** Standard face model

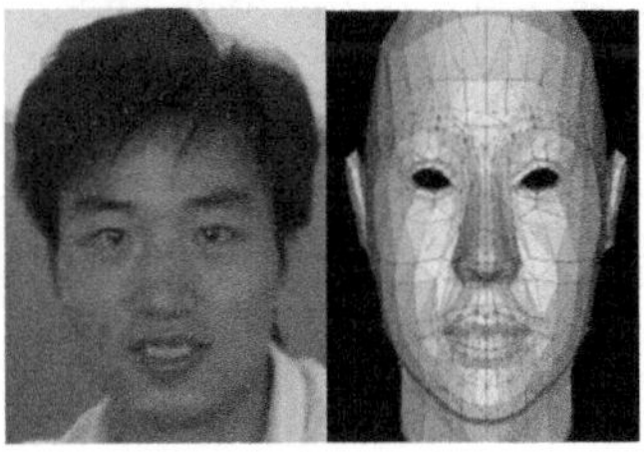

**Fig. 4.** Feature points of the photo (left); Feature points of the model (right)

Manually label grid vertexes of standard face model which corresponding to the 65 feature points detected by ASM. These feature points are utilized to generate personalized fame model which is grid deformation adaption.

The process of transforming standard model into personalized model by grid deformation is the personalization adaption of the model. Our system adopts RBF to realize grid deformation based on constraint. RBF can be utilized in interpolation of three dimension scatter points. As a typical interpolation function, it can satisfy minimum energy and interpolation requirements. The advantages of this method first are deformation based on space and second are independent with grid topology and third are fit the feature points group with any constraint and last are providing the linear analysis expression of interpolation without optimizing and iteration. It meets the need of grid deformation with constraint well. Result shows that, after deformation, the grid consecutiveness and smooth.

This system consists of modeling and animation parts. Modeling subsystem accepts two kinds of input, the photo input and camera input. And the common camera is enough. The image needs frontal face, upright and exposure well. The process and effect is shown in figure 5.

**Fig. 5.** Face capture; Feature points detection; Model generation

## 4 Conclusions

The implement of "Online expo key technology research and application" project aims at supporting the Shanghai Expo and large virtual system and large industry application. It will promote the creative ability and development of high technologies.

The system constructs a personalized face model from a frontal face model and builds a virtual avatar. The results show that the system has advantages of easy input, high automatic process, high sense of reality, lifelike animation and real-time animation. As the system relies on the result of ASM, the results are not perfect when photo are of low quality. So, the robust of the system should be improved.

## References


1. Pan, Z., Jiang, X., Shi, J.: Overview of distributed virtual environment. Journal of Software 11(4), 461–467 (2000)
2. Pan, Z., He, G., Su, S., Li, X., Pan, J.: Virtual Network Marathon: Fitness-Oriented E-Sports in Distributed Virtual Environment. In: Zha, H., Pan, Z., Thwaites, H., Addison, A.C., Forte, M. (eds.) VSMM 2006. LNCS, vol. 4270, pp. 520–529. Springer, Heidelberg (2006)
3. Gómez-Martín, M.A., Gómez-Martín, P.P., González-Calero, P.A.: Game-Driven Intelligent Tutoring Systems. In: Rauterberg, M. (ed.) ICEC 2004. LNCS, vol. 3166, pp. 108–113. Springer, Heidelberg (2004)
4. Yan, J., Gao, W., Yin, B.: Generation of Realistic 3D Specific Human Face. Chinese J. Computers 22(2), 147–153 (1999)
5. Yan, J., Gao, W.: Specific Face Synthesis Based on the Modefication of the General Face Model. Journal of Computer-aided Design & Computer Graphics 11(5), 385–394 (1999)

6. Chen, Y., Gao, W., Wang, Z., Jiang, D.: A Speech Driven Face Animation System Based on Machine Learning. Journal of Software 14(2), 215–221 (2003)
7. Mei, L., Bao, H., Peng, Q.: Quick Customization of Particular Human Face and Muscle-Driven Expression Animation. Journal of Computer-aided Design & Computer Graphics 13(2), 1077–1082 (2001)
8. Zhang, Q., Chen, G.: Realistic 3D Hnman Fadal Animation. Journal of Software 14(3), 643–650 (2003)
9. Cootes, T., Graham, J.: An Introduction to Active Shape Models. In: Baldock, E. (ed.) Image Processing and Analysis, pp. 223–248. Oxford University Press, Oxford (2000)
10. FaceGen Modeller 3.2(free version), `http://www.facegen.com`
11. Wang, J.: Study on Video-Based Face Expression Modeling. Ph. D.Thesis, Zhejiang University, pp. 32–34 (2003)
12. Yue, Z.: Personalized face modeling study. Master's Thesis, Zhejiang University (2008)

# 3D Face Texture Stitching Based on Differential Coordinates

Yun Ge*, Baocai Yin, Yanfeng sun, and Hengliang Tang

Beijing Municipal Key Laboratory of Multimedia and Intelligent Software Technology
Beijing University of Technology, 100124, China
{geyun,ybc,yfsun,tanghengliang}@emails.bjut.edu.cn

**Abstract.** In this paper, we present a new method for 3D face texture stitching based on Differential Coordinates in which 3D texture patch from different face samples can be seamless stitched patch together. Usually, traditional stitching methods for geometric textures involve two works: stitching on shape and stitching on textures. None of them combine these two works. 3D face model is composed of two parts information: surface geometry and texture elements. A natural and realistic face model can be created by interactions between them. So, the approach presented in this paper can get good result. We demonstrate that our approach enables to edit texture elements while considering the shape of face sample.

**Keywords:** Texture Stitching; 3D face model; Differential Coordinates.

## 1 Introduction

Over the past decades, face research have made great progress in theory and algorithm. But these methods are mainly carried out on 2D face samples. It has been proved that pose and lighting variation have a great impact on algorithm performance. Compare with 2D facial image, 3D face sample can provide us with more information, such as spatial information and pose parameters. Therefore, it is effective way to do research using 3D face sample. However, numbers of 3D face samples in current database are relatively insufficient and it is a tedious work to get prototype face model. An alternate way is graphics technology to model realistic 3D face sample.

At present, modeling methods in literature can be categorized into three types: parametrical model, generic model deformation and 3D morphable model. The parametrical method allow user to control face appearance directly. But it is a difficult work to define a complete parameter set. Parke was the first one to use parametrical model to build 3D face [1]. Cohen use a set of animation parameters to controlling face shape [2].The second method is deforming genetic face according to shape information which is calculated by graphics technology. Compare with the former way, it is easy to implement and has a better result. Pighin use five facial images taken from different direction to build a 3D face model [3-5]. Won-Sook Lee

* Corresponding author.

Z. Pan et al. (Eds.): Transactions on Edutainment VI, LNCS 6758, pp. 20–26, 2011.

proposed a method to compute face feature from two images: a frontal image and a profile one [6-8]. The most difficulty for this way is that is a tedious work to detect feature points in face image. By far the most successful approach is morphable model [9]. Matching the model to given facial images, even a single image, realistic 3D face model of the person can be synthesized automatically by adjusting combination parameters of prototypic faces. The method based on the morphable model is automatic and has good results. All these methods are complex and difficult to perform in practical. Based on this analysis, we proposed a modeling way based on organ exchange. Because different face has same topological, new sample can be generated by resampling existing samples. The key point of the method is stitching different organs which are derived from different samples seamless. 3D face model are composed of two parts information: surface geometry and texture elements. Stitching methods for geometric textures involve two works: stitching on shape and stitching on textures. The stitching way for shape information can be accomplished by classic interpolation methods. However there is no appropriate approach for 3D texture stitching. Traditional stitching methods are poxel-based way which can only solve the stitching problem for 2D image. A natural and realistic face model can be created by interactions between the shape and texture elements.

Because intrinsic quality of object can be accurately described by PDE, majority of 2D texture editing task can be effectively accomplished by PDE-based interpolation methods, such as inpainting techniques and image cloning based on Poisson equation. Inspired by these works, we present an editing method for 3D face texture e with which organ texture patches from different samples can seamless stitched together. Basis work of the PED way is to find a good operator. The operator proposed in this paper is base on differential coordinates. First, we use differential coordinates to describe interrelation between texture elements. Then, the discrepancies along the boundary to the entire cloned area are smoothly spread according to differential coordinates operator. The same as Poisson Equation, we also introduce a constraint in the form of a guidance field which is derived from the source patch. Unlike pixel-based image editing way, our algorithm stitch texture elements directly on the surface of the model. Remainder of the paper is organized as follows: The way of 3D face model pretreatment is introduced in the following section. The proposed algorithm will be examined in section 3. In section 4 we will test our approach on 3D face texture stitching operation. Conclusions are presented in section 5.

## 2 3D Face Pretreatment

To perform the stitching work, prototypical 3D face samples are selected from existing 3D face database. The samples employed in this paper are derived from BJUT-3D face database [10]. This database is composed of over 1500 3D faces ranging in age from 16 to 49 years. Half of them are male and the other is female. Each data in this database contains 125601 vertices and 240000 triangle patches.

To ensure the consistency of 3D face samples, all samples in the BJUT-3D database are corrected to a unified coordinate system. The upward direction is z-axis and oriented direction is y-axis.

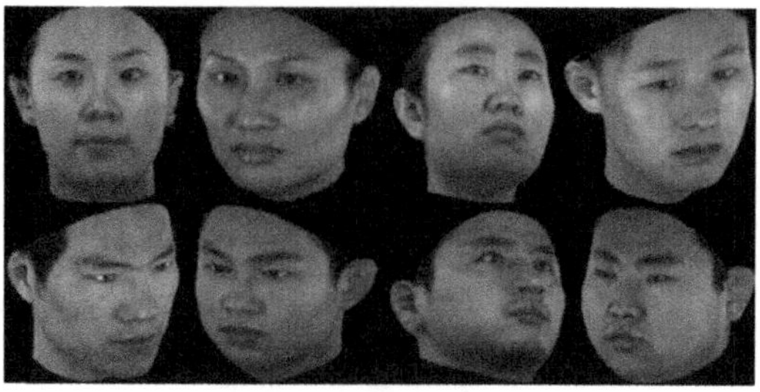

**Fig. 1.** BJUT 3D Faces

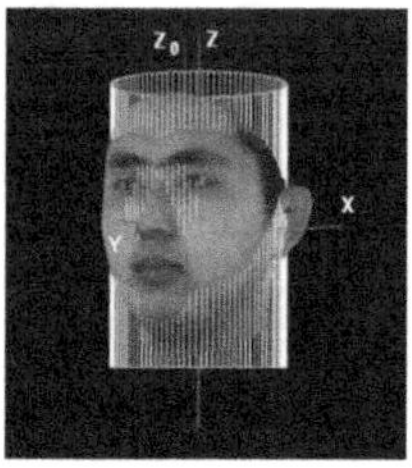

**Fig. 2.** Corrected Face Model

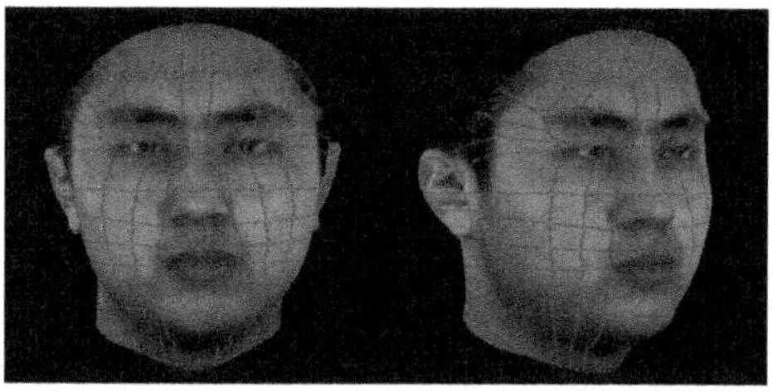

**Fig. 3.** Divide the 3D Face into Patches

**Fig. 4.** Face organ patch

In order to facilitate operation, all samples in the database are aligned based on the facial characteristics. There is a dense corresponding between them in terms of facial organ distribution. First, each sample is divided into 122 patches. Then mesh resample operation are performed on the model to have the dense corresponding.

As the stitching way is stitching new texture patch which is derived from other sample with other face model, the corresponding patch in different face samples must have same num of points. We select some regions that can affect the identification very much as the candidate patches. The selected ones are defined according to the existing face patch. Some of the classic regions are shown in Fig 4.

# 3 3D Geometry Texture Stitching

Here, we present a 3D texture stitching method based on differential coordinates for face model. This method is constructed based on differential coordinates and can solve the stitching problem for texture elements on geometry surface. It thoroughly considers the characteristic of the texture and the correlation between texture elements and surface geometry. First, to describe the correlation of texture elements between points, we devise a new differential operator which can reflect the interrelation between texture elements and surface geometry. Then an interpolation framework is proposed based on PDE. Because of the unsatisfactory interpolation result, a guidance vector is introduced into the minimization problem.

## 3.1 Differential Operator

Purpose of texture stitching is to merge different texture patches at the boundary and keep their local structure at the same time. Traditional stitching methods are to construct a harmonic interplant that smoothly spreads the discrepancy along the boundary to the entire source patch. The key point of harmonic interplant is to find an appropriate operator which can fully represent local structure information of texture elements. However, compare with a great deal of efforts on image stitching, few of them pay attention to the field 3D texture stitching. For the pixel based editing situation, the structure information is computed according to the diversity information on each point. But the adjacency relationship in geometry surface is totally different from the 2D image. The number of adjoin point are not fixed and the geometry characteristic varies from each other. The new operator should consider all the factors at the same time. Inspired by the Yaron's[15] work, we proposed a operator based on differential coordinates. The differential coordinates can represent the details and are defined by a linear transformation of the mesh vertices. The simplest form of differential coordinates is Laplacian coordinates. The powerful properties of Laplacian coordinates for mesh representation have been exploited in various ways. it can effectively used for morphing and free-form modeling and would be more suitable to constrain under a global deformation of the mesh. On the geometry surface, different points have different normal and the distance between each other are not same. All these difference will have impact on the distribution of texture elements on it. After thoroughly analysis based on statistical, we found that the similarity of texture information between points is high when the normal discrepancy and distance between them are all small. On the contrary, the similarity decreases either the normal discrepancy become wide of distance long. According to above analysis, we design the new operator.

Let $G=(V,\ E,\ T)$ be a 3D mesh, where V denotes the set of vertices, E denotes the set of edges and T denotes the set of texture on point. $t_i$ is defined as the texture information on vertex $i$. So the approximation of $t_i$ is defined by linear combination of its adjoin points:

$$t_i \approx \sum_{j\in \text{supp(i)},\text{i}\neq \text{l}} a_{ij} t_j \tag{1}$$

Where $\text{supp}(i)$ denotes the set of vertex indices that belong to set of adjoin points of $v_i$ and $a_{ij}$ is defined as by the following equation:

$$a_{ij} = \frac{1}{w_1 d_{ij} + w_2 \left|\overrightarrow{n_i} - \overrightarrow{n_j}\right|} \tag{2}$$

where $w_1$ and $w_2$ are experience value, $d_{ij}$ is the distance between $v_i$ and $v_j$, $\left|\overrightarrow{n_i} - \overrightarrow{n_j}\right|$ is the normal discrepancy. Then new operator can be defined as following:

$$D(t_i) = t_i - \sum_{j \in (i,j) \in E} a_{ij} t_j = \delta_i \tag{3}$$

where $\boldsymbol{\delta}_i$ is used to describe the texture structure on geometry surface. $D$ is defined as differential representation of the geometry texture.

### 3.2 Interpolation Equation

In this section we explain in detail how differential operator can be used to perform seamless 3D texture stitching. To stitch two texture patches, the stitching criteria should be constructed in advance. Usually we stitch two patches by changing both of their boundary values. However, it is too complex and unstable to change both of them at the same time. In this paper, we set one of them as target patch and other as source patch. In that case, the complex stitching work is change to transform source patch so that these two patches can be seamless stitched.

To merge source texture patch with the target patch, we should let the boundary texture value of source patch agree with the target patch. Since we have defined the new operator, discrepancy of texture elements are spread accord to this new operator. Let $G_S \in R^3$ be the domain of the source geometry texture patch and $G_T \in R^3$ be the target patch. We would like to stitch $G_S$ seamless with $G_T$. Typically the stitching work is performed by finding an interpolating function which can make the transformed patch had a smooth variation according to the new boundary value. The interpolating function is computed by solving the following minimization problem:

$$\min_t \iint_G \left|D(t) - \delta\right|^2 \quad with \quad \delta(t)\big|_{\partial G_S} = \delta^*(t)\big|_{\partial G_T} \tag{4}$$

where $\partial G$ is the boundary of mesh G and $\delta$ is guidance vector derived from the source patch. Its discrete solution satisfies the following simultaneous linear equations:

$$t_i - \sum_{j \in N_i \cap G_S} a_{ij} t_j = \sum_{j \in N_i \cap \partial G_S} a_{ij} t_j^* + \delta_i \tag{5}$$

where $t_j^*$ is the texture value of the i-point on target patch. According to the above equations, we can get a harmonic interpolation which cans seamless stitch the source patch onto target patch. This equation is solved in the least-squares sense. Except that the source patch can also keep its local structure.

## 4 Experiments

We demonstrate our experiment result generated by our proposed algorithm on the BJUT-3D face database. Among this database, 500 individuals are used in our experiment. Half of them are male and the other is female. The subjects being captured keep neutral expression, without glasses of accessories. All the samples are pretreatment according to section 2. In order to analysis the effect of the proposed method, we change some organ patches of the source face model. Then the new organs are stitched with the original face model. The stitching result is shown in the following picture:

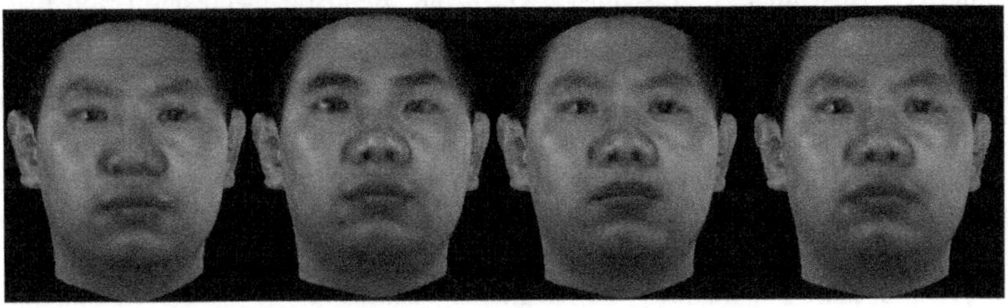

**Fig. 5.** Stitching result of texture

From figure 5, we can see that the stitching results are much natural and we cannot find out an obvious seam between patches. The new organs are seamless stitched with the target face model. The original face models are shown in the right side. The first models have been changed in the nose region, the second one in eye nose region model and the third one in mouse region. Because of the big difference in lighting condition between the texture of new face patch and target face sample, the new must be pretreatment before merged into the target face sample. In this paper we modify new patch's lighting condition through changing the color distribution. Correspondences between two textures spatial in three channels are derived by linear regression. As shown in Figure 5, the results by the proposed algorithm have a good appearance.

## 5 Conclusion and Future Work

In this paper, a new texture stitching method based on Differential Coordinates for 3D face modeling. The traditional texture editing method is promoted to geometric field. Experimental results show our new stitching method based on Differential Coordinates have a good performance on face texture model. Although we have presented a editing way on texture, it still has not fully utilized impact information derived from geometry surface. In the future, we will keep on improving the result of texture stitching.

**Acknowledgments.** The authors would like to thank the anonymous reviewers for their constructive comments on improving this paper. This paper is supported by the National Natural Science Foundation of China (N0.60973057, 60825203, 60973056, U0935004). National Key Technology R&D Program (2007BAH13B01), Beijing Natural Science Foundation (4102009).

## References

1. Eason, G., Noble, B., Sneddon, I.N.: On certain integrals of Lipschitz-Hankel type involving products of Bessel functions. Phil. Trans. Roy. Soc. London A247, 529–551 (1955)
2. Parke, F.I.: A Parametric Model of Human Faces, Ph.D. Thesis, University of Utah, Salt Lake City, UT, UTEC-CSc-75-047 (December 1974)
3. Cohen, M., Massara, D.: Modeling co-articulation in synthetic visual speech. In: Magnenat Thalmann, N., Thalmann, D. (eds.) Model and Technique in Computer Animation, pp. 139–156 (1993)
4. Pighin, F., Auslander, J., Lischinski, D., et al.: Realistic facial animation using image based 3d morphing. Technical Report TR-97-01-03, University of Washington, Computer Science Department (January 1997)
5. Pighin, F., Hecker, J., Lischinski, D., Szeliski, R., Salesin, D.H.: Synthesizing Realistic Facial Expressions from Photographs. In: Synthesizing Realistic Facial Expressions from Photographs, In Proceedings of SIGGRAPH 1998, pp. 75–84 (1998)
6. Pighin, F.: Modeling and animating realistic faces from images. Ph.D dissertation, University of Washington (1999)
7. Lee, W., Escher, M., Sannier, G., Magnenat-Thalmann, N.: MPEG-4 Compatible Faces from Orthogonal Photos. In: International Conference on Computer Animation, Geneva, Switzerland, pp. 186–194 (1999)
8. Lee, W.S., Kalra, P., Magnenat-Thalmann, N.: Model Based Face Reconstruction for Animation. In: Proc. Multimedia Modeling (MMM 1997), Singapore, pp. 323–338 (1997)
9. Lee, W.-S., Magnenat-Thalmann, N.: Fast Head Modeling for Animation. Journal Image and Vision Computing 18(4), 355–364 (2000)
10. Blanz, V., Vetter, T.: A morphable model for the synthesis of 3D faces. In: Proceeding of SIGGRAPH 1999, pp. 187–194. ACM Press, Los Angeles (1999)
11. BJUT-3D Face Database (2005), `http://www.bjpu.edu.cn/sci/multimedia/mui-lab/3dface/facedatabase.htm`
12. P´rez, P., Gangnet, M., Blake, A.: Poissonimage editing. ACM Trans.Graph. 22(3), 313–318 (2003)
13. Reinhard, E., Ashikhmin, M., Gooch, B., Shirley, P.: Color transfer between images. EEE Computer Graphics and Applications 21(4), 34–41 (2001)
14. Welsh, T., Ashikhmin, M., Mueller, K.: Transferring color to grey scale images. In: Proceedings of SIGGRAPH2002, pp. 277–280. ACM Press/ACM SIGGRAPH (2002)
15. Lipman, Y., Sorkine, O., Cohen-Or, D., Levin, D.: Differential coordinates for interactive mesh editing. In: International Conference on Shape Modeling and Applications, pp. 181–190

# Physically-Based Tree Animation and Leaf Deformation Using CUDA in Real-Time

Meng Yang[1,3], Meng-cheng Huang[1,3], and En-hua Wu[1,2]

[1] State Key Laboratory of Computer Science, Institute of Software, Chinese Academy of Sciences, Beijing 100190, P.R. China
[2] Department of Computer and Information Science, Faculty of Science and Technology, Uni. of Macau, Macau, P.R.China
[3] Graduate University of Chinese Academy of Sciences, Beijing 100049, P.R. China
{yangm,hmcen}@ios.ac.cn, EHWu@umac.mo

**Abstract.** This paper presents a novel physically-based parallel approach to animate tree motion in realtime and the leaf deformation is accelerated on a CUDA-based platform. Since physically-based tree animation can hardly achieve realtime performance due to the complicated geometry and expensive calculation. Therefore in this paper, three main measures are taken to overcome this problem. Firstly, we briefly introduce a method of physically-based tree motion called hierarchical matrix structure model driven by the external forces such as the wind; then we analyze the model on a parallel platform in detail; finally, all the tree data structures will be redefined as arrays which are suitable for parallel implementation on GPU. In addition, leaf deformation with a double layer structure, caused by its internal forces, will also be well mapped from CPU to GPU using a similar parallel mechanism. Experimental results show that many species of trees can animate realistically and naturally in realtime; Meanwhile, leaf deformation can be plausibly simulated and the performance will be improved by up to ten times.

**Keywords:** physically-based simulation, realtime tree animation, leaf deformation, CUDA.

## 1 Introduction

Animation of plants especially trees has been an active topic in virtual reality for several decades. Tree animation is widely applied in lots of fields such as advertisement, cartoon, computer aid-design, educations, military, and so on. However, animation of tens of thousands of tree branches and leaves is quite difficult due to the huge quantity and complicated geometry of trees. Influenced by natural forces such as the wind, trees may turn out to have various appearances, such as light vibration in breeze or swaging crazily in gale. Meanwhile, leaves, as an important part of a tree, may deform when the seasons alternate from summer to autumn due to the loss of water in their internal organs. In addition, numerical solver of physics theory for tree animation and leaf deformation is usually treated in a sequential way, making it a time-consuming process. All the reasons above make it hard to animate/deform

Z. Pan et al. (Eds.): Transactions on Edutainment VI, LNCS 6758, pp. 27–39, 2011.

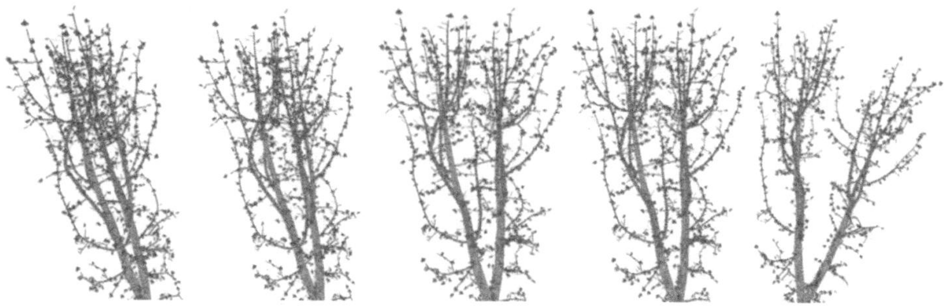

**Fig. 1.** Snapshot of tree swaying in the wind

trees in realtime. To address this issue, in this paper, we mainly put the focus on how to design a parallel mechanism to speedup physically-based tree animation and leaf deformation by taking full advantage of the computational ability of GPU.

Graphic Processing Unit (GPU) has become a useful tool for parallel computing since the Nvidia company developed the Compute Unified Device Architecture (CUDA)[1]. The CUDA platform has a parallel computation framework of three levels: *thread*, *block* and *grid*. The potential capability of hardware calculation brings us a chance for realtime tree animation. Therefore, how to fully take advantage of hardware resource seems to be more important to accelerate physically-based parallel simulation.

In this paper, we propose a novel GPU-based accelerating algorithm for realtime tree animation and leaf deformation in parallel. We exploit a hierarchical tree model, as represented in [2], which can realistically animate by taking a physically-based transformation matrix calculations (namely PTMC) driven by the wind force. According to PTMC, the transformation matrix of the child branch is accumulated by its parent branch matrix as a recursion till the root branch. However, this recursive process is not suitable to be performed in parallel. In order to overcome this problem, we should analyze the recursive structures and then extract all the essential information for each local system. Finally we can perform independent calculation between each two local systems. Thus it is suitable for us to migrate all these independent calculations to GPU. In our implementation, all the independent information is defined in CUDA format. In addition, we also exploit a parallel approach for leaf deformation on GPU. The main contribution of this paper can be list as follow:

- Propose a physically-based parallel method to animate trees in realtime, which is suitable to run on CUDA platform.
- Accelerate leaf deformation effectively by a physically-based parallel method, which can achieve up to even ten times speedup on GPU than CPU.

The remainder of this paper is organized as following: Section 2 gives a short survey of the related work, and Section 3 presents parallel algorithm for tree animation on a CUDA platform in detail. The accelerating method for leaf deformation on GPU is described in Section 4. Experimental results are demonstrated in Section 5. In Section 6, we will make a conclusion on the summary of our ideas presented in this paper.

## 2 Related Work

Previous research on tree animation can be roughly categorized into two main categories: (1) physically-based strategies; (2) procedurally-based strategies. In this section, we will review the related work in tree animation and their GPU implementations.

### 2.1 Physically-Based Animation

Physically-based animations generally take use of numerical integration of the dynamics driven by physical forces. Armstrong and Green [3] proposed an approach to simulate the dynamics of rigid bodies, which was considered as a form of rigid links joined at hinges to form a tree. Another segment-based approach of tree animations was proposed in [4] which considered tree branches as connected springs. In this way the dynamic equation of branch's displacement can be solved. Both [5] and [6] represented the tree motion in the wind using a physically-based simulation system. Habel et.al [7] used a physically guided approach to synthesize tree animation in the wind. [8] raised a physically-based approach of leaf deformation using two layer spring model. But this approach was hard to simulate the deformation of several pieces of leaves at one time. Although many physically-based methods above have been proposed in decades, it is hard for them to simulate tree motion in realtime.

### 2.2 Procedurally-Based Animation

Procedurally-based animations are generally driven by experimental results which hardly take into account the physical properties of trees. [9] and [10] proposed a method to sway individual leaves and branches in a wind field for a simulation of natural motions. A hybrid approach was represented in this paper to combine a stochastic method and a simulation method together. An approach of synthesizing tree motion was proposed in [11] by using dynamics data extracted from video. Stam [12] carried out the simulation in the Fourier domain using a filter constructed by a modal analysis of the tree. The periodic motions of given trees can be pre-computed using a spectral synthesis algorithm. Chuang et.al [13] proposed a spectral method for tree animation in which trees are considered as a dynamic system and each branch is considered as a harmonic oscillator. However, these procedurally-based methods can only achieve branch motions, in addition they are lack of physical exactness.

### 2.3 GPU Implementation

Zioma [14] animated tree motion in realtime on GPU using a user-defined procedural method. However, this method exploited a simple structural tree model which didn't take leaf animation into consideration thus was difficult to achieve realistic tree motion simulation.

# 3 Real-Time Tree Animation

## 3.1 Tree Structure and Dynamics Principle

In this paper, we take advantage of a hierarchical structure, as first proposed in [2], to describe tree branch model. Figure 2 shows a *three-level* tree branch model. The branches in the first level are represented by red segments, the second are by green ones, and the third level by blue ones.

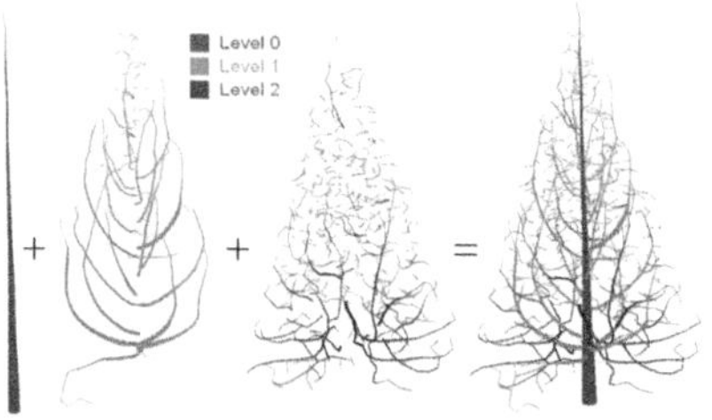


**Fig. 2.** Hierarchical tree model

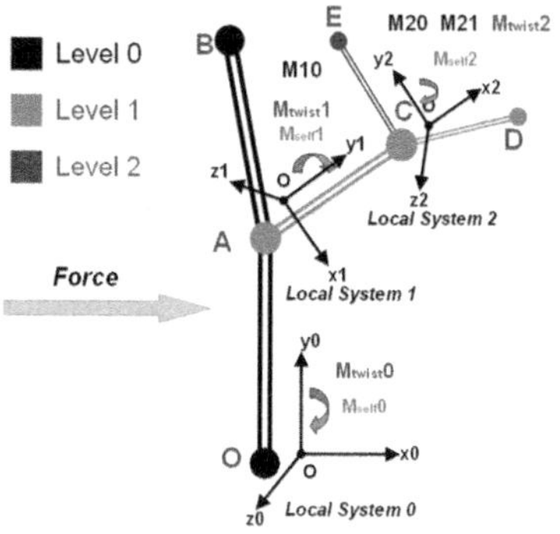


**Fig. 3.** Illustration of hierarchical animation model

We describe a novel tree animation model illustrated in Figure 3, the round nodes indicate the joint nodes and the lines are the branch segments. The original $O$ of the local coordinate system is set to the position of the lower end node of the branch, and the $x$ and $z$ axes are set on the plane perpendicular to the branch direction. The branch nodes $O$, $A$ and $B$ constitute the $level_0$ branch system; similarly, $A$, $C$ and $D$ constitute $level_1$ branch system; $C$ and $E$ constitute $level_2$ branch system. Since $O$, $A$, $C$ are the root nodes of these branch systems respectively, we define the local coordinate system for each branch system according to the root node direction of the parent level branch system. Initially, we can compute the transformation matrix according to the world coordinate system $M_{i0}$, where $i$ indicates the level of the current local branch system. And then we can compute the relative transformation matrix $M_{ij}$, which translate the tree branches from level $i$ branch system to level $j$. Therefore the world position of every node ($level\ i$) can be computed by using matrix $M_{totali}$, which is defined as

$$M_{totali} = M_{total(i-1)} * M_{i(i-1)}^{-1} * M_{i\_self}^{-1} \tag{1}$$

And $M_{i\_self}^{-1}$ is defined as the transformation matrix of itself at the time point $T$. Also the local coordinate can be obtained by computing all the $M_{totali}$, when the tree model is stationary, and $M_{i\_self}$ is the identity matrix.

After constructing the tree branch transformation matrix, the next task is to move a local branch system according to the external forces such as a wind field. According to Newton's law: $F=ma$, and the branch movement equations: $X=X_0+X'*t$, $X'=X''*a$.

Then we can simulate the tree motion by measuring the angle movement using $X$, $X'$, and $X''$. We define $X=vector(a, b, c)$, which shows the transformation related to the local coordinate system. Here we consider the total external force as the arithmetical sum of the forces of all the nodes inside the local branch systems. Therefore we can get the angular accelerator $a$ easily. Here we adopt the implicate integral to achieve the computation convergence. In this way our physically-based simulation can animate the tree branches naturally.

In order to simplify the calculations, we define the wind as a two-dimensional force field over the terrain. A wind primitive is defined as an analytical function: $V_w=G_W(x,t)$. We use several mathematical functions to simulate its characteristic. In summary, the *Algorithm 1* about tree animation on CPU can be listed as following Table 1.

### 3.2 GPU-Based Algorithm of Tree Animation in Real-Time

As discussed above, the algorithm of tree animation on CPU includes two main processing: one is to calculate local self-motion for each local tree branch; the other is to accumulate global self-motion from sequential parents to itself for each local branch system according to Equ. 1. Let us first look at step 1-6 in Table 1, local self-motion matrix only depends on local wind vector and is independent on the other local branch system, hence we can easily migrate it onto GPU for parallel implementation. In step 7-10, calculation of total transformation matrix $M_{totali}$ is dependent on the corresponding parent transformation matrix $M_{totali}^{parentj}$, while the global root node position $R_i$ for $i_{th}$ local branch system is dependent on corresponding parent root node position $R_i^{parentj}$. Obviously, both of these two operations are sequential and not suitable for parallel implementation.

To overcome this problem, firstly we should redefine all the data as a 1D arrays which is suitable for implementation within a CUDA framework. The redefinition guarantees each CUDA *thread* is corresponding to one single element of data indexed by a certain thread ID.

Taking a *three-level* tree model shown in Figure 3 for example, step 1-8 in *Algorithm 1* can be implemented in parallel as shown in Figure 4, correspondingly. $thd_i$ $(i=0,1,2)$ expresses one of the three parallel *threads* issued by GPU, and each of them corresponds to a local branch system $level_i(i=0,1,2)$, respectively. Thus we can gain each twist angle vector $X_i(i=0,1,2)$ at time $T$, which is similar to the solver of self-transformation matrix $M_{selfi}(i=0,1,2)$. However, total transformation matrix $M_{totali}(i=0,1,2)$ can't be dealt with in parallelism as discussed above due to Euq. 1. Therefore, three temporary variables $M_{tempi}(i=0,1,2)$ are introduced to solve this problem. At this moment, step 8 of *Algorithm 1* can be divided into three-pass solvers: (1)computing $M_{totali} = M_{selfi} * M_{inversei}(i=0,1,2)$, where $M_{totali}$ is treated as a midterm temporary variable; (2)computing $M_{tempi} = \Pi_{j=0}^{i} M_{totalj}(i=0,1,2)$, where $M_{tempi}$ is also a midterm temporary variable; (3)assigning value of $M_{tempi}$ to $M_{totali}(i=0,1,2)$. By using this method, we can successfully achieve parallel processing on GPU in dealing with the simulation of tree animation.

**Table 1.** Pseudo-code of the tree animation on CPU

---

**Algorithm 1: Tree animation on CPU**

---

**void** TreeAnimationOnCPU(void){

1: for (each branch system $Branch_i$) {

2: external force: $F_i \leftarrow V_{w_i}$;}

3: for (each branch system $Branch_i$){

4: angle vector: $X_i \leftarrow$ *Newton 2rd Law* & $F_i$;}

5: for (each branch system $Branch_i$){

6: self-matrix: $M_{self_i} \leftarrow$ **Transformation**($X_i$);}

7: for (each branch system from $Level_0$ to $Level_n$){

8: total transformation matrix :$M_{total_i} \leftarrow$ Euq. 1;}

9: for (each branch system from $Level_0$ to $Level_n$){

10: temporary root node position: $R_i \leftarrow \sum_{j=0}^{m} R_i^{parent_j}$;}

11: for (each node $Node_j$){

12: global node position: $W_j \leftarrow W_j + R_i$;}

13: }

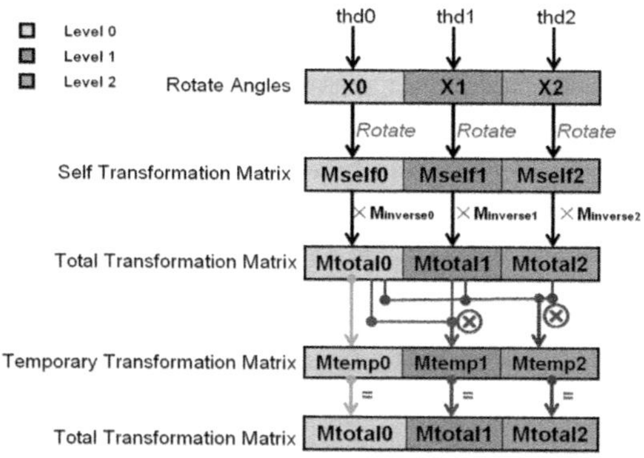


**Fig. 4.** Accumulation of total transformation matrix $\boldsymbol{M_{totali}}$

If the temporary variables $M_{tempi}$($i$=0,1,2) were not employed, the reading-writing conflicts may occur when solving Euq. 1. That is because the current values of $M_{totali}$($i$=0,1,2) may have been changed before the next access on it. Obviously, midterm temporary variables play an important role in alleviating the conflicts and realizing parallel implementation on GPU.

Similar to the calculation of $M_{totali}$, global position $R_i$($i$=0,1,2) of root node in step 9-10 of *Algorithm 1* can be designed as shown in Figure 5. We firstly multiply local position $L_i$($i$=$o,a,...,e$) (known) by corresponding total transformation matrix $M_{totali}$ which was calculated above for every tree node. Next we assign the value of the computing results to the corresponding $W_i$ ($i$=$o,a,...,e$) as a midterm temporary value. At last we should accumulate $R_i$ by equation:

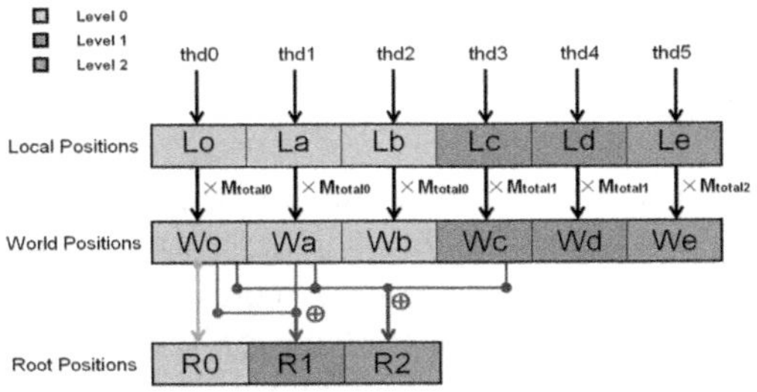


**Fig. 5.** Accumulation of global position $\boldsymbol{R}_i$

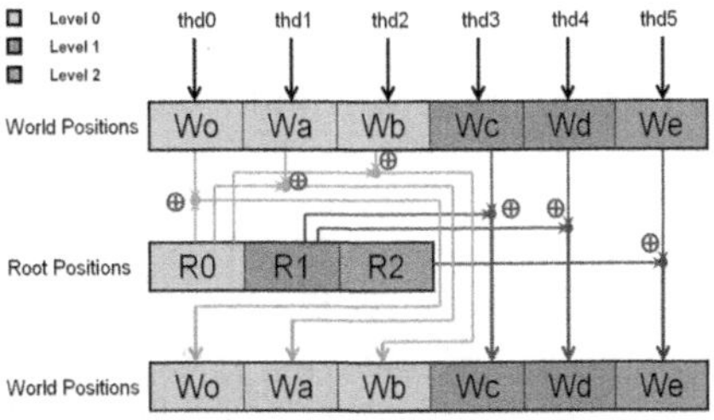


**Fig. 6.** Accumulation of global position $\boldsymbol{W}_i$

$$R_i = \sum_{j=0}^{i} W_{parent_j} \tag{2}$$

where $i$=0,1,2; $parent_j$=$o, a,...,e$. Taking $R_2$ for example, it can be computed as:

$$R_2 = W_o + W_a + W_c \tag{3}$$

After getting global position $R_i(i=0,1,2)$ of each root node, we need map the temporary position to global position $W_j\,(j=o,a,...,e)$ for each node, as shown in Figure 6. In practice, we can easily update $W_j\,(j=o,a,...,e)$ by equation $W_j = W_j + R_i$ ( $i$=0,1,2; $j=o,a,...,e$).

Once the global positions of all skeleton nodes have been known, a *six-prism* branch geometry will be established around corresponding skeleton segments.

### 3.3 Implementation on CUDA Platform

We have discussed one of the important factors which can influence the speed of tree animation. However, it is not the only one. In the following paragraph, we will introduce other potential factors which can affect the performance of tree animation simulation.

In practice, a tree model usually can contain a magnitude of about fifty or sixty thousands nodes. In order to make enough *threads* to cover all nodes at one time, we should elaborately select suitable dimensions for *block* and *thread.* Taking a tree model of 52348 nodes for example, we can select 65536 *threads* in total to fit this situation. We can either take advantage of *256 blocks* and *256 threads* (*65536 = 256*256*) or select *128 blocks* and *512 threads* (*65536 = 128*512*) and so on. Which solver is the most suitable selection is dependent on the capability of special hardware architecture. If the *threads* on GPU can't handle all the model nodes at one time, we can make a loop implementation to throughout all the nodes.

In summary, we can speedup tree animation in three ways: parallel design for data structure; full usage of midterm temporary variables; and exhaustion of computing capability of the hardware.

# 4 Acceleration of Leaf Deformation

## 4.1 Leaf Structure and Dynamic Analysis

Leaves deform when seasons alternate from summer to winter due to the loss of their internal moisture. A novel approach was proposed to simulate leaf deformation using a *double layer spring model* (namely *DLM*) in paper [8]. According to *DLM* definition, leaf model is composed of two types of springs: blade springs and vein ones. The blade springs are described as red lines with only one layer springs while the vein springs are denoted as blue ones with two layer springs, as shown in Figure 7(a). In this paper, we illustrate all the blade springs in a 2D flat plane simply, as shown in Figure 7(b). The double layers of vein springs are shown in Figure 7(c).

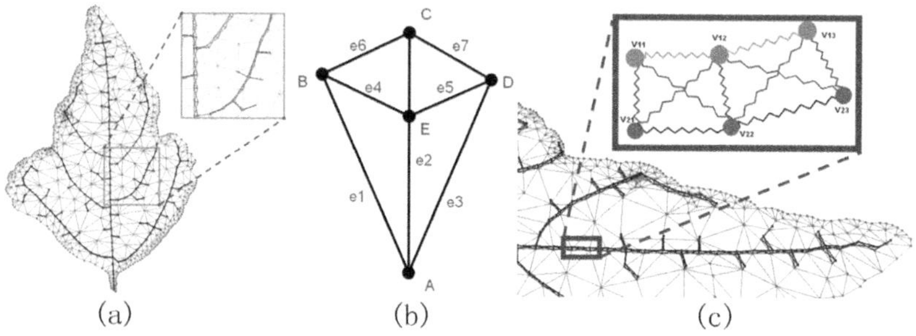


**Fig. 7.** (a) Leaf ***DLM***; (b) Illustration of blade springs; (c) Double layer vein springs

As shown in Figure 7(b), the letter $X$ ($X$=$A, B, C, D, E$) denotes blade node, and the line $e_i$ ($i$=1,...,7) denotes blade springs. Hence leaf deformation can be well controlled by spring shrinkage realistically and naturally. The elastic force of springs can be driven by Euq. 4:

$$f_{ij} = -\left\{ h_{ij} * (|l_{ij}| - r_{ij}) + d_{ij} * \frac{v_{ij} * l_{ij}}{|l_{ij}|} \right\} * \frac{l_{ij}}{|l_{ij}|} \tag{4}$$

where $i,j$=$\{A,...,E\}$, they describe the indices of two ends of a spring; $l_{ij}$ denotes the current length of the spring; $r_{ij}$ expresses the length of the remained spring; $h_{ij}$ is the elastic coefficients of the spring and $d_{ij}$ represents damping coefficients; the relative velocity from $i_{th}$ node to $j_{th}$ node can be defined as $v_{ij}$.

Double layer vein springs are illustrated in Figure 7(c), which are the uppermost factors to control the shape of the leaf during deformation. The bisque nodes ($V_{11}$, $V_{12}$, $V_{13}$) denote upper ends of vein springs; the blue nodes ($V_{21}$, $V_{22}$, $V_{23}$) denote lower ends of vein springs. A spring with upper end and corresponding vertical lower end is called *structural vein spring*, such as $V_{11}V_{21}$; while a spring with upper end and neighbor shared lower end is called *shared vein spring*, such as $V_{11}V_{22}$, $V_{12}V_{21}$.

## 4.2 GPU-Based Accelerating Approach for Leaf Deformation

The numerical solution to the leaf deformation is generally generated using the *Newton Second Law* and *Euler Exploit Integration*. In practice, this solution can be simply represented using an iterative program to update external forces and states for each node. However, this implementation is a time-consuming process due to a rather fine geometry of leaf model [8]. Therefore in this paper, we target to speedup this deformation on a *CUDA-based* platform. Similar to realtime approach of tree animation, firstly we need reorganize leaf data as 1D arrays in parallel structures which suit to run on GPU.

A novel approach for accelerating leaf deformation is described in Table 2 which expresses the deformation algorithm on GPU. Steps 1-5 in *Algorithm 2* explain the

**Table 2.** Pseudo-code of leaf deformation on GPU

**Algorithm 2: Leaf deformation on GPU**

**void** LeafDeformationOnGPU(void){
1: for (each node $Node_i$){
2: velocity: $V_i \leftarrow 0$;}
3: for (each spring $Spring_i$){
4: new rest length: $L_{r_i} \leftarrow L_i * \lambda$;
5: spring force: $S_i \leftarrow$ **Equ.** 4;}
6: ***update state for each node***:{
7: looping times: $N \leftarrow \alpha$;
8: for (each node $Node_i$){
9: damping force: $D_i \leftarrow -V_i \times \beta$; }
10: for (each node $Node_i$){
11: external force: $F_i \leftarrow D_i + \sum_{j=0}^{m} S_j$; }
12: for (each node $Node_i$){
13: new state: $V_i, P_i \leftarrow F_i$ & *Newton Second Law*;}
14: $N \leftarrow (N-1)$;
15: if($N = 0$) goto 17; else goto 8;
16: }
17: repeat 1-16 till terminated conditions.
18: }

**Table 3.** Statistics of tree animation

| Tree | Vertex Number | Segment Number | Platform | FPS | Speedup Ratio |
|---|---|---|---|---|---|
| 1 | 76848 | 230520 | GPU | 9.62 | 7.4 |
| | | | CPU | 1.29 | 1.0 |
| 2 | 23336 | 69984 | GPU | 60.97 | 2.2 |
| | | | CPU | 27.81 | 1.0 |
| 3 | 35784 | 107328 | GPU | 20.00 | 4.3 |
| | | | CPU | 4.62 | 1.0 |
| 4 | 26792 | 75328 | GPU | 23.28 | 3.5 |
| | | | CPU | 6.70 | 1.0 |
| 5 | 16352 | 49032 | GPU | 64.10 | 1.4 |
| | | | CPU | 45.66 | 1.0 |

method of initializing leaf states and calculating each the elastic force of the spring. Obviously, these five steps are suitable to run in parallel because of the independence between each two nodes/springs. In step 4, $\lambda$ is a user-defined constant shrinking coefficient within the interval [0, 1.0].

The main operation for leaf deformation is to update states for each node. This operation is listed from step 7 to step 16. At the beginning, we need to initialize a variable $N$ by a user-defined constant $\alpha$, and $N$ denotes the looping times from the current balanced state into a new one. Then the damping force $D_i$ can be easily computed by equation $D_i = -V_i*\beta$ independently as shown in steps 8-9, where $\beta$ is the damping coefficient, and flag "-" means the direction of damping force vector $D_i$ is opposite to velocity vector $V_i$. Steps 10-11 show us the calculation of total external forces for each node, that is $F_i=D_i+ \Sigma_{j=0}^{m} S_j$, here $S_j$ denotes force of $j_{th}$ spring connecting to $i_{th}$ node. Thus new states for each node can be updated using *Newton Second Law*(steps 12-13) similar as discussed above. Finally steps 14-15 are branch statements to control which step will be run next. Step 17 indicates the terminated conditions of *Algorithm 2*.

In practice, taking leaf model in Figure 7(b) for example, steps 1-2 in *Algorithm 2* can obviously be mapped to GPU. Figure 8 illustrates operations of steps 3-9 in parallel. $thd_i(i=1,...,8)$ denotes $i_{th}$ thread issued by GPU hardware; $S_i(i=1,...,8)$ expresses the external force of $i_{th}$ leaf spring; $F_j(j=a,...,e)$ denotes the total external force for each node. Hence the total external force $F_a$ of node $A$ shown in Figure 7(b) can be expressed by $F_a = S_1 + S_2 + S_3 + D_a$, where $D_a$ is damping force of node $A$, and $S_1$, $S_2$, $S_3$ are elastic forces of springs which share the common node $A$. In this practical implementation, we select calculation of spring force for each spring rather than for each node. As we have known, a spring has two ends, if we select calculation of spring force to each node, it will cause a repetitive computing, which certainly will reduce the simulation efficiency greatly. In addition, this selection for each spring can also avoid reading-writing conflict similar to discussion of tree animation above.

After $F_j(j=a,...,e)$ is calculated, we can update the states for each node using *Newton Second Law* and *Euler Explicit Integration* in parallel (see Figure 9). Therefore, velocity $V_j(j=a,...,e)$ for each node can be updated by $V_j= V_j + (F_j / m_j) * t$, where $m_j$ is the mass of $j_{th}$ node; In addition, position $P_j(j=a,...,e)$ for each node can be updated by $P_j = P_j + V_j* t$.

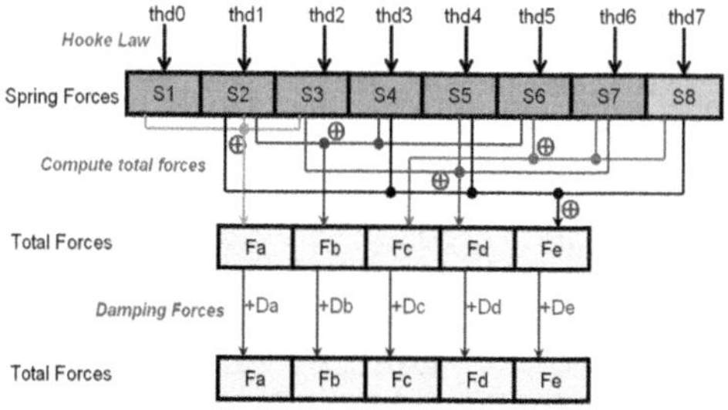


**Fig. 8.** Accumulation of external forces for leaf node

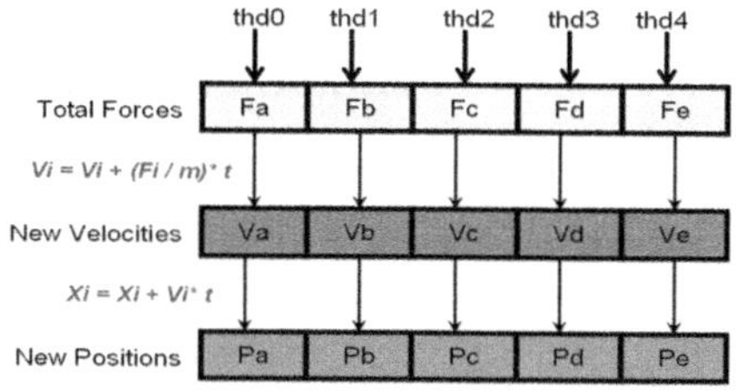


**Fig. 9.** Euler integral for leaf node

### 4.3 Implementation on CUDA Platform

There is a bottle-neck in leaf deformation calculation with *Algorithm 2* to get high quality results, which is caused by the uncertain value of looping times *N*. Experimental results show that: the larger the value of *N*, the smoother the animation frames are, but the less efficient of the implementation, vice versa.

In practice, number of leaf model nodes in our experiments may be up to about 100 thousands. Therefore a parameter selection may be 256 *blocks* and 512 *threads*, which can cover all the nodes at one time due to *256*512=131072>100000*. In addition, it can speedup by a certain amount by putting constants in constant/texture or registers. Finally, similar to tree animation, we should optimize the *CUDA kernel* definition and reduce unnecessary branch controlling codes in program.

## 5 Results

The proposed approaches are developed on an *Intel Core(TM) 2.6GHz* CPU, together with *nVidia GeForce 8800* GPU and *3G* RAM. Figure 10 shows realistic tree animations under the influence of wind by using our realtime tree motion system; Another result of tree swaying is shown in Figure 1. Two natural results for deformation of leaves of different shapes are illustrated in Figure 11, the left and center pictures show different viewports in front and back, respectively, while the right picture shows a second type of leaf deformation. Table 3 lists the statistical data for five different species of trees animations. In these animations, tree leaves are treated as the highest level branch, therefore the leaf and branch animations can be realized in the same motion system. As shown in Table 3, the frame per second (namely *FPS*) of tree animation can reach up to about 64 at most, which achieves a realtime simulation. Meanwhile, the *FPS* is speeded up by about 1.4-7.4 times from GPU implementation to CPU. Table 4 explains the influence of leaf quantity accelerating ratio of deformation on GPU compared to CPU, and this deformation only involves leaves, rather than branches. The data in Table 4 indicates that the more pieces of leaves, the higher accelerating ratio. In addition, the accelerating ratio can reach up to over 10 times at most. Table 5 indicates the influence of *N* to accelerating ratio of deformation. Taking five pieces of leaves for example, when the value of *N* varies from 500 to 10000, the accelerating ratio of *FPS* from GPU to CPU almost keeps changeless. This indicates that the value of *N* contributes little on speed up efficiency of leaf deformation. Therefore, a recommended value of *N* may be 1000 to keep a realistic and smooth enough result.

**Fig. 10.** Results of tree animations in wind field

**Fig. 11.** Results of leaf deformations

**Table 4.** Statistics of leaf deformation with different quantity of leaves (*N*=1000)

| Leaf Number | 1 | 5 | 10 | 30 | 50 | 100 | 200 |
|---|---|---|---|---|---|---|---|
| FPS on CPU | 6.41 | 1.19 | 0.59 | 0.20 | 0.10 | 0.04 | 0.02 |
| FPS on GPU | 8.00 | 3.56 | 1.88 | 0.67 | 0.42 | 0.26 | 0.22 |
| Speedup Ratio | 1.2 | 3.0 | 3.0 | 3.4 | 4.3 | 5.9 | 10.6 |

**Table 5.** Statistics of leaf deformation with different values of *N* (5 pieces of leaves)

| Value of *N* | 500 | 1000 | 2000 | 4000 | 6000 | 8000 | 10000 |
|---|---|---|---|---|---|---|---|
| FPS on CPU | 2.38 | 1.19 | 0.59 | 0.29 | 0.20 | 0.15 | 0.12 |
| FPS on GPU | 7.14 | 3.56 | 1.78 | 0.88 | 0.59 | 0.44 | 0.35 |
| Speedup Ratio | 3.01 | 3.00 | 3.03 | 2.97 | 2.99 | 3.02 | 3.01 |

## 6 Conclusions and Future Work

In this paper, we presented a novel method to construct realistic tree animations and leaf deformations using GPU on a *CUDA-based* platform. Our system was presented on purpose of accelerating simulations of trees/leaves. To realize this target, we devised a parallel technique to design data structure of trees/leaves, which is suitable to run on GPU. Meanwhile, we achieve results of the physically-based tree animation in realtime using our parallel algorithm. Meanwhile, we accelerate the tree animation or leaf deformation up to about 10 times on GPU compared to CPU. In future, we plan to extend our parallel algorithms for forest animation and attempt to find an auto-detecting method for selecting the number of CUDA *thread* per *block*. Furthermore, we are interested in using other GPU-based methods to accelerate plant animations.

**Acknowledgements.** This research work is supported by National Natural Science Foundation of China (Grant No. 60833007, 60773030, 60973066), National 863 High-Tec. Program of China (Grant No. 2008AA01Z301) and University of Macau Research Grant.

## References


1. Diener, J., Reveret, L., Fiume, E.: Hierarchical retargeting of 2d motion fields to the animation of 3d plant models. In: ACM-SIGGRAPH/EG Symposium on Computer Animation (SCA), ACM-Siggraph/Eurographics, pp. 231–240 (2006)
2. Chi, X., Sheng, B., Chen, Y., Wu, E.: Simulation of autumn leaves. In: SIGGRAPH 2007: ACM SIGGRAPH 2007 posters, San Diego, California, p. 36 (2007)
3. Ono, H.: Practical experience in the physical animation and destruction of trees. In: Eurographics Workshop on Animation and Simulation, pp. 149–159 (1997)
4. Yang, M., Sheng, B., Wu, E., Sun, H.: Multi-resolution tree motion synthesis in angular shell space. In: ACM VRCAI 2009, pp. 47–52 (2009)
5. Stam, J.: Stochastic dynamics: Simulating the effects of turbulence on flexible structures. In: Computer Graphics Forum (Proceedings of Eurographics 1997), vol. 16(3), pp. 159–164 (1997)
6. NVidia: NVIDIA CUDA Programming Guide: CUDA toolkit, `http://www.nvidia.com/object/cudaget.html`

7. Akagi, Y., Sanami, S., Kitajima, K.: Computer animation of swaying trees based on physical simulation. Computers & Graphics 30(4), 529–539 (2006)
8. Chuang, Y.-Y., Goldman, D.B., Zheng, K.C., Curless, B., Salesin, D.H., Szeliski, R.: Animating pictures with stochastic motion textures. In: ACM Transactions on Graphics (Proc. SIGGRAPH 2005), vol. 24(3), pp. 853–860 (2005)
9. Ota, S., Fujimoto, T., Tamura, M., Muraoka, K., Fujita, K., Chiba, N.: 1/fb noise-based real-time animation of trees swaying in wind fields. Computer Graphics International, pp. 52–59 (2003)
10. Ota, S., Tamura, M., Fujimoto, T., Muraoka, K., Chiba, N.: A hybrid method for real-time animation of trees swaying in wind fields. The Visual Computer 20(10), 613–623 (2004)
11. Wu, E., Chen, Y., Yan, T., Zhang, X.: Reconstruction and physically-based animation of trees from static images. Computer Animation & Simulation, 47–61 (1999)
12. Habel, R., Kusternig, A., Wimmer, M.: Physically guided animation of trees. In: Computer Graphics Forum (Proceedings EUROGRAPHICS 2009), vol. 28(2), pp. 167–7055 (2009)
13. Armstrong, W.W., Green, M.W.: The dynamics of articulated rigid bodies for purposes of animation. The Visual Computer 1(4), 231–240 (1985)
14. Zioma, R.: Gpu-generated procedural wind animations for trees. In: GPU Gems 3, ch. 6, pp. 231–240 (2007)

# Simulation of Implosion and Transportation of Ore in Digital Mine

Xixi Huang[1,2], Dongyong Yan[2], Fuli Wu[2], Nan Xiang[1], and Mingmin Zhang[1,*]

[1] State Key Laboratory of CAD&CG, Zhejiang University, Hangzhou, 310058
zmm@cad.zju.edu.cn
[2] School of Computer Science and Technology, Zhejiang University of Technology, Hangzhou, 310023
hxxfighter@163.com

**Abstract.** Digital mining technology and software development are essential for informatization in China coal industry. We adopt .net3.0 platform and OpenGL graphics library to develop a system to simulate the process of ore's implosion and the process of ore's transportation. In order to implement these functions, the particle system principle and some physical algorithms are used in this system. Besides, other additional functions such as scenes navigating and data statistics are included. Experimental results show that this system can dynamic simulate excavation situations in different mines and has high application value.

**Keywords:** Digital mine, Simulation of implosion, Transportation of ore, Particle system.

## 1 Introduction

Digital mine is the combination of the development of mining science, information science, artificial intelligence, computer technology, and it will change the traditional production activities of mining. Constructing the "Digital Mine" must have a huge impact on mining enterprises in all ways, and it will make the production, safe management and operation mode of mining enterprises more precise, more scientific and more reasonable, in order to promote the realization of sustainable development in mining enterprises[1-2]. The degree of informational mine in developed mining countries has already taken solid steps, and some countries even have made long-term planning. In the country, as a class of typical traditional mining industry, Chinese mine industry has already been facing the challenges of informational technology.

Digital mine system[1-4] is a huge project, which combines several systems and uses lots of science technologies[5-10]. Virtual reality[11] technology is one of the most important technologies, the goal of this system is to use virtual reality to simulate the entire mining process and to make mining process visualization and offer some mining methods according to computer. For example, with the help of computer, it can simulate blasting process of mine, and compute the best point to blast, and get the

* Corresponding author.

Z. Pan et al. (Eds.): Transactions on Edutainment VI, LNCS 6758, pp. 40–48, 2011.

routes and programs about mining ores, and predict the safety of mining by person simulation. Therefore, the system can be used to virtually simulate the mining process and make the mining process safer, more efficient and more convenient.

In this paper, firstly some backgrounds and related work on digital mine are introduced, then the functional framework of system is presented, and design features of main functions are introduced. Finally, conclusions about this research project are drawn, and some future works are proposed.

## 2 Functional Framework

The main functions of the system are to simulate the processes of mine blasting and ore transportation. The framework of system is shown in Fig.1. The functions of system include three parts. The first part is to draw the scenes that are required. The second part is to simulate some mining processes on the foundation of the first part, including scene navigating, mine blasting, and ore transportation. The third part is to get the statistics of useful data that is provided by the simulations from the second part.

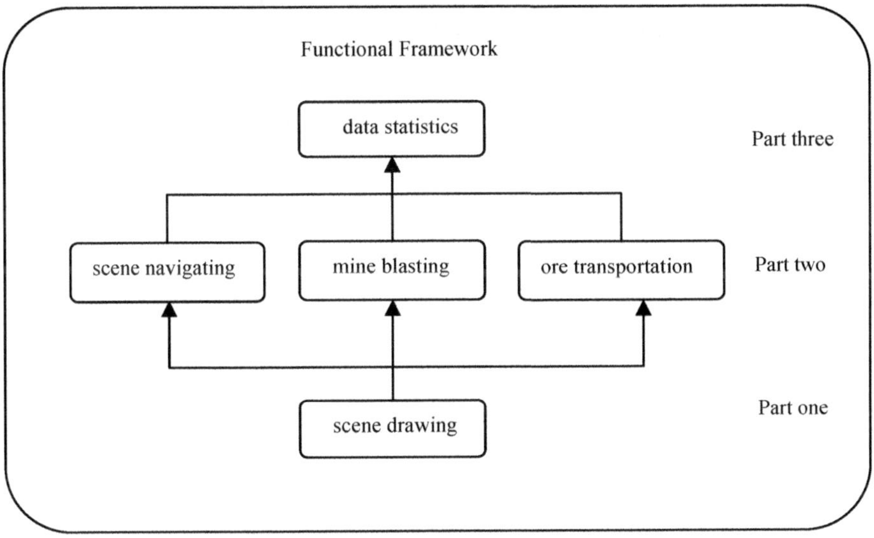


**Fig. 1.** Functional framework

Firstly, the function of scene drawing is to draw environment scenes, including mine, sky, land, pit, mining area, transporter and so on. Virtual scene is the foundation of constructing models such as mining equipments and mineral. Then, in the second part, this function of scene navigating can help the user change the location of observation points and angles, for example, the user can observe around mine hills, or observe the processes of mine blasting and ore transportation. Mine blasting reasonably designed by the particle system[12-15] and some physical algorithms are to simulate the process of implosion, such as the falling and collision of broken ores, the falling and color changing of sparks, the upward motion of smoke which is created in the blasting process, and the forming process of rupture areas. Ore transportation is to simulate the process that transporter can transport the broken ores produced in the blasting. The whole transportation process consists of several steps, including moving ores into transporter and pulling ores into ore area. In the third part, generally, the data includes two kinds. One kind is the information of mine field, such as the progresses of mining, mining capacity, and the amounts of explosives. Another one is the information of the whole mine hill, such as the number of mine hill, the amount of mine field, the location of mine hill, the whole progress of mining, and the whole mining capacity.

## 3 System Design and Implementation

### 3.1 Scene Drawing

The scenes that we draw include mine, sky, land, pit, mining area, and transporter. Each scene requires specific models in order to make a realistic simulation. Details of the above models are described as following:

Mine hill model: The feature about mine hill is irregular. Therefore, the model of mine hill can create different shapes of hills. The model is shown as Fig.2.

Broken ore model: The broken ores are produced after blasting, they are always irregular. The model is shown as Fig.3.

Land model: The grid model always is used when a large scale terrain is drawn. The model is shown as Fig.4.

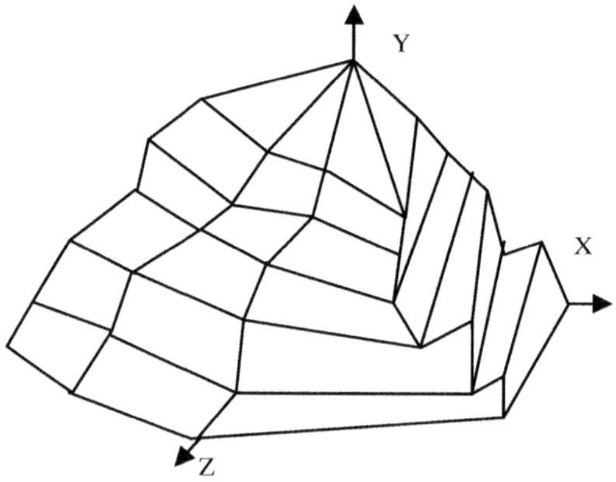


**Fig. 2.** Mine hill model

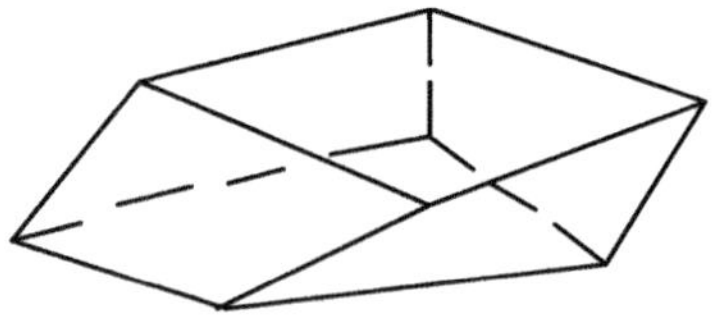

**Fig. 3.** Ore model

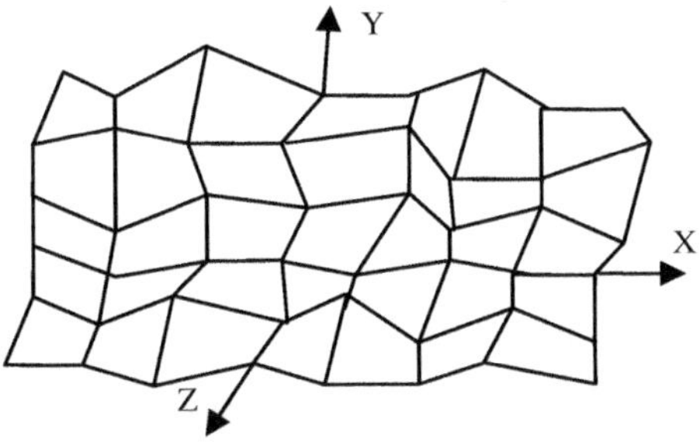


**Fig. 4.** Spatial grid model

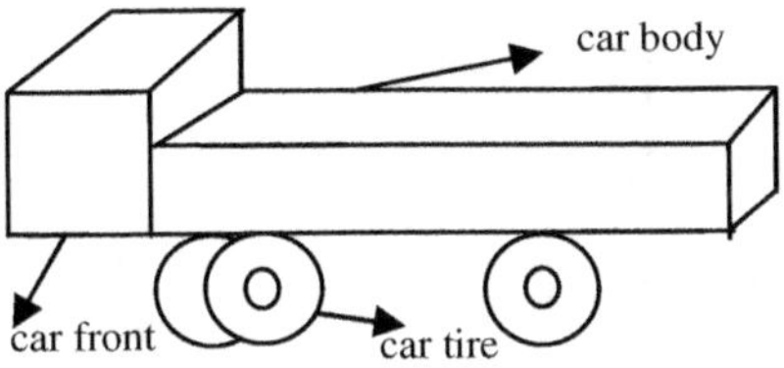


**Fig. 5.** Transporter model

Transporter model: The transporter is used to transport the broken ores. It includes three parts, such as car front, car body, and car tire. The model is shown as Fig.5.

## 3.2 Mine Blasting

We exploit particle system principle to simulate the implosion process, and the physical detection algorithm is applied to predict the position of ores. The whole process includes the motion of broken ores, the motion of sparks, and the motion of smoke. The main part of mine blasting is the motion of ores which contains the following steps. The flow chart of all ores' motion states is shown as Fig.6.

Step1: It produces a number of broken ores in the area which is required to blast. What's more, the parameters of ores should be initialized, such as the size, location, speed, acceleration speed, and rotation speed. And the state of ores becomes the falling state in the air.

Step 2: After a period of time, the ores can change each location on the basis of the speed, acceleration speed, and rotation speed. Different actions will be taken based on the following situations:

(1) If the locations of ores are closing to the surface, the ores need to be judged whether the state is changed or not. One state is that the ores stop on the surface of mining area. Another state is that the ores keep the original state which is the falling state in the air.

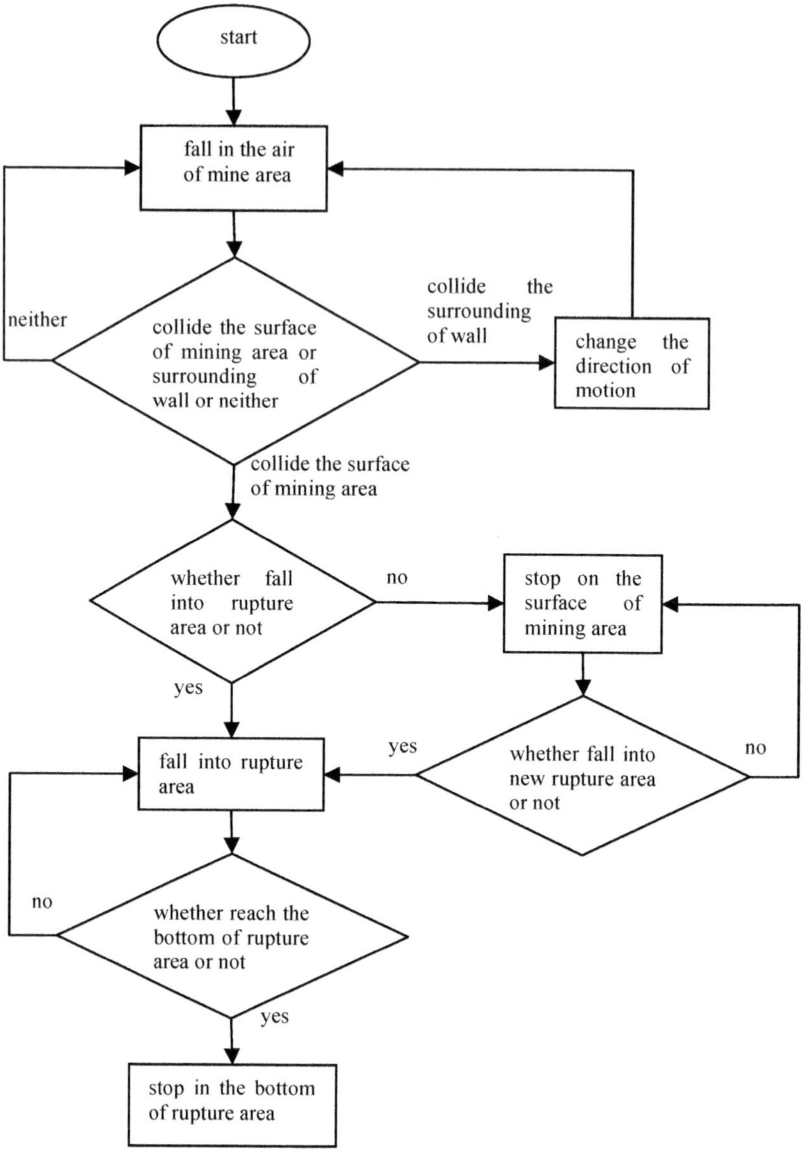


**Fig. 6.** The flow chart of all ores' motion states

(2) If the ores stop on the mining area surface, and when a new blast is happened on the surface, the ores need to be judged whether they are in the new rupture area or not.

(3) If the ores reach the surrounding walls of mining area, the directions of the ores' movements should be changed.

Step3: If the ores are in the new rupture area, the state of ores should be changed to the falling state in the rupture area. Otherwise they should keep original state.

If the ores are falling in the rupture area, the locations of the ores should be judged. When the ores reach the bottom of rupture area, they should stop falling, and the state should be changed to the state of stopping on the bottom surface of rupture area.

Step4: If the state of ores are stopping on the surface of mining area or rupture area, they should keep original locations and states when no new blasting occurs.

The motions of sparks and smoke are similar to the motion of ores, and they are all based on particle system principle. The different points are that the spark has color parameter and the parameter always keep changing. What's more, the motion of smoke is upward moving and the smoke disappears at last.

### 3.3 Ore Transportation

In the system, the transporter is used to transport the broken ores that are produced in the blasting from mining area to ore area. The whole process includes several parts.

Firstly, the chosen ores are picked up into transporter. The target ores are chosen by the mouse, and they are put into transporter. The realization principle is that the location of ores should be changed into the free area of car body. The area of car body can be logically divided into many same size cube spaces (they don't exist in fact). These virtual cube spaces are numbered (start from one), when one ore is put into transporter, the next number cube space is chosen (for example, if the last time number n space is chosen, number n+1 will be chosen in the next time). Then, transporter is started. When the transporter is started, the state of transporter is changed from static state to moving state. Continued, transporter is moved. The principle of transporter moving is that the location of transporter is changed in real time. Specifically, the points of transporter are changed after a period time. Then, transporter is turned around. The main principle of turning around the transporter is complex, not only the car should be changed, but also the ores in the transporter should be kept relatively static to the transporter.

After that, the ores are pulled into ore area. This process can be divided into two steps, the first step is that the ores slide down in the transporter, and the second step is that the ores leave the transporter and fall into the ore area. The demands of the first step are that the ores in the transporter should be pulled up while they should slide down along the car body as some degree speed. The implementation principle is following: the car body slopes after a period of time. As Fig.7 shows, the sloped angle of car body has positive correlation with $\theta$. So when $\theta$ is changed, the sloped angle is also changed. Supposing that the displacement is named AB as car body changed, the length of AB is $L$, if the coordinate of point A is known as ($Xa$, $Ya$, $Za$), and the coordinate of point B can be computed as ($Xb$, $Yb$, $Zb$) with Formula 1.

$$\begin{cases} Xb = Xa + L * \cos\theta; \\ Yb = Ya + L * \sin\theta; \\ Zb = Za. \end{cases} \tag{1}$$

The changing situation of every point in the transporter is similar with the point A. After changing, all the locations of the ores in the transporter can be computed according to Formula 1.

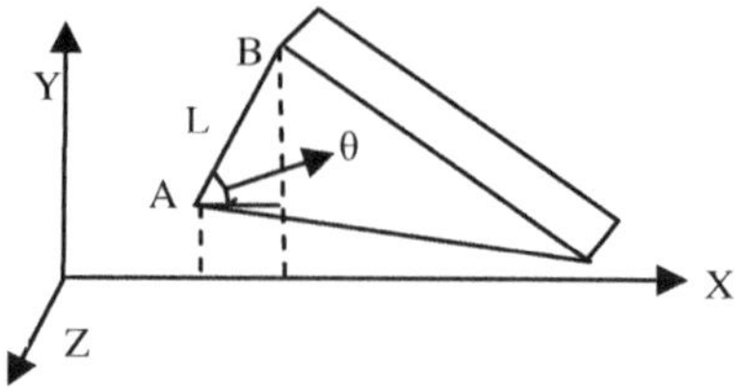


**Fig. 7.** Slope diagram of transporter

The demands of the second step are also complex. After the ores leave the transporter, they would have new speed, new acceleration speed, and new motion direction. And then with the influence of gravity acceleration speed, the ores fall into the ore area, and they stop on the surface of ore area at last.

Finally, the transporter leaves the ore area. When the transporter leaves ore area, the process need deal with two conditions. One condition is that there are no ores in the transporter, and the other condition is that there are some ores in the transporter. In the latter condition, when the transporter leaves the ore area, the car pulls down, so do the ores in the car. Furthermore, the ores should be kept relatively static with car body. The process is opposite to the process which the ores are pulled into the ore area. With the use of the Formula 1, supposing the coordinate of point B is known as (*Xb*, *Yb*, *Zb*), and then the coordinate of point A can be computed as (*Xa*, *Ya*, *Za*).

## 4 Experimental Results

The results of experiments are as following. Fig.8 shows the function of navigating the mine hill. As Fig.9 shows, when the users click a place to blast, there occurs blast. As Fig.10 shows, the broken ores are carried to the transporter. As Fig.11 shows, when the transporter is moved to ore area, then the car body of transporter slopes, in order to make the ores pull into ore area.

**Fig. 8.** Navigate the mine hill

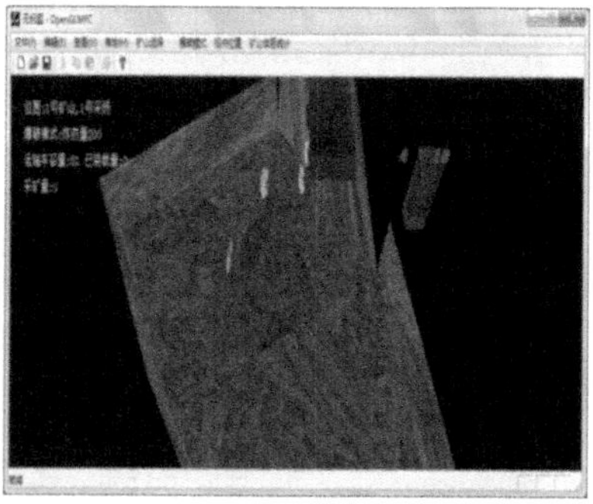

**Fig. 9.** Implosion result

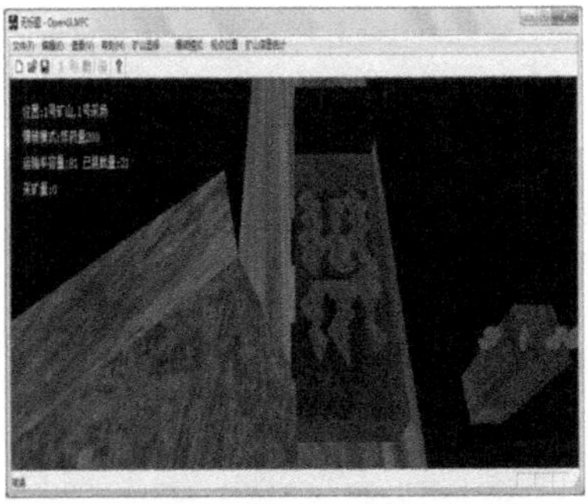

**Fig. 10.** Carry broken ores

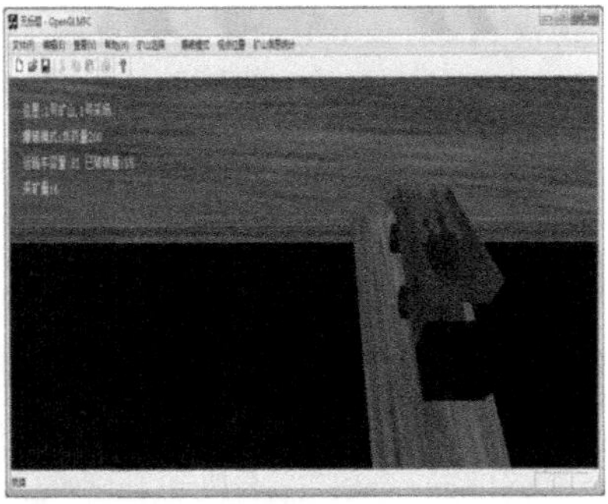

**Fig. 11.** Transport ores into ore area

## 5 Conclusion

In this paper, we design and implement a prototype to simulate the production process of coal mine by drawing lots of scenes such as mine hill, land, sky, mining area, and visualizing the blasting and transportation process of ore. In addition, we also consider some information affecting the mining process, including mining capacity, the amounts of explosives and so on.

As to the future work, we plan to improve the performance of the prototype system. First, some models are required be improved. Then the blasting effect should be enhanced to be more realistic. Finally, some other functions should be completed, such as integration of virtual actors, and the virtual navigation.

**Acknowledgments.** This research work is supported by "Key technology and software development of digital mining", with grant no.2009AA062704. The authors would like to give thanks to some other team members, such as Qingfeng Mi, Kangkan Wang et al. for their kind help.

## References

1. Wu, L., Zhu, W., Zhang, R.: Digital mine and the future development in China. Science and Technology Review 7, 29–31 (2004)
2. Liu, K.: The research of digital mine and mine information system. West-China Exploration Engineering 17(12), 309–310 (2005)
3. Wang, Y.K., Ma, D.F.: Research on SVG-based Remote Visualization System of Digital Mine Information. In: Proceedings of the 2009 International Conference on Computer Modeling and Simulation, pp. 270–272 (2009)
4. Wu, L., Zhang, R., Qi, Y., Qi, A., Li, B.: 3D Geoscience Modelling and Virtual Mine System. Journal of Surveying and Mapping 31(1), 28–33 (2002)
5. Kuenzer, C., Zhang, J., Tetzlaff, A., van Dijk, P., Voigt, S., Mehl, H., Wagner, W.: Uncontrolled coal fires and their environmental impacts-Investigating two arid mining regions in north-central China. Applied Geography 27(1), 42–62 (2007)
6. Li, M., Liu, Y.: Underground Coal Mine Monitoring with Wireless Sensor Networks. ACM Transactions on Sensor Networks 5(2), 10–28 (2009)

7. Xu, M., Li, H., Lv, P., Chen, W., Liu, G., Zhu, P., Pan, Z.: L4RW: Laziness-based Realistic Real-time Responsive Rebalance in Walking. Computer Graphics Forum 29(7), 2187–2196 (2010)
8. Liu, G., Pan, Z., Cheng, X.: A stylistic human motion editing system based on a subspace motion model. International Journal of Computer Applications in Technology 38(1/2/3), 10–18 (2010)
9. Yun, R., Zhang, B., Pan, Z.: Research on Using Cult3D and Java to Realize Virtual Assembly. In: Chang, M., Kuo, R., Kinshuk, Chen, G.-D., Hirose, M. (eds.) Learning by Playing. LNCS, vol. 5670, pp. 363–370. Springer, Heidelberg (2009)
10. Chen, T., Pan, Z., Zheng, J.: EasyMall - An Interactive Virtual Shopping System. In: Proceedings of the 2008 Fifth International Conference on Fuzzy Systems and Knowledge Discovery, vol. 4, pp. 669–673 (2008)
11. Guan, E., Guo, Z., Wu, S.: The application of virtual reality technology in mine system. Mining Engineering 7(1), 59–61 (2009)
12. Xiao, H., He, M., Bai, Z.: Fountain simulation bases on particle system in OpenGL. Computer Simulation 24(12), 201–204 (2007)
13. Hastings, E.J., Guha, R.K., Stanley, K.O.: Interactive evolution of particle systems for computer graphics and animation. IEEE Transactions on Evolutionary Computation 13(2), 418–432 (2009)
14. Su, W.Y., Hart, J.C.: A programmable particle system framework for shape modeling. In: International Conference On Shape Modeling and Applications 2005, pp. 114–123 (2005)
15. Xiao, H., He, C.: Real-time Simulation of Fireworks Based on GPU and Particle System. In: Proceedings of the 2009 First International Workshop on Education Technology and Computer Science, vol. 1, pp. 14–17 (2009)

# An Automatic and Robust Chessboard Corner Extraction

Xifan Shi, Ning Hong, and Tiefeng Cai

Zhijiang College, Zhejiang University of Technology, Hangzhou 310024, China
zjufan@hotmail.com, hning@zjut.edu.cn, ctf@zjc.zjut.edu.cn

**Abstract.** Camera calibration is crucial in many applications. Our lab uses the world wide used camera calibration toolbox for Matlab and finds its two major drawbacks, i.e., manual selection of the four extreme corners and inability to process images larger than 2MP. In this paper, a new method to eliminate these drawbacks is presented. The original chessboard is modified slightly and based on the added boundary composed of four narrow rectangles, the four extreme corners can be forecast. In addition, because it is implemented by C++, the 2MP limitation no longer exists. The experiment shows that even without multithread optimization and even for a 50MP photo, the corners can be extracted within 20 seconds on a 3GHz CPU.

**Keywords:** Camera Calibration, Corner Extraction, 3D Scanner.

## 1 Introduction

Camera calibration is an important task in computer vision, motion analysis, three-dimensional object reconstruction and texture mapping [1]. It is a hot research topic in computer vision as well as virtual reality in recent decades [1-11]. The purpose of camera calibration is to find the transformation between world coordinates and image coordinates. Evidently, a pixel in an image corresponds to a line in the world frame and only after calibration, the line can be expressed. This correspondence enables many applications. For example, if two pixels in two different images are the image of the same voxel in the world frame, then, by this triangulation method, the world coordinates of the voxel can be determined. Thus camera calibration is a prerequisite for any application where the relation between 2D image coordinates and 3D world coordinates is needed [2]. The most commonly used camera calibration model is the pinhole model [1], as shown in equation (1), where $a_x$, $a_y$, $u_0$ along with $v_0$ are the intrinsic parameters, ***K*** the intrinsic parameters matrix and ***E*** the extrinsic parameters matrix.

In practice, it is found that sometimes the transformation between world and image deviates from this pinhole model, especially at the four corners of an image. As a result, the lens distortion and the skew coefficient are introduced to solve this issue. The $s$ in equation (2) is the skew coefficient and a nonzero value means that the $u$ axis and $v$ axis of the image is not perpendicular strictly. The lens distortion was first introduced by Brown in 1966 [12] and called "Plumb Bob" model (radial polynomial + "thin prism"). The tangential distortion is due to "decentering", or imperfect centering of the lens components and other manufacturing defects in a compound lens. With this model, the lens distortion can be corrected effectively.

Z. Pan et al. (Eds.): Transactions on Edutainment VI, LNCS 6758, pp. 49–56, 2011.

$$Z_c\begin{bmatrix}u\\v\\1\end{bmatrix}=\begin{bmatrix}\frac{1}{dx}&0&u_0\\0&\frac{1}{dy}&v_0\\0&0&1\end{bmatrix}\begin{bmatrix}f&0&0&0\\0&f&0&0\\0&0&1&0\end{bmatrix}\begin{bmatrix}R&T\\0^T&1\end{bmatrix}\begin{bmatrix}X_w\\Y_w\\Z_w\\1\end{bmatrix} \qquad (1)$$

$$=\begin{bmatrix}a_x&0&u_0&0\\0&a_y&v_0&0\\0&0&1&0\end{bmatrix}\begin{bmatrix}R&T\\0^T&1\end{bmatrix}\begin{bmatrix}X_w\\Y_w\\Z_w\\1\end{bmatrix}=\begin{bmatrix}K&0\end{bmatrix}E\vec{X}_w=M\vec{X}_w$$

$$Z_c\begin{bmatrix}u\\v\\1\end{bmatrix}=\begin{bmatrix}a_x&s&u_0&0\\0&a_y&v_0&0\\0&0&1&0\end{bmatrix}\begin{bmatrix}R&T\\0^T&1\end{bmatrix}\begin{bmatrix}X_w\\Y_w\\Z_w\\1\end{bmatrix}=\begin{bmatrix}K&0\end{bmatrix}E\vec{X}_w=M\vec{X}_w\,. \qquad (2)$$

Camera calibration is the process of determination of the intrinsic parameters (the focal length $a_x$, $a_y$; the principal point $u_0$, $v_0$; the lens distortion and the skew coefficient $s$) as well as the extrinsic parameters (the location $\boldsymbol{T}$ and the orientation $\boldsymbol{R}$).

Camera calibration can be classified into two categories: the conventional approach [1][5-11] and the self calibration approach [2]. The former requires predefined calibration object such as chessboard or its variation while the latter uses only information in the image. Self calibration requires solving high degree binary equations (Kruppa's Equations), which makes the calibration less stable. In addition, the precision also suffers from the less calibration information. Hence, to construct a 3D scanner for scanning utensil in a museum, we decide to use the conventional approach. The 3D scanner developed by our lab is composed of a projector and a camera. Obviously, both of them must be calibrated to make the scanner function correctly.

The work is initiated with searching "camera calibration" in Google and the first page is a camera calibration toolbox for Matlab [5]. Having tried it for many times, we find this toolbox is extremely useful (robust and precise) except for two obvious drawbacks which hinder its further use on our 3D scanner. One is the manual selection of the four extreme corners, as shown in Fig. 1. According to the specification, the selection of the corners must be within 5 pixels; otherwise some of the corners might be missed by the detector. Nowadays, the resolution of a camera is much higher than that of a display. As a result, the user must magnify the image (100% instead of fit screen) and move in four directions to guarantee the selection error of each corner not to exceed 5 pixels, which costs about 6 seconds for a 4000 × 3000 image. The resolution of a camera is growing continuously. For instance, Leaf has just announced Leaf Aptus-II 12 boasting a worshiping resolution of 10320 × 7752. But the time to select the corner is proportional to the image resolution, so how long will it takes to do the selection of a high resolution photo in future. The manual selection must be automated by a computer. Another drawback is that the Matlab procedure can only process images no larger than 1600 × 1200, or else the program will not respond, which prevents us from making full use of the full resolution of a camera. The main reason is that it is implemented by Matlab and we decided to port it to C++.

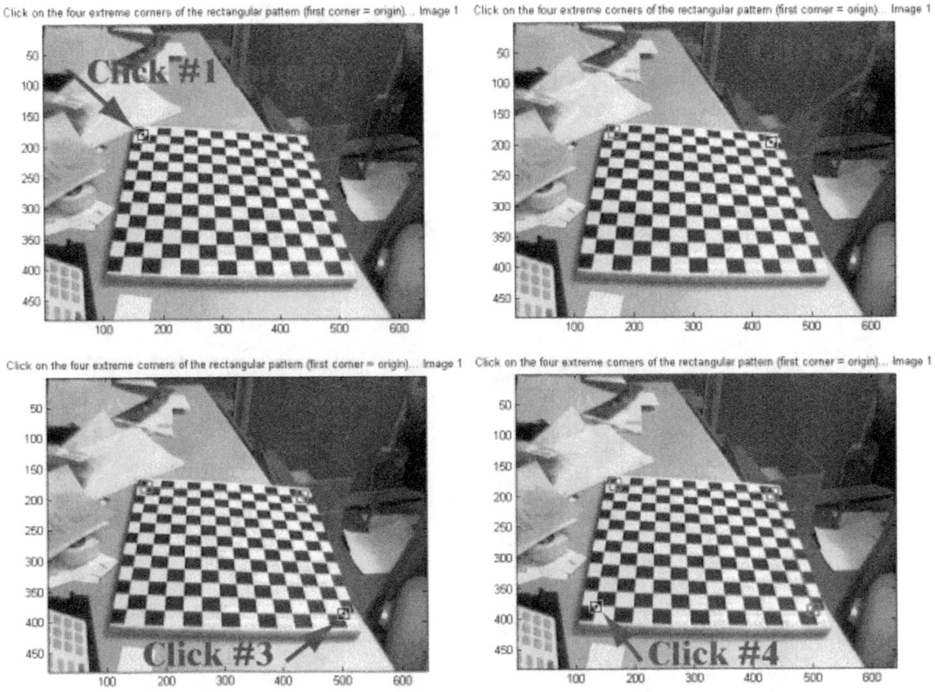


**Fig. 1.** Manual selection of the four extreme corners

In this paper, first a modified calibration pattern is proposed. Then in section 2.1 and 2.2, the algorithm to locate the added rectangular bar is presented. Section 2.3 shows the method to forecast the corners by using the property of cross ratio invariance and the forecast results. Finally, the conclusion and next work are discussed in chapter 3.

## 2 The Modified Calibration Pattern and Algorithm

### 2.1 Thresholding and Erosion

The original calibrate pattern is modified to achieve automatic calibration (see Fig. 2). With the help of the four added narrow rectangles, the center of the chessboard can be found by intersecting the diagonal and based on the property of cross ratio invariance, the corner can be forecast.

**Fig. 2.** The modified calibration pattern

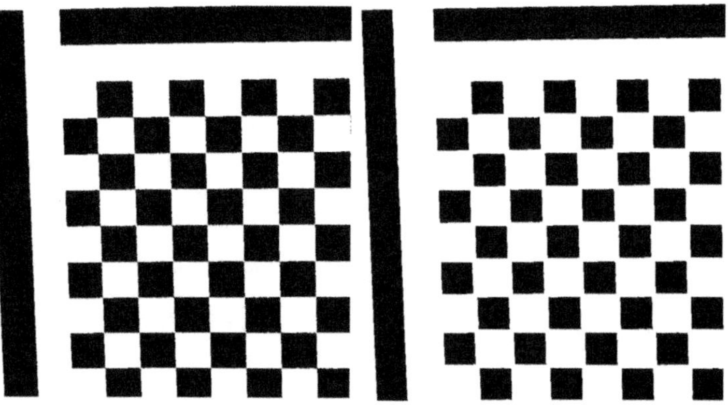

**Fig. 3.** Before and after erosion

Since during the calibration process, the camera is disallowed to move. So first a reference photo is taken when there is no chessboard. Then the chessboard is placed in the scene and several calibration images are photographed. By comparing the reference image and the calibration images, the chessboard can be easily located. To speed up this procedure, only the pixels whose *u* and *v* coordinates are both a factor of 4 is visited.

Then, the chessboard region is extracted and converted into gray scale image. The *k* (*k*=2) means cluster algorithm is employed and the chessboard region is thresholded.

After that, the image is eroded three times, as illustrated in Fig. 3. After erosion, the chessboard is disconnected into small black blocks, which make the location of the four added rectangles rather easily, i.e., counting the number of connected pixels of each block.

## 2.2 Locating the Four Rectangles

Let us define a connect region is a region that each of its pixels satisfies the following two criteria:

1) the pixel is black,
2) at least one of its adjacent pixel is black.

In this way, all the boundaries of the regions are found, as shown in Fig. 4 left.

It is obvious that the newly added rectangles should have the maximum number of connected pixels and thus by counting the number of connected pixels and selecting the regions that have the top four maximum numbers of connected pixels, the four rectangular bars can be easily identified. But to make the algorithm more robust, the shape factor is also considered.

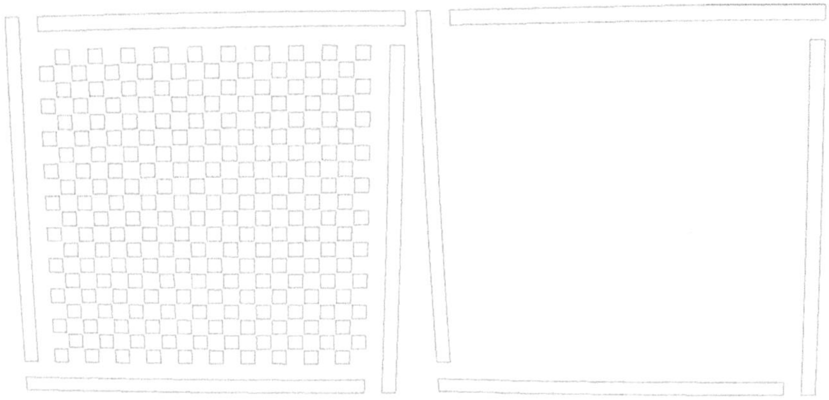

**Fig. 4.** The extracted boundaries (left) and the extracted four added rectangles (right)

The shape factor $f$ is defined as the ratio of the square of a region's circumference to its area. In formula form, let $a$ and $b$ be the length of the long and short edge of a rectangle respectively. Then, for an arbitrary rectangle, the shape factor is:

$$f = \frac{(2a+2b)^2}{ab} = \frac{4(a+b)^2}{ab} = \frac{4\left(1+\frac{b}{a}\right)^2}{\frac{b}{a}} = \frac{4(1+r)^2}{r} = 4\left(\frac{1}{r}+r+2\right), \tag{3}$$

where $0 < r <= 1$. Partial derivative to $r$ gives:

$$\frac{df}{dr} = 4\left(1-\frac{1}{r^2}\right). \tag{4}$$

When $0 < r < 1$, the derivative of $f$ to $r$ is negative, which means $f$ is monotonically decreasing. That is to say, when $a$ is equal to $b$, the shape factor $f$ has the minimum value: 16. The objective function is area times shape factor. Since by theory, the four added rectangles should have the maximum area and shape factor, by selecting the regions whose values of objective function are top four will safely find the rectangular bars, as shown in Fig. 4 right.

### 2.3 Corner Forecasting

In this stage, first, each of the central line piercing the added rectangles in the long direction is fitted. In section 2.2, the boundaries of the added rectangles have been successfully located. The central line is depicted by the following equation:

$$x\cos a + y\sin a + b = 0, \tag{5}$$

where the sum of the square of all the pixels' coordinates substituting into the above equation is minimum. Or in formula form: let

$$G = \sum_i \left(x_i \cos a + y_i \sin a + b\right)^2, \tag{6}$$

then by minimizing $G$ the coefficients $a$ and $b$ are solved. When $G$ is minimized, its partial derivatives to $a$ and $b$ must be both zero, which result in two equations which can be numerically solved.

Now it is ready to forecast the corners. Cross ratio invariance is a well-known property in projective geometry that states the ratio of the distance between four collinear points is the same as that between their projections (see Fig. 5 upper left).

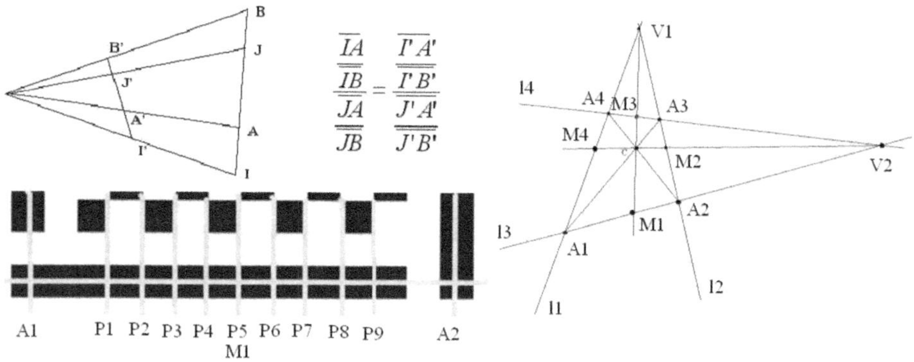


**Fig. 5.** Illustration of the cross ratio invariance (upper left)

(Locating the other points on the central lines by cross ratio invariance (lower left). Locating the center of the chessboard (right)).

As illustrated in Fig. 5 right, $l_1$, $l_2$, $l_3$ and $l_4$ are the central lines piercing the added rectangles computed by minimizing $G$ in equation (6). $l_1$ and $l_2$ intersect at $V_1$ while $l_3$ and $l_4$ intersect at $V_2$. The other four intersections of $l_1$, $l_2$, $l_3$ and $l_4$ are $A_1$, $A_2$, $A_3$ and $A_4$. Evidently, the intersection (denoted as $C$) of $A_1A_3$ and $A_2A_4$ is the center of the chessboard. Suppose $V_1C$ intersect $l_4$ and $l_3$ at $M_3$ and $M_1$, respectively while $V_2C$

**Fig. 6.** The forecast corners

intersect $l_1$ and $l_2$ at $M_4$ and $M_2$, respectively. The point $I$, $A$, $J$ and $B$ are on the world coordinate system (WCS) while the point $I'$, $A'$, $J'$ and $B'$ are on the image coordinate system (ICS). If the points $I$, $A$, $J$ and $B$ refer to $A_1$, $M_1$, $A_2$ and $P_i$ ($i$=1...9) in lower left of Fig. 5 on WCS and $I'$, $A'$, $J'$ and $B'$ refer to $A_1$, $M_1$, $A_2$ and $P_i$ ($i$=1...9) in lower left of Fig. 5 on ICS, then only the location of $P_i$ on ICS is unknown and can be calculated.

In this way, all the points ($P_i$) on the central lines are solved. Then, connecting the corresponding points on the two non-adjacent sides will give the rough positions of all the corner points. As shown in Fig. 6, the results are very close to the actual corners. The rest corner extraction code is just rewriting the Matlab program in C++.

## 3 Conclusions and Future Work

In this paper, an automatic and robust chessboard corner extraction algorithm is presented. The algorithm is rather efficient and precise. On Intel E6850 (3GHz), for a 8000 × 6000 / 12000 × 9000 image (The two images are interpolated from a 4000 × 3000 image.), the corner points are extracted within 20 / 45 seconds.

The future works are two folds. For one thing, the forecast procedure should be multithreaded, especially when multi-core CPU becomes common. And indeed, the procedure can be multithreaded since there is no dependence during the process of pixels. Or more drastically, the code will be port to CUDA to run on GPU if the speed of multithreaded code is not fast enough. For another, more cases should be tested to prove the effectiveness and correctness of the algorithm.

## References


1. Shi, X., Diao, C., Lu, D.: An Efficient and Robust Camera Extrinsic Parameters Calibration Algorithm. Journal of Computational Information Systems 3(1), 285–293 (2007)
2. Faugeras, O.D., Luong, Q.T., Maybank, S.J.: Camera Self-Calibration: Theory and Experiments. In: Sandini, G. (ed.) ECCV 1992. LNCS, vol. 588, pp. 321–334. Springer, Heidelberg (1992)
3. Shi, J.: Fundamental of Virtual Reality and Its Practical Algorithm. Science Press, Beijing (2002)
4. Ma, S., Zhang, Z.: Computer Vision - Fundamental of Computational Theory and Algorithm. Science Press, Beijing (1998)
5. Camera Calibration Toolbox for Matlab, `http://www.vision.caltech.edu/bouguetj/calib_doc`
6. Heikkila, J., Silven, O.: A Four-step Camera Calibration Procedure with Implicit Image Correction. In: IEEE Computer Society Conference on Computer Vision and Pattern Recognition, pp. 1106–1112 (1997)
7. Zhang, Z.: A Flexible New Technique for Camera Calibration. IEEE Transactions on Pattern Analysis and Machine Intelligence 22(11), 1330–1334 (2000)
8. Bakstein, H.: A Complete DLT-based Camera Calibration with a Virtual 3D Calibration Object, Thesis, Prague (1999)
9. Tsai, R.: A Versatile Camera Calibration Technique for High-Accuracy 3D Machine Vision Metrology Using Off-the-Shelf TV Cameras and Lenses. IEEE Journal of Robotics and Automation (legacy, pre - 1988) 3(4), 323–344 (1987)
10. Rosenhahn, B., Zhangm, Y., Sommer, G.: Performance of Constraint Based Pose Estimation Algorithms. In: DAGM-Symposium on Informatik Aktuell, Mustererkennung 2000, pp. 277–284. Springer-Verlag, Heidelberg (2000)
11. Liu, Y., Holstein, H.: Pseudo-linearizing Collinearity Constraint for Accurate Pose Estimation from a Single Image. Pattern Recognition Letters 25(8), 955–965 (2004)
12. Brown, D.C.: Photometric Engineering, vol. 32(3), pp. 444–462 (1966)

# An Adaptive Gradient Enhanced Texture Based Tracking Algorithm for Video Monitoring Applications

Huibin Wang, Xuewen Wu, and Rong Hong

College of Computer and Information Engineering, Hohai University, 210098
Nanjing, China
hhuwhb@gmail.com

**Abstract.** Object tracking is an important technology in video surveillance. The main approach is Mean Shift algorithm and its improved version. Studies show that the traditional Mean Shift algorithm adopts a fixed searching window in the tracking process, which cannot adjust the template adaptively. The improved algorithm, CamShift, overcomes this problem with an adaptively changing searching window. However, these algorithms are both based on color tracking, which requires that the colors of the foreground targets are unique. If the color of the target is similar to the color of the background, tracking errors will occur or tracking targets will be lost. In this study, we developed an adaptive gradient enhanced texture based tracking algorithm for traffic monitoring applications. This algorithm combines the characteristics of the color and texture of objects. The algorithm builds a joint histogram template of color and texture for targeting, which solves the problems of tracking targets losing when the color of the object is similar to the color of the background. The experiments show that the algorithm can improve the accuracy and robustness of object tracking.

**Keywords:** video surveillance; object tracking; Camshift; texture feature.

## 1 Introduction

In recent years, video surveillance system has been widely used in many areas, with the development of video analysis and processing techniques. Object tracking is very import issue in video surveillance application. Meanwhile, it is also the difficulty of computer vision technology. The purpose of object tracking is to check, identify and track the interested objects in a series of video frames, and to extract the movement parameters of the moving targets further. Nowadays, in the field of traffic monitoring, the main difficulties in video-based vehicle tracking are as follows:

- The features of vehicles being difficult to be extracted when the vehicles are far away from the camera.
- The moving of the cameras.
- Occlusion among the vehicles.
- Disturbance caused by the light change to object tracking.

Z. Pan et al. (Eds.): Transactions on Edutainment VI, LNCS 6758, pp. 57–66, 2011.

In order to solve all these problems, there have been various kinds of tracking methods, such as the deterministic methods [1] and statistical methods [2, 3], feature based methods and model based methods [4, 5, 6, 7]. All these methods have their respective advantages and are suitable for different tracking objects and different surroundings. There are some commonly used algorithms such as particle filtering, Kalman filtering, Mean-shift and so on. Particle filtering algorithm [8] has a phenomenon of degeneration, that is, after several times of iterations, most of the particles own a small value of weight, which is a waste of time. Kalman filtering [9] needs amounts of computation and is hard to describe the flexible movements of objects, so it is not suitable in real time tracking of moving objects. Mean shift [10] is a classical algorithm in deterministic algorithms, which is first introduced to the field of object tracking by Comaniciu. Mean Shift needs low computation cost and can be successfully used in real time monitoring.

Mean Shift is not adaptive in updating model. When the size of the moving objects has some changes, there would be some problems of tracking losing or tracking mistake. Nevertheless, mean shift has its own advantages such as low computation, non parameters, kernel histogram modeling and so on. For the above reasons, mean shift is robust in edge occlusion, object rotation and background changing. There are lots of improvements in mean shift algorithm by different scholars. Yang [11] introduced a similarity measuring mean shift that has a strong resolving power and adopted fast Gaussian transformation to decrease its computation cost. Alper Yilmaz [12] proposed an object tracking method based on the asymmetric kernel mean shift, in which the scale and orientation of the kernel adaptively change depending on the observations at each iteration. Jeehyun Goya Choe [13] proposed a kernel model containing both the color and distance information to reduce the computing time. In addition, Bradski [14] proposed Camshift algorithm, that is Continuously Adaptive Mean Shift, which is a kind of improved Mean Shift Algorithm. Camshift algorithm solves the problems that the traditional template of the Mean Shift algorithm cannot be updated, and cannot track moving targets adaptively.

In this paper, an adaptive gradient enhanced texture based tracking algorithm (AGETA) is proposed. The algorithm bases on Camshift, Meanwhile, for the problem of only color information used in tracking, AGETA is adopted when color based tracking failed. The paper was organized as follows. Section 2 describes the design ideas and methods of this paper. There is a detailed analysis on the basic principles and characteristics of color based tracking algorithms (including Meanshift and Camshift) in Section 3. In Section 4, it gives the processes of adaptive tracking algorithm based on gradient enhanced texture, which is followed by simulation results of algorithms are shown in Section 5.

## 2 Methodology

Object tracking is different from object detection. Object tracking needs to establish a matching relation based on position, speed, shape, color and texture feature.

In object tracking, the continuous movement of the objects can lead to the change of distances between camera and objects, which leads to the size changing of objects in video frames. So, it will be a big shortcoming if the object model cannot be updated or the kernel window cannot be changed. It is specifically expressed in the following two aspects:

(1) When the size of moving objects decreases continuously, the kernel window can be somewhat larger relatively. So, it will contain extra background pixels which have a great impact on the comparison between the histogram of searching window and model. The final positioning of the moving object can be distracted and the object maybe roams between several modes.

(2) When the size of the moving objects grow fast and outrange the kernel window, the relatively smaller kernel window can make the searching result wander in several modes. The inaccurate positioning leads to bad tracking or lost of tracking.

So, one of the focuses in this paper is how to updating tracking models. Meanwhile, when modeling the moving objects we can choose another feature space. Therefore, if the tracking based on a certain feature space fails, another space feature can replace the above one to improve the tracking. Also, a second tracking behavior can be added to increase the robustness and accuracy of object tracking.

Considering the above problems, we propose a scheme of cascade control. The architecture and methodology is showed in Figure 1. First, a color based fast tracking is introduced, and then we adopt a method to solve the problem of model updating. Finally, when tracking based on color information fails, another feature space of texture feature space is proposed to replace the color space.

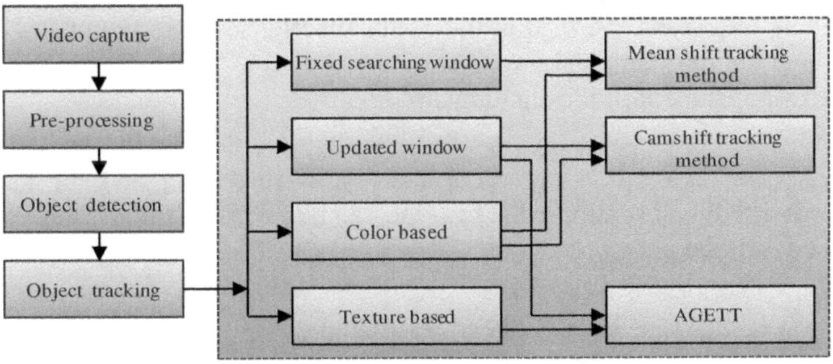


**Fig. 1.** Architecture and methodology

# 3 Tracking Algorithm Based on Color Information

## 3.1 Fixed Kernel Window Based Tracking

As the classical color based tracking, the traditional mean shift tracking is the most representative one. The tracking algorithm based on mean shift adopts color histogram to represent the interested objects. Color histogram is a simple description of the probability density function of the color distribution. Suppose the color histogram of the object model is $\hat{q}$, the histogram of the candidate region centered at y is $\hat{p}(y)$, the similarity function between the object model and the candidate

is $\hat{\rho}(y) = \rho(\hat{p}(y), \hat{q})$. The local maximum of the similarity function means the most likely candidate in the region of interesting, so the object position is the position of y which make $\hat{\rho}(y)$ reach its local maximum. The mean shift vector derived by the similarity function directs the right direction of original position to the forward position. The proof of the convergence of mean shift vector guarantees the existence of the local maximum of the similarity function. So, the tracking problem is converted to a problem of finding the best matching model.
The tracking by mean shift can be described by the following three steps:

(1) The establishment of object model

Color based mean shift uses the probability of color distribution as the feature vector of the moving objects, and the probability density centered at $x_0$ can be represented as

$$\hat{q}_u = C_1 \sum_{i=1}^{n} k(\| \frac{x_0 - x_i}{h} \|^2) \delta[b(x_i - u)], \tag{1}$$

Where $x_0$ is the central coordinate of the searching window; the amount of pixels in the window is n; $x_i$ stands for the coordinate of the $i$th pixel in the window; h stands for the width of the kernel window, which is also the radius of the searching window. $C_1$ is the normalization constant; $k(\| x \|^2)$ is a convex and decreasing kernel function which allocates lower weight values for the far away pixels and larger weight values for the pixels near the center; $\delta$ is the Delta function used to count the amount of pixels owned u in the statistical histogram.

(2) The establishment of the candidate region

Suppose $\{x_i \mid i = 1, 2, ..., n_h\}$ is the position of the pixel in the candidate region respectively; we take the central coordinate y as reference, and the same kernel function k and radius h is adopted. Then, the candidate probability of level u centered at y can be described as

$$\hat{p}_u(y) = C_h \sum_{i=1}^{n_h} k\left( \left\| \frac{x_i^s - y}{h} \right\|^2 \right) \delta\left[ b\left(x_i^s\right) - u \right]. \tag{2}$$

(3) The measurement of the object model and candidate model

In order to measure the similarity between the object model and the candidate model, we use the distance between them as the similarity criterion. The most likely position y of moving object can be reached by minimizing the distance between the moving object and the candidate model. The process of minimizing the distance can be equal to maximizing the similarity coefficients of the histogram.

The searching in current frame starts in the position $\hat{y}_0$, which is an evaluation of the moving object in the previous frame. Suppose the center of the searching widow is $y_0$, by the measurement criterion, we will seek the local optimization value of $y_1$ in the neighborhood of $y_0$. When $\hat{\rho}$ reaches its greatest value, the mean shift vector is as follows:

$$m_s = y_1 - y_0 = \left( \sum_{i=1}^{n} x_i w_i k(\| \frac{y_0 - x_i}{h} \|^2) \right) / \left( \sum_{i=1}^{n} w_i k(\| \frac{y_0 - x_i}{h} \|^2) \right) - y_0, \tag{3}$$

Suppose the color probability of candidate model centered at $\hat{y}_0$ in the current frame is described as $\{\hat{p}_u(\hat{y}_0)\}_{u=1,2,\ldots,m}$, by using the Taylor expansion of function $\hat{p}_u(y)$ at $y_0$, then the Bhattachyya coefficient describing the similarity of histogram can be described as follows:

$$\rho[\hat{p}(y),\hat{q}] \approx \frac{1}{2}\sum_{u=1}^{m}\sqrt{\hat{p}_u(y_0)\hat{q}_u} + \frac{1}{2}\sum_{u=1}^{m}\hat{p}_u(y)\sqrt{\frac{\hat{q}_u}{\hat{p}_u(y_0)}}. \tag{4}$$

In (5), $\hat{p}_u(y)$ and $\hat{q}_u$ represents the value of level u in the two histograms respectively, the similarity of $\hat{p}_u(y)$ and $\hat{q}_u$ is measured by Bhattachyya coefficient $\hat{\rho}(y)$:

$$\hat{\rho}(y) \equiv \rho[p(y),q] = \sum_{u=0}^{m-1}\sqrt{\hat{p}_u(y)\hat{q}_u(y_0)}. \tag{5}$$

The distance between object model and candidate model is shown as

$$d(y) = \sqrt{1-\rho(\hat{p}(y),\hat{q})}. \tag{6}$$

When Bhattachayya coefficient $\hat{\rho}(y)$ between the color histograms representing object model and candidate model reaches maximal, it means the distance between object model and candidate model reaches a minimal value. The task of seeking the moving object can be converted to the problem of seeking the density function $\hat{p}(y)$ which is most like $\hat{q}(y_0)$.The greater of $\hat{p}(y)$, the more likeliness between object model and candidate.

### 3.2 Adaptive Tracking

As for adaptive tracking of color information, Camshift is a classical one. In the tracking process of mean shift, the size of kernel window determines the amount of samples iterated, and also the size of the tracking window. In the process of object tracking, we need to find the peak value of a series of frames. The fixed size of kernel window may lead to the problems previously mentioned.

Camshift [14] is an improvement of mean shift and it solves the problem of fixed window. The basic idea of Camshift is to operate mean shift algorithm on each video frame, and to use the previous location of the moving object as the original position of the current frame. It means that the size and location of the previous searching window is the original value of the next mean shift iteration. Meanwhile, in the process of iteration, by extracting the zeroth moment of the searching window, the size of the kernel window can be adjusted inside the window and outside the searching window. The width or radius of the searching window is set as a function of the zeroth moment of the kernel window.

Suppose $(x, y)$ as the coordinates in the searching window, and $I(x, y)$ is the pixel value of $(x, y)$ corresponding to the histogram of moving object. The zeroth moment and the first moment of the searching window can be described as follows:

$$M_{00} = \sum_{i=0}^{m-1}\sum_{j=0}^{n-1} I_{(i,j)}(x, y) \tag{7}$$

$$M_{01} = \sum_{i=0}^{m-1}\sum_{j=0}^{n-1} y \cdot I_{(i,j)}(x, y) \tag{8}$$

$$M_{10} = \sum_{i=0}^{m-1}\sum_{j=0}^{n-1} x \cdot I_{(i,j)}(x, y) \tag{9}$$

The size of the video frame is $m \times n$, which means the amount of the pixels in the frame is $m \times n$. According to the solving method of center of gravity, the center of gravity in the searching window is as follows:

$$(x_c, y_c) = (\frac{M_{10}}{M_{00}}, \frac{M_{01}}{M_{00}}) \tag{10}$$

The key point of Camshift algorithm is to adjust the size of the searching window according to the zeroth moment $M_{00}$, and to move the center of the searching window to the mass center of the searching window. If the distance of movement is larger than the preset threshold, another new adjustment of the window size and location is processed. When the movement of the searching window center and the mass center is smaller than the preset threshold, or the number of iterations is larger than a maximal value, the iteration in the current frame is finished. The next video frame will take its value as the start of the iteration itself, and use $M_{00}$ to update the window size.

Camshift algorithm uses color information to track moving object by establishing its color histogram. It can also adjust the width of searching window by the zeroth moment of the previous window size, which is adaptive with the size of the moving object.

## 4 Adaptive Gradient Enhanced Texture Based Tracking

The tracking algorithm, such as camshaft, uses color information as the basis of tracking. It is quite effective when the moving object has a unique color compared with the background. However, when the moving object has a very similar color compared with the background color, color information will be not enough to describe the object model. This shortcoming restricts the wide use of the tracking algorithm.

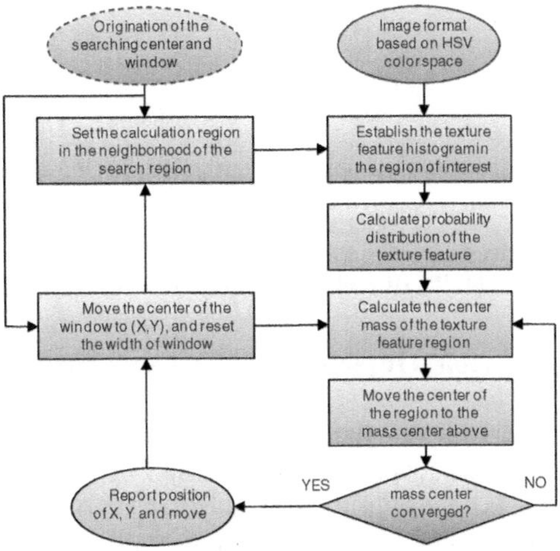


**Fig. 2.** The flowchart of gradient enhanced texture based algorithm

To solve the above problem, we can choose another feature besides the color information as the object model when the moving object has a similar color with the background. In this paper, we choose gradient enhanced texture as the substitute. Figure 2 is the flowchart of GETA.

Generally speaking, different kinds of objects have different kinds of texture features. When texture feature is chosen, we consider the local half tone characteristic and the grey dependency of the pixels.

By imitating the color histogram in Camshift, we establish texture feature histogram. In this histogram, we can choose the gradient direction of each pixel. By quantizing the gradient direction we can establish the texture feature histogram. The texture feature histogram counts the probability of all levels of the direction angles in the frame just as the color histogram counting the probability of all levels of color information. The similarity between the texture feature histogram of the object model and the candidate model is also measured by Bhattacharyya coefficient. Since the gradient direction angle is not sensitive to the change of the object size and light, the AGETT method can somewhat avoid occlusion and lighting.

# 5 Experiments Results

## 5.1 Vehicle Tracking Based on Camshift

Figure 3 shows the tracking result of color based Camshift in a relatively simple background, when car flow in traffic is not crowded. From the figures, we can see that the red ellipse can contain the moving object well. Also, the tracking can satisfy real-time application. In the operation of the algorithm, we choose the color based model of the car excluding the window, plate number or wheels.

(a) the 39th frame (b) the 52nd frame

**Fig. 3.** The moving object tracking in simple background

### 5.2 Tracking of Non-rigid Objects Based on Camshift

In this section, Figure 4 shows the tracking result of non-rigid moving object of Camshift algorithm. In the video, someone dressed in red is running over a lawn. In order to testify the tracking results of Camshift, the moving one changes her speed and gesture continuously. The experiment results show a satisfied tracking.

(a) the 506th frame (b) the 725th frame (c)the 2222nd frame

(d) the 2552nd frame (e) the 2633rd frame (f) the 2789th frame

**Fig. 4.** The tracking result of Camshift algorithm

### 5.3 Tracking of Moving Objects Based on Different Models

The characteristic of Camshift algorithm makes it sensitive to the choice of moving object model. In the operation, the tracking can be based on different kinds of models. Figure 5 shows the tracking results based on plate number and the whole car respectively. The experiments show that the geometric center of the red ellipse can be located on the center of the moving object approximately.

When choose the color information of the whole car as object model, shown by Figure 5(c), 5(d), we can see that the red ellipse is trying to include the whole car in the entire tracking process. And the size of the searching window is obviously larger than Figure 5(a), 5(b) which uses plate number as an object model.

(a) the 13rd frame (b) the 19 th frame (c) the 12nd frame (d) the 23rd frame

**Fig. 5.** Tracking result. (a) and (b): tracking results of using plate number; (c) and (d): tracking results of using the whole car.

## 5.4 Tracking Results of Gradient Enhanced Texture Based Algorithm

Figure6(a), 6(b) are the result of the tracking based on color information by Camshift algorithm; Figure 6(c), 6(d) are the result of the tracking based on gradient enhanced texture algorithm(GETA).

(a) the 12nd frame (b) the 15th frame (c) the 14th frame (d) The 18th frame

**Fig. 6.** The tracking result.(a) and (b): tracking results of color based Camshift;(c) and (d): tracking results of GETA.

From Figure 6 we can see that the moving object has a very similar color as the background. So, the searching window cannot locate the moving object correctly by adopting the traditional Camshift based on color information; while somewhat locate correctly by taking texture feature. Therefore, we can see that in a situation of mis-tracking or tracking losing, the gradient enhanced texture based tracking can be used and show a relatively satisfied result.

# 6 Conclusion

The algorithm of Camshift updates the size of the searching window in the process of tracking to fit the distribution of the object, and then overcomes the shortcomings of mean shift algorithm. However, the requirement of the color uniqueness restricts the wide use of Camshift algorithm. By establishing texture feature histogram, we can somewhat avoid the phenomenon of mis-tracking or tracking losing when moving objects have similar color with the background. Since the algorithm uses kernel histogram modeling, it is not sensitive to the edge occlusion, object rotation, shape change and background change. Our future research will be focused on improving the extraction of the texture feature and the real time implementation of object modeling.

**Acknowledgement.** This work is supported by the National High Technology Research and Development Program of China (863 Program) (No.2007AA11Z227), and Supported by National Natural Science Foundation of China (60872096).

## References

1. Zhou, S.K., Chellappa, R., Moghaddam, B.: Visual tracking and recognition using appearance adaptive models in particle filters. IEEE Transactions on Image Processing 13(11), 1491–1506 (2004)
2. Boyd, J.E., Meloche, J., Vardi, Y.: Statistical tracking in video traffic surveillance. In: IEEE International Conference on Computer Vision 1999, pp. 163–168 (1999)
3. Cucchiara, R., Grana, C., Tardini, G.: Probabilistic people tracking for occlusion handling. In: 17th International Conference on Pattern Recognition, pp. 132–135 (2004)
4. Pece, A.E.C., Worrall, A.D.: A comparison between feature-based and EM-based contour tracking. Image and Vision Computing 24(11), 1218–1232 (2006)
5. Hu, W.M., Tan, T., Wang, L., Maybank, S.: A Survey on Visual Surveillance of Object Motion and Behaviors. IEEE Transactions on Systems, Man, and Cybernetics - PART C: Applications and Reviews 34(3), 334–352 (2004)
6. Ottlik, A., Nagel, H.-H.: Initialization of Model-Based Vehicle Tracking in Video Sequences of Inner-City Intersections. International Journal of Computer Vision 84(2), 211–225 (2008)
7. Magee: Tracking multiple vehicles using foreground, background and motion models. Image and Vision Computing 22(2), 143–155 (2004)
8. Arulampalam, M.S., Maskell, S., Gordon, N., Clapp, T.: A tutorial on particle filters for online nonlinear/non-Gaussian Bayesian tracking. IEEE Transactions on Signal Processing 50(2), 174–188 (2002)
9. Julier, S.J., Uhlmann, J.K.: A new extension of the Kalman filter to nonlinear systems. In: 11th International Symposium on Aerospace/Defense Sensing, Simulation and Controls, Orlando, pp. 182–193 (1997)
10. Comaniciu, D., Meer, P.: Mean shift: A robust approach toward feature space analysis. IEEE Transactions on Pattern Analysis and Machine Intelligence 24(5), 603–619 (2002)
11. Yang, C., Duraiswami, R., Davis, L.: Similarity measure for nonparametric kernel density based object tracking. In: Eighteenth Annual Conference on Neural Information Processing Systems, Vancouver (2004)
12. Yilmaz, A.: Object Tracking by Asymmetric Kernel Mean Shift with Automatic Scale and Orientation Selection. In: IEEE Computer Society Conference on Computer Vision and Pattern Recognition, pp. 1–6 (2007)
13. Choe, J.G., Seok, J.H., Lee, J.J.: Mean-shift Tracker with Face-adjusted Model. In: International Conference on Control, Automation and Systems, Seoul, pp. 816–819 (2008)
14. Bradski, G.R.: Real Time Face and Object Tracking as a Component of a Perceptual User Interface. In: IEEE workshop on Applications of Computer Vision (WACV 1998), Princeton, pp. 214–219 (1998)

# A Novel Method for Large Crowd Flow

Xiaoxi He, Leiting Chen, and Qingxin Zhu

University of Electronic Science and Technology of China,
No. 2006, Xiyuan Road, Chengdu Hi-tech Zone, China
Chengdu College of UESTC, No. 1, Baiye Road, Chengdu Hi-tech Zone, China
microwest@163.com, {richardchen,qxzhu}@uestc.edu.cn

**Abstract.** Large scale crowd simulation can be difficult using existing techniques due to the high computational cost of the update to large number of crowd. We present a novel technique for simulating detailed groups quickly. Coarse grid is used to represent the macroscopic crowd distribution and motion tendency consistent with fluid dynamics, allowing for a fast implicit update to a few agents for local path planning and Congestion Avoidance. This allows our simulations to run at a fraction of the cost of existing techniques while still providing the fine scale structure and details obtained. Our method scales well to very large crowd and is suitable to dynamically changing environment.

**Keywords:** crowd, fluid dynamics, large scale, potential force.

## 1 Introduction

Real-time crowd simulation is difficult because large groups of people exhibit behavior of enormous complexity and subtlety. Recent researches mostly start from some kind of behavior exhibited in large crowds. Bring up the model, establish rules and produce the algorithm to solve the problem. A crowd model must not only describe people's distribution and motion tendency globally, but also solve individual human behaviors and dynamic interactions with other people and environment.

Previous work has mostly been agent-based. It is attractive for real crowds clearly operate with each individual making independent decision. In addition, different simulation parameters may be defined for each crowd member, yielding complex heterogeneous motion. But the computation for each agent becomes too expensive particularly in real-time contexts with the increase of population size.

Other major approaches have been field-based such as potential-field based. They generally employ attraction and repulsion to resolve local collision avoidance and global path planning, considering density and velocity of crowd, terrain slope and obstacles. But it inevitably becomes a bottleneck while updating potential forces for people out of sight unnecessarily.

This paper presents a real-time motion synthesis model for large crowds. We view crowds as fluids, and adopt fluid dynamic on the system. This formulation yields a set of dynamic density and velocity fields that represent the crowd distribution and guide a small portion of agents' motion. Our approach unifies global navigation, congestion avoidance, environment interactions and other specific cases into optimal equations of

Z. Pan et al. (Eds.): Transactions on Edutainment VI, LNCS 6758, pp. 67–78, 2011.

fluid dynamic. Global path planning is pre-computed and constant before environment changes or emergency occurs. The status of crowd flow is recorded in the coarse grid without computing or updating most of the individuals. Locally, the motion of each individual in sight is driven by a simple equation considering interactions with his neighbors. Our approach scales well to very large crowd in the scene of fine occlusion level and appropriate rasterization size.

## 2 Related Work

Researches of crowd animation start in the 19th century, spreading widely to other fields, such as architectonics, psychology and sociology. Reynolds [1] gave a complete control model of the group behaviors in 1987. He modeled the autonomous group behavior similar to birds, fish or bees, with rules (center attraction, speed to follow and repulsive force) to simulate individuals' interaction with environment and others. Bouvier [2] and [3] combined particle system with grids to analog people in the virtual city, group motion in which was driven by attraction field (to make people moving to goal) and repulsion field (yielded by obstacles).

Musse [4] proposed a hierarchical model for real-time crowd simulation, based on the group, rather than individuals. The programmable group followed the pre-defined behaviors, and autonomous groups use the event and the anti-force to generate more complex behaviors. Ulicny and Thalmann [5] proposed hierarchical rules of group animation. In their system, behavior captured determined its rules of conduct by level, and hierarchical finite state machines handled behaviors. Jin [6] realized interactive control of crowd navigation by Radial Basis Functions (RBF) based vector fields. Treuille [7] handled the changing environment with a globally dynamic potential field (other work see Helbing [8]), simultaneously considering the density and velocity of crowd, terrain slope and discomfort. They unified global path planning and local collision avoidance into a single framework but required the group as a unit. This effectively solved the movement of a large number of virtual groups without a precise mechanism for collision avoidance. Narain [9] used a dual representation both as discrete agents and as a single continuous system for Dense Crowd Simulation. Our approach has been partly inspired by the concepts of potential force, grouping, discomfort and hierarchical path planning.

Other work inspired us is related to the field of fluid dynamics. Many authors (such as Foster and Metaxas [10]; Stam [11]; Fedkiw et al. [12]) have used grid based techniques to produce visually compelling results, the size of the grids that these techniques can use is limited by the amount of computational power available. A kind of approach is to improve the baseline simulation on the existing grid. This can be done by using higher order methods in space, such as BFECC, QUICK, and MacCormack methods (see Dupont and Liu [13]; Kim et al. [14]; Selle et al. [15]), or in time. Although these methods increase the accuracy and fidelity of the resulting simulation, they are more expensive than traditional fluid simulation and are still limited by the Nyquist frequency of the grid. To increase the grid resolution while keeping the increase in cost to a minimum, adaptive grid techniques were introduced such as AMR [16] and octrees [17]. These techniques are effective at reducing the computational cost in cells where there is not much detailed motion while maintaining details where needed.

## 3 The Governing Equations

In this section we develop a mathematical model of crowd dynamics. We begin with a set of observations about crowd flow. Crowd behaviors are consistent at the macro with many of the characteristics of fluid dynamics found, such as flowing from high density region to low density region, pressure being interrelated to the density of the fluid, convective acceleration caused by a (possibly steady) change in velocity over position, acceleration caused by external forces, etc.

The focus is that crowd flow meets conservation of mass and is non-viscous. In fact, momentum is not conserved here. As descriptions in equation (6), the forces upon the unit area of crowds generate the acceleration. The viscosity comes from the interaction of fluid molecules (like friction). For some fluid of little viscosity and small gradient of velocity, such as water and air, their viscosity can be ignored. Our crowd flow is also this kind of fluid. Ignoring little friction between people, we view crowds as non-viscous fluid.

External forces on crowd flow are composed of the Optimal Routing force, the Discomfort force and other potential forces. The Optimal Routing force is produced by our global path planning algorithm, which makes the crowd flow follows the intended path. The Discomfort [7] force represents the terrain slope and obstacles. It will bring resistance on the grids which should influence the moving direction.

So we represent the macroscopic motion tendency and status with fluids equations, bring about microscopic behaviors with velocity fields.

### 3.1 Global Governing Equations

Navier-Stokes equations for the conservation of mass and momentum, given by

$$\rho\left(\frac{\partial v}{\partial t}+v\cdot\nabla v\right)=-\nabla p+\rho f+\mu\nabla^2 v \tag{1}$$

,

$$\frac{\partial \rho}{\partial t}+\nabla\cdot(\rho v)=0 \tag{2}$$

.

Here $\rho$ is the density of the fluid; $\frac{\partial v}{\partial t}$ is the unsteady acceleration; the convective acceleration $v\cdot\nabla v$ is an acceleration caused by a (possibly steady) change in velocity over position; $-\nabla p$ is the pressure gradient; $f$ is the external forces upon fluid; $\mu$ is the viscosity of fluids.

Note that our fluid equations focus on the macroscopic motion of crowd flow. That is the velocity we require to solve is the average vector value. The next step in local governing equation, we will further discuss the details of flow characteristics of group. The convective acceleration $v \cdot \nabla v$ will be simulated by Congestion Avoidance. Simultaneously, our crowd flow is non-Viscous ($\mu = 0$). So deleting the two items, we get a new equation.

$$\frac{\partial v}{\partial t} = -\frac{1}{\rho} \nabla p + f \tag{3}$$

Formula (2) and (3) make up the simplified fluids equations. We solve the pressure $p$ and external forces $f$ as follows.

**Crowd Flow Pressure.** People move at the maximum speed possible and always tend to the direction of low density. There is more pressure (so called congested) where there is high density, and the maximum speed of crowd is lower. So the pressure gradient accords with the density gradient in the direction and the acceleration is reversed to the pressure gradient in the direction. The gradient of Crowd Flow Pressure in the unit space given by

$$\nabla p = \nabla(\alpha \rho), (0 \le \rho \le \rho_{\max}) \quad . \tag{4}$$

Here $\alpha$ is the coefficient of $p$ than $\rho$ . The value of $\rho$ isn't greater than $\rho_{\max}$ , which is the maximum of crowd in the unit space. The Crowd Flow Pressure that we get is not the precise value. It depends on $\alpha$ valued experimentally. That will be further discussed in equation (6).

**Route Force.** In our model, external forces upon crowd flow consist of 3 parts: the Route force $f_R$ , the Discomfort force $f_D$ and other forces $f_O$ .

We use an algorithm of hierarchical path finding on grid-based maps similarly to HPA*[18]. We abstract a map into linked local clusters. At the local level, the optimal distances for crossing the cluster are pre-computed and cached. At the global level, an action is to cross a cluster in a single step rather than moving to an adjacent atomic location. At the local level, we use uniform grid maps; at the global level, a quadtree map is used.

A* returns a complete path. In contrast, HPA* returns a complete path of sub-problems. The first sub-problem can be solved, giving a unit the first few moves along the path. As needed, subsequent sub-problems can be solved providing additional moves. So the hierarchical framework is suitable for static and dynamically changing environments. When we find a path, $\vec{f_R}$ is given along this path. At any point $\vec{f_R}$ is consistent with the path in the direction and the value is a Constant. This will be the potential force for a population movement to the target site.

**Discomfort Force.** There exist a "discomfort field" which represents the gradient of the terrain and obstacles. It will bring resistance on the grids which should influence the moving direction. The force put on an individual in the environment is opposite to the direction of discomfort.

$$f_d = -\int_\theta D ds\,, \quad f_d \leq f_{max}\,. \tag{5}$$

Here $f_d$ is the discomfort force and not more than the threshold $f_{max}$; $\int_\theta D ds$ is sum of the discomfort in the $\theta$ direction; D (see paper [7]) is the discomfort in a unit which consists of terrain discomfort and obstacle discomfort. Terrain discomfort in the $\theta$ direction increase with the gradient, which means there is more resistance on the steep ramp than the gentle slope. The obstacle discomfort is generally a max value, which means obstacles are constantly impenetrable.

**Other Forces.** Other forces $f_O$ are used to explain the emergency or specific situations in crowd simulations, such as disasters or alarms to make people away from some areas, marshland slowing down the movement, traffic lights stop or make people through, and etc. Not all the specific situations are represented through forces. Sometimes we directly change the velocity of crowd or individuals in the specific areas. This will simplify the problem without losing details of crowd.

With equation (4) and (5), we may rewrite equation (3) and give our global governing equations as

$$\frac{\partial v}{\partial t} = \underbrace{-\frac{\alpha}{\rho}\nabla\rho}_{Crowd\ Flow\ Pressure} + \underbrace{\beta f_R}_{Route\ Force} - \underbrace{\gamma\int_\theta D ds}_{Discomfort\ Force} + \underbrace{\omega f_O}_{Other\ Force}\,, \tag{6}$$

$$\frac{\partial \rho}{\partial t} + \nabla\cdot(\rho v) = 0\,. \tag{7}$$

Here $\alpha$, $\beta$, $\gamma$ and $\omega$ are weights for individual terms, and we solve the gradient $\nabla *$ as $\left(\frac{\partial *}{\partial x}, \frac{\partial *}{\partial y}\right)$ for the two-dimensional characteristics of crowds. We solve these equations to get density map and velocity map. With predefined density map we first calculate $\frac{\partial v}{\partial t}$ to get $\overline{v}_T$, and with equation (7) we calculate $\rho_T$. The density map $\rho_T$ of crowd at time T shows the population distribution over the domain. The velocity map $\overline{v}_T$ will be used to simulate the local movement of individuals.

Every force's value can not exceed a threshold $f_{max}$. $f_R \equiv f_{max}$, $\beta$=1, for the route to the goal is always the max desire for crowds. Crowd pressure makes people to the low density area but can't exceed $f_{max}$, so $\alpha$ is assigned between 0 and 1; the small the value of $\alpha$, the more congestion the crowd can endure. Discomfort force represents the environmental obstruction, so $\gamma$ is always no greater than 1. Other force explain the emergency, when $\omega$=1, $\beta$=0. For the scene of terrain and dense crowd, we set these constants as: $\alpha$ =0.15, $\beta$=1, $\gamma$=0.4 and $\omega$=0.

### 3.2 Local Governing Equations

Globally we get the velocity map of the crowd flow, which means in a unit space many individuals move at the average velocity $\overline{v}_T$. But it seems ridiculous that a group of people move at the same speed and in the same direction. In the actual observation, it is obvious that the individual's movement influences by his neighbors. If his neighbors move at roughly the same direction, he always moves at his max speed. If his neighbors move on his contrary, he will slow down to avoid collision. While the most popular circumstance is that people move in various directions, an individual prefer to find a way in the cracks of the crowd to his goal, which is called Congestion Avoidance.

With these hypotheses, the velocity of each individual is given by

$$v_{iT} = (1-\eta)\overline{v}_T + \frac{\eta}{k}\sum_{k\in R}\frac{v_{k(T-1)} \times L_{\min}}{L_{ki}}, \text{ where } \quad 0<\eta<1,\ L_{\min} < L_{ki} \ . \tag{8}$$

Here the velocity $v_{iT}$ of the individual $i$ consists of the average velocity $\overline{v}_T$ of the crowd flow and the average value of his neighbors' velocity over distance. $\eta$ is the weight for the neighbor item. $v_{k(T-1)}$ is the velocity of the neighbor k at the previous moment. $L_{ki}$ is the distance between the neighbor k and the individual. $L_{\min}$ is the minimal distance between two individuals. To calculate the velocity $v_{iT}$, we initialize each individual velocity $v_k$ with the average value $\overline{v}_T$.

The solution of our governing equations is a procedure of recursion. With the initial density map $\rho$ and the zero velocity map $v$ we calculate the average velocity map $\overline{v}_T$ and the density map $\rho_T$. It is very important that for only the visible area we calculate the individual velocity, which means only the visible crowd near the camera to be rendered as 3D objects, the mass of the crowd out of sight represented by density map.

## 4 Implementation

To simulate our system, the model described in the previous section must be discretized in time and space. The simulator advances through each timestep as follows:

Initial step:

Give the initial density map $\rho$ and the zero-velocity map $v$;

Initialize each individual velocity $v_k$ with the average value $\overline{v}_T$.

For each group at each timestep:

Calculate each group's velocity map $\overline{v}_{mT}$ .

Calculate each group's density map $\rho_{mT}$ and

construct the summation of density maps $\rho_T$ .

Calculate locally each individual velocity $v_{iT}$ .

Update the people's locations.

Enforce the minimum distance between people.

Our simulating model consists of two parts. As shown in Figure 1, we use a quadtree to represent the virtual environment, and a pair of density map and velocity map for each group to represent the crowd flow.

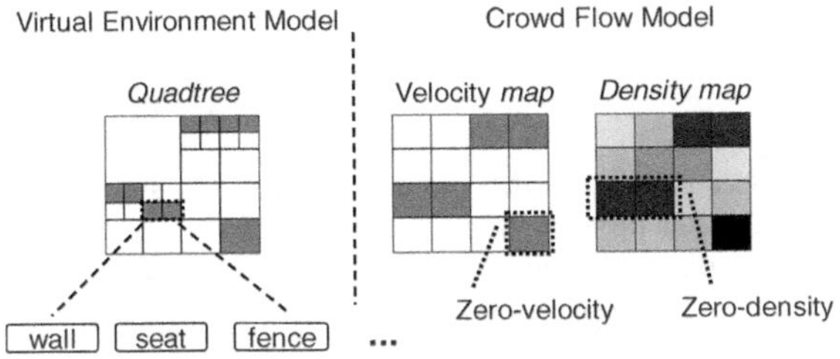


**Fig. 1.** Our simulating model consisted of virtual Environment Model and Crowd Flow Model

The quadtree conducts the Visibility Segmentation for the virtual scene and limits the areas that groups can not enter (such as obstructions) to some nodes. With the quadtree, we conclude which region is visible in the scene and use the velocity map to control of the detailed behaviors of the group. As for the rest of the invisible region, we just record the density of the population without the need for each individual simulation. The quadtree has also recorded the unreachable regions in the scene which are represented as static obstacles such as walls, seats and fences. So the quadtree provides the basis for environmental perception.

Each node of the quadtree map stores information about its level in the quadtree, the position of the area covered by the node, the occupancy type (ground, obstacle, seat, etc.), and pointers to neighboring nodes, as well as information for use in path planning, such as a distance variable (i.e., how far the node is from a given start point).

Our path planning includes the quadtree map which supports global, long-range path planning and the velocity map which supports short-range path planning. The velocity map is a coarse grid projection to the scene, each grid cell of which records the velocity of the group. Together with the quadtree map, it is employed to compute quasi-optimal paths to desired goals for groups (hierarchical path-finding) [18] [19]. The deep colored cells in the velocity map record the zero velocity which indicates the unreachable regions. If unfortunately, a person is "squeezed" in the region. It must immediately get away at the end of this timestep.

The density map has the same raster size to the velocity map. It records the crowd density at time T. The meaning of zero density is representative of the unreachable region. We calculate the density map and velocity map regularly rather than each frame. The interval between two calculations depends on the moving speed of the view point.

## 4.1 Global Crowd Flow

To compute these fields, we discretize space into two regular grids, with physical variables defined in each grid cell.

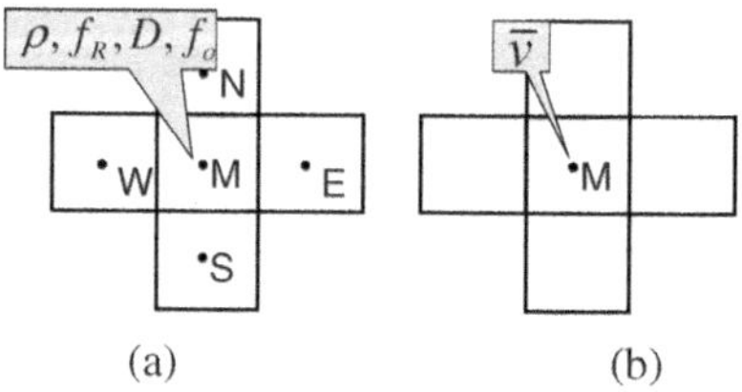


**Fig. 2.** All fields are defined at the center of each grid cell. As shown in *(a)*, we store density as scalar, route force and other forces as pairs of floating point numbers. Discomfort Force is an anisotropic field depending on the direction, so it is stored with four floats per cell corresponding to $\theta = \{0^\circ, 90^\circ, 180^\circ, 270^\circ\}$, which is the east, north, west, and south faces of each cell. Finally, the average velocity is stored as a pair of floating numbers per cell in *(b)*.

With equations (6), (7) and given density and velocity maps, we can calculate density and velocity maps next frame. That is the global motion tendency and status of the crowd flow and will not be simulated as visual objects. The part of the crowd to be displayed on the screen is just near the simulating camera or within the space segment can be seen.

## 4.2 Local Individual Behaviors

With the quadtree, we conclude which region is visible in the scene and use the density and velocity map to update a group of visual agents representing detailed behaviors.

A dynamic array is used to store all of the visual agents, while the status of each agent is store in a structure variable.

```
Struct agent
{
        location: float3;
                v_iT :  float2;
                j  :  integer; //row number of the grid
                k  :  integer; //column number of the grid
             // other status
}
```

For the simulation initialization, a group of visual agents are generated within the visible grid cells according to the density map. For each timestep, we use velocity map to update each agent's status, such as their location and velocity.

We also add other status variables into the agent's structure for the individual diversity, such as max speed, degree of hunger, endurance, etc. So the individual locomotion or behavior not only depends on equation (8). The finite state machine should decide what agent status output by specific inputting.

There are inevitably computational errors between the density of global governing equations and which results from local agents' behaviors. We use a "transition region" coordinating global density map and local agents' distribution, which consists of a group of grid cells just around the local visible region. We regularly update the visual agents (generate new ones or destroy redundancy) in the "transition region" according to the density map. This update rates by moving speed of the camera and the space segment.

## 5 Results

We have run a diverse set of crowd simulations with our system and found it can produce smooth behavior for thousands of people at interactive rates. Our implementation was in a mixture of C++, Microsoft DirectX 10 and NVIDIA CUDA. All simulations ran on a 2.6GHz Pentium Dual-Core with a NVIDIA GeForce 9600GT graphics card. The computations of the density and velocity map were distributed to GPU for multi-thread execution. CPU executes a rendering thread and another thread for visual agents update. The frame rate of our simulation depended mainly on the occlusion of the scene and the crowd scale. In the good obturated (indoor or city block) scene, it ran at 24 fps for 130,000 persons. Outdoors or in the terrain it ran at 17 fps for 10,000 persons.

(a) (b)

**Fig. 3.** Outdoor crowd simulated with the 32×32 *(a)* or 64×64 *(b)* coarse grids, allowing a maximum of 20 persons in each grid cell. Global status of crowd flow was updated but a fraction of the crowd need to interact with others and be rendered in the scene. Calculation mainly costs in the interaction between people.

(a) (b)

**Fig. 4.** *(a)* City block crowd was simulated with the 64×64 coarse grids. *(b)* When we pause the simulation and move the spectator around, it will be seen that there is no agent out of the sight. Which means our method simulates a few agents of the crowd and reduces the cost of both updating agents' states and computing their interactions.

(a) (b)

**Fig. 5.** *(a)* Crowds were tending to form lanes to avoid obstacles and adapt to terrain. When environment changed, lanes rebuilt. With external force, we could add emergency event to the system. *(b)* People rushing for the plaza in the earth-quake while some of them dying on the way. With extra properties of agents, we could simulate diverse behaviors such as suffering, death and etc.

Our method benefits a lot from the approaches of continuum dynamic (e.g. Treuille's [7]), but is much different from them. In continuum dynamic model, the velocity is not directly correlated to the density. In fact Treuille "splatter the crowd particles onto a density grid in order to compute the speed field". They could not directly compute the density field with the continuum equations. That means there has to be a heavy cost on the update to all people, such as 10,000 persons' locations.

In contrast, our equations of crowd flow represent the direct correlation between velocity and density as shown in (6) and (7). We compute density map to exhibit the crowd distribution instead of updating to thousands of people. Simultaneously a few

| | 32×32 grids to be calculated | | |
|---|---|---|---|
| | 2,000 | 5,000 | 10,000 |
| Continuum Dynamic | 2,000 | 5,000 | 10,000 |
| Our Method | ≈53 | ≈161 | ≈297 |
| | Agents to be updated | | |

(a)

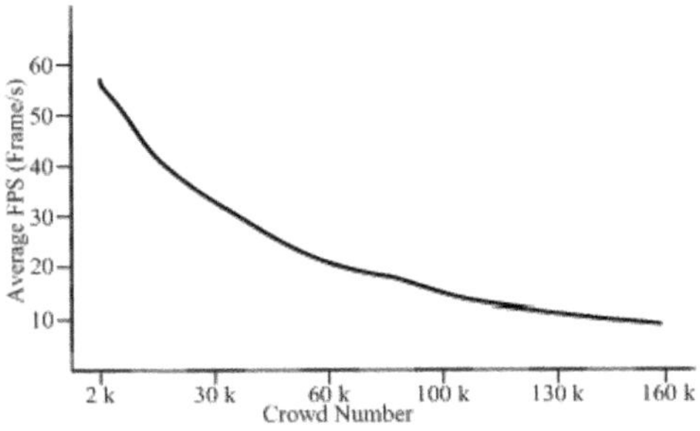


(b)

**Fig. 6.** *(a)* At the same grids size (32x32), our method updates a fraction of the crowd. The number of agents to be updated is experimental data and could be instable for the camera moving and agents in sight. *(b)* There is a rapid decline in frame rate between 2k and 100k people due to the increase of agents in sight. For more than 100k, crowd number takes less effect on frame rate.

(e.g. 300) agents were updated to render in the scene due to their visibility. Under the same conditions, we could simulate more crowds. For the truth is, we just update a fraction of them.

**Acknowledgements.** The authors would like to thank the anonymous reviewers for their helpful comments. This work was sponsored by the National High Technology Research and Development Program ("863" Program) of China under Contract No. 2007AA01Z322 and Provincial Key Technology R&D Program of Sichuan under Contract No. 2009GZ0017.

## References

1. Reynolds, C.W.: Flocks, herds, and schools: A distributed behavioral model. In: Computer Graphics Proceedings of SIGGRAPH 1987, vol. 21, pp. 25–34 (1987)
2. Bouvier, E., Guilloteau, P.: Crowd simulation in immersive space management. In: Proceedings of the 1996 Eurographics Workshop on Virtual Environments and Scientific Visualization, pp. 104–110. Springer, Berlin (1996)
3. Bouvier, E., Cohen, E., Bajman, L.: From crowd simulation to airbag deployment: Particle systems, a new paradigm of simulation. Journal of Electrical Imaging, 94–107 (1997)
4. Musse, S.R., Thalmann, D.: A hierarchical model for real time simulation of virtual human crowds. IEEE Transactions on Visualization and Computer Graphics 7, 152–164 (2001)
5. Ulicny, B., Thalmann, D.: Crowdbrush: Interactive authoring of real-time crowd scenes. In: Proceedings of the 2004 ACM SIGGRAPH /Eurographics Symposium on Computer Animation, pp. 243–252. ACM Press, New York (2004)
6. Jin, X., Xu, J., Wang, C.C.L., Huang, S., Zhang, J.: Interactive Control of Large Crowd Navigation in Virtual Environments Using Vector Fields. IEEE Computer Graphics and Applications 28(6), 37–46 (2008)
7. Treuille, A., Cooper, S., Popovic, Z.: Continuum crowds. In: SIGGRAPH 2006: ACM SIGGRAPH 2006 Papers, pp. 1160–1168 (2006)

8. Helbing, D., Farkas, I., Vicsek, T.: Simulating dynamical features of escape panic. Nature 407, 487–490 (2000)
9. Narain, R., Golas, A., Curtis, S., Lin, M.C.: Aggregate Dynamics for Dense Crowd Simulation. In: ACM Transactions on Graphics (Proceedings of SIGGRAPH Asia), vol. 28(5), pp. 122–122 (2009)
10. Foster, N., Metaxas, D.: Controlling fluid animation. In: Proceedings CGI 1997, pp. 178–188 (1997)
11. Stam, J.: Stable fluids. In: Proceeding of SIGGRAPH 1999, pp. 121–128 (1999)
12. Fedkiw, R., Stam, J., Jensen, H.: Visual simulation of smoke. In: Proc. of ACM SIGGRAPH 2001, pp. 15–22 (2001)
13. Dupont, T., Liu, Y.: Back and forth error compensation and correction methods for removing errors induced by uneven gradients of the level set function. Journal of Computational Physics 190, 311–324 (2003)
14. Kim, B.M., Liu, Y., Llamas, I., Rossignac, J.: Using BFECC for fluid simulation. In: Eurographics Workshop on Natural Phenomena (2005)
15. Selle, A., Fedkiw, R., Kim, B., Liu, Y., Rossignac, J.: An unconditionally stable MacCormack method. Journal of Scientific Computing 35, 350–371 (2008)
16. Berger, M., Oliger, J.: Adaptive mesh refinement for hyperbolic partial differential equations. Journal of Computational Physics 53, 484–512 (1983)
17. Losasso, F., Gibou, F., Fedkiw, R.: Simulating water and smoke with an octree data structure. In: Proceedings of ACM SIGGRAPH 2004, vol. 23, pp. 457–462 (2004)
18. Botea, A., Müller, M., Schaeffer, J.: Near optimal hierarchical path-finding. Journal of Game Development 1, 7–28 (2004)
19. Shao, W., Terzopoulos, D.: Autonomous Pedestrians. In: Proceedings of the 2005 ACM SIGGRAPH/Eurographics symposium on Computer animation, pp. 15–28 (2005)

# Evoking Panic in Crowd Simulation

Tianlu Mao, Qing Ye, Hao Jiang, Shihong Xia, and Zhaoqi Wang

Institute of Computing Technology, Chinese Academy of Sciences,
Beijing 2704 mail box, Beijing, China, 100190
{ltm,yeqing,jianghao,xsh,zqwang}@ict.ac.cn

**Abstract.** In order to exhibit panic phenomenon in the crowd simulation, special rules or parameters setting is needed for a given scene. In this paper, we present a panic model, named PPIB (Panic, Propagation and Influence on Behavior), which could evoke panic automatically under dangerous situation without manual intervention. PPIB describes panic behavior in three perspectives, including human mental factors and their variation caused by local situation, panic propagation, and influence of panic over the basic factors of pedestrian dynamic. Experiments show that combined with a dynamical crowd model, PPIB could evoke a wide variety of panic behaviors and exhibit emergent phenomena in crowd simulation.

## 1 Introduction

Mass-panic is one of the most disastrous crowd phenomena. Simulating crowd with panic has an important value not only in the entertainment and games, but also in the emergency planning for great events or architectures with high-density crowd. Although some empirical work in behavioral sciences show that panic is seldom happened during emergent evacuation [1-3], it is still very necessary to simulate crowd with panic and arrange in advance to avoid tragic situation. This year, the crowd disaster occurred in Duisburg during the Love Parade music event and stampede occurred on a bridge in Cambodia during the water festival, remind us the necessity of simulating the worst situation.

In crowd simulation, considerable efforts on navigation, path planning and locomotion have been made to generate lifelike and collision-free crowd motion. However, very little attention has been focus on simulating crowd with panic. Some existing crowd models could exhibit part of panic behaviors by adjusting the value of parameter [4] or combining with some specific psychological rules [5]. Using these models, special setting or combination is needed for a given scene. Therefore, in the view of practicability, a full-formed panic model which could perceive dangers, automatically evoke panics and naturally generate panic behaviors is valuable.

In this paper, we designed a novel panic model which could be used in games or evacuating simulation to evoke panic behavior automatically without manual intervention. We called it as PPIB model, which means panic, propagation and influence on behavior. PPIB model describes mass panic in different perspectives, from individuals to crowd, and from mentality to behavior. In mental layer, PPIB

Z. Pan et al. (Eds.): Transactions on Edutainment VI, LNCS 6758, pp. 79–88, 2011.

models the variation of mental factors caused by the dangers in the environment and the propagation of panic among crowd. In influence layer, it models the variation of basic factors in pedestrian dynamic caused by panic. By evoking and propagating panic among individuals, and transforming mental variation into dynamical variation, PPIB could automatically and naturally change the behaviors of crowd.

PPIB describes the influence on crowd dynamics caused by the panic, instead of the motion mechanism of crowd. It could be combined with dynamical crowd models, such as empirical social forces model [6] or continuum field models [7, 8] in simulation, and could evoke them to express a wide variety of panic phenomena naturally and automatically.

## 2 Related Work

In this section, we give a brief review of previous work in the crowd simulation which has relatively high expressiveness for crowd phenomena, especially for the panic phenomena.

Helbing's empirical social forces model [6] is one of the most significant dynamical models in this area. By applying socio-psychological and physical forces among pedestrians and obstacles, it could exhibit a lot of dynamical features observed in the real world. Additionally, controlled by a single "nervousness" parameter, it could transform the crowd from rational status to panic status [4]. Some work have focused on extending empirical social forces model [9, 10], however the expressiveness of panic phenomenon are the same. The main problem of these models is that the propagation of panic is ignored, which has been certificated in the real life [11]. Furthermore, it needs manual intervention when controlling panic behaviors by the "nervousness" parameter.

Continuum field method is another type of dynamical model with high expressiveness for crowd phenomena [7]. By projecting discomfort on the potential field and increasing speed in front of the danger, continuum field method could exhibit several emergent phenomena. It has been extended to generate more conflict-free motion under high density when using small grids in complex environments [8]. However, like social forces model, continuum field methods ignore the propagation of panic. Additionally, the control of panic behavior in a higher layer is lacked, thus special setting of low layer parameters is needed to achieve a desired result.

Rule-based models [12] introduced by Reynolds could generate emergent flocking behavior by combining several simple local rules. In order to expand the set of possible behaviors, different behavior rules are mixed and applied selectively [13-15], and cognitive models are combined into the rule-based model [16]. However, they can't simulate high density crowds and can't generate 'pushing' behavior in panic situation [5].

By applying a combination of psychological and geometrical rules with a forces model, HiDAC model could exhibit many emergent behaviors, especially in the high density [5]. It is further expanded by adding OCEAN personality model to demonstrate personality influences on the crowd motion [17]. The disadvantage of HiDAC model is that the number of rules increases rapidly when a wide range of behaviors need to be exhibited in one scene, as a result organizing and selection for rules might be tough since contradiction between rules will be frequent. For example, stopping rule is used to handle 'shaking' problem in high-density, however, when pushing behavior should be exhibited, stopping rule must be canceled.

Contrasted with rule-based methods, dynamical crowd models could exhibit features in evacuation which match the observation in real world [6] and could simulate high density crowd [8]. We try to design a panic model which could be used to control dynamical models in the mental layer so as to evoke panics and panic behaviors automatically.

# 3 PPIB Model

PPIB aims to, first evoking panics in the mental layer when an individual perceives dangers or infected by people around, and then transforming the mental variation into the dynamical variation to evoke panic behaviors.

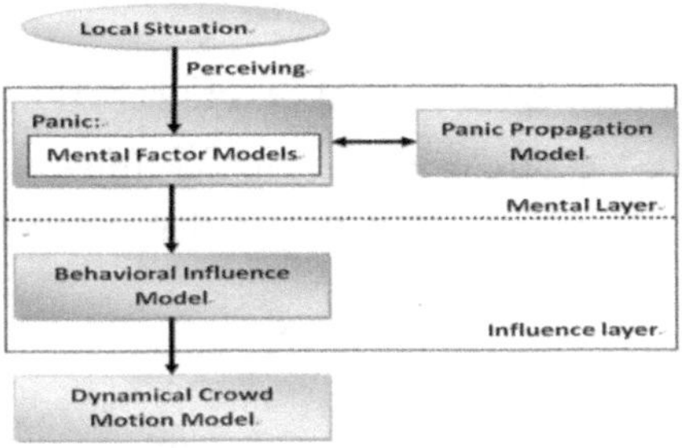


**Fig. 1.** Architecture overview

Fig. 1 shows an overview of PPIB model. In the mental layer PPIB describes the variation of mental factors caused by the dangers in environments and the propagation of panics among individuals. Thus panics could be evoked mentally. In the influence layer, PPIB models the variation of basic factors in the pedestrian dynamic caused by panics. This layer describes transition from psychology to behavior. It enables PPIB have the power to change the motion of crowd and evoke panic behaviors without any explicit rules or manual intervention. In the crowd simulation, PPIB need to be combined with a dynamical crowd motion model. Continuum fields methods, or social forces models combined with a navigation method, are optional selections.

# 4 Mental Layer

## 4.1 Mental Factors

Panic is assumed to occur in situations where people compete for scarce or dwindling resources like safe space or access to an exit [1]. It is also characterized by selfish or irrational behavior which affects large groups through propagation [1, 6]. In the disaster research, conditions evoking panic and basic elements of panic have been studied [2, 19-21]. Based on these works, we defined the mental layer of panic.

$$E = \{E_{fear} E_{urgency} E_{helpless} \cdots\} \tag{1}$$

- $E_{fear}$ *: Evading against danger source*
- $E_{urgency}$ *: Desire of escape quickly*
- $E_{helpless}$ *: Fluctuations from normal behaviour state because lack of escape information*

$E_i$ denotes the mental factor related with panic and triggered by the environment for a given individual. Their values are ranged from 0 to1, and are changed relative to the current situation and personalities of the individuals. If these factors accumulated to a certain extent will evoke panic in the mental layer. The set E is includes, but is not limited to, the aforementioned elements: fear, urgency and helpless. It is extensible. Factors like adherence and aggressive could be included if they are needed. Here we give the functions for three basic mental factors.

$$E_{fear} = \sum \sigma_i \exp\{-\xi(\|\vec{r} - \vec{r_{di}}\|, R_i)\} \tag{2}$$

where $\sigma_i$ is the weighted coefficient representing different influence from danger sources i ($i = 0,1,2,\ldots$), $\|\vec{r} - \vec{r_{di}}\|$ represents the distance from a given individual to danger source i. $R_i$ is the influence radius of danger source i. Function $\xi(x, y)$ is defined as:

$$\xi(x, y) = \begin{cases} x & \text{if } x < y \\ 0 & \text{otherwise} \end{cases} \quad (3$$

Different danger sources should have different weights and ranges. Some dangers, like fire, would have a large power to keep people far away from the burning position. Others, like toxic gas, will have less weight but would spread widely.

$$E_{urgency} = \begin{cases} 0 & \text{if time} \le 0 \\ (2/\pi)\left|\tan^{-1}(\pi(t - t_0))\right| & \text{else} \end{cases} \tag{4}$$

where $t_0$ is the expected escape time.

$$E_{helpless} = 1 - A_{local}/A_{global} \tag{5}$$

where $A_{local}$ is the amount of information the given individual holds, and $A_{global}$ is that of the information on the whole escape path.

### 4.2 Panic

Panic could be evoked in the mental layer when an individual perceives dangers or infected by people around. We defined panic as a time variation function, and composed by two types of component. For a give individual, at time step t, his/her panic value is $P(t)$, which is:

$$P(t) = \mu P(t-1) + (1-\mu)\big(M(t) + G(t-1)\big) \tag{6}$$

where $P(t-1)$ is the panic value in the last time step. $\mu$ represents the rate of psychology delay, $0 < \mu < 1$. $M(t)$ denotes the panic component generated by the given individual himself/herself. It is defined as the comprehensive value of mental factors $E_i$ in current time step:

$$M(t) = \sum \lambda_i E_i \tag{7}$$

where $\lambda_i$ is the weighted coefficient representing different contributions from different mental factors. It meets $\sum \lambda_i = 1$. $G(t-1)$ denotes the panic component infected by other people. It is related to the panic value of people around at last time step. We will define it in next section.

### 4.3 Propagation

For a given individual i, its panic component, G, is infected by other people. It is defined as:

$$G = \sum_{P_j > P_0} (\widetilde{\emptyset_{ij}} \cdot P_j) \tag{8}$$

It means that individual i infected by neighboring individual j, if $P_j$ (panic value of individual j) is higher than a threshold $P_0$. $\widetilde{\emptyset_{ij}}$ is a weighted coefficient, it comes from $\emptyset_{ij}$ after normalized.

$$\emptyset_{ij} = \begin{cases} 0 & \text{if } \|\vec{r_i} - \vec{r_j}\| > 3R \\ \exp\left\{-\frac{\|\vec{r_i} - \vec{r_j}\|}{R}\right\} \omega(\varphi_{ij}) & \text{else} \end{cases} \tag{9}$$

where $\|\vec{r_i} - \vec{r_j}\|$ is the distance between i and j, R is the decay length and there is a cutoff at 3R. $\omega(\varphi_{ij})$ is the anisotropic function means different weight of impact in different direction.

## 5 Influence Layer

In the influence layer of PPIB, panic affects the behaviors of crowd by changing the basic dynamic factors of individuals. We will demonstrate the method by a serial of panic behaviors it evokes.

**Herding behavior.** In panic situations, people show a tendency to do what other people do [6]. For example, follow the flow, flock to some exits, but ignore others. In PPIB, we model herding behavior as:

$$B_i(t) = \{B_j(t) \mid P_j > P_0, \emptyset_{ij} \text{ is the max one }\} \tag{10}$$

where $\emptyset_{ij}$ is a weighted influence coefficient as in formula (9). Here it represents a possibility of individual i follow the behavior of individual j. $B_i(t)$ and $B_j(t)$ is a set of basic motion factors of i and j at time t respectively, include travel goal and motion state.

**Pushing behavior.** We evoke the pushing behavior by enhancing the repulsion among individuals according to panic value as following:

$$U_i' = U_i \exp(P_i) \tag{11}$$

In the social force model, since it is under an agent-based framework, $U_i$ represents repulsion force from individual i to another individual. In continuum methods, $U_i$ represents the discomfort field individual i generated.

**Vicious competition.** The phenomena of vicious competition in escaping can be fully explained by the Prisoner's Dilemma (PD) game [18]. Applying the PD game into our PPIB model, in panic situation, if one runs faster he could soon gain the critical resource. Then other individuals would become aggressive and tend to pull him back. To evoke vicious competition, we define:

$$V_i' = V_i \exp(P_i) \tag{12}$$

In continuum methods, $V_i$ represents the discomfort field individual i generated. In social force model, $V_i$ represents sliding friction force from individual i to another individual.

**Small group.** PPIB also facilitates the construction of small group upon the social force model. It is very common in the every-day life, people standing closer to his/her familiars and forming small groups. In panic situation, people relatively tend to gather together closer.

In order to evoke grouping phenomenon, first, we model the clinging force in the common situation as following:

$$I_{ij} = k\,l\,(\vec{r_j} - \vec{r_i})/\|\vec{r_i} - \vec{r_j}\|\ \mathrm{sign}\,(l - \gamma_i) \tag{13}$$

$I_{ij}$ is the clinging force exerted on i to follow j. $R_i$ and $R_j$ are the radius of i and j respectively, l means the blank space between i and j, k is a const parameter. To consider the potential collision between i and j, we set a minimum threshold $\gamma$ to represent the personal space radius. sign() is a sign function. If the blank space between i and j is smaller than $\gamma_i$, the clinging force will take the opposite direction to avoid potential collision.

In the panic situation, the personal space radius $\gamma$ and the clinging force will be changed as following:

$$\gamma_i = \varepsilon_i \exp(-P_i) \tag{14}$$

$$I_{ij}' = I_{ij} \exp(P_i) \tag{15}$$

where $\varepsilon_i$ is the minimum value of the personal space radius of i. In such a way, when the panic occurs, people are more likely to stay or run together with groups. However, PPIB evokes grouping phenomena only upon the social force model, since it is an agent-based model.

## 6 Results

In this section, we demonstrate the simulation results of panic crowds. All experiments are run by PPIB with a developed social forces model, which adds an orientation constraint on Helbing's social force model to handle the problem of "shake" in the high-density crowd and adds a clinging force as in formula (13) to expand the set of possible behaviors.

**Panic and propagation.** First, we demonstrate the propagation of panic in crowd. Fig. 2 shows one of the results. An individual is in panic (red cylinder in the first sub-figure), then the panic is propagated to others around, gradually spreading to whole crowd. When the panic of an individual increases, his/her color will changes from blue to red. In last sub-figure, cylinders with shining star over head represent individuals who can influence the individual in yellow. Fig. 3 shows another result in which the fear increases and panic spreads as the fire gets nearer and nearer. Fig. 4 demonstrates another situation in which individuals want to escape from a locked room, as time flying over the expected leaving time, the value of $E_{urgency}$ increases.

**Pushing and vicious competition.** Fig. 5 demonstrates the pushing phenomenon when two individuals go vis-à-vis. The upper row in Fig. 5 represents situation without panic, in which individuals (blue cylinders with white disks as their personal spaces) avoid running into each other. The lower figures represent a panic individual (red cylinder) pushing away another normal one.

Fig. 6 shows pushing behavior when two groups go vis-à-vis. In the left, a group of panic individuals are rushing to their goal and several normal ones give way to them. In the right, several panic individuals are rushing into and dispersing the group of normal ones. In addition, we could find that the group in panic tends to stay closer than the normal group.

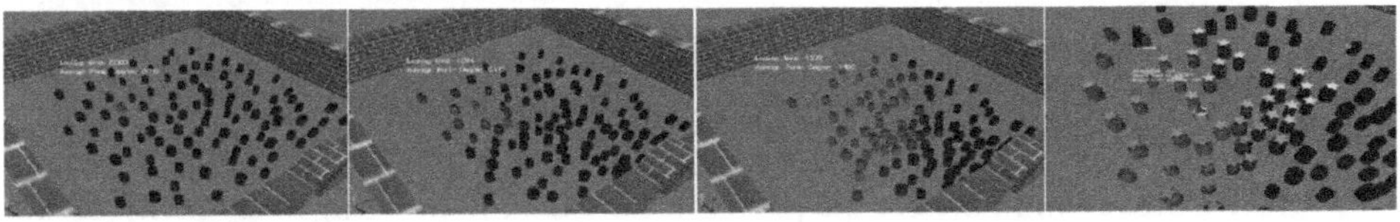

**Fig. 2.** Panic propagation in crowd. Red denotes individuals with higher panics, blue denotes ones in normal statue.

**Fig. 3.** Panic evoked by fire and propagation in crowd

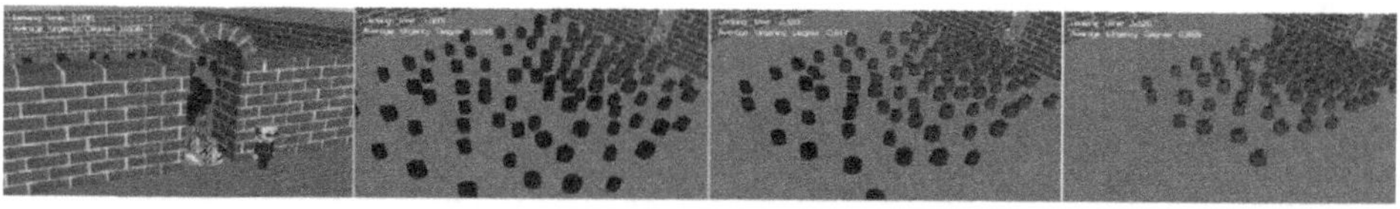

**Fig. 4.** Panic evoked as time flying over the expected leaving time

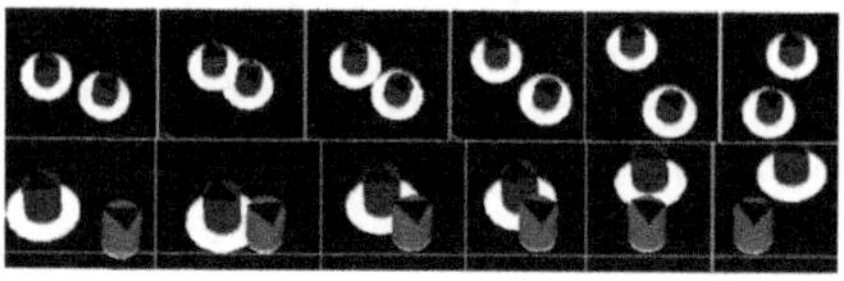

**Fig. 5.** Push behavior in two person scene, contrast with normal situation

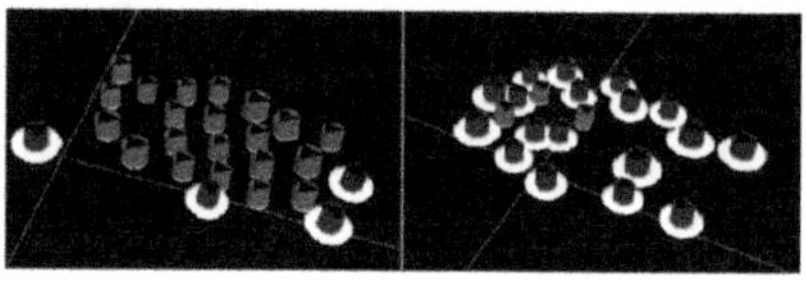

**Fig. 6.** Pushing behavior in two groups

Fig. 7 and Fig. 8 show the simulation results of vicious competition when individuals compete for the access to an exit or a door. In Fig. 7, individuals are going up to a train at a subway station, a panic passenger (red cylinder in right sub-figure) rushes in more quickly than the one in normal state (yellow cylinder in left sub-figure) and others waiting in order. In Fig. 8, when normal individuals walking out to a passage in order, a few panic individuals (with red ball over head) rushing through the others.

**Fig. 7.** Vicious competition caused by a panic individual, contrast to the normal situation

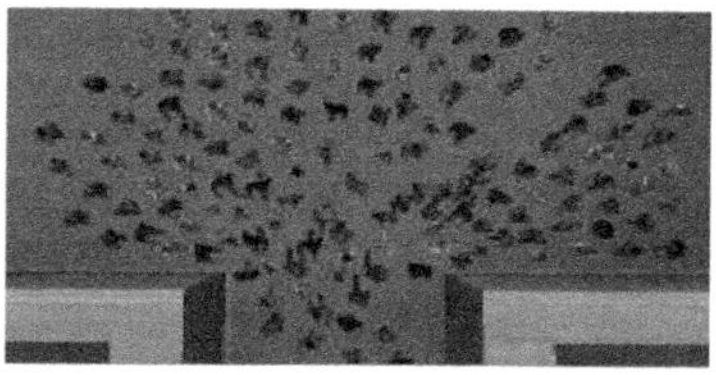

**Fig. 8.** Vicious competition and rushing through the crowd

**Control transform.** In the escape panic, it is difficult to move against the direction of the crowd, like swimming against the stream. Control transfer phenomenon may happen in such situation, which means the individual's power of motion control has been transferred to the mass no matter on one's own will. Fig. 9 shows three different situations to demonstrate the phenomena of control transform. An individual with direction reserved to crowd flow: if the individual is calm (blue ball) and the crowd in normal state, he could slowly get out from the crowd (left sub-figure); if the agent is panic (red ball) and crowd in normal state, he could quickly get out (middle sub-figure); if the agent is calm but crowd is panic, he could not get out from the crowd and have to move with the flow (right sub-figure).

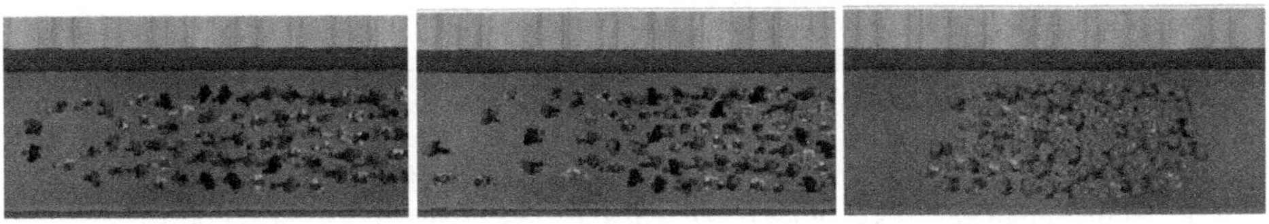

**Fig. 9.** Control transform in panic, contrast with normal situation

## 7 Conclusion

In this paper, we introduce a panic model named PPIB, which could be used upon a dynamical crowd model to evoke panics and panic behaviors automatically under dangerous situations without manual intervention.

We demonstrate a wide range of emergent phenomena evoked by PPIB in our simulation, including panic propagation, pushing, vicious competition and control transform. We also demonstrate the small group phenomenon in either normal or panic situation. The main contribution of PPIB is not only the ability to express panic behaviors, but also the ability to evoke panic behaviors naturally and automatically.

**Acknowledgments.** This work is supported and funded by the National Natural Science Foundation of China No. 60703019, No. 60903140 and No. U0935003. It is also supported by Co-building Program of Beijing Municipal Education Commission. Furthermore, we would like to thank the anonymous reviewers for their valuable comments and suggestions.

## References

1. Schadschneider, A., Klingsch, W., Klupfel, H., Dretz, T., Rogsch, C., Seyfried, A.: Evacuation Dynamics: Empirical Results, Modeling and Applications. In: Meyers, R.A. (ed.) Encyclopedia of Complexity and System Science. Springer, New York (2009)
2. Keating, J.P.: The myth of Panic. Fire Journal, 57–62 (May 1982)
3. Sime, J.D.: The Concept of Panic. In: Canter, D. (ed.) Fires and Human Behaviour, vol. 1ch. 5, pp. 63–81. John Wiley & Sons Ltd. London (1990)
4. Helbing, D., Farkas, I., Molnar, P., Vicsek, T.: Simulation of pedestrian crowds in normal and evacuation situations. In: Proceedings of Pedestrian and Evacuation Dynamics (2002)
5. Pelechano, N., Allbeck, J.M., Badler, N.I.: Controlling individual agents in high-density crowd simulation. In: Proceedings of Eurographics/ ACM SIGGRAPH Symposium of Computer Animation (2007)
6. Helbing, D., Farkas, I., Vicsek, T.: Simulating dynamical features of escape panic. Nature 407, 487–490 (2000)
7. Treuille, A., Cooper, S., Popivic, Z.: Continuum Crowds. In: ACM Transactions on Graphics (SIGGRAPH 2006), pp. 1160–1168 (2006)
8. Jiang, H., Xu, W., Mao, T., Li, C., Xia, S., Wang, Z.: Continuum Crowd Simulation in Complex Environments. Computers & Graphics 2010 34(5), 537–544 (2009)
9. Helbing, Buzna, Johansson, Werner: Self-Organized Pedestrian Crowd Dynamics. Transportation Science 39(1), 1–24 (2005)

10. Lakoba, T.I., Kaup, D.J., Finkelstein, N.M.: Modification of the Helbing-Molnar-Farkas-Vicsek Social Force Model for Pedestrian Evolution. Simulation 81(5), 339–352 (2005)
11. Gelder, B., Snyder, J., Greve, D., Gerard, G., Hadjikhani, N.: Fear fosters flight: A mechanism for fear contagion when perceiving emotion expressed by a whole body. Proc. Natl. Acad. Sci. 101(47), 16701–16706
12. Reynolds, C.W.: Flocks, herds, and schools: A distributed behavioural model. In: Computer Graphics Proceedings of SIGGRAPH 1897, vol. 21, pp. 25–34 (1987)
13. Reynolds, C.: Steering behaviours for autonomous characters: Steering behaviours for autonomous characters. In: Game Developers Conference, pp. 763–782 (1999)
14. Silverman, B., Bharathy, G., Cornwell, J., O'brien, K.: Human Behaviour Models for Agents in Simulators and Games: Part II - Gamebots for a Foreign Culture. Presence 15(2), 163–185 (2006)
15. O'sullivan, C., Cassell, J., Vilhjalmsson, H., Dobbyn, S., Peters, C., Leeson, W., Giang, T., Dingliana, J.: Crowd and Group Simulation with Levels of Detail for Geometry, Motion and Behaviour. In: Third Irish Workshop on Computer Graphics (2002)
16. Shao, W., Terzopoulos, D.: Autonomous pedestrians. In: Proceedings of ACM SIGGRAPH / Eurographics Symposium on Computer Animation, pp. 19–28 (2005)
17. Durupinar, F., Allbeck, J., Pelechano, N., Badler, N.: Creating crowd variation with the OCEAN personality model. In: Proceedings of the 7th International Joint Conference on Autonomous Agents and Multiagent Systems (May 12-16, 2008)
18. Flood, M., Dresher, M.: On game-learning theory and some decision-making experiments. In: RAND Research Memorandum (1952)
19. Drabek, T.E.: Human System Responses to Disaster: An Inventory of Sociological Findings. Springer, New York (1986)
20. Tierney, K.J., Lindell, M.K., Perry, R.W.: Facing the Unexpected: Disaster Preparedness and Response in the United States. Joseph Henry Press (2001)
21. Dynes, R., Quarantelli, E., Kreps, G.: A Perspective on Disaster Planning. Disaster Research Center. University of Delaware, New York, DE(1981)

# A Behavior Model Based On Information Transmission for Crowd Simulation

Ting Dong, Yan Liu, and Lin Bian

School of Computer Science and Technology, Tianjin University,
No. 92, Weijin Road, Nankai District, 300072 Tianjin, China
{dongting1129,linyaya212}@163.com, daisy_liu@tju.edu.cn

**Abstract.** In this paper, a crowd behavior model based on information transmission processes is presented. In crowds, human behaviors are easily influenced by information. The information is transferred to them by other people and surrounding environment. When emergencies occur in crowds, people get danger information when they see an emergency occurs or other people tell them. People in the crowd are intelligent agents. They get information from their surroundings, make decisions according to certain events and take some actions according to the decisions. The contribution of this paper would be that information transmission processes is used and taken into account by the agents. This behavior model can simulate how information about danger is transferred in crowd in emergency situations. By combining the information transmission processes with people's personalities, it can achieve good crowd evacuation simulation.

**Keywords:** behavior model, crowd simulation, information transmission, intelligent agent.

## 1 Introduction

Crowd simulation now becomes an important research area, which has a wide application in education, entertainment, architecture, training, urban engineering and virtual heritage. In general, there are two main approaches in this research area that should be taken into account: (1) control all the people in crowd as an entity, make it moving to an appointed place, (2) make the individual in crowd owning his own personality which is different from others', he decides where to go and what to do by himself. The first approach is low-request on hardware when simulating large scale crowd, but as a result of ignoring the personality of each individual, the realism of simulation is not good. The other one looks much more realistic. But because system has to maintain a relatively larger attributes list, when the number of agents in crowd is increased, the computational cost is increased too. When an emergency occurs in crowd, the responses of people in crowd to certain events are also an important research area in crowd simulation.

Because the backgrounds of research are different, the crowd simulation models presented by research groups from all over the world are various. That is, much work has been done to make the behaviors of crowd realistic [9] or to achieve real time

Z. Pan et al. (Eds.): Transactions on Edutainment VI, LNCS 6758, pp. 89–98, 2011.

simulation for very large crowds [10]. However, relatively little effort has been placed upon the information transmission in crowd simulation.

A behavior model based on information transmission processes is described in this paper. On the basis of information transmission, the model can simulate the information transmission processes when an emergency occurs in crowd. To achieve good result in crowd simulation, the model uses method of combining individual personality and information transmission processes. In addition, an interface which uses our behavior model is provided to users to control motions of the crowd. As a result, our model can not only exhibit realistic simulation of crowd behaviors, but also can provide convenience to users.

This paper is organized as follows: in section 2, related works are briefly reviewed. Section 3 focuses on the details of our crowd behavior model which is based on information transmission. In section 4, the experimental results are described. Our conclusions and future work are discussed in section 5.

## 2 Related Works

To get better results in crowd simulation, it is essential to endow people abilities to perceive environment where they stay. In literature, we can get some related works. Monzani and Thalmann [11] proposed simple methods for sound spread. Each agent's influence area is radial and angular distribution. If agents are far from each other, they cannot get information from each other. Funge, Tu and Terzopoulos [12] have worked on behavioral simulation for artificial life which is endowed with synthetic vision. In Reynolds [1] and Musse's [13] researches, agent can get their neighbors positions directly. Reynolds concerns flocks of birds and schools of fishes, and Musse concerns crowds of human. Smell simulation is complex and difficult. Mamlouk [14] presented a robust infrastructure to analyze and interpret psychophysical and neurophysiological experiments in olfactory. Cony et al. [5] proposed a multi-perceptive model to simulate the movement of virtual human in emergency situations. Conde and Thalmann [15] presented a multi-sensorial perception model for autonomous agents. In these multi-perceptive models, intelligent agents get information from several ways: hearing, vision, smell and touch.

In traditional crowd simulation, all people have the same simple behavior set. Their reactions to particular event are same. Helbing et al. [2] solves Newton's equation for each individual and considers repulsive interaction, friction forces, dissipation and fluctuations to simulate the interaction between people and obstacles. Reynolds [1] first used a distributed behavior model to produce flocking behavior. In multi-agent crowd system, each individual has his own action rules. Braun et al. [8] presented model to control each agent by individual rules and physical laws. Pelechano and Badler [6] animate evacuation in complex building and try to make people have different roles such as trained personnel, leaders and followers. Pelechano et al. [7] presented an architecture integrated psychological model, roles and communication.

# 3 Our Works

## 3.1 Intelligent Agent Control Structure

The behavior control structure is described in Fig.1. In macroscopic, the structure adopts layered architecture of Perceptual-Control-Motion, the control system is divided into three subsystems: behavior system, planning system and reflex system.

Reflex system controls agent behavior in a simple method. The method is that agent responds to stimulation directly without thinking and reasoning processes. Planning system is in charge of memory analysis and real time percept. It implements virtual human's path planning and collision avoidance. Behavior system is in charge of higher level behaviors: behaviors generation and behaviors abstraction. It makes virtual human more intelligent.

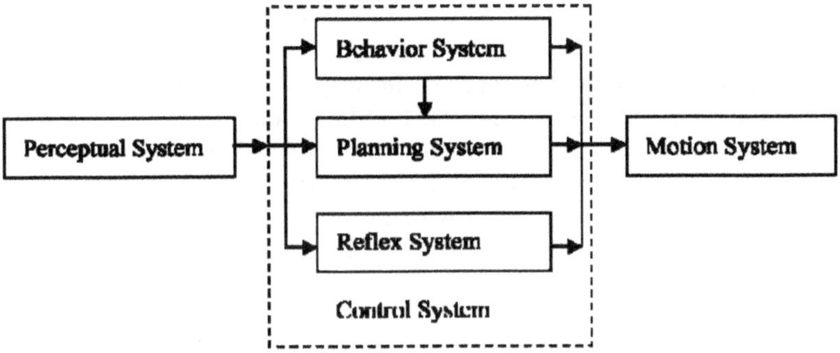


**Fig. 1.** The agent control structure adopts layered architecture of Perceptual-Control-Motion. This structure can describe human behaviors clearly and exactly.

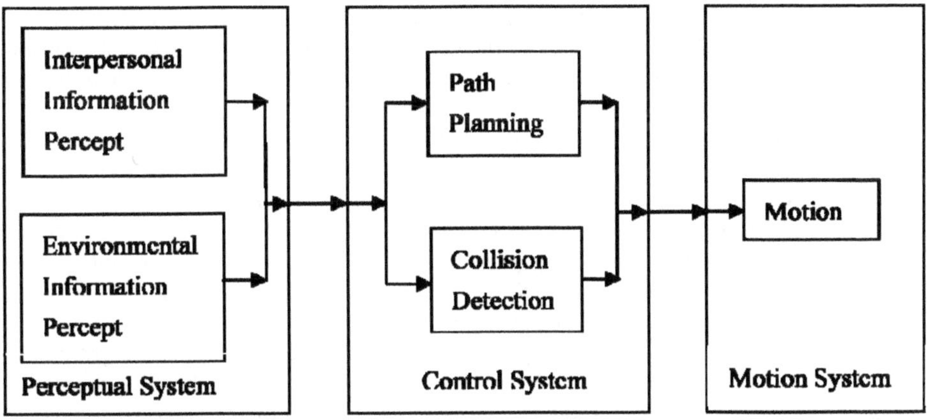


**Fig. 2.** The simplified intelligent agent control structure we used in our behavior model. In this structure, behavior system and reflex system are neglected.

The agent control structure in Fig. 1 can describe human behaviors clearly and exactly. But if there are thousands of agents in the scene, it is really a waste of computer resources when behavior model focus on so many details. The serial process of Perceptual-Control-Motion corresponds with the primary features of human behaviors, so a simplified intelligent agent control structure is used in our behavior model. In this simplified structure, behavior system and reflex system are neglected. It is described in detail in Fig. 2.

In perceptual system, each agent not only can receive information from other agents, but also can receive information from their surrounding environment. For example, when fire breaks out in a public place, an agent can get this information from two ways: (1) other agents tell him that there is fire; (2) he sees the fire by himself. The agent gets information, so he has to take some actions, running away or doubting the information is true or not.

In control system, an agent gets information from perceptual system. He will take actions according to the information and surrounding environment. For example, if the information is fire alarm and he believes it, the agent who gets this information will run to a safe place. At first he needs to choose a path which leads to the destination, it is called path planning. On the way to the destination, the agent might run into obstacles such as other agents, buildings and some other things. How to detect obstacles and how to avoid obstacles are also problems needed to solve.

In motion system, an agent takes some actions. For example, a person wants to run to a safe place, he will decide to adopt which method to go to the destination, running, walking or other methods. At the same time he transfers this information to other agents.

### 3.2 Crowd Motion Characteristics Analysis

A crowd is composed by many individuals who are regarded as independent intelligent agents, every agent has five characteristics: independence, sociality, responsiveness, mobility and consciousness. When an agent exists as an independent individual, his characteristics of independence and consciousness perform obviously. When an agent exists as a member of the crowd, his independence and consciousness will decrease. Owning to the differences among all of the agents, the decrement of independence and consciousness will be different [16].

In general, psychology research shows that the agent behaviors in crowd can be divided into seven types: gather, perceive, obstacle avoid, follow, escape, communicate and respond [16]. These behaviors are influenced not only by surrounding environment, but also by the agent's attributes such as characters, gender, age and etc. Decisions made by agent in particular condition are result of these factors. If an agent is in the crowd, he is influenced by others relatively easily, and his decisions are mainly determined by surroundings.

For example, when an emergency occurs in an enclosed place, people get panicky mood easily, a woman gets fluster much more easily than a man, because women are usually likely to depend on others. So a woman is much easier to accept the information which others tell her, and run out the place quickly. People analysis is added to our behavior model. It is described in detail below.

### 3.3 Behavior Model Based On Information Transmission

In general, crowd simulation is divided into two categories: (1) simulate crowd as an entity, (2) crowd behaviors are made up by individuals' behaviors. The second method is used to control the crowd behaviors in our behavior model.

It is supposed that when emergencies occur, the information about danger is not spread by the broadcast method. In some places, there is not broadcast equipment or the broadcast equipment is down. So the assumption proposed by us is reasonable. The information transmission processes in crowd are very crucial when people escape dangerous scene. In our behavior model, there are two ways to get the information about danger: (1) get information from the danger source, such as fire origin, (2) if the distance is little enough, the agent can get information about danger from other agents who have already got the information. By parity of reasoning, information is spreaded in method of flooding. The agent gets information through either of the two ways, and he will make corresponding decision according to his own attributes and other factors.

The agents' motion statuses in crowd behavior model are mainly determined by two factors: (1) their own attributes, (2) surrounding environment information. For example, when a woman who has dependent trend receives information about danger from surroundings, she might make a decision to escape the place quickly. And then, it is described that how the agents' attributes and danger information influence their decisions in our crowd behavior model.

**Agent Attributes Setting**

Each agent's behaviors contain three factors: destination, movement detail and speed. According to these factors and psychological factors, the agent attributes are defined, which is showed in Fig.3. Values are illustrated below.

personality (-1, 0, 1): there are three types of agents according to characters. The agent valued -1 tends to believe what he hears and sees. The agent valued 0 tends to analyze what he hears and sees rationally. The agent valued 1 tends to stick to his own opinion and does not accept what he hears and sees.

age (-1, 0, 1): We classify agents into three types according to their ages. Value 1 represents people whose ages are from 20 to 35 and they tend to stick to their own opinion and do not accept what they hear and see. Value 0 represents people whose ages are from 35 to 50 and they tend to analyze what they hear and see rationally. Value -1 represents people whose ages are from 50 to 70 and they tend to believe what they hear and see.

gender (-1, 1): value -1 represents female and value 1 represents male. Female are much easier to be information accepters than male.

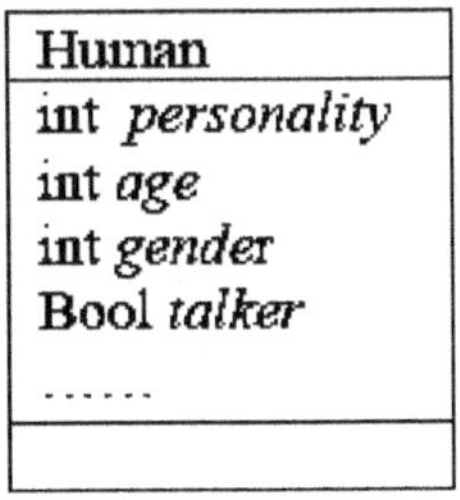


**Fig. 3.** Agent attributes list

talker (true, false): if the value is true, the agent is an information source, he will pass the information to other agents when they come across. If the value is false, the agent has not received the information, so he cannot become an information source.

**Attributes Influence on Human Behaviors**

Human attributes influence human behaviors directly. Agents get information passively. Although an agent gets information from other agents who are information sources, his behaviors in crowd are also determined by his own attributes such as personality, age, gender and etc. Agents' attributes influence motion details much more little. Motion details mainly refer to path planning and collision detection. So agent attributes' influences on destinations and speed will be described below.

*Influence on Speed*

Basic speed is determined by the initial attributes of agent which is loaded into the scene.

$$\text{nowSpeed=baseSpeed=initialSpeed} \div \left(\text{realAge-gender} \times \text{genFactor-personality} \times \text{perFactor}\right) . \quad (1)$$

nowSpeed represents current speed. At the beginning of agent loaded into scene, current speed is equal to basic speed baseSpeed. initialSpeed represents initial speed, which is defined according to demand. realAge represents the agent's age. gender represents people's gender which value is -1 or 1. personality represents agent's character which value is 1, 0 or -1. genFactor and perFactor are defined according to demand. genFactor represents the percentage that gender factor influence on speed. perFactor represents the percentage that agent attributes factor influence on speed. A conclusion is got from Formula 1 that speed is getting lower as the age increasing, at the same time gender and characters also have influences on speed.

When agent receives information about danger and the information is confirmed, the speed will raise. It is showed in Formula 2. raiseFactor is defined according to demand.

$$\text{nowSpeed} = \text{nowSpeed} \times \text{raiseFactor} . \quad (2)$$

When the crowd density is increased, the speed will decrease. When crowd density unitHumNum is bigger than density factor densityFactor, we use Formula 3. densityFactor is defined according to demand.

$$\text{nowSpeed} = \text{nowSpeed} \div \left(\text{unitHumNum} \div \text{densityFactor}\right) . \quad (3)$$

*Influence on Destination*

There are two ways to generate destination:

1. When the agent is not an information source, he is in free moving situation. The agent has no stationary destination, so destination is generated randomly.

2. When the agent is an information source, he will run to the exit which is nearest to him, so the exit is his destination.

**Information Source Generation**

Before information source generation processes are described, a word talkerArea must be defined. talkerArea is the area of information spread when the information source is regarded as the center. When an agent who is not information source enters the area of an information source, he can get information about danger. talkerArea is a circle with information source as center, and a radius of r. r is determined according to demand.

The method of information source generation and judgment is described in detail below. Whether an agent is information source, it depends on the agent's status. If he transforms from free movement to directional movement, the agent becomes a new information source.

In Fig. 4, there are two statuses and two transformation methods. Method A: the agent receives information about danger, for example he sees fire, and the agent transforms from free movement to directional movement. Method B: when the dicideFactor is greater than critical value (criticalValue = 0), the agent transforms from free movement to directional movement.

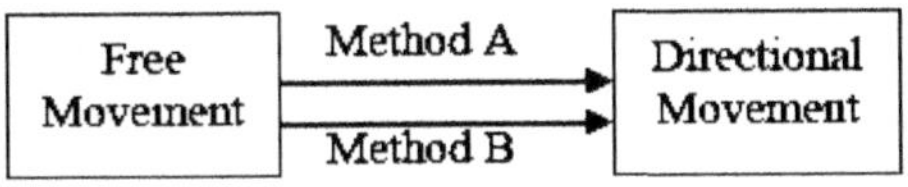


**Fig. 4.** Two methods of transforming from free movement to directional movement

The method of calculating dicideFactor in Method B shows in Formula 4.

$$\text{dicideFactor} = -(\text{personality} + \text{age} + \text{gender}) + \text{messageTimes}\ . \tag{4}$$

messageTimes represents the times of the agent receives information from other information sources. The calculating processes of dicideFactor are described clearly through the two examples below.

Example 1:

Human1 personality = 1; age = 1 (age between 20 and 35); gender = 1 (male)
dicideFactor = - (personality + age + gender) + messageTimes = -3 + messageTimes

When messageTimes is greater than 3, the agent accepts information about danger, and run to the exits. The agent becomes a new information source, and spreads information to other agents.

Example 2:

Human2 personality = -1; age = -1 (age between 50 and 70); gender = -1 (female)
dicideFactor = -(personality + age + gender) + messageTimes = 3 + messageTimes

No matter how many messageTimes is, dicideFactor is greater than 0, so when the agent gets information about danger just one time, he will accept the information, and run to the exits. The agent becomes a new information source, and spreads information to other agents.

# 4 Implementation and Results

The proposed behavior model based on information transmission is validated through a series of experiments.

## 4.1 Implementation

A platform is built to simulate crowd motion. Visual Studio .NET is used as development platform, C++ as development language, OGRE (Object-Oriented Graphics Rendering Engine) as graphics rendering engine and XML files as storage files of crowd data. In order to get better simulate result, LOD (Levels of Detail) and GPU (Graphics Processing Unit) accelerate technologies are used to increase rendering speed, conjunction and bounding box collision detection method and real time path planning method are used to make scene looks much more realistic.

## 4.2 Result Analysis

The platform runs on our PC. The computer configuration is that operating system Windows XP, CPU 2.8GHz, memory 2G and display card Geforce 9600 GT. 55 agents are loaded into scene at the beginning. They are distributed randomly in the scene.

Fig. 5 shows experiment results of crowd behaviors model based on information transmission. There are six parts in Fig. 5. A shows the situation at moment 0. Danger information generates, the agents around the fire point get information about danger,

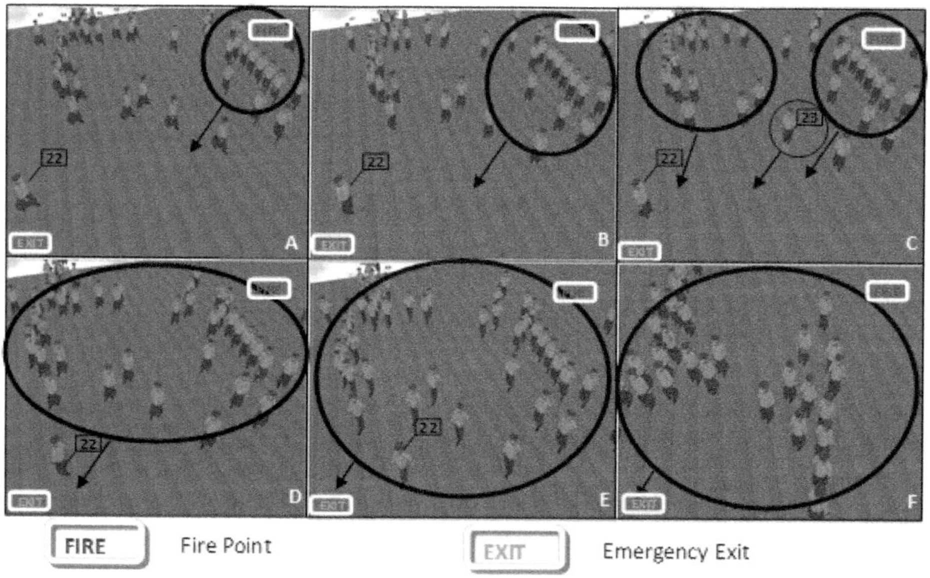


**Fig. 5.** Experiment results of crowd behavior model based on information transmission

and run to the emergency exit. At this moment, 11 agents choose to run away and they are information sources. B shows the situation at moment 1. As the agents moving, more and more agents get danger information and run to the exit. At this moment, the number of runaway rises to 14. C shows the situation at moment 2. The information source group becomes bigger and bigger. Information about danger spreads to the left scene by No.23 agent. The number of runaway is 30. But there are some agents still do not accept the information because of their own attributes. They are still in free movement. D shows the situation at moment 3. Information about danger almost spreads to all of crowd, 41 agents choose to run away, but No.22 agent has not get the information yet, he is still in free movement. E shows the situation at moment 4. Danger information spreads to all crowd, all agents run to the exit. F shows the situation at moment 5. The crowd is gathering toward the exit.

From the fire breaks out to all people in crowd run out of the exit, it takes about 5 minutes. The experiment results are in accordance with human behaviors and our anticipations.

## 5 Conclusions and Future Work

A crowd behavior model based on information transmission processes is proposed. The contributions of our works may be summarized as below.

1. A simplified intelligent agent control structure is used in our behavior model.
2. Information transmission processes combined with people's personalities are used in crowd behavior model. It can achieve good results in crowd evacuation simulation.
3. A platform is developed according to the behavior model we presented. It provides an interface to users to control crowd behaviors conveniently.

Our future works mainly include these things:

1. Find a validate method to verify the realism of the crowd behaviors.
2. Find method to solve the bottleneck of rendering speed.
3. Optimize information transmission processes which are used in our behavior model. Make crowd behaviors in simulation much more realistic.

**Acknowledgements.** A special thanks to Wenjing Zhang, Yunshuai Liu, Wei Zhang and members of the Virtual Reality Group in School of Computer Science and Technology of Tianjin University for assisting in this work.

## References

1. Reynolds, C.: Flocks, Herds, and Schools: A Distributed Behavior Model. In: Proc. ACM Siggraph, pp. 25–34. ACM Press, New York (1987)
2. Helbing, D., Farkas, I., Vicsek, T.: Simulating Dynamical Features of Escape Panic. Nature 407, 487–490 (2006)
3. Chenney, S.: Flow Tiles. In: Eurographics/ACM Siggraph Proc. Symp. Computer Animation, pp. 233–242. ACM Press, New York (2004)

4. Musse, S.R., Thalmann, D.: Hierarchical model for real time simulation of virtual human crowds. IEEE Transaction on Visualization and Computer Graphics, 152–164 (2001)
5. Cony, C., et al.: A perceptive model for virtual agents in crowd. In: 25th Computer Graphics International Conference, pp. 141–149 (2007)
6. Pelechano, N., Badler, N.: Modeling crowd and trained leader behavior during building evacuation. IEEE Computer Graphics and Applications 26(6), 80–86 (2006)
7. Pelechano, N., et al.: Crowd simulation incorporating agent psychological models, roles and communication. In: First International Workshop on Crowd Simulation, pp. 21–30 (2005)
8. Braun, A., et al.: Simulating virtual crowds in emergency situations. Virtual reality software and technology, 244–252 (2005)
9. Pelechano Gomez, N.: Modeling realistic high density autonomous agent crowd movement: social forces, communication, roles and psychological influences. PhD thesis, Philadelphia, PA, USA. Adviser-Badler, Norman I (2006)
10. Treuille, A., Cooper, S., PopoviC, Z.: Continuum crowds. In: SIGGRAPH 2006: ACM Siggraph 2006 Papers, pp. 1160–1168. ACM Press, New York (2006)
11. Monzani, J.S., Thalmann, D.: A sound propagation model for interagents communication. In: Heudin, J.-C. (ed.) VW 2000. LNCS (LNAI), vol. 1834, pp. 135–146. Springer, Heidelberg (2000)
12. Funge, J., Tu, X., Terzopoulos, D.: Cognitive Modeling Knowledge, Reasoning and Planning for Intelligent Character. In: Proc. ACM Siggraph, pp. 29–38. ACM Press, New York (1999)
13. Musse, S.R., Thalmann, D.: A model of human crowd behavior. In: Computer Animation and Simulation 1997, pp. 39–51. Springer, Heidelberg (1997)
14. Mamlouk, A.M., Chee-Ruiter, C., Hofmann, U.G., Bower, J.M.: Quantifying olfactory perception: mapping olfactory perception space by using multidimensional scaling and self-organizing maps. Neurocomputing 54-54, 591–597 (2003)
15. Conde, T., Thalmann, D.: An artificial life environment for autonomous virtual agents with multi-sensorial and multi-perceptive features. Journal of Computer Animation and Virtual Worlds 15(3), 311–318 (2004)
16. Hou, Y.: Social Psychology. Peking University Press (2002)

# Pattern Based Motion for Crowd Simulation

Nan Hu[1], Michael Lees[1], Suiping Zhou[2], and Vaisagh Viswanathan T[1]

[1] School of Computer Engineering, NTU, Singapore
{huna0002,vaisagh1}@e.ntu.edu.sg, mhlees@ntu.edu.sg
[2] School of Computing, Teesside Univesity, United Kindon
s.zhou@tees.ac.uk

**Abstract.** We present a pattern-based approach for simulating the steering behaviour of pedestrians, which aims to imitate the way that real pedestrians perceive spatial-temporal information and make steering decisions in daily-life situations. Novel representations of spatial-temporal patterns are proposed that allow modellers to intuitively and naturally specify some prototypical patterns for various steering behaviours. Based on the spatial-temporal patterns, a hierarchical pattern matching process has been developed, which simulates how pedestrians process spatial temporal information and make steering decisions. Experimental results show that this new approach is quite promising and capable of producing human-like steering. We hope that the idea presented in this paper can direct researchers in this area with a fresh perspective.

**Keywords:** steering behaviour, spatial-temporal patterns, crowd simulation, motion planning.

## 1 Introduction

Simulation of pedestrian navigational behaviours has a wide range of applications in crowd simulation, digital entertainment, and safety planning etc. Although humans are able to move smoothly almost effortlessly even in crowded places, it is still a challenging task for computer programs to imitate such behaviours realistically.

From a computational modelling point of view, the complex navigational behaviours are typically generated from activities of an agent at two levels: *path planning* and *locomotion*. Path planning can be considered as the higher-level behaviour that generates a global path directing the agent to the goal. This typically considers static aspects of the environment, such as walls and doorways. Locomotion is considered as the lower-level behaviour that actuates the agent's motion in order to avoid dynamic obstacles. This bi-level methodology is effective in some applications, but is lacking when it comes to the generation of realistic human motion. Our work describes a level between the traditional two, which uses higher-level cognitive information to adjust routes dynamically. These adjustments essentially try to reduce the likelihood of collisions by adopting strategies. Our work focuses on this middle level by describing and modeling *strategic steering behaviours*.

Z. Pan et al. (Eds.): Transactions on Edutainment VI, LNCS 6758, pp. 99–110, 2011.

Strategic steering behaviours are commonly observed during pedestrians' navigation in daily life. Pedestrians use the strategies to ensure their movement is smooth and efficient in avoiding collisions. However, we argue that such phenomenon does not necessarily reflect any smart mechanism to guarantee collision-free movement. In fact, we believe that pedestrians do not need to make complex decisions in most situations. Instead, they are adapted to relying on simple steering strategies corresponding to different situations that they are familiar with. One characteristic of such strategic steering behaviours, which distinguishes it from locomotive movement, is that proactive planning is involved. When comparing to path planning, the steering strategies generally consider sequences of actions in relative short term of both space and time.

Most existing agent-based approaches rely on various mechanical or steering rules to prevent agents from colliding with each other. There are two major disadvantages of this approach: 1) rules are specific to different situations and are hard to design, it is difficult to naturally relate these rules with human behaviours; 2) the realism of the generated behaviours is largely determined by the experience of the designer in tuning the parameters involved.

We adopt a different approach. Our work is motivated by some basic assumptions which are based on our observations and existing literature on pedestrian behaviours. It seems that pedestrians achieve efficient steering behaviours relying on certain implicit criteria to assist their decision. Such criteria reflect the current situation comprehensively while in a sufficiently simple and aggregated form such that it leads to fast decisions efficiently. We regard such implicit criteria as the formed *patterns* in our work. We assume that experienced pedestrians proactively match the perceived spatial-temporal patterns in the situation with some prototypical cases in their experience to retrieve similar steering strategies and apply them in an empirical way.

The major advantages of this pattern-based approach include: 1) *Intuitiveness*: it allows modellers to understand and specify patterns intuitively according to their experience; 2) *Efficiency*: complex steering behaviours can be achieved through proper scheduling among several simple steering strategies based on the pattern-matching results; and 3) *Human-like information processing*: human are efficient in processing information through grouping [1]. They are capable of handling more chunks of information at the same time in a parallel manner. In our approach, spatial-temporal information is implicitly processed in a parallel manner and represented in an aggregated form (3D array).

We have proposed a generic framework based on this pattern-based approach in our previous work [2]. In this paper, we focus on the design of the spatial-temporal patterns based on the agent's attention in 2-dimensional space along a period of time. The pattern-matching process is hierarchical along both spatial and temporal domains, with differing significance defined by the proposed attention model, which aims to better imitate pedestrians' decision-making process.

The rest of the paper is organized as follows: Section 2 describes related work on steering behaviour modelling. The pattern-based framework will be reviewed in Section 3. The design on the spatial-temporal patterns is detailed in Section 4.

Section 5 describes the hierarchical matching process and includes a concrete example of the pattern-matching process. Simulation results that demonstrate the unique features and capabilities of the approach are shown and discussed in Section 6. Section 7 concludes the paper and outlines ideas for future work.

## 2 Related Work

There have been many attempts to simulate people's steering behaviours ever since Reynolds's pioneering work on *boids* [3]. As one of the essential goals, collision avoidance plays an important role in these works. As motion control and motion planning have been broadly studied, most previous work focuses on generating optimal, collision-free motion for all entities in the simulation environment. One representative work is the *Reciprocal Velocity Obstacle (RVO)* model [4] and its variants [5,6]. It generally provides a single optimal solution for all cases. However, we argue that humans are non-optimal in their movement behaviour. For example, collisions do occur in some real world situations.

Another popular approach, rule-based models [7,8,9] achieve collision avoidance based on pre-defined rules. Visually appealing simulation is achievable. However, rules are likely tightly coupled to specific scenario conditions, thus such models may not function well in general case. It also poses a challenge for the modellers to specify a complete set of rules capable of generating realistic simulation results for many different situations.

Example-based approaches have been proposed and applied in steering behaviour simulation recently [10,11]. Real-life examples of the moving trajectories of people are recorded, extracted and stored as the input to a simulation model. Agents in the simulation analyze the simulation environment and compare it with the stored examples. Certain stored moving trajectories in the example situations are applied. Although this work target to replicate realistic steering behaviours, the model realism is limited as paths for agents are explicitly *synthesized*. Only external factors can be extracted from the image based examples, unique traits of individual persons are difficult to incorporate with this approach.

There is currently a trend to incorporate different human cognitive components into behavioural models aiming to achieve higher level of realism. [12,13,14] focus on *psychological factors*. In [15], *prediction* is taken into account and [16] uses *egocentric affordance field* for space-time planning in short term. [17] follows a *visual stimuli/motor response* control flow by taking captured image from the real world as input to form the visual stimuli. These models demonstrate a good perspective in modelling navigational behaviours, that is the *realism* of the model.

## 3 Pattern-Based Decision-Making Framework

In our previous work, we have proposed a pattern-based decision-making framework [2]. In this section, we briefly review the previously described framework and highlight those parts that have been further developed. It is assumed that

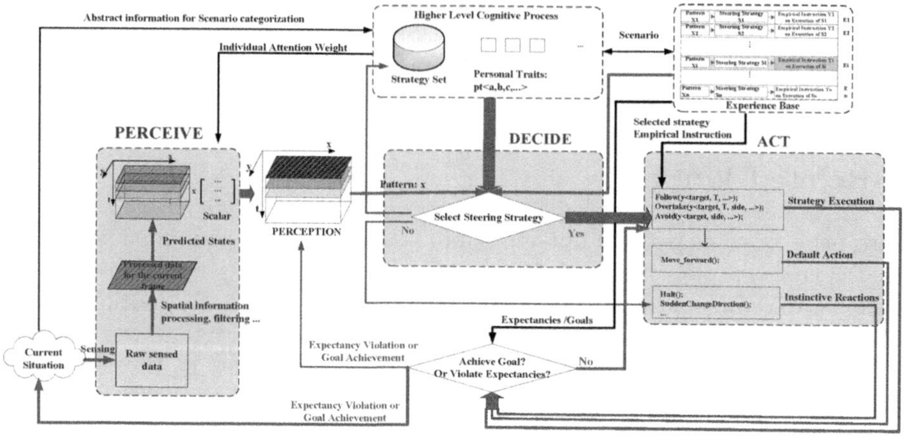


**Fig. 1.** Overview of the pattern-based decision-making framework

pedestrians proactively adopt a limited number of steering strategies to minimize the chances of performing certain reactive or instinctive reactions to resolve imminent collisions. The scheduling and execution of these steering strategies result in various complex navigational behaviours of individual pedestrians. Decisions on steering strategies in a given situation at a specific time instance are mainly based on the matching results between the currently perceived and the prototypical *patterns* in their experience base. They are also influenced by certain internal factors such as *personal traits.* Particularly in this work, we consider the *commitment levels* to their strategic plan and their *preferred speed* for agents. As will be illustrated later, different commitment levels specify different temporal constraints in the pattern-matching process. The overall cognitive process is modelled as a continuous process following the "perceive-decide-act" paradigm as shown in Fig.1. We will demonstrate the pattern-matching process based on a given steering strategy set for a restricted bi-directional passageway context. In this context, our model currently includes three steering strategies: *follow*, *overtake* and *side-avoid.* Due to the page limit, readers are referred to [2] for more details on the framework design.

In the abstract framework level, our current framework is highly consistent with the well-known *RPD* model. Each experience instance consists of a *pattern* (*cues* in RPD terms) and a *steering strategy.* The steering strategy is characterized by the empirical instructions on how to execute in a specific situation corresponding to the prototypical pattern. *Goals*, *expectations* and *actions* in RPD terms are included in the empirical instructions to represent different experience levels of individual agents. An agent has two states, one in which a steering strategy is selected and one in which no steering strategy is selected. When no steering strategy is matched, the patterns (cues) will be used to select a matching strategy. Once a strategy is selected, matching is no longer necessary. Instead, the selected steering strategy is executed according to the empirical instructions until such time as the expectancies are violated or the goals have been achieved. Iterations of sensing, perception, steering strategy selection (when necessary) and execution continue in the simulation. An important new feature of the current framework compared with the previously designed one is the use of *violation-check* during the strategy execution process as shown in Fig.1. Perception formation and the pattern-matching process only occur when a new steering strategy needs to be made due to the violation of the current strategy. We argue this may reflects the naturalistic decision-making process of humans as assumed in the RPD model.

## 4 Spatial-Temporal Patterns

In our framework, patterns function as the implicit criteria to assist agents make fast decisions during steering strategy selection and execution. The designed pattern should be *comprehensive* in its content and *succinct* in its representation. Specifically, significance of information should be considered at different positions along both the spatial and temporal domains based on their impact on the decision. Information should be processed in a bulk/parallel manner so as to imitate humans' information grouping and parallel processing capabilities. The patterns also naturally reflect some qualitative criteria that are commonly used by pedestrians rather than precise computations to make steering choices. Thus, modellers can design these patterns intuitively based on their experience. This is one of the major advantages of our pattern-based approach compared with most existing rule-based models.

To achieve the goal of collision avoidance in the steering behavioural level, information on the potential obstacles (static objects or dynamic agents) in both spatial and temporal domains needs to be captured. The spatial information is predominantly processed through visual sensing and attention filtering; the temporal information is generally formed through predicted changes on the spatial information. In previous work [2], we proposed a novel array-based representation for the situation awareness and defined spatial-temporal patterns in the form of a 2D array (1D spatial + 1D temporal) as shown in Fig. 2(a). The spatial information was represented by a 1D array with values 0, 1(-1) representing available space, obstacles with same (or opposite) moving directions respectively within the single attention range on a relative visionary direction. The model oversimplifies the perceived patterns in 1D space based on the single attention range value. Such 1D spatial patterns obviously lose some useful information that may result in different decisions during navigation. To mimic the attention range more realistically, we have made three assumptions in the use of attention for human in real life:

1. People tend to pay more attention to the area immediately in front of them within a relatively short visual range.
2. People tend to consider currently relevant information with higher significance as opposed to any future predictions.
3. People may pay more attention to some salient features such as size, colour of certain objects in the situation.

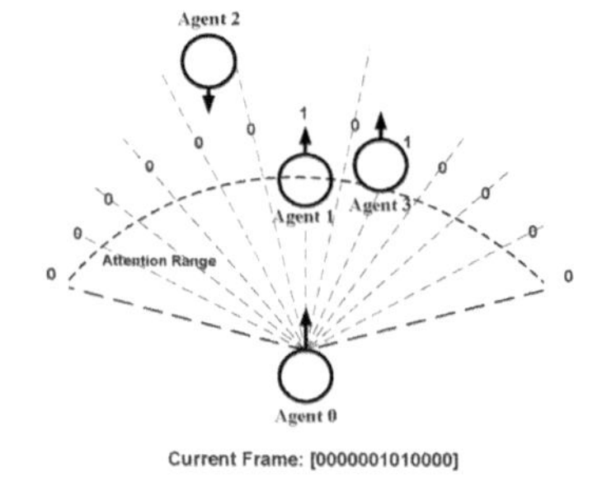


(a) Drawbacks of the single attention range representing 1D spatial information

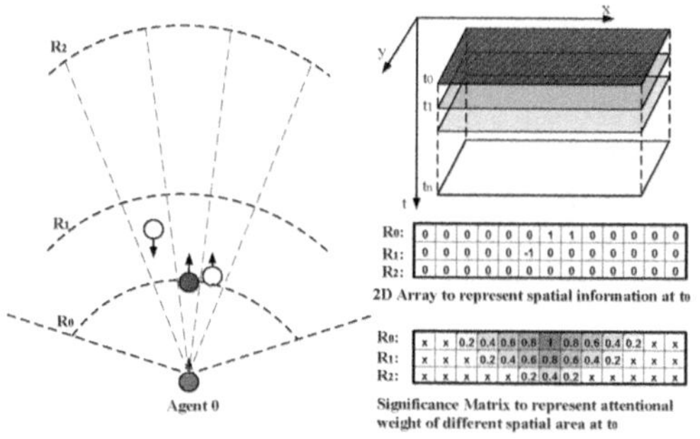


(b) Multi-Level attention range capturing 2D spatial Information with differing significances along spatial and temporal domains

**Fig. 2.** The previous and the current attention systems

Based on the assumptions, comprehensive perception of an agent on the situation are defined based a multi-level *attention range* as shown in Fig.2(b). 2D spatial information are captured in a 2D array with significance difference for different areas in both spatial and temporal domains. Each row in a 2D array represents the spatial information for the area within a specific attention range at a specific point in time. In the demonstrated model, we use 3 levels of attention range with the distance of the first range $R_0$ set to a proper value such that one agent can just fully occupy one visionary section at the boundary of $R_0$ as demonstrated by the red agent in Fig.2(b). $R_1$ and $R_2$ exponentially increase with regard to $R_0$. The significance of an area is inversely proportional to its relative distance to the agent, its relative deviation from the agent's vision center, and how further ahead it is predicted. For illustration purpose, we demonstrate different attention weights with different darkness in Fig.2(b). The darker the colour is, the higher the attention weight on that area. A 3D array is aggregated from several such 2D arrays using a linear dead reckoning method to measure the positions of other agents currently within the farthest attention range, along the prediction time $t$ based on their current relative velocities to "me" agent.

Spatial-temporal patterns are defined as certain *subsets* in the 3D array that emphasize the area of interest addressed by the attention in different situations. Fig.3 demonstrates one example of a prototypical spatial-temporal pattern used for the selection of the *overtake* steering strategy. The pattern is highlighted as the subset within the 3D array; it reflects the agent's perception on the current situation that *front center is blocked by some target agents with other oncoming agents from the right in the near future.* Thus, if the agent's preferred speed is high, it may choose to *overtake* the agents in front from their left-hand side. In this example, a prototypical pattern to trigger the *overtake* steering strategy can be seen from the first frame of the 3D array in Fig.3. We can describe the pattern as *front center is blocked with available space aside.* It naturally follows the way that people describe the spatial configuration of a situation during their steering. Note that several prototypical patterns may trigger the same steering

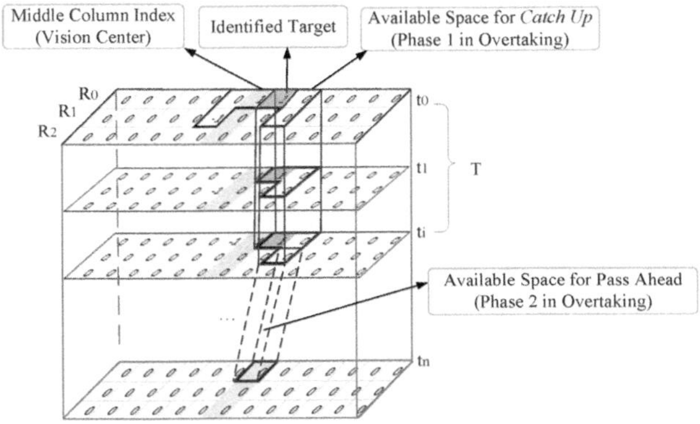


**Fig. 3.** An example of spatial-temporal pattern as a subset of the 3D array

strategy. The modellers can specify the association of a prototypical pattern and its corresponding steering strategy to represent different experience base of different people.

## 5 Hierarchical Pattern Matching

In the pattern-matching process, an agent needs to check for the presence of the constituents of certain prototypical patterns in the 3D array representation of the perceived spatial-temporal information. We adopt a hierarchical approach. Specifically, the 3D patterns are divided into slices of 2D spatial patterns for each time instance. The matching result of the perceived information against the prototypical patterns is aggregated from the matching results of these 2D patterns with different significance values according to the different attention weights as discussed. Such a hierarchical matching process naturally reflects the cognitive process of pedestrians with different significance to different areas. More specifically, we start to search for the constituents of prototypical patterns in the first 2D array at current time step $t_0$. If a suitable match is found, the process continues to the next predicted frame slice $t_1$. This process continues until such time as the pattern fails or succeeds to match. According to different steering strategies, the match between the 2D spatial patterns is also determined by different temporal constraints. Some require certain spatial patterns to exist for a period of time $T$ and some just require their existence at a specific frame. Such temporal constraints also relate to the agent's specific characteristic of commitment. The commitment parameter defines the number of slices of the current 2D pattern that must be successfully matched before proceeding to the next 2D pattern matching. Those agents with high commitment require many matches; this intends to represent people who will only select strategies when they are confident of their success.

Consider the pattern-matching process for the *overtake* steering strategy as an example shown in Fig.4.

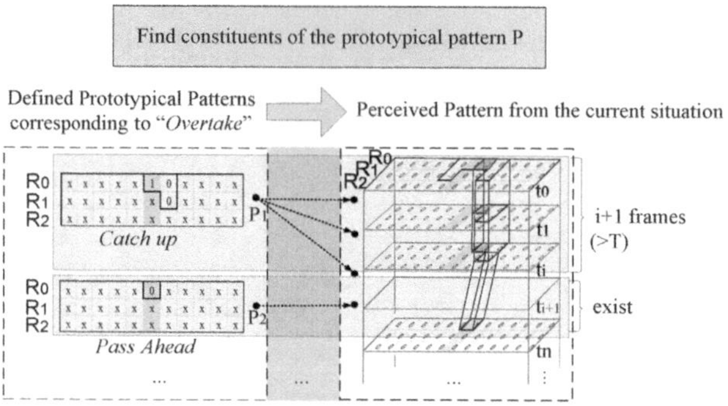


**Fig. 4.** Hierarchical pattern-matching process

The execution of the *overtake* steering strategy can be generally modelled in three phases as *catch up*, *pass ahead* and *resume to original courses*. The prototypical pattern needs to represent the situations where *overtake* is usually triggered. To trigger the attempt to *overtake*, *the agent's center front should be blocked by some target and there should be available space that can accommodate the comfortable personal space beside the target* so that there is space for the agent to occupy during the *catch-up* phase. Such condition can be represented by the prototypical patterns [xxx10xx] or [xx01xxx] in the first row of a 2D array as shown in Fig.4. The 2D arrays representing prototypical spatial patterns along different temporal frames to characterize how the overtake steering strategy is empirically executed in phases are shown on the left side of Fig.4; while the perceived spatial-temporal information from the current situation are represented in the 3D array on the right side of the figure. In this example, the "1" in the first row of the first 2D array in the prototypical pattern represents the group of target that has blocked "me" agent's way, it should be around the middle column index in the array. The "0" represents the available space beside the target that is larger than "me" agent's personal space. To match such prototypical patterns with the current situation, we search for such patterns in the perceived 3D array. In this example, such patterns exist in the 3D array in $R_0$ at $t_0$ as highlighted in Fig.4. Note that only the specific area of interest is considered in the pattern-matching process. This ensures our approach capable of handling a certain degree of uncertainty in the situation. For example, any area other than the highlighted area in the 3D array is not important to the decision of *overtake*, thus given the value *do not care* as indicated as $x$. Along the temporal domain, such spatial patterns need to exist for certain frames (e.g., larger than $T$) so that the agent could reach the observed available space within the number of frames in the *catch up* phase. In Fig.4, spatial patterns for *catch up* last for $i+1$ frames (i.e. from $t_0$ to $t_i$), and the agent starts from frame $t_{i+1}$ to match the prototypical spatial patterns for *pass ahead* in the second phase of overtaking as shown in the second 2D array on the left side of the figure. The "0" in row $R_0$ of this array represents the available space for "me" agent to *pass ahead* beside the target agent. Note that, the column index of the "0" changes to the middle column index from frame $t_{i+1}$ onwards. This is because in the predicted frames, the agent should consider its relative position with the other agents. Since the patterns matched successfully for phase 1 in overtaking, the agent is to occupy the space beside the target and its subsequent steering behaviours in phase 2 should be based on the new position. In the decision-making process, these changes need to be taken into account though the agent has not started to execute the actions in practice.

## 6 Simulation Results

We have implemented the improved pattern-based decision-making framework using the MASON multi-agent Toolkit [18]. We also design a number of prototypical patterns in the model to mimic the experience of the agents. We test the model by tracking the steering behaviours of individual agents in typical test cases and analyzing their steering choices together with their perceived spatial-temporal patterns. To investigate individuals' steering choices reflected by their velocity change in locomotion, we demonstrate their steering trajectories in 2D in this part for demonstration purpose.

It is still challenging to evaluate the realism of steering behaviours generated by simulation models. Comparison is one of the most common way to measure the performance. However, comparing motion of two different models is not a straight forward task; this is especially true when trying to indicate which model is more human-like. In this paper we do not propose a measure of how human-like of the behaviours our model can generate. Our results and comparison are provided for the reader to compare the output of both models and make their own assessment. Our analysis is based on our personal observations of human movement. The comparison does highlight that our model is capable of producing different behaviours when compared to the more mechanical motion planning systems. Specifically, we compare the simulation results of our model with the RVO model (based on the latest RVO2 library [19]) under the same specific set of test cases. The RVO model is a representative efficient motion control approach to achieve collision free motion for steering behaviour simulation.

Consider the situation as shown in Fig.5, one agent is attempting to avoid two oncoming agents. It is a commonly observed scenario in any passageway situation. The steering trajectories of the agents are shown in the figure by a thicker line; the thinner line in front of an agent indicates its current velocity.

Results from the RVO model are shown in Fig.5(a) and 5(b). The group of two agents coming from the right side split (see Fig.5(a)) in order to avoid collisions and the agent starting from left decreases its speed significantly until the other two agents have deviated to a collision free path. The results from our model are shown in Fig. 5(c) and 5(d), where the single agent coming from left will deviate its route proactively to avoid collision with the oncoming group of two agents. The group of two agents also change their velocities accordingly to avoid the collision. Both the individual and the group of two agents perceived the pattern that triggers the *side-avoid* steering strategy at 5(c) and start to execute the strategy at 5(d). In real life, we usually observe that people on their

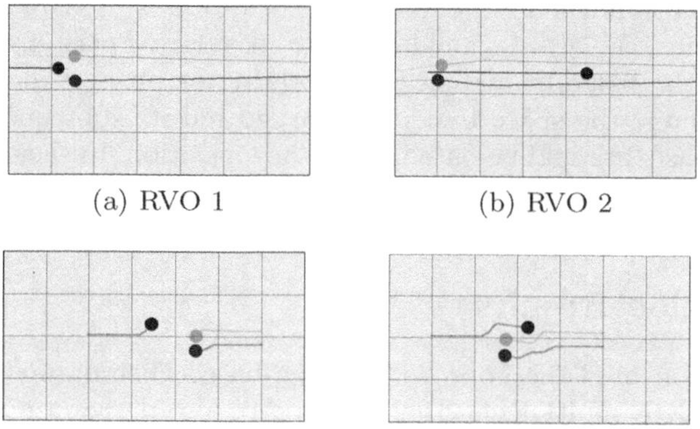

(a) RVO 1 (b) RVO 2

(c) PBM 1 (d) PBM 2

**Fig. 5.** Avoiding oncoming collisions in RVO model and our model

own or in a smaller group are likely to give way to a bigger group. With this test cases, we want to demonstrate this behaviour with our model, which is lacking in the current RVO models.

In another test case shown in Fig.6, one agent is trying to *overtake* the other two agents in front. Simulation results from the RVO models are shown in Fig.6(a), 6(b) and 6(c). The agent behind reduces its speed when approaching to the agents in front, and the two agents in front will deviate to the side to give way to the agent coming from behind (see Fig.6(a)). After the agent moves in front of them (see Fig.6(b)), the two agents steer back to their original course and continue moving towards their goals (see Fig.6(c)). The results from our model are shown in Fig.6(d), 6(e) and 6(f). The agent behind deviates its route to avoid collision with the other two agents in front. It is shown clearly that there are three phases(*catch up*, *pass ahead* and *resume to original course*) as discussed in previous sections in the *overtaking* process. In this case, the agent coming from behind perceives the two agents in front as a blockage in the vision center with available space beside them in the pattern. Thus, *overtake* steering strategy is triggered and executed. In real-life situations corresponding to this test case, the group of two persons in front are less likely to proactively give way to the one behind due to two reasons: 1) they may not detect the person coming from behind; 2) they are in a group. On the other hand, the person behind is also likely to overtake the group of people from side rather than cutting through them in-between due to the social norms. Such commonly observed overtaking behaviour is replicated in our model while it is still lacking in the RVO model.

Due to the page limit, we do not illustrate other test cases in the paper. While both models achieve collision avoidance through different steering choices, we have the following observations: Though RVO model generally achieves more smooth steering behaviour at locomotive level, it can hardly reflect how pedestrians behave in similar situations in real life. On the contrary, our approach generates more realistic steering behaviours in these situations. We can describe such behaviours naturally in terms of several steering strategies. The less smooth

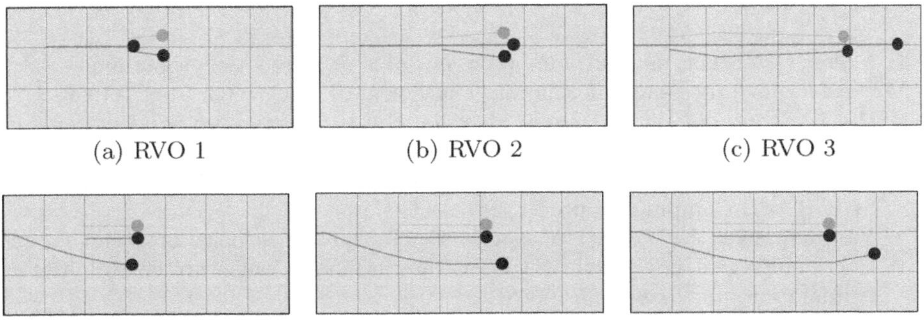

(a) RVO 1 (b) RVO 2 (c) RVO 3

(d) PBM 1 (e) PBM 2 (f) PBM 3

**Fig. 6.** Overtaking a group of two agents in RVO model and our model

locomotive movement generated by our model is mainly because we focus on the steering choices at the strategic level, thus our current model has less control directly at the locomotive level. This can be improved by specifying more constraints on the velocities of agents in locomotion based on the pattern-matching results in the future work. Though more comprehensive tests and systematic evaluation are still in progress, the current simulation results demonstrate some unique features of our approach.

## 7 Conclusions and Future Work

We present a pattern-based approach that aims to imitate how real pedestrians perceive and make steering decisions in daily-life situations. With the pattern-based approach, the complex cognitive processes involved in steering decision making are essentially transferred to pattern-matching processes between the perceived spatial-temporal patterns and the prototypical cases in agents' experience base. 3D arrays have been used to capture some important spatial-temporal information. This representation allows modellers to intuitively specify various spatial-temporal patterns and also facilitate efficient information processing for making steering decisions. The hierarchal pattern matching mechanism aims to model how real pedestrians make sense of spatial temporal information and make steering decisions.

The simulation results are quite promising and demonstrate some unique features of this new approach. We plan to further refine the model under the pattern-matching mechanism and we are designing a comprehensive evaluation method for our model.

## Acknowledgments

This work is supported in part by the Singapore National Research Foundation under Grant NRF2007IDM-IDM002-052.

## References


1. Miller, G.A.: The magical number seven, plus or minus two: some limits on our capacity for processing information. Psychological Review 63, 81–97 (1956)
2. Hu, N., Zhou, S., Wu, Z., Zhou, M., Cho, B.E.K.: Spatial-temporal patterns and pedestrian simulation. Computer Animation and Virtual Worlds 21, 387–399 (2010)
3. Reynolds, C.W.: Flocks, herds and schools: A distributed behavioral model. SIGGRAPH Comput. Graph. 21, 25–34 (1987)
4. Van den Berg, J., Lin, M., Manocha, D.: Reciprocal velocity obstacles for real-time multi-agent navigation. In: IEEE International Conference on Robotics and Automation, pp. 1928–1935 (2008)
5. Snape, J., van den Berg, J., Guy, S.J., Manocha, D.: Independent navigation of multiple mobile robots with hybrid reciprocal velocity obstacles. In: IEEE/RSJ International Conference on Intelligent Robots and Systems, St. Louis, MO, pp. 5917–5922 (2009)
6. Van den Berg, J., Guy, S.J., Lin, M.C., Manocha, D.: Reciprocal n-body collision avoidance. In: International Symposium On Robotics Research (2009)
7. Loscos, C., Marchal, D., Meyer, A.: Intuitive crowd behaviour in dense urban environments using local laws (2003)
8. Lamarche, F., Donikian, S.: Crowd of Virtual Humans: a New Approach for Real Time Navigation in Complex and Structured Environments. Computer Graphics Forum 23, 509–518 (2004)
9. Musse, S.R., Thalmann, D.: Hierarchical model for real time simulation of virtual human crowds. IEEE Transactions on Visualization and Computer Graphics 7, 152–164 (2001)
10. Lee, K.H., Choi, M.G., Hong, Q., Lee, J.: Group behavior from video: a data-driven approach to crowd simulation (2007)
11. Lerner, A., Chrysanthou, Y., Lischinski, D.: Crowds by example. Computer Graphics Forum 26, 655–664 (2007)
12. Pelechano, N., O'Brien, K., Silverman, B., Badler, N.: Crowd simulation incorporating agent psychological models, roles and communication. In: Proceedings of the First International Workshop on Crowd Simulation (2005)
13. Rymill, S.J., Dodgson, N.A.: A psychologically-based simulation of human behaviour (2005)
14. Sakuma, T., Mukai, T., Kuriyama, S.: Psychological model for animating crowded pedestrians: Virtual humans and social agents. Comput. Animat. Virtual Worlds 16, 343–351 (2005)
15. Paris, S., Pettre, J., Donikian, S.: Pedestrian reactive navigation for crowd simulation: a predictive approach. Computer Graphics Forum 26(1), 665–674 (2007)
16. Kapadia, M., Singh, S., Hewlett, W., Faloutsos, P.: Egocentric affordance fields in pedestrian steering. In: 3D 2009: Proceedings of the 2009 Symposium on Interactive 3D Graphics and Games, Boston, Massachusetts, pp. 215–223. ACM Press, New York (2009)
17. Ondrej, J., Julien, P., Olivier, A.H., Donikian, S.: A synthetic-vision based steering approach for crowd simulation. ACM Transactions on Graphics 29, 1–9 (2010)
18. Luke, S., Claudio, C.R., Liviu, P., Keith, S.: Mason: A new multi-agent simulation toolkit (2004)
19. Van den Berg, J., Guy, S., Snape, J., Lin, M., Manocha, D.: Rvo2 library: Reciprocal collision avoidance for real-time multi-agent simulation (2011)

# Adding Physical Like Reaction Effects to Skeleton-Based Animations Using Controllable Pendulums

Ahmad Abdul Karim[1,2], Thibaut Gaudin[2], Alexandre Meyer[1], Axel Buendia[2,3], and Saida Bouakaz[1]

[1] Université de Lyon, CNRS
Université Lyon 1, LIRIS, UMR5205, F-69622, France
[2] Spir.Ops Artificial Intelligence, Paris, France
[3] CNAM – CEDRIC, 292, rue St Martin, 75003 Paris, France

**Abstract.** We propose a system capable in real time of adding controllable and plausible oscillating physical like reaction effects in response to external forces (perturbations). These oscillating effects may be used to modify a motion or to customize it in a cartoon like way. The core of our system is based on several connected 3D pendulums with a propagating reaction. These pendulums always return to a preferred direction that can be fixed in advance or can be modified during the motion by external predefined data (such as keyframe). Our pendulums are fully controllable, concerning reaction time and damping, and the results are completely deterministic. They are easy to implement, even without any prior knowledge of physical simulations. Our system is applicable on articulated body with predefined motion data (manually set or captured) or procedural animation.

## 1 Introduction

There is a lot of research into developing convenient methods for adapting existing articulated body animations to suit other environments and characters. The joints in a given articulated body can typically have many degrees of freedom, many constraints of length or angles, and additionally are generally required not to allow the body to self-penetrate. Thus, the physics that govern its movement is computationally expensive, numerically imprecise, and often difficult to predict and to control. A recent survey by Welbergen *et al.* [15] gives a good overview of the different methods and paradigms used and most importantly the trade offs between animation control and motion naturalness. In this context, there is a crucial demand for real-time methods providing physically plausible, but controllable effects [3].

We propose an original system, to our knowledge, that adds physical like reaction effects to any skeleton-based object, in real-time with a full user control using our 3D pendulums. The effects we seek to obtain are based on damped oscillatory motions that propagate through an articulated chain. The effect may

Z. Pan et al. (Eds.): Transactions on Edutainment VI, LNCS 6758, pp. 111–121, 2011.

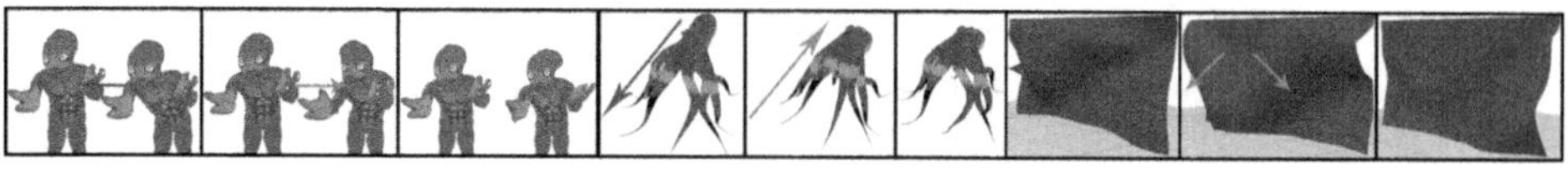

**Fig. 1.** Some example uses of our system. Red arrows represent external perturbations. Green arrows represent the system's response.

be visually plausible like a rope moving in the wind, or a body reacting to external forces. They may also be made more cartoonish which is shown in the accompanied video by giving a dancing like effect. In our system each bone of the articulated body is animated by a 3D pendulum. The pendulum is guided by a spring-damper that pulls it toward a user-definable target direction. Our approach has two objectives. Firstly, we ensure body length constraint between any two joints by only working on the angle between the bodies. Secondly, we make a predictable real-time system in which we can control the reaction time to reach a user-defined direction and also the regime (critical or underdamped) of the oscillations around this direction. Our pendulums have three degrees of control: reaction time, damping and target direction. This concept of 3D pendulums may be applicable in a multitude of scenarios with some of them illustrated in Figure 1. We must emphasize that our system is better suited for acyclic bodies and that we do not address the balancing problem in the case of the biped example. Our system is really easy to implement, as we will see in section 3, with no need for a full physics simulation, nor any kind of complex calculations (like the inertia matrix). The mesh of the 3D model is animated with the classical linear blend skinning technique [8].

## 2 Related Work

Our pendulums oscillate visually like real 3D pendulums by computing their movements with a mass-spring approach. A mass-spring approach is a very simple way to simulate physics-based animation [13], as it offers an intuitive and flexible means of modeling a mechanical system. In Pixar's movie WALL-E [10], they used a mass-spring system in a derived fashion to animate large crowds of humans and robots in a believable way.

Editing the motion of an articulated body (producing or modifying an existing animation) is an important topic in computer animation. For instance, some methods aim at warping the time of an existing motion [9], or combining/blending existing motions (often represented in an animation graph) [14]. Others propose the use of signal processing tools to modify animations [4].

Parallel of these approaches, an important aspect is to add physical reactions to animations, like blending an existing motion with a physical response [2]. Zordan *et al.* in [18,17] use a Proportional-Derivative (PD) controller to drive the dynamic body motion toward a re-entry in motion capture data. Our method may be related to a PD controller, and also to the MRAC controller that uses the Adaptive Control proposed by [12] and used in [11]. All of these controllers are like our pendulum bringing a bone to a preferred direction but we differ in several essential ways. Firstly, the other methods always try to return to a preferred direction (or position), even if there is no external perturbations. This introduces a delay in the produced animation between the target pose (keyframe or motion capture data) and the response of the PD controller (as seen in [19]). On the other hand, our system is a superimposed layer over the motion data and only reacts when there is an external perturbation. Our system plays exactly the motion data with no delay, and only adds the reaction effects when needed. Another difference is the controllability; our system is designed to be temporally controlled (control over the reaction time). Temporal control in the case of the PD controller is hard to achieve and demands some hand tuning of the gain constants. In [1] they show the ability to temporally control PD controllers (using adaptive calculation of the gain constants), but it involves some heavy calculations of the inertia matrix of each joint on each keyframe, with specific calculations in the case of an external perturbation (calculating the re-entry key frame). Finally, all the mentioned controllers are always critically damped. On the other hand, our pendulums can be critically damped or underdamped while maintaining the temporal control. An MRAC controller is designed to be temporally controlled but it calculates and adapts its gain constants on each frame using forces and torque calculations. Our pendulums do not need any adaptive pass once the user sets the reaction time and damping. Additionally, they can be modified in real time.

We differ from other systems of skeleton-driven deformations like [5] in that we concentrate only on deforming the skeleton of the articulated body, without any specific treatment to the mesh. Our mesh is animated by the classical linear blend skinning [8]. With no intention to compete against realistic fabric simulation seen in [16], we show a rigid tissue represented by a tree of bones animated by our approach with a large time-step and controllable computation.

## 3 3D pendulums

In our system, a bone of an articulated body is animated as a pendulum with a configurable target direction as illustrated in Figure 2(a). A pendulum is an anchored bar, with a fixed length L, attracted to its target direction by a spring. This spring pulls the pendulum toward this direction (described in Section 3.1). This idea allows the system to easily add plausible oscillations to any animation with a temporal control (explained in Section 3.2). In Section 3.3 and 3.4 we present our linear algorithm that deals with a tree of pendulums or a skeleton, by propagating the motion of a single pendulum to its father and sons.

### 3.1 3D Pendulum Principle

We design a pendulum $\overrightarrow{V}$ as a rotating bar attracted to its preferred direction by two springs: one spring on each 2D plane $XY$ and $ZY$ as illustrated in Figure 2(b). We choose this scheme with two springs instead of one spring to avoid spiral rotation motion around the target direction. The computation

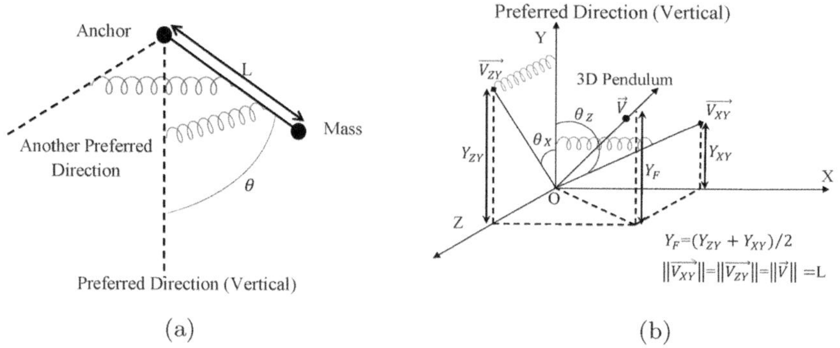


**Fig. 2.** (a) 3D pendulum (b) A 3D pendulum composed of two 2D pendulums with Y as their preferred direction

of pendulum $\vec{V}$ motion is done using its projections $\overrightarrow{V_{XY}}$,$\overrightarrow{V_{ZY}}$ independently. During the motion, after calculating the two new spring positions in 2D $\overrightarrow{V_{XY}}$ and $\overrightarrow{V_{ZY}}$, the 3D position $\vec{V}$ is obtained by combining them and ensuring that $\|\vec{V}\| = \|\overrightarrow{V_{XY}}\| = \|\overrightarrow{V_{ZY}}\| = L$. In the current implementation we omit the twist component around the axe of the 3D pendulum $\vec{V}$ which is the third degree of freedom, we plan to add it in a future work. It is interesting to notice that by using the target direction $\overrightarrow{-Y}$, we can give the impression of gravity that always pulls the bodies toward the ground.

### 3.2 Time Based Control for Spring Dampers

Let $m$ be a mass connected to a spring with stiffness constant $k$. This mass oscillates around a rest position $x_0$ with a viscous damper that has a damping coefficient $c$. Based on Newton's second law of physics the acceleration is $\ddot{x} = -(k(x - x_0) + c\dot{x})/m$ where $x$ is the current position of the mass, and $\dot{x}$ is its velocity. We integrate this motion using the Verlet scheme [13] which was numerically stable during our experiment described in Section 4. Giving a random position $x$ to the mass, it oscillates around the rest value $x_0$, seeking to minimize the error $(x - x_0)$ until reaching zero. This oscillation depends directly on the constants $(k, c, m)$. In order to achieve temporal control on the spring damper movement, we use the *Settling Time* $T_s$ principle. It is the time required for the mass position $x$ to reach its max amplitude inside a given error interval (See Figure 3(a)) and remains inside it. This interval is symmetrical around $x_0$.

$$T_s = -\frac{ln(tolerancefraction)}{\zeta * w_0} \tag{1}$$

Where the *tolerance fraction* is the needed error interval shown in Figure 3(a), $w_0$ is the natural frequency and $\zeta$ is the damping of the ordinary differential equation governing a damped harmonic oscillator:

$$m\ddot{x} + c\dot{x} + k(x - x_0) = 0$$

or

$$\ddot{x} + 2 * \zeta * w_0 * \dot{x} + w_0^2 * (x - x_0) = 0$$

with

$$\zeta = \frac{c}{2mw_0}, w_0 = \sqrt{\frac{k}{m}} \tag{2}$$

By fixing the tolerance fraction to 5% in equation (1) and by using the user provided settling time and damping (critically damped or underdamped), the spring damper constants $k$ and $c$ are calculated from equation (2), achieving total control over the curve of the spring damper while maintaining its dynamic aspect.

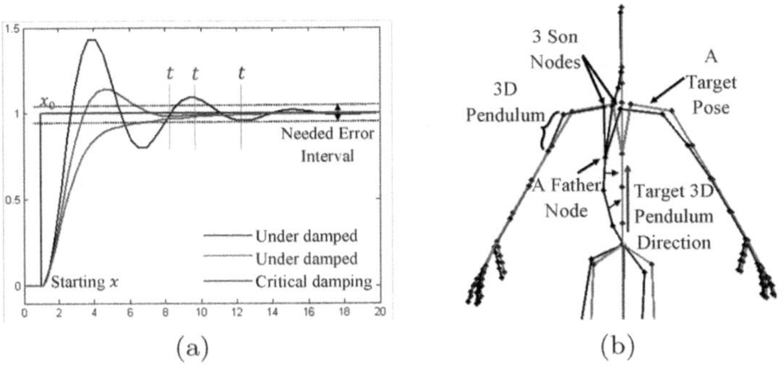


**Fig. 3.** (a) Spring oscillation under different damping (b) 3D pendulums Tree in Black with target direction in Grey

Figure 3(a) illustrates springs oscillating under different damping values. They oscillates around their $x_0$ until full stop, with their respective settling time. The third spring damper is a critical spring damper which converges toward $x_0$ faster than the others, and without oscillation.

### 3.3 Tree of 3D Pendulums

The skeleton of an articulated body is a tree of connected joints (articulations). By connecting several 3D pendulums and by defining the target direction for each one of them, the final result is a tree of pendulums that map the articulated structure, as shown in Figure 3(b). Some of the 3D pendulums act as a father node for several others. When they move, the anchor points of their children move. In order to have a visually believable reaction, these 3D pendulums need to interact with each other. We define two strategies used in conjunction to achieve this goal: Father Pursuit strategy and Son Pursuit strategy. In the accompanying video we show the similarities between the motion of a chain of pendulums fully-physically simulated and our chain of 3D pendulums that incorporate these strategies. For simplicity, these strategies will be described in a 2D plane.

**3.3.1 Father Pursuit Strategy.** The objective of this strategy is to propagate the motion of the father 3D pendulum toward its children, thus they need to incorporate this movement in their own motion. Figure 4(a) illustrates two connected pendulums $P_A$,$P_B$, A,B are the positions of each mass, $L_A$,$L_B$ are the lengths of the bars, and $\theta_A$,$\theta_B$ are the errors that each pendulum seeks to minimize. In this example the preferred direction of the pendulums are identical (the dashed -$\overrightarrow{Y}$).

The update system is a top-down system scheme, starting from the anchor toward the leaf. First, on time $t_1$ (in black) the error that we try to minimize is $\theta_{A1}$ in $P_A$ and $\theta_{B1}$ in $P_B$. Now, on time $t_2$ (in red):

1. $P_A$ moves, its spring damper tries to minimize the error, and has a new position $A2$.
2. $P_B$: the angle $\varepsilon_{AB}$ between the two vectors $\overrightarrow{B1A1}$ and $\overrightarrow{B1A2}$ is added to its own error, $\alpha_B = \theta_{B1} + \varepsilon_{AB}$.
3. $P_B$: letting the spring damper integrate its equations, we obtain a new angle value $\theta_{B2}$ which contains the new pursuit error.
4. $P_B$: based on $L_B$ the new position $B2$ (in blue) is calculated.

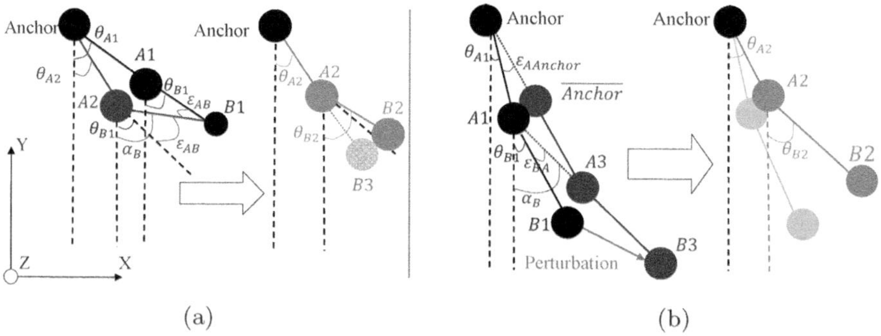


**Fig. 4.** (a) Father Pursuit Strategy (b) Son Pursuit strategy

Without this process, the new position of $P_B$ would have been $B3$ (in green), which is not correct and would have produced a non-logical disconnected motion. This Father Pursuit process is extended to every pendulum in the chain. A third pendulum $P_C$ follows the motion of its father $P_B$, and so on. By extending this process in 3D we have a totally plausible physical chain of 3D pendulums (as seen in the accompanying video). Each one reacting to its father's movement while oscillating around its target direction.

**3.3.2 Son Pursuit Strategy.** The objective of this strategy is to reflect the perturbation that can occur on the son level, to reflect it on its father. It occurs when the mass of $P_B$ takes a perturbation as seen in Figure 4(b) (in green). The perturbation is regarded as a change in the position, as if we only take the final position resulted of an impulse applied to a rigid body.

1. The perturbation induces its full impact as if the mass $P_B$ was not attached (in red).
2. $P_B$'s mass has two positions: $B1$ (the old one) and $B3$ (the new one). Inverting the previously detailed computation of the father induced error $\varepsilon_{AB}$, we calculate the child error $\varepsilon_{BA}$, the angle between $\overrightarrow{A1B3}$ and $\overrightarrow{A1B1}$ and adding it to $\theta_{B1}$, we obtain $\alpha_B = \theta_{B1} + \varepsilon_{BA}$.
3. The mass of $P_A$ should follow, as it is being pulled by its son now. The new position $A3$ is calculated easily by choosing on the line $A1B3$ the point $A3$ where $\|A1B1\| = \|A3B3\|$.
4. This process propagates toward the anchor.
5. The new positions are recalculated based on the fixed anchor position.

With this scheme, all the errors that the spring dampers need to minimize because of a perturbation are calculated in a bottom-up way starting from the son that took the perturbation toward the anchor.

**3.3.3 Final workflow.** In a tree of pendulums, calculation cycles may occur when two nodes are influencing each others in an endless loop (father influencing its son, then the son influencing its father, and so on.). To avoid these kinds of loops, we use an update system inspired by Featherstone's divide and conquer algorithm [6,7]. This algorithm eliminate any cyclic calculation problems and breaks the computation into two main linear passes. The first is a bottom-up pass through the articulated body tree, and the second is carried out from the top to the bottom. We adopt this paradigm completely. Only the calculations differ, as listed below:

1. For each 3D pendulum perturbed in the tree: resolve this perturbation by applying it on its mass then calculate the errors $\varepsilon$ in a bottom-up iteration toward its ancestors according to the Son Pursuit strategy.
2. For each father 3D pendulum integrate all the children errors ($\varepsilon_1$,$\varepsilon_2$ *etc.*) to its own error $\theta$.
3. Start the standard top-down pass starting from the anchor toward the leaf according to the Father Pursuit strategy.

In the previous step 2, there are many ways to calculate the integration:

- Summing up all the perturbation errors coming from its children: it is the method used to produce all of our results. It is the simplest method, and the one we chose after testing.
- Calculating an average: the father node will be perturbed in the same direction as the previous method, but with less amplitude. It is useful when the application decides that the father should be less affected by its children.
- Doing a weighted average based on:
  - The Mass: the heavier son has more influence on its father.
  - The importance of each branch: assigning predefined priorities on the children.

We can imagine many other possibilities based on a specific application's needs. Our system is quite easy to implement and the actual calculations in each strategy require only basic knowledge of 3D vector math. No prior knowledge of physics systems is required; we do not compute the inertia matrix nor we use the notion of force. At the same time we can use physics principles to enhance the end result like in the case of the father pendulum integrating its children's errors based on the inertia matrix.

### 3.4 3D Model Skeleton Vs. 3D Pendulums Tree

In the following section we demonstrate our system with skinned 3D models, using a predefined skeleton to construct the pendulums tree. Starting from the bind pose (rest pose) of the skeleton, we create a 3D pendulum for each skeletal connection (bone) with the same length and with its preferred rest direction calculated from the bone rest pose orientation. By maintaining the hierarchy of the base skeleton, we have a pendulums tree that maps this skeleton perfectly. While playing motion data, we modify the target direction of each corresponding pendulum, mimicking the base animation exactly. If the 3D pendulums start to react to an external perturbation, each of the 3D pendulums orientation and position is applied to its corresponding bone.

## 4 Applications and Results

In this section, we present several ways to use the 3D pendulums tree: adding physical effects to lifeless models like an octopus, modifying pre-defined motion data with physics reactions, and anecdotally a cloth simulation (which is normally a closed-loop problem). In all cases, the pendulum's reaction time, damping, and target direction is totally controllable. The results were computed on an Intel Core 2 Duo 2GHz, 2 GB RAM, with an ATI X1400, 256 MB. Our experimentation does not manage collisions, but we can easily imagine a system that creates an impulse (change in the position) on each 3D pendulum to counter any penetrations that occur.

### 4.1 Adding Physical Reaction Effects to Any Skeleton-Based Bodies

In Figure 5, we use our system on a lifeless octopus model. By adding some simple procedural animation to its tentacles (pulling only the root node of each tentacle toward the center at random intervals) the rest of the model reacts in a passive way, modifying the animation and adding plausible physics effects. The octopus model consists of 150 joints and the computation time of our superimposed physical effects is only 0.3 ms.

We can also use our system on animated models. In that case on each frame, the motion data takes control of the skeleton changing the preferred direction of each pendulums. With no external perturbations, the 3D pendulums rigorously follow the animation data. When an external perturbation occurs, our system reacts to this while continuously trying to return to the desired target pose.

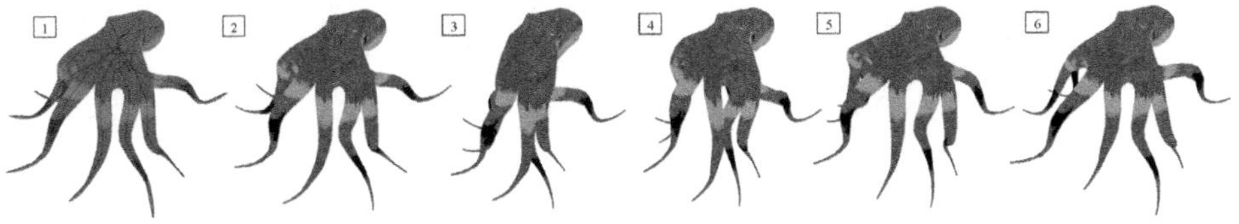


**Fig. 5.** From top left: [1] the model with its 3D pendulums, [2] rest pose, [3] we pull all the tentacles toward the center, [4] reacting, [5] tentacles overshooting (underdamped regime), [6] return to rest pose

With such a technique, our system adds plausible physical reaction effects to predefined animation data, as a superimposed animation layer. These reactions can furthermore be customized by making a section of the body more rigid, more flexible, changing the reaction time, or tuning the damping. This gives the end user a powerful tool to modulate the reaction of the body in a very easy and intuitive way.

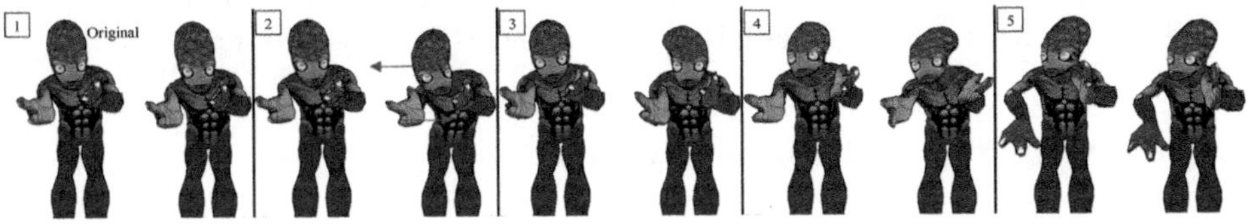


**Fig. 6.** From top Left: [1] Original (on the left) and our simulated articulated body (on the right), [2] Two perturbations, [3] to [5] Reaction and returning to the original keyfarme

By playing only the animation data on our test machine, for the previous model in Figure 6 with 92 joints, the average computation time for each frame is 0.06 ms. When playing the same animation using our pendulums and two perturbations, the computation time rises to an average of 0.46 ms, which stays negligible. This added cost is the result of reading the motion capture data in order to change the pendulum's target direction, integrating the perturbation, and then performing the main integration (as previously described).

### 4.2 Cloth Simulation

Although cloth is a closed loop problem, we are capable of giving the impression of an animated cloth by simply creating several vertical 3D pendulums that cover the cloth, plus attaching several horizontal 3D pendulums to each vertical one (one vertical is shown in Figure 7(a)). By doing a weighted average between the positions of all horizontal pendulums activated by their vertical father, weighted based on the distance between each horizontal pendulum and its vertical father, we compute the final cloth position. This results in a fully reactive cloth, without any tearing problems, that maintains its horizontal and vertical dimensions, while giving total control over the reaction time. We are not aiming to compete against more general, visually and physically accurate cloth simulators that are

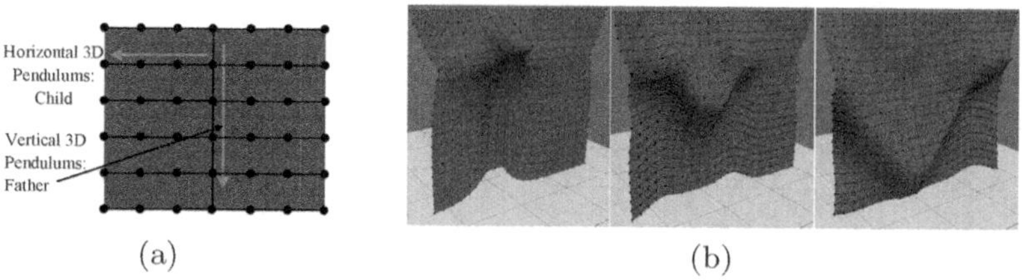


**Fig. 7.** (a) A cloth represented as a tree of pendulums (b) Cloth being pulled in the middle with a visual representation of the 3D pendulums

better suited to simulate actual human cloth, for example. We are just proposing a less sophisticated, but stable and relatively fast method that can plausibly simulate the motion of reactive cloth. In Figure 7(b), an external perturbation is applied to the middle three vertical pendulums. In order to optimize calculation time, those three vertical pendulums are the only ones actively being simulated (with the horizontal children of each one of them). The mesh is simulated using approximately 1500 3D pendulums. The average calculation time of these pendulums with the post calculations for the final cloth is around 5 ms.

## 5 Conclusion and Future Work

Our system is linear, straightforward, and based on simple 3D pendulums. It is capable of adding physical like reaction effects to skeleton-based body very easily. Additionally it is highly customizable: we can control reaction time, target direction and damping of the motion. The current system does not enforce angular constraints. We need to incorporate them into our future work in order to simulate real-life joint constraints that exists in most skeleton-based bodies. In addition to this, we are investigating coupling the system with a balance solver. This work would provide a body with the ability to actively work to maintain its balance, in opposition to the passive reactions described in this paper. Our system could also be used to mimic hair, which is an acyclic system and fits neatly in the domain that the 3D pendulums system can simulate.

## References

1. Allen, B., Chu, D., Shapiro, A., Faloutsos, P.: On the beat!: timing and tension for dynamic characters. In: Proceedings of the ACM SIGGRAPH/Eurographics symposium on Computer animation (2007)
2. Arikan, O., Forsyth, D.A., O'Brien, J.F.: Pushing people around. In: Proceedings of the ACM SIGGRAPH/Eurographics Symposium on Computer Animation (2005)
3. Barzel, R., Hughes, J.F., Wood, D.N.: Plausible motion simulation for computer graphics animation. In: Proceedings of the Eurographics Workshop on Computer Animation and Simulation (1996)
4. Bruderlin, A., Williams, L.: Motion signal processing. In: Proceedings of the Annual Conference on Computer Graphics & Interactive Techniques, SIGGRAPH (1995)

5. Capell, S., Green, S., Curless, B., Duchamp, T., Popović, Z.: Interactive skeleton-driven dynamic deformations. In: Proceedings of 29th Annual Conference on Computer Graphics& Interactive Techniques, SIGGRAPH (2002)
6. Featherstone, R.: A divide-and-conquer articulated body algorithm for parallel o(log(n)) calculation of rigid body dynamics. part 1:basic algorithm (1999)
7. Featherstone, R.: A divide-and-conquer articulated-body algorithm for parallel o(log(n)) calculation of rigid-body dynamics. part 2:trees,loops,& accuracy (1999)
8. Gain, J., Bechmann, D.: A survey of spatial deformation from a user-centered perspective. ACM Trans. Graph. 27, 107:1–107:2 (2008)
9. Hsu, E., da Silva, M., Popović, J.: Guided time warping for motion editing. In: Proceedings of the ACM SIGGRAPH/Eurographics Symposium on Computer Animation (2007)
10. Kanyuk, P.: Brain springs: Fast physics for large crowds in wall-e. IEEE Computer Graphics and Applications 29, 19–25 (2009)
11. Kokkevis, E., Metaxas, D., Badler, N.I.: User-controlled physics-based animation for articulated figures. In: Proceedings of the Computer Animation (1996)
12. Landau, Y.D.: Adaptive control: the model reference approach / Yoan D. Landau. Dekker, New York (1979)
13. Müller, M., Stam, J., James, D., Thürey, N.: Real time physics: class notes. In: SIGGRAPH 2008: ACM SIGGRAPH 2008 Classes, pp. 1–90. ACM, New York (2008)
14. Reitsma, P.S.A., Pollard, N.S.: Evaluating motion graphs for character animation. ACM Trans. Graph. 26 (October 2007)
15. van, H.W., van, B.B., Egges, A., Ruttkay, Z., Overmars, M.H.: Real time character animation: A trade-off between naturalness and control. In: Eurographics (2009)
16. Volino, P., Magnenat-Thalmann, N., Faure, F.: A simple approach to nonlinear tensile stiffness for accurate cloth simulation. ACM Transaction on Graphics (2009)
17. Zordan, V., Macchietto, A., Medina, J., Soriano, M., Wu, C.C.: Interactive dynamic response for games. In: Sandbox: Proceedings of the ACM SIGGRAPH symposium on Video games (2007)
18. Zordan, V., Majkowska, A., Chiu, B., Fast, M.: Dynamic response for motion capture animation. In: ACM SIGGRAPH 2005 Papers (2005)
19. Zordan, V.B., Hodgins, J.K.: Motion capture-driven simulations that hit and react. In: Proceedings of the ACM SIGGRAPH/Eurographics Symposium on Computer Animation (2002)

# Movement Classes from Human Motion Data

Kang Hoon Lee[1], Jong Pil Park[2], and Jehee Lee[2]

[1] Kwangwoon University, Seoul 139-701, Korea
kang@kw.ac.kr
[2] Seoul National University, Seoul 151-742, Korea
{jppark,jehee}@mrl.snu.ac.kr

**Abstract.** We present a new method for identifying a set of movement types from unlabelled human motion data. One typical approach first segments input motion into a series of intervals, and then clusters those into a set of groups. Unfortunately, the dependency between segmentation and clustering causes trouble in alternate tuning of parameters. Instead, we unify those two tasks in a single optimization framework that searches for the optimal segmentation maximizing the quality of clustering. The genetic algorithm is employed to address this combinatorial problem with our own genetic representation and fitness function. As the primary benefit, the user is able to obtain a repertoir of major movements just by selecting the number of classses to be identified. We demonstrate the usefulness of our approach by providing visual descriptions of motion data, and an intuitive animation authoring interface based on movement collections.

**Keywords:** computer animation, human motion data, movement classfication.

## 1 Introduction

Captured human motion data is widely used today in various applications such as game development, film production, and sports analysis. Given a large amount of motion data for practical use, it is often challenging for the user to quickly recognize what kinds of motions are available, or whether some specific kinds of motions need to be additionally acquired. For example, let us assume that we have a motion clip in which hundreds of dance steps are included. Manually examining the entire sequence not only is cumbersome, but also hardly provides a complete view of major dance steps, such as 'box step', 'free spin', and so on.

Many researchers have addressed this problem by presenting automatic methods of identifying a set of movement types from unlabelled motion data. A typical approach first partitions input motion data temporally into a collection of motion segments, and then clusters those into several groups such that similar segments can be included in the same group. The result of this two-phase approach strongly depends on the first phase, motion segmentation. As an extreme case, if we use a uniform segmentation scheme of partitioning input motion at regular intervals, it is hardly expected for any clustering algorithms to produce

Z. Pan et al. (Eds.): Transactions on Edutainment VI, LNCS 6758, pp. 122–131, 2011.

meaningful categories. In fact, there are a lot of more elaborate segmentation schemes than uniform partitioning, and suitable combinations of segmentation and clustering methods can yield much better results. However, there is not yet a consensus about any specific combinations that guarantee reasonable quality without respect to the domain of input motion.

We present an alternative approach to automatic motion classification from unlabelled human motion data. Instead of regarding segmentation and clustering as two separate procedures, we unify those into a single optimization framework in which both the segmentation of input motion and the clustering of segmented intervals can be simultaneously achieved. Given only the number of classes to be identified, we search for an optimal segmentation that produces the most concise and precise collection of movement classes. In order to cope with a large diversity of lengths and arrangements of basic movements, we allow both the lengths and the number of segments to vary within a pre-defined ranges through our optimization process. As a result, hundreds of irregular size segments as well as dozens of regular size segments can be equally treated as candidate segmentations for the same motion. Such a few constraints give us a huge size of search space for optimization, which could not be practically handled by exhaustive search.

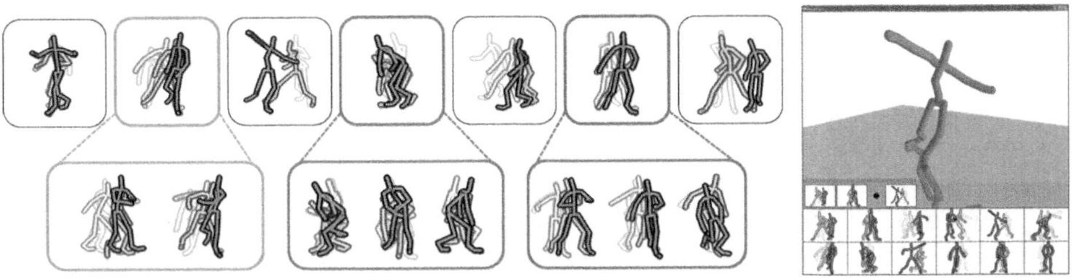

**Fig. 1.** Movement classes from breakdance motion data of about two thoudsands of frames. (Left top) The centroid motion segment of each class. (Left bottom) Some example motion segments other than the centroids. (Right) Our interactive animation authoring interface based on classified movements.

We employ the genetic algorithm to find a good approximate of the global optimum from such a large combinatorial space. To do so, we devise a genetic representation of the solution domain so that any feasible segmentations can be compactly encoded as binary strings (see Section 3). The fitness of a string, in other words, the goodness of a segmentation, is evaluated according to the quality of the clusters formed by running the *K-medoids* algorithm on the segmented intervals. Our measure of clustering quality prefers more compressed, and less lossy classifications (see Section 4). In optimization, a population of initial strings are randomly generated, which iteratively evolve into the next generations through selection, crossover, and mutation (see Section 5). When the optimization terminates, the string of the highest fitness is regarded as the best segmentation. The clusters formed by running the *K-medoids* finally on the best segmentation corresponds to our collection of movement classes, each of which is best represented by the centroid segment of its cluster (see Figure 1 (Left)).

The main benefit of our method is that the user can acquire a precise repertoire of major movements easily and consistently. The user provides only the number of motion classes without caring about which segmentation scheme is appropriate and how finely or coarsely input motion should be partitioned. We demonstrate the flexibility and usefulness of our approach by summarizing a variety of input motion data visually with a concise set of still images of classified movements (see Figure 2). Furthermore, our experimental interface system shows that the user can intuitively author new animation sequences just by arranging movement classes at any intended orders (see Figure 1 (Right)).

## 2 Background

The motion capture technology opened a new way of expressing highly realistic motion within virtual worlds for computer games and movies. In order to express a large diversity of motions using a limited amount of motion data, a lot of methods for processing motion data have been investigated. Currently, we are able to edit a motion sequence to satisfy geometric constraints [1], blend multiple sequences into intermediate motions [2], rearrange sub-sequences into arbitrarily long sequences that satisfy high-level constraints [3,4,5,6].

Data-driven motion synthesis often requires input motion data be pre-processed into computationally efficient and easily recognizable structures. Identifying movement types is an important step for compact representation of original data. Clustering after segmentation has been a popular approach to address this problem, using various segmentation schemes. Barbič et al. employed the principal component analysis (PCA) to find cutting locations where intrinsic dimensionality is changed [7]. Fod et al. identified zero-crossing frames, where angular velocities of joints reverse, as segmenting positions [8]. Kwon and Shin decided cutting positions based on the vertical peaks of the center-of-mass trajectory [9]. These methods regard segmentation and clustering as two separate tasks, while we simultaneously perform both tasks in a single unified procedure.

Our problem is closely related to another problem of retrieving a set of similar motions from motion database given a query motion. Typically, this involves the measure of evaluating the similarity of any two motion sequences, which has been addressed by several different approaches based on joint angles [3], point clouds [4], geometric relational characteristics [10]. Efficient methods for motion retrieval has been explored based on those measures. Kovar et al. presented a match web structure for searching over a large motion database to identify a set of similar motions efficiently [11]. Meng et al. pre-computed the best matches for each frame in a compact structure that supports fast motion retrieval [12].

Recently, there have been efforts for handling segmentation and clustering in a coupled manner as in ours. Beaudoin et al. presented a method of finding repetitive motion patterns, called motion-motifs [13]. This method is highly scalable to the size of input motion, and produces a well-organized view of the entire motion data. However, its randomized approach does not guarantee clear distinction among identified motifs, which is the goal of this paper. The most similar approach to ours is found in the work of Zhou et al. [14], where they also formulate the segmentation problem as an optimization of clustering. The key difference from ours is that the number of segments is constant, and regarded as the input parameter in Zhou et al. On the other hand, an arbitrary number of segments are allowed in our segmentation, which leaves only the number of classes as the input parameter, and gives much higher flexibility.

## 3 Genetic Representation

Let us denote the number of classes and the maximum number of segments as $K$ and $N$, respectively. Then, the number of segments $n$ is allowed to have an arbitrary value within the range of $[K, N]$ in our method. The lower boundary condition $n \geq K$ guarantees that every cluster includes at least a single segment. On the other hand, the upper boundary condition is to limit the size of search space, which grows exponentially according to $N$.

We further reduce the search space by pre-allocating $N-1$ possible cut locations within the range of $(1, T)$ where $T$ is the number of motion frames. For example, let the maximum number of segments $N$ be two. Then, just a single location, e.g. $T/2$, is pre-allocated, where a cut can be inserted or not. If inserted, we obtain two disjoint segments $[1, T/2)$ and $[T/2, T]$. Otherwise, only a single segment is obtained, corresponding to the entire interval $[1, T]$.

This simplification allows us to rephrase our problem as determining whether to accept or not each element from the ordered set of every possible cut location $\mathbf{T} = \{T_1, T_2, \cdots, T_{N-1}\}$. Denoting acceptance by 1 and rejection by 0 allows us to encode any segmentations in the solution domain compactly as binary strings $\mathbf{b} = b_1 b_2 b_3 \cdots b_{N-1}$, where $b_m \in \{0, 1\}$. Note that at least $K-1$ values of $\mathbf{b}$ should be 1 to satisfy the lower boundary condition $n \geq K$ as mentioned above.

In our experiments, we built the set of possible cut locations $\mathbf{T}$ simply by sampling the entire interval regularly (e.g. every half or one second). Any other more elaborate schemes, such as sampling where the contact states of feet are changed, might also be employed in deciding $\mathbf{T}$ to obtain more meaningful and smaller search spaces. However, manually selecting and tuning a specific scheme for each kind of input motion is tedious and error-prone, which reduces the main benefit of our approach, that is, removing the need of such a special attention in segmetnation. Our experimental results show that the brute-force regular sampling yields satisfying quality for a diversity of input motions.

## 4 Fitness Evaluation

In order to evaluate the fitness of a string $\mathbf{b}$, we first decode it into a series of cutting locations $\mathbf{t} = \{t_1, t_2, \cdots, t_{n-1}\} \subset \mathbf{T}$ by including only the $m$-th elements of $\mathbf{T}$ whenever $b_m = 1$. Those cutting locations are easily interpreted as a series of segment intervals, which are then clustered into $K$ groups according to their similarity. Finally, the quality of clustering is measured as the score of $\mathbf{b}$ based on our fitness function. This section explains three orthogonal components involved in this process in detail: motion similarity measure, clustering algorithm, and clustering quality measure.

### 4.1 Motion Distance

Let the input motion data of our method be a sequence of motion frames $\{\mathbf{x}_t|1 \leq t \leq T\}$ where $\mathbf{x}_t$ denotes a skeletal pose at an instance. Each pose is described as a root position $\mathbf{p}_t$ and a set of joint orientations $\{\mathbf{q}_{t,j}|1 \leq j \leq J\}$. Given any two frames $\mathbf{x}_t$ and $\mathbf{x}_{t'}$, we evaluate the dissimilarity $\mathrm{d}(\mathbf{x}_t, \mathbf{x}_{t'})$ between the corresponding poses by using the measure of Lee et al. [3].

This pose-to-pose distance measure can be easily extended to evaluate the distance between any two motion intervals $[t_s, t_e]$ and $[t'_s, t'_e]$. Because any two target intervals can have different lengths, temporal alignment of those intervals is a prerequisite for pose-to-pose comparison. The dynamic time warping is a well-known approach to this problem ensuring optimal alignment, but its computational cost is relatively expensive for our purpose.

Instead, we use a simple uniform time warping such that the $m$-th frame of the longer interval corresponds to the $\lfloor ml'/l \rfloor$-th frame of the shorter one, where $l$ and $l'$ are the lengths of the longer and shorter intervals, respectively. If the matched pairs of frames after alignment are $\{(t_m, t'_m)|1 \leq m \leq L = max(l, l'), t_s \leq t_m \leq t_e, t'_s \leq t'_m \leq t'_e\}$, then our motion distance is evaluated as follows.

$$\mathrm{D}([t_s, t_e], [t'_s, t'_e]) = \frac{1}{L} \sum_{m=1}^{L} \mathrm{d}(\mathbf{x}_{t_m}, \mathbf{x}_{t'_m}) \tag{1}$$

This calculation is one of the most frequently used operations in our optimization process, so reducing its computational cost can significantly increase the overall performance. For this purpose, we pre-compute $\mathrm{d}(\mathbf{x}_t, \mathbf{x}_{t'})$ for every pair of $(t, t')$ and just look up the resulting distance table at the optimization phase.

### 4.2 Motion Clustering

The cutting locations $\mathbf{t} = \{t_1, t_2, \cdots, t_{n-1}\}$ are interpreted as $n$ segment intervals $\{\mathbf{s}_1 = [1, t_1), \mathbf{s}_2 = [t_1, t_2), \cdots, \mathbf{s}_n = [t_{n-1}, T]\}$. We use the *K-medoids* algorithm to parition those segment intervals into a set of clusters $\mathbf{C} = \{\mathbf{C}_k|k = 1, \cdots, K\}$. We define each cluster $\mathbf{C}_k$ as a collection of segments $\{\mathbf{s}^i_k|1 \leq i \leq N_k\}$ where $N_k$ is the number of segments included in the cluster.

The overall process of the *K-medoids* algorithm is almost equivalent to the *K-means* algorithm except that the *K-medoids* algorithm allows more general distance measures other than the Euclidean distance. The objective function of the *K-medoids* is defined as follows.

$$\mathrm{E}(\mathbf{C}) = \sum_{k=1}^{K} \sum_{i=1}^{N_k} \mathrm{D}(\mathbf{s}_k^i, \mathbf{s}_k^c) \tag{2}$$

where $\mathbf{s}_k^c$ and $\mathbf{s}_k^i$ represent the central segment (i.e. centroid) and the $i$-th segment beloning to the $k$-th cluster, respectively, and $\mathrm{D}(\mathbf{s}, \mathbf{s}')$ corresponds to $\mathrm{D}([t_s, t_e], [t'_s, t'_e])$ in Equation 1 when $\mathbf{s} = [t_s, t_e]$ and $\mathbf{s}' = [t'_s, t'_e]$.

In order to minimize this objective function, we first initialize the centroids of $K$ clusters as the first $K$ segments $\mathbf{s}_1, \mathbf{s}_2, \cdots, \mathbf{s}_K$, and then iteratively update clusters and their centroids until convergence. When updating clusters, we associate every segment with its closest cluster based on the distances to centroids. For each new cluster, its centroid is updated to a new one that has the minimal sum of distances to every other segment within the same cluster. We terminate this iteration when no change of segment-to-cluster association is found.

### 4.3 Cluster Evaluation

We evaluate the result of clustering $\mathbf{C}$ via two contradictory features, compression ratio and reconstruction error, to achieve a reasonable trade-off between the conciseness and the preciseness of the action classes. The compression ratio measures how short segments are required to summarize the input motion data in comparison with the entire length as follows, denoting the length of a segment $\mathbf{s}$ as $L(\mathbf{s})$.

$$\mathrm{R}(\mathbf{C}) = \frac{1}{T} \sum_{k=1}^{K} L(\mathbf{s}_k^c) \tag{3}$$

On the other hand, the reconstruction error measures how much distortion is produced when we summarize the original motion only with the identified actions. This roughly corresponds to the data loss after replacing every segment $\mathbf{s}_k^i$ with the centroid segment $\mathbf{s}_k^c$ for every cluster in the input motion data. We evaluate this error by slightly modifying the function $\mathrm{E}(\mathbf{C})$ as follows in order to limit its range to $[0, 1]$ without respect to the length of input motion and the diversity of poses, where $\mathrm{d}_{max}$ is the maximum among the distance of every pair of two poses $\mathrm{d}(\mathbf{x}_t, \mathbf{x}_{t'})$.

$$\mathrm{E}'(\mathbf{C}) = \frac{1}{\mathrm{d}_{max}} \sum_{k=1}^{K} \sum_{i=1}^{N_k} \frac{L(\mathbf{s}_k^i)}{T} \mathrm{D}(\mathbf{s}_k^i, \mathbf{s}_k^c) \tag{4}$$

Choosing only one of these two features might cause undesirable effects in our optimization. Simply igonoring the reconstruction error, low compression ratio means just a large number of short segments that are grouped into arbitrary action classes without regard to thier similiarities. On the other side, low reconstruction error corresponds to a small number of long segments. At its extreme, the lowest error can be easily achieved by segmenting the input motion into $K$ intervals, and assigning a single segment for each cluster.

We take the inverse of the weighted sum of both features as our fitness function as follows in order to generate higher score for lower sum of compression ratio and reconstruction error, where the weight $\omega$ controls the relative contributions of the two features to the final fitness ($0 \leq \omega \leq 1$).

$$\mathrm{F}(\mathbf{C}) = \frac{1}{\omega\mathrm{R}(\mathbf{C}) + (1-\omega)\mathrm{E}'(\mathbf{C})} \tag{5}$$

## 5 Optimizing Classifications

We are now ready to perform the genetic algorithm with our genetic representation of the solution domain and the fitness function for any given solutions. A set of initial solutions, called a population, is randomly generated first. Then, the population is iteratively reproduced into a new population in the next generation based on three basic rules: selection, crossover, and mutation. This iteration terminates when the population converges to a local optimum, or the number of generations reaches to a pre-defined threshold. Finally, the best string in the last generation is selected as our classfication.

The initial population $\{\mathbf{b}_p | p = 1, \cdots, P\}$ is randomly generated by selecting each value of the string $\mathbf{b}_p$ from $\{0, 1\}$ with an equal probability. Then, we need to check if the number of 1's in $\mathbf{b}_p$ is greater than or equal to $K - 1$ for every string, as discussed in Section 3. If not, we locally update some 0's to 1's to obtain a valid string. This validation process applies not only to the initialization phase, but also to every reproduction step.

We adopt *elitism* and *roulette-wheel selection* schemes when producing the next generation. The score for every string $\{\mathbf{b}_p\}$ is evaluated by our fitness function as discussed in Section 4. A small portion of the entire population that obtains the topmost score is regarded as the *elite*, which is transferred to the next generation in its original form. For the rest of the population, we associate each string with its reproduction probability as the ratio of its own score to the total score. Then, each new string in the next generation, e.g. a child, is produced by probabilistically selecting a pair of existing strings, e.g. parents, and performing crossover and mutation operations.

Among many crossover techniques, we use the one-point crossover that cuts two existing strings $\mathbf{b} = b_1 \cdots b_{N-1}$ and $\mathbf{d} = d_1 \cdots d_{N-1}$ at a common location $p$, and exhanges the resulting substrings with one another to reassemble two new strings $\mathbf{b}' = b_1 \cdots b_{p-1} b_p d_{p+1} \cdots d_{N-1}$ and $\mathbf{d}' = d_1 \cdots d_{p-1} d_p b_{p+1} \cdots b_{N-1}$. Both new strings are accepted into the population of the next generation in our implementation. When deciding cut locations, we prefer the locations where both values $b_p$ and $d_p$ are 1 to preserve existing segment intervals. If there are no such locations, we randomly select one among the locations where either $b_p$ or $d_p$ is 1.

We probabilistically mutate each new string with the probability being decreased through iterations. In other words, a large portion of the population mutates at the early phase of our optimization for extensively exploring the

**Fig. 2.** Movement classes from boxing (Left) and basketball (Right) motion data of about three and five thousands frames, respectively

search space, while little portion is mutated at the late phase for finely tuning the existing solutions. In our implementation, the mutation probability is determined as $e^{-5g/G}$ where $g$ and $G$ is the current and the total number of generations, respectively. Once a string is determined to be mutated according to the probability, we randomly choose a single location in the string, and negate its value.

## 6 Experimental Results

We experimented with a variety of input motions including boxing, breakdance, and basketball. The number of classes for each motion data was determined by running optimizations with various numbers between 5 and 20, and selecting the best one yielding the highest score. In optimization, we used the same parameters for every test data. We represented a segmentation as a string by arranging possible cut locations at every one second. The population consisted of one hundred strings, which reproduced for 500 generations. For each generation, the topmost 10 strings were selected as elites, and transferred to the next generation without crossover. The usefulness of our approach is qualitatively demonstrated by visually summarizing each movement class in Figure 2. We rendered a small number of poses belonging to each segment in a cartoon style, and layered the rendered poses in sequence of time. Additionally, we utilized the same visualization techniques in creating an interface system for animation authoring (see Figure 1 (Right)). Regarding the movement classes as animation building blocks, the user can intuitively design new animation sequences by arranging movement classes in the time domain.

In order to demonstrate the effectiveness and robustness of our approach, we plot the maximum scores obtained from a short basketball motion clip of 500 frames with respect to the number of generations $g$ on the left and the number of classes $K$ on the right. For the left graph, we fixed $K$ to 13, sampled possible cut locations at every 10 frame, and produced 200 generations. The resulting graph shows that the maximum score sharply increases at irregular intervales due to our policy of elitism, and eventually converges to a local optimum around the 100th generation. For the right graph, we varied $K$ from 1 to 50, and run our optimization process 5 times for each $K$ to cope with the randomness of the genetic algorithm. When $K$ is 1, every segment belongs to the same cluster, leading to the lowest compression ratio and the highest reconstruction error. On the other hand, when $K$ equals to the number of maximum segments (50), every cluster includes a single segment, thus yielding the highest compression ratio (1), e.g. no compression, and the lowest reconstruction error (0), e.g. no error. The score is equal to 4.0 because the weight $\omega$ is 0.25 in this experiment. Between 1 and 50, the scores roughly draw an arc, whose maximum occurs at the ideal number of classes (13 in this case) with respect to our fitness measure.

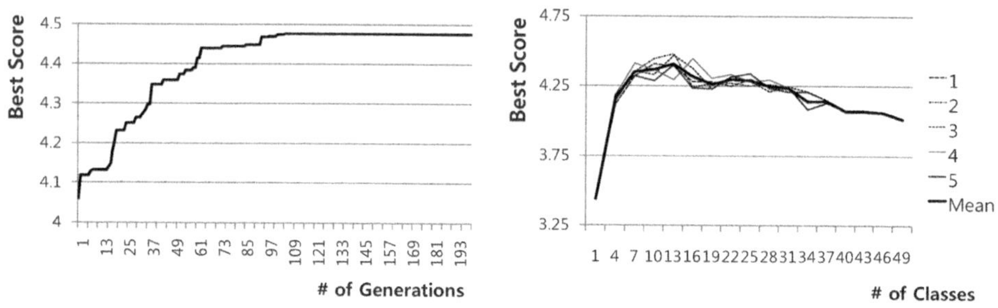


**Fig. 3.** The best scores obtained from our genetic algorithm with respect to the increasing numbers of classes

## 7 Discussion

We have presented a new method for identifying a user-given number of motion classes from an unlabelled human motion data. The key characteristic of our method is in its unified process of obtaining the optimal segmentation that produces a high quality classification. Our experimental results demonstrate that our method based on the genetic algorithm is highly flexible to a large diversity of human motions without exhaustive tuning of parameters.

The primary advantage of our method is that the user can easily obtain a simplified view of his/her motion data that summarizes the entire motion into a small set of representative movements. Furthermore, such movement collections can be utilized for interactively authoring new animation sequences. We plan to improve our authoing system introduced in this paper to incorporate path editing, pose editing, and multi-character synchronization.

Our solution domain allowing an arbitrary number of segments causes a challenging problem of combinatorial explosion, which makes it hard for our method to scale well with the size of input motion data. As an idea of dealing with this problem, we are interested in a hierarchical extension that first processes a set of short motion sequences into a large number of classes, and then merge those classes into a small number of more comprehensive classes.

**Acknowledgments.** We would like to thank Sang Won Lee for his help in video editing. This research was supported by Basic Science Research Program through the National Research Foundation of Korea(NRF) funded by the Ministry of Education, Science and Technology (No. 2010-0008243 and No. 2010-0012759).

## References

1. Lee, J., Shin, S.Y.: A Hierarchical Approach to Interactive Motion Editing for Human-Like Figures. In: 26th Annual Conference on Computer Graphics and Interactive Techniques, pp. 39–48. ACM Press, New York (1999)
2. Kovar, L., Gleicher, M.: Flexible Automatic Motion Blending with Registration Curves. In: 2003 ACM SIGGRAPH/Eurographics Symposium on Computer Animation, pp. 214–224. Eurographics Association, Switzerland (2003)
3. Lee, J., Chai, J., Reitsma, P.S.A., Hodgins, J.K., Pollard, N.S.: Interactive Control of Avatars Animated with Human Motion Data. ACM Trans. Graph. 21(3), 491–500 (2002)
4. Kovar, L., Gleicher, M., Pighin, F.: Motion Graphs. ACM Trans. Graph. 21(3), 473–482 (2002)
5. Arikan, O., Forsyth, D.A., O'Brien, J.F.: Motion Synthesis from Annotations. ACM Trans. Graph. 22(3), 402–408 (2003)
6. Treuille, A., Lee, Y., Popović, Z.: Near-Optimal Character Animation with Continuous Control. ACM Trans. Graph. 26(3), 7 (2007)
7. Barbič, J., Safonova, A., Pan, J.-Y., Faloutsos, C., Hodgins, J.K., Pollard, N.S.: Segmenting Motion Capture Data into Distinct Behaviors. In: Graphics Interface, pp. 185–194. Canadian Human-Computer Communications Society, Ontario (2004)
8. Fod, A., Mataric, M.J., Jenkins, O.C.: Automated Derivation of Primitives for Movement Classfication. Auton. Robots 12(1), 39–54 (2002)
9. Kwon, T., Shin, S.Y.: Motion Modeling for On-Line Locomotion Synthesis. In: 2005 ACM SIGGRAPH/Eurographics Symposium on Computer Animation, pp. 29–38. ACM Press, New York (2005)
10. Müller, M., Röder, T., Clausen, M.: Efficient Content-Based Retrieval of Motion Capture Data. ACM Trans. Graph. 24(3), 677–685 (2005)
11. Kovar, L., Gleicher, M.: Automated Extraction and Parameterization of Motions in Large Data Sets. ACM Trans. Graph. 23(3), 559–568 (2004)
12. Meng, J., Yuan, J., Hans, M., Wu, Y.: Mining Motifs from Human Motion. In: Eurographics 2008–Short Papers, pp. 71–74 (2008)
13. Beaudoin, P., Coros, S., van de Panne, M., Poulin, P.: Motion-Motif Graphs. In: 2008 ACM SIGGRAPH/Eurographics Symposium on Computer Animation, pp. 117–126. Eurographics Association, Switzerland (2008)
14. Zhou, F., de la Torre, F., Hodgins, J.K.: Aligned Cluster Analysis for Temporal Segmentation of Human Motion. In: IEEE International Conference on Automatic Face and Gesture Recognition (2008)

# Front View vs. Side View of Facial and Postural Expressions of Emotions in a Virtual Character

Matthieu Courgeon[1,2], Céline Clavel[1], Ning Tan[1,2], and Jean-Claude Martin[1,2]

[1] LIMSI-CNRS, B.P. 133, 91403 Orsay, France
[2] University Paris South XI, France
{courgeon,clavel,ntan,martin}@limsi.fr

**Abstract.** In 3D virtual environments and social scenes, virtual characters are not always visible from a front view. Nonverbal expressions of emotions should be designed so as to be properly perceived when viewed from multiple angles. Our platform enables the design of facial expressions including 3D expressive wrinkles and 3D postures. It was used to generate stimuli for studying the impact of front versus side views on the perception of blends of facial and postural expressions of emotions. Results observed in previous studies for front views of incongruent images are confirmed for side views. Furthermore, subjects were less confident in their ratings for side views images than for front view images.

**Keywords:** facial expressions, posture, emotions, evaluation study, 3D rendering.

## 1 Introduction

Users do not always interact with a single virtual character that is displayed in a front view. Instead, they often have to interact with virtual characters that are embedded in complex 3D environments and social scenes featuring other virtual characters. The face and the posture of the virtual character are thus no longer visible by the user from a single front view but rather from a side view when the character is pointing at virtual objects or is displaying non-verbal cues of social interactions towards other characters. This requires a virtual character platform that enables the virtual character to properly display 3D expressions of emotions while being viewed from the front, from the side, and possibly from a distance. User's perception of these expressions of emotions from various angles and distances needs to be assessed.

Emotion theories need to be considered in order to understand how these nonverbal expressions of emotions are perceived. Discrete emotion theories claim a limited number of basic or fundamental emotions. Six basic emotions are often considered: fear, happy, anger, sadness, surprise and disgust [1]. Dimensional theorists define dimensional spaces that account for the similarities and differences in emotional experience. Three dimensions are often used [2]. Pleasure is a continuum ranging from extreme pain or unhappiness at one end to extreme happiness or ecstasy at the other end. Arousal ranges from sleep to frenzied excitement. Dominance ranges

Z. Pan et al. (Eds.): Transactions on Edutainment VI, LNCS 6758, pp. 132–143, 2011.

from feelings of total lack of control or influence on events and surroundings to the opposite extreme of feeling influential and in control.

In everyday life, it is frequent to express blends of several emotions [1, 3]. Producing congruent expressions in different modalities requires important skills given the difficulty of monitoring and controlling different cues at the same time [4].

Several studies explore how emotions are expressed by the face or by the body. Ekman suggests that a single emotion is expressed using a family of facial expressions. He lists distinctive clues to six basic emotions [1]. Baron-Cohen proposes a more detailed list of 416 so-called mental states (e.g. Relaxation). The MindReading database includes six audiovisual performances for each of these mental states [5].

Whereas Ekman suggests that posture might provide information regarding the intensity of emotion [6], Wallbott observes discriminative features of emotion categories in posture and movement quality [7]. Basic gestural form features might also be related somehow to emotions (e.g. the left hand was observed to be used more frequently when in a relaxed and positive mood) [8].

Viewing angle is becoming a relevant issue for studying how emotions are expressed or perceived. Coulson studies the attribution of emotion to static body postures without facial expressions from three points of view [9]. Correlations across the three viewpoints for each emotion category shows that, for anger, happiness and surprise, the attributions are more likely for front views; for fear, the attributions are more likely when perceived from behind and from side; for sadness, the attributions are more likely when perceived from front and from side. The AffectMe database contains motion capture postural expressions of some basic emotions [10]. The GEMEP corpus contains front views and side views of facial and postural expressions of acted emotions [11]. The system designed by Pantic and Patras aims at the automatic recognition of facial action units and their temporal models from profile-view face image sequences [12]. Other systems process full 3D scans of facial expressions [13].

3D techniques are also used for animating and rendering facial expressions. Bump-mapping 2D texture-based rendering of expressive wrinkles are observed to improve various aspects of the recognition and subjective perception of facial expressions of emotions when displayed with a front view [14, 15]. Yet, when viewed from the side, such 2D techniques might be not enough for rendering realistic wrinkles, as the skin surface remains flat. Instead, 3D rendering of such facial details might improve the perception of facial expressions of emotions [16]. 3D Wrinkles can be computed from physical biomechanical models [17] or displayed using parametric models [18]. Parametric 3D wrinkles can be included directly in facial blend shapes, or mapped from displacement textures, deforming the mesh. The final image is rather similar, the quality of the wrinkles depending on the complexity of the mesh rather than on the rendering technique. The only way to improve wrinkle rendering would be on-the-fly local mesh refinement. Wrinkles can be extracted from 3D video captures [18] of manually edited using image edition tools (bump maps) or 3D edition software (3d mesh).Video captured wrinkles require costly 3D capture equipments, but can be more accurate and natural.

The perception of facial and postural expressions of emotions also depends on the framing. In a tight framing of the virtual character, the rendering details of the face are more visible.

Models of blends of face-only expressions of emotions use either interpolations between predefined basic emotions' expressions for the whole face, spatial facial region decomposition, dimensional models of emotions or sequenced expression models [19]. But face and body appear together in daily experience. Several studies observe that congruent combinations of facial and postural expressions of emotions improve emotion recognition [20, 21, 22]. De Gelder observes that, when a face is accompanied by a body expressing the same emotion, the judgment accuracy and speed increase [23]. In a study using virtual character stimuli, a similar effect is observed for congruent combinations [24]. But, in incongruent combinations of face and posture expressions (e.g. anger facial expression combined with a posture expressing sadness), subjects report the emotion category that is displayed in the face, whereas they report the level of activation of the emotion displayed via the body.

In summary, previous research suggests that face and posture might convey different aspects of emotion when occurring in incongruent combinations and displayed in frontal view. Yet, little is known about how such facial and postural expressions are perceived when viewed from the side or from a distance. Most studies are limited to the frontal display, some to the upper body, and with limited 3D rendering (e.g. no expressive wrinkles in 3D). The present aim is to study the impact of the viewing angle and distance on the perception of combinations of 3D facial and postural expressions of emotions.

## 2 System

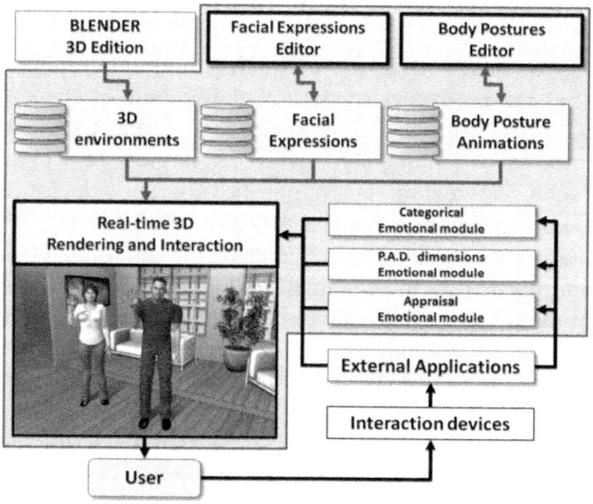


**Fig. 1.** MARC's architecture

In order to investigate the perception of 3D facial and postural expressions of emotion from front and side views, we used the MARC system, extended with 3D wrinkles [25]. MARC is a set of tools and models for the design and the animation of virtual characters. It features three main applications: the facial expression editor, the body posture editor, and the real-time rendering application (see Figure 1).

The system uses GPU computing through OpenGL and GLSL to render and animate virtual characters and their environments. The face of the virtual characters is bound to a list of about 100 MPEG-4 standard keypoints [26].

In order to create realistic 3D wrinkles, we extended the system with a second set of keypoints dedicated to wrinkles. Areas of influence of keypoints are edited manually. Figure 2 shows the area of influence for a wrinkle keypoint, and the resulting geometric deformation.

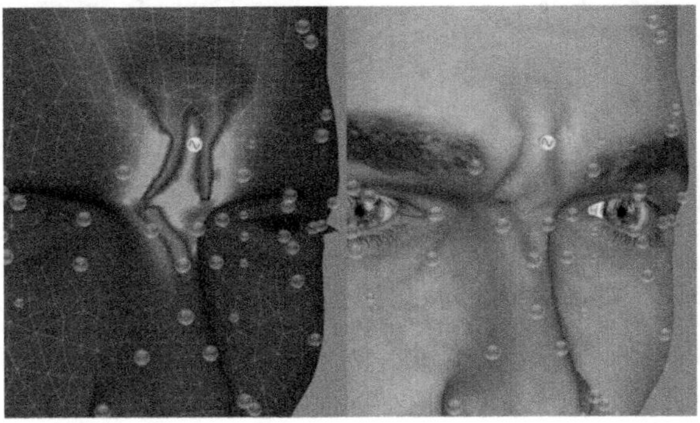

**Fig. 2.** Influence of a wrinkle keypoint (left): red means negative influence, green means positive influence; the resulting effect (right)

The location of the wrinkle keypoints were defined based on Ekman's descriptions of expressive facial wrinkles [27]. Three keypoints are defined on the forehead (left, center, right). Two keypoints are defined for the nose (frown and nose wrinkles). Two keypoints are defined for crow's feet wrinkles (left and right). Two keypoints are defined for managing nasolabial furrows (left and right). Finally, two keypoints are defined to render the folding lines under the eyes (left and right).

These 3D geometric wrinkles enable a more realistic rendering. They are more visible from a side view than from a front view. Figure 3 shows a side view of geometric wrinkles using the 3D technique, versus wrinkles rendered using the usual 2D bump mapping technique.

The 3D geometric deformation is possible thanks to the high-resolution meshes that we use: 20.000 polygons for the face only. Using only low-resolution polygons would not allow rendering fine geometric wrinkles without expensive on-the-fly local mesh refinement techniques. Moreover, this 3D wrinkle rendering method does not cost much computational time for the GPU. We use keypoints for both facial deformations and wrinkling effects. Thus, the animation GPU programs (shaders) do not make any distinction between MPEG4 keypoints and wrinkle keypoints. This approach uses on-the-fly computation of the deformed mesh normal vectors to create proper shadow effects. Unlike 2D bump mapping techniques, the 3D wrinkles rendering method enables the rendering of geometric wrinkles from various points of view without the complexity of a muscle model [28]. MARC is designed for real-time interactive animation. Using a muscle based model is not possible in our applications since we aim at real-time interaction. Thus, we implemented a parametric 3D wrinkles model.

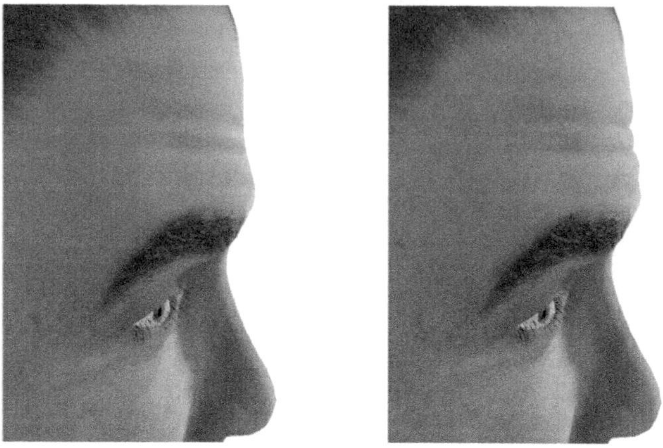

**Fig. 3.** Forehead wrinkles: 2D bump mapping wrinkles (left) vs. 3D geometric wrinkles (right)

Similarly to facial expressions, body postures were edited manually. The body animation system is based on standard skeleton rigging. The body posture editor of MARC enables to specify sequences of postures on a timeline, defining a whole animation.

The facial and postural expressions presented in the following sections were designed using this system. They were rendered using the Real-time Rendering Application from which we extracted static pictures of the combined display of facial expression and body postures.

## 3 Experiment

Our experiment aims at evaluating the impact of the point of view and the expressive modalities on perception of emotional perception.

Regarding the observer point of view, we consider two factors: the view angle (front versus side) and the distance (close-up versus more distant).

Regarding the expressive modalities, we consider 1) mono-modal expression (posture only and face only) versus 2) congruent combinations (face and posture expressing a single emotion) versus 3) incongruent combinations (face and body expressing different emotions).

We have the following hypotheses:

- **H1: The congruent combinations should be better recognized than face-only and posture-only images.**
- **H2: The close-up of the face should be better recognized than the more distant view.**
- **H3: The point of view should have an impact on emotion recognition.**
- **H4: In incongruent combinations, subjects should perceive the category of emotion expressed in the face but the level of arousal expressed in the body.**
- **H5: Subjects' confidence should be lower for side views than for front views; lower for incongruent than for congruent combinations.**

We selected 4 emotions for the study: Joy, Anger, Sadness, and Relaxation. These emotions were selected because they are balanced in terms of valence and arousal [2]. Joy is a positive emotion with high arousal. Relaxation is a positive emotion with low arousal. Anger is a negative emotion with high arousal. Sadness is a negative emotion with low arousal. Furthermore, incongruent combinations of Joy, Anger and Sadness were already used in a similar study using front views [24]. Selecting these three basic emotions enables us to compare the results with this previous study.

The specification of a facial expression for each of the three basic emotions (Joy, Anger and Sadness) was inspired by the visual and textual descriptions of Ekman [1]. The specification of the facial expression of Relaxation was inspired by the MindReading database [5]. The specification of postural expressions was inspired by the AffectMe database [10] for Joy, Sadness and Anger. The postural expression for Relax was inspired by a study on basic gestural form features and emotions [8].

To investigate the perception of combined facial and postural expressions of emotions from various angles and distances, four modalities were considered: close face, far face, posture, face+posture.
We used 56 pictures rendered by the MARC system described in the previous section (Figure 4, 5):

- **16 face-only images (the body is hidden):**
  8 front views + 8 side views; 8 close-up + 8 more distant shots
- **8 body-only images (the head is hidden):**
  4 front views + 4 side views
- **8 congruent face and body images:**
  4 front views + 4 side views
- **24 incongruent face and body images:**
  12 front views + 12 side views

36 subjects participated in the experiment (12 females, 24 males, average age 27). The order of presentation of the 56 images was randomized. Each image was displayed with a 560x650 pixels size. Aside to the image, a questionnaire was displayed with a set of eight sliders. For each image, users had to rate the levels of valence, arousal and dominance they perceived. They also had to rate how much they perceived each of the four emotions and to report their confidence in their ratings Each question was answered using a five points Likert scales. In order to detect

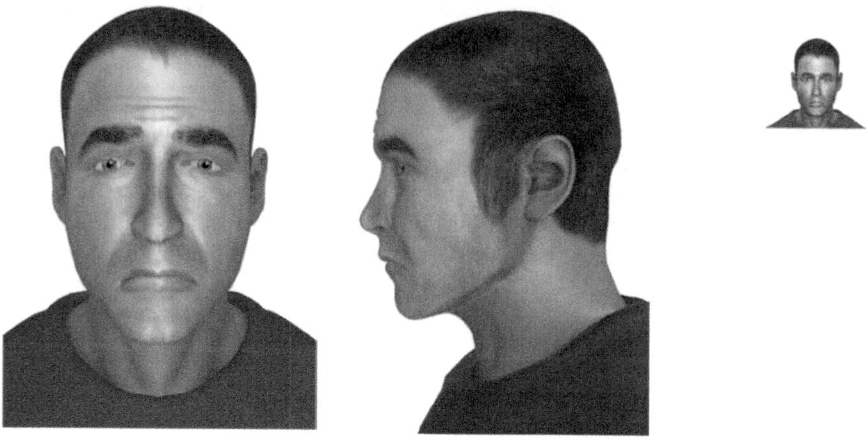

**Fig. 4.** Sadness face-only pictures. Front close-up (left), side close-up (center) and front from a distance (right)

**Fig. 5.** Congruent expressions of Sadness (a) and Joy (b), Incongruent expressions of Joy (face) and Anger (body) from front (c) and side (d)

blends of emotions, we used Likert scale instead of a forced choice as used by Coulson et al. [9]. Thus, subjects were able to moderate their answers and to report blends of emotions.

## 4 Results

We computed repeated measures ANOVA in order to estimate the degree of emotional and dimensional recognition in each modality.

## Categorical recognition

*Anger* was the most perceived emotion in our images of Anger whatever the point of view for the four modalities (close face, far face, posture, congruent face+posture).

*Sadness* was the most perceived emotion in our images of Sadness for the face-only images or for the face+posture images whatever the point of view. However the front-view posture-only image designed for Sadness was equivalently perceived as being an expression of Relax.

*Joy* was the most perceived emotion in the face-only and face+posture images designed for Joy. Nevertheless the posture-only side view image designed for Joy was equivalently perceived as an expression of Relax.

*Relax* was the most perceived emotion only in the front view posture-only image designed for Relax. The face-only and face+posture images designed for Relax were equivalently perceived as Joy or Relax whatever the point of view. The side view of the posture-only image of Relax was perceived as a blend of the four emotions.
These results validate the categorical recognition of 25 images out of 32. The images designed to express Relax were frequently misperceived as Joy, which is also a positive emotion.

**Table 1.** Average values for dimensions (-1/+1)

| Emotion | Valence | Activation | Dominance |
|---|---|---|---|
| Anger | -0,86 | 0,5 | 0,52 |
| Sadness | -0,62 | -0,78 | -0,8 |
| Joy | 0,6 | 0,62 | 0,14 |
| Relax | 0,1 | **0,06** | -0,16 |

## Dimensional recognition

We analyzed the attribution of P.A.D. dimensions to each congruent image (face + posture). We used ANOVA and Post Hoc Analysis HSD of Tukey. The average values for each emotion (Table 1) are in the correct quadrant of the PAD space [2], except for Relax activation, which is slightly positive.

***H1.*** Regarding congruent emotions (mono-modal and congruent combinations), we observed that the categorical recognition rates are equivalent in congruent combination and face-only images. Posture-only images recognition rates were lower than congruent combination and face-only images. Yet posture-only images were correctly recognized. These results partly confirm H1. Face-only was indeed recognized as well as congruent combination.

***H2.*** Close-up images of face were not better recognized than distant views. Thus, we can hypothesize that using prototypical expressions of emotions enable to display virtual characters from distance without reducing emotional perception.

However, if we consider side view versus front view, we observed that close-up front view image of Joy was better recognized than the more distant view. We also observed a tendency effect for the negative emotions (Sadness and Anger). The perception of side view images conveying these emotions tended to be better recognized in close-up than in the more distant view.

***H3.*** We observed that the point of view influences the recognition of emotions: 1) the perception of the face-only and posture-only images of Anger was equivalent whatever the point of view. But the front view face+posture image of Anger was better perceived than in side view. 2) The face-only image and the face+posture image of Joy were better perceived in side view than in front view. 3) The front view of Relax was better recognized than the side view, whatever the modality. Finally, 4) the face-only and face+posture images of Sadness were better recognized in front view than in side view. Yet, the posture-only image of Sadness was better recognized in side view than in front view. Thus, the point of view does influence the recognition of emotions. H3 is confirmed.

***H4.*** We only considered incongruent images of two emotions with either constant activation (e.g. Anger / Joy), or constant valence (e.g. Joy/Relax). We obtained 8 images in which we can assess the impact of valence and activation independently. The results show that for 6 images out of these 8 images, subjects attribute the emotion category conveyed by the facial expression. For the remaining 2 images, subjects perceived a blend of emotions conveyed by facial and postural expressions. The image combining the facial expression of Relax with the postural expression of Joy, was equivalently perceived as Joy and Relax whatever the point of view.

The rating of Activation depends on the emotion conveyed by postural expression whatever the point of view. For example, subjects judged that the image combining the facial expression of Anger with the postural expression of Sadness was less active than the image combining the facial expression of Sadness with the postural expression of Anger. On the contrary, the rating of Valence depends on the facial expression and not on the postural expression. For example, subjects judged that the image combining the facial expression of Joy with the postural expression of Anger was more positive than the image combining the facial expression of Anger with the postural expression of Joy. These results confirm our hypothesis H4.

***H5.*** Confidence was rated lower on incongruent images than congruent images. Confidence was also rated lower on side view images than front view images. This confirms hypothesis H5.

We also considered the interaction between congruence and viewing angle. The level of confidence reported for the incongruent images was lower in side view than in front view. The level of confidence was lower for the incongruent images in side view than for the congruent images in side view. The level of confidence was lower for the incongruent images in side view than for the congruent images in front view. To summarize, incongruent profile images show a low confidence rate, but congruent combinations and/or front view images shows an equivalent high confidence report.

## 5 Conclusion

In conclusion, we observed high recognition rates for congruent images of emotion whatever the point of view and the distance. Yet, these factors have an impact on the reported confidence.

In this experiment we only used two angles (front and side). Using intermediate angles might provide interesting results about the limit upon which the viewing angle becomes problematic for perception and leads to a decrease in the reported confidence.

Regarding facial expressions, similar studies need to be conducted using photos of real humans' expressions, using physical biomechanical facial simulations, and using different face models. It would enable to assess the impact of simplified parametric wrinkles models on the perception of facial expressions of emotions,. However, using human faces would introduce a new challenge: how to control precisely all facial parameters.

Regarding expressive modalities, our results confirm previous findings [24]. In incongruent combinations of face and posture, subjects report the emotion category that is displayed in the face, whereas they report the level of activation of the emotion which is displayed via the posture.

Several studies pointed the impact of dynamic versus static stimuli on the perception of expressions of emotions [11]. We intend to extend the present study to more emotions, and to animations of the virtual character. MARC's animation system features an event-based system to precisely synchronize facial expressions with postural animations. The dynamics of these expressions should not be limited to interpolation of prototypical expressions. In this study, we used only one expression for each emotion. Our system features an appraisal module that produces more complex facial animations [4, 28], the dynamics of which requires to be properly integrated with body movements. Our system is also capable of importing motion capture files, enabling to render more realistic postural animations. Following similar studies by de Gelder [23], we intend to explore the combinations of face with other contextual modalities such as the speech and the surrounding scene.

Our platform was recently integrated in a virtual reality setup enabling the user to interact with multiple virtual characters in life-sized audiovisual spatial social scenes. In such applications, the virtual characters might be visible only from some angles, as users' displacements are limited. It is thus important to have experimental results on how their expressions of emotions will be perceived from different angles.

## References


1. Ekman, P., Friesen, W.V.: Unmasking the face. A guide to recognizing emotions from facial clues. Prentice-Hall Inc. Englewood Cliffs (1975)
2. Russell, J.A., Mehrabian, A.: Evidence for a three-factor theory of emotions. Journal of Research on Personality 11(3), 273–294 (1977)
3. Scherer, K.R.: Analyzing emotion blends. In: 10th Conf. of the Int. Society for Research on Emotions, pp. 142–148 (1998)
4. Scherer, K.R.: Emotion and emotional competence: conceptual and theoretical issues for modelling agents. In: Scherer, K.R., Bänziger, T., Roesch, E. (eds.) Blueprint for Affective Computing, pp. 3–20. Oxford University Press, Oxford (2010)
5. Golan, O., Baron-Cohen, S., Hill, J.: The Cambridge Mindreading (CAM) face-voice battery: testing complex emotion recognition in adults with and without asperger syndrome. Journal of Autism and Developmental Disorders 36(2), 169–183 (2006)
6. Ekman, P., Friesen, W.V.: Nonverbal behavior and psychopathology. In: Friedman, R.J., Datz, M.M. (eds.) The Psychology of Depression: Contemporary Theory and Research, pp. 203–232. Winston & Sons, Washington (1974)

7. Wallbott, H.G.: Bodily expression of emotion. European Journal of Social Psychology 28, 879–896 (1998)
8. Kipp, M., Martin, J.C.: Gesture and emotion: can basic gestural form features discriminate emotions? In: Int. Conf. on Affective Computing and Intelligent Interaction. IEEE Press, New York (2009)
9. Coulson, M.: Attributing emotion to static body postures: recognition accuracy, confusions, and viewpoint dependence. Journal of Nonverbal Behavior 28(2), 117–139 (2004)
10. Kleinsmith, A., de Silva, R., Bianchi-Berthouze, N.: Cross-cultural differences in recognizing affect from body posture. Interacting with Computers 18(6), 1371–1389 (2006)
11. Bänziger, T., Scherer, K.R.: Using actor portrayals to systematically study multimodal emotion expression: The GEMEP corpus. In: Paiva, A.C.R., Prada, R., Picard, R.W. (eds.) ACII 2007. LNCS, vol. 4738, pp. 476–487. Springer, Heidelberg (2007)
12. Pantic, M., Patras, I.: Dynamics of facial expression: recognition of facial actions and their temporal segments from face profile image sequences. IEEE Transactions on Systems, Man and Cybernetics 36(2), 433–449 (2006)
13. Maalej, A., Amor, B.B., Daoudi, M., Srivastava, A., Berretti, S.: 3D face analysis for facial expression recognition. In: Int. Conf. on Pattern Recognition (2010)
14. Courgeon, M., Buisine, S., Martin, J.C.: Impact of expressive wrinkles on perception of a virtual character's facial expressions of emotions. In: Ruttkay, Z., Kipp, M., Nijholt, A., Vilhjálmsson, H.H. (eds.) IVA 2009. LNCS, vol. 5773, pp. 201–214. Springer, Heidelberg (2009)
15. de Melo, C., Kenny, P., Gratch, J.: Influence of autonomic signals on perception of emotions in embodied agents. Applied Artificial Intelligence 24(6), 494–509 (2010)
16. Huang, Y., Fan, H., Li, Y.: Robust symbolic dual-view facial expression recognition with skin wrinkles: local versus global approach. IEEE Transactions on Multimedia 12(6), 536–543 (2010)
17. Zhang, Y., Sim, T.: Realistic and efficient wrinkle simulation using an anatomy-based face model with adaptive refinement. In: Proc. Computer Graphics International 2005, pp. 3–10 (2005)
18. Bickel, B., Botsch, M., Angst, R., Matusik, W., Otaduy, M., Pfister, H., Gross, M.: Multi-Scale Capture of Facial Geometry and Motion. ACM Transactions on Graphics 26(3) (2007)
19. Hyniewska, S., Niewiadomski, R., Mancini, M., Pelachaud, C.: Expression of affects in embodied conversational agents. In: Scherer, K.R., Bänziger, T., Roesch, E. (eds.) Blueprint for Affective Computing, pp. 213–221. Oxford University Press, Oxford (2010)
20. Gunes, H., Piccardi, M.: Fusing face and body display for bi-modal emotion recognition: Single frame analysis and multi-frame post integration. In: Tao, J., Tan, T., Picard, R.W. (eds.) ACII 2005. LNCS, vol. 3784, pp. 102–111. Springer, Heidelberg (2005)
21. Hietanen, J.K., Leppänen, J.M.: Judgment of other people's facial expressions of emotions is influenced by their concurrent affective hand movements. Scandinavian Journal of Psychology 49, 221–230 (2008)
22. Meeren, H.K.M., van Heijnsbergen, C., de Gelder, B.: Rapid perceptual integration of facial expression and emotional body language. In: Proc. of the National Academy of Sciences of the USA, vol. 102(45), pp. 16518–16523 (2005)
23. de Gelder, B., Van den Stock, J.: Real faces, real emotions: perceiving facial expressions in naturalistic contexts of voices, bodies and scenes. In: Calder, A.J., Rhodes, G., Haxby, J.V., Johnson, M.H. (eds.) The Handbook of Face Perception. Oxford University Press, Oxford (in press)

24. Clavel, C., Plessier, J., Martin, J.C., Ach, L., Morel, B.: Combining facial and postural expressions of emotions in a virtual character. In: Ruttkay, Z., Kipp, M., Nijholt, A., Vilhjálmsson, H.H. (eds.) IVA 2009. LNCS, vol. 5773, pp. 287–300. Springer, Heidelberg (2009)
25. Courgeon, M., Martin, J.C., Jacquemin, C.: MARC: a Multimodal Affective and Reactive Character. In: Proceedings of the ICMI 2008 Workshop on Affective Interaction in Natural Environments (2008)
26. Pandzic, I., Forchheimer, R.: MPEG-4 facial animation: the standard, implementation and applications. John Wiley and Sons Inc., West Sussex (2003)
27. Ekman, P.: Emotions revealed. Weidenfeld & Nicolson (2003)
28. Fratarcangeli, M., Schaerf, M.: Realistic modeling of animatable faces in MPEG-4. Computer Animation and Social Agents. Computer Graphics Society (CGS) (2004)
29. Courgeon, M., Clavel, C., Martin, J.C.: Appraising emotional events during a real-time interactive game. In: ICMI 2009: Int. Workshop on Affective-Aware Virtual Agents and Social Robots (2009)

# Evaluating Emotional Content of Acted and Algorithmically Modified Motions

Klaus Lehtonen and Tapio Takala

Aalto University,
School of Science,
Department of Media Technology,
Espoo, Finland
{klaus.lehtonen,tapio.takala}@tkk.fi

**Abstract.** Motion capture is a common method to create expressive motions for animated characters. In order to add flexibility when reusing motion data, many ways to modify its style have been developed. However, thorough evaluation of the resulting motions is often omitted. In this paper we present a questionnaire based method for evaluating visible emotions and styles in animated motion, and a set of algorithmic modifications to add emotional content to captured motion. Modifications were done by adjusting posture, motion path lengths and timings. The evaluation method was then applied to a set of acted and modified motions. The results show that a simple questionnaire is a useful tool to compare motions, and that expressivity of some emotions can be controlled by the proposed algorithms. However, we also found that motions should be evaluated using several describing dimensions simultaneously, as a single modification may have complex visible effects on the motion.

**Keywords:** computer animation, motion capture, emotional motion, evaluation of motion style, motion editing.

## 1 Introduction

We can see emotions in facial expressions, poses and motions of animated characters. Motion capture is a convenient way to record the visible emotions. However, doing new motion capture for each different case requires time and money and is not practical in all situations [1]. New ways to reuse motion data can lower the costs. Reusing and modifying motions are especially beneficial in games, because game characters need to move and react in many different ways in real time.

Much research has been done to change the style of captured motions, but there has been less effort in validating the effects of the modifications. Many published modifications create changes in motions, but how significant the changes are to people viewing the motions has not been investigated [2,3,4,5]. In a case where motion style of modified motions was evaluated with many viewers, it was found out that the modification was not always noticed by the viewers [6].

Z. Pan et al. (Eds.): Transactions on Edutainment VI, LNCS 6758, pp. 144–153, 2011.

We present a questionnaire based method for evaluating the emotional and stylistic content of motions with a large audience. This evaluation is used to compare the effects of three algorithmic modifications to motion data. These modifications change the posture, motion path length, and timing of the motions. The results show that a questionnaire is an effective method for measuring emotional content of motions and to compare the modification methods. The questionnaire can also reveal if a modification produces unwanted side effects to the style of the motions.

## 2 Related Works

### 2.1 Evaluating Motions

We found an earlier evaluation of modified motions that used valence, arousal and dominance as the dimensions in their questionnaire [6]. However, some stylistic properties like masculinity and femininity are not easily mapped to the three dimensions. In another study, dynamic and geometrical features of dancing motions were assessed using Laban motion analysis [7]. This approach requires expert knowledge from the evaluators. Enabling untrained people to evaluate everyday actions requires a simpler approach.

Evaluating emotions seen in facial expressions is a common practice [8]. Facial expressions are a simpler case than bodily motions, because the face is mainly used for communication and much less for other actions, whereas in bodily motion both appear. Questionnaires used to evaluate facial expressions often force labeling one face image with one emotion. This is a justified approach as prototypical faces are associated with basic emotions in commonly used models. Defining similar prototypical bodily motions is hard and, since motions can have many stylistic properties in addition to visible emotions, the task is even harder.

Based on these observations we decided to limit our study to assessing emotional content of bodily motions only. We animated motions with a simplified human model without face and fingers. In the questionnaire we asked evaluation of multiple simultaneous dimensions instead of a single choice.

### 2.2 Modifying Motions

Neff and Kim state that important components affecting motions are posture, transitions between poses, simplification and exaggeration [9]. We wanted to use modifications that would directly affect these components. Some of these aspects of motion can be changed in motions that are defined with a low number of keyframes per second (around 1 Hz) [10]. For example transitions between poses in keyframes can be easily edited without changing the keyframes themselves. Same methods cannot be used straight away with motion defined with a high number keyframes per second (over 10 Hz), such that motion capture produces, as transitions between the keyframes are too fast.

Many modification methods of motion styles are based on the difference between two recorded motion signals [2,3,4]. The way these methods treat the motion data differ greatly, but the results are all dependent on the styles of the input motions. In our study, we used a method based on differences between still poses for changing postures of characters. For other changes, however, we used procedurally generated modifications.

Bruderlin and Williams presented multiresolution filtering that we used for exaggerating and diminishing the length of motion paths [5]. The transitions between poses can be changed by the speed transform described by Amaya et. al. [2]. However, the speed transform is not a direct method as it requires two motions for defining the changes made to a third motion. To make the method more direct, we developed a new heuristic approach that defines the changes in timings based on the velocity of the input motion.

# 3 Implementation

## 3.1 Capturing Motions

To create suitable motions, we asked one female and one male actor to perform a short walk and a knocking motion with ten different styles that were used earlier by Pollick et. al.: *afraid*, *angry*, *excited*, *happy*, *neutral*, *relaxed*, *sad*, *strong*, *tired* and *weak* [11]. Both of the actors had acted in theater performances, but they did not have previous experience with motion capture. We also captured several standing poses. For recording the motions, we used Optitrack Full Body Motion Capture system, consisting of twelve cameras capturing motions with 100 frames per second. The system gives coordinates and orientation of the hips, and rotations for 18 joints.

## 3.2 Modifying Motion Paths

To change the length of the motion paths, multiresolution filtering described by Bruderlin and Williams was used [5]. The basic idea is to divide an original motion signal into frequency bands that are modulated separately in a way that adds no phase shift. Then we can return to the original signal format by summing up the modified frequency bands. We observed that multiplying the middle bands (between 1.0 and 12.5 Hz) makes the motion paths exaggerated or reduced.

With this method we can make a short and slow walk longer and faster or vice versa. During the process, the modification exaggerates or diminishes the poses as seen in Figure 1. Our hypothesis was that this modification would make motions look more *excited*, *tired* and *weak*. The hypothesis was based on the findings that high movement activity has been connected with *elated joy*, *hot anger* and *terror*, while low movement activity has been connected to *boredom* and *contempt* [12].

Multiresolution filtering suffers from stretching bones if applied to joint positions as input signals. Using joint rotations can also be problematic as unnatural rotations may happen when the angles are near a gimbal lock. To avoid these problems, we represented the joint rotations with two orthogonal vectors pointing the direction of the bones. This way the bone lengths are not affected by the modification and gimbal lock is not an issue.

Multiplying frequency bands can make the feet of the character slide. This was fixed in post-processing by recalculating the coordinates of the hips. The fix was done by measuring the original supporting periods of the feet and forcing the feet to stay still during these periods in the new motions.

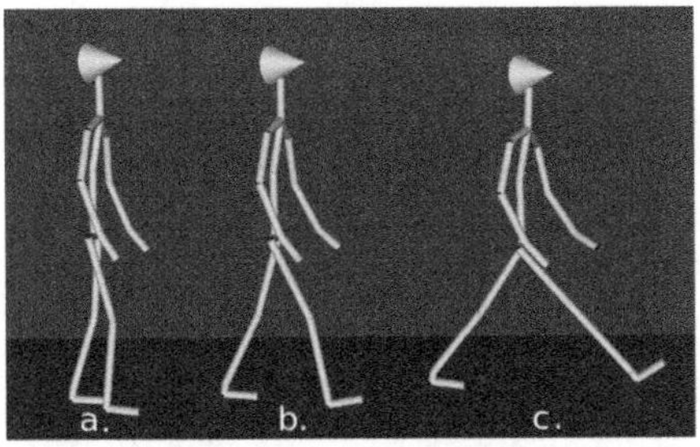


**Fig. 1.** Changes in pose when a walking motion (*b*) is modified by making motion paths shorter (*a*) and longer (*c*)

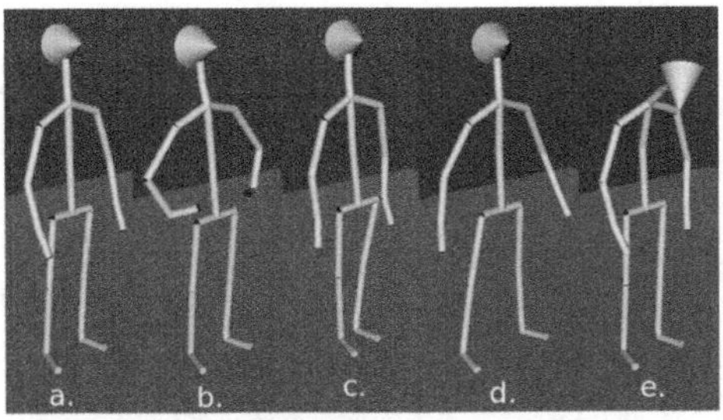


**Fig. 2.** Still poses used in changing posture of animated characters. Pose (*a*) is the neutral pose of the actor.

### 3.3 Modifying Posture

For creating motions with varying posture we need a motion with *neutral* posture, a *neutral* still pose and varying expressive poses (Fig. 2). Next we calculate the differences between joint rotations in the *neutral* pose and the other poses. Then we can add the desired difference to each frame of the motion to change the posture of the animated character. If we need to reduce or exaggerate the change of the posture, we can multiply all the changes with a constant. We made a hypothesis that modification to posture could make motions look more *sad* or more *confident*, as earlier studies show that those emotion types have stereotypical positions of upper body, shoulders and head [12].

With a motion like a regular walk the change of posture works quite well as it is. If the motion has parts where pose of the character is very different compared to the *neutral* pose, the technique can have unwanted side effects. For example, if the character is reaching forward with a straight arm, the arm can become twisted by the change of the posture. This can be fixed by fading the changes gradually out when the end of a limb goes too far from its position in the *neutral* pose. The fade-out must be done to all the joints that affect the position of the limb.

### 3.4 Modifying Timings

Amaya et al. adjusted the speed of motions by time warping the motions according to differences between two reference motions [2]. Their approach depends on the quality of the original motions and requires motion segmenting to find links between the reference motions. To bypass these requirements, we developed two heuristics that define the time warps without any reference motions. The heuristics aim to produce motions with either constant speed or added acceleration while keeping the total duration of the motion unchanged (Fig. 3). Our hypothesis was that these changes would make motions look more *relaxed* and *angry*, respectively. The hypothesis was based on findings that high movement dynamics are connected with *hot anger* [12].

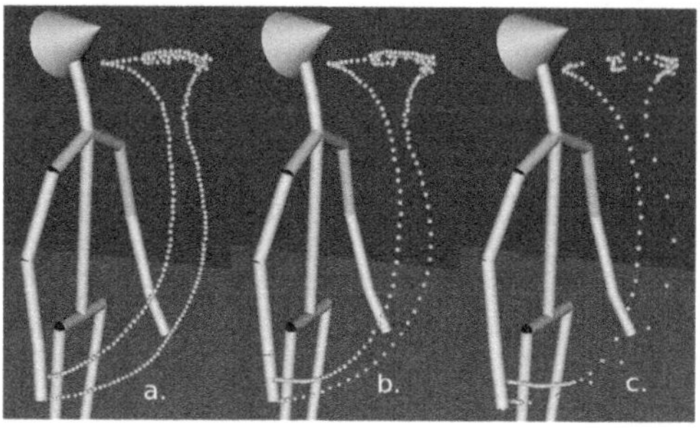


**Fig. 3.** Trajectories of the right hand during a knocking motion. Original motion ($b$) is modified to nearly constant speed ($a$) or with exaggerated acceleration ($c$).

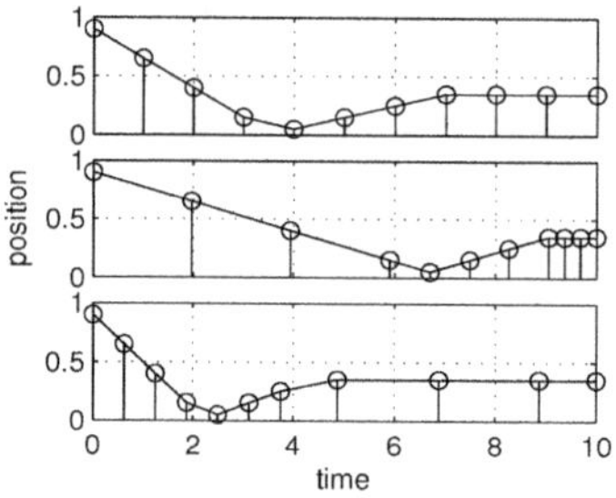


**Fig. 4.** Timewarping motion: evenly timed original frames (*top*) are repositioned in time to form constant speed (*middle*) or added acceleration (*bottom*)

Transforming a motion to constant speed can be done by taking evenly timed motion samples, spreading out frames with fast movement and compressing frames with slow movement, as depicted in figure 4. New motion is then formed by resampling between these as keyframes. The frames where the position does not change at all, would be compressed completely together to get constant speed, but this would cause all pauses of the motion to be skipped. More natural motion results if the pauses are preserved by enforcing a minimum duration between frames (as seen in the last four frames in the middle plot of figure 4).

In practice time warping is done separately for each limb of the character. When constant speed for each frame is desired, we can use the velocity values of the limb limited by a minimum value as the durations between frames and then scale all frames to preserve original total duration of the motion. When adding acceleration to a motion, we use original durations of the frames and increase the durations next to frames that are local minima of velocity and then scale as in the previous case. This makes the pauses of the motion last longer and other parts faster as seen in the lowest plot of figure 4.

### 3.5 Combining Modifications

To use the modifications interactively, the path lengths of an original motion are modified to produce a motion with short motion paths and another with long motion paths. Next, the sliding feet are fixed. Then, the timings of the three motions are modified to produce versions with constant speed and added acceleration. Once these steps are done we can create new motions by interpolating between the produced motions. Modification of posture is done last to the interpolated motion.

Modifying path lengths, fixing the sliding feet and modifying timings requires off-line processing. When they are done an animator controlling the system has real-time feedback as the interpolation of motions and changing the posture are both very fast operations.

## 4 Questionnaire

Evaluation of emotional and stylistic content of motions is necessary for comparing the motions and for testing methods that create modifications. We were also concerned with the validity of a questionnaire based evaluation. This led to three research questions: 1. Can acted styles and emotions be distinguished by viewing motions animated with a stick figure? 2. Do the three implemented modifications change emotions seen in the motions? 3. What are suitable dimensions to be rated when evaluating motions?

The captured acted motions were used as material for the first question. For the second question, we created pairs from the *neutral* motions to each of the acted motion styles. The pairs were created according to our hypotheses of the effects of the modifications and intended to have the same emotional and stylistic content as the acted motions. We also created motions with intended styles *masculine* and *feminine* that attempted to change the gender of the characters. Motion *energetic sadness* was created by combining modifications that we had hypothesized to increase *sadness* and *excitement*. The emotion *happy* was omitted because it was not known which modifications could affect *happiness*. The final combinations of the modifications are in figure 7.

40 videos were created from the acted and modified motions. The videos were shown in randomized order. The participants were able to play the videos many times, but it was instructed that viewing the videos once should be usually enough.

We included in the questionnaire all the emotional descriptions given to the actors. However, *neutral* was not included as it was assumed to fall in the middle of a scale. *Confident* was not part of the original set of emotions recorded with actors, but it was necessary to have a pair for *afraid*. To make the questionnaire simpler to answer, we combined opposite motion styles, making scales between pairs *sad-happy*, *tired-excited*, *angry-relaxed*, *weak-strong*, *afraid-confident* and *masculine-feminine*.

For each video, the participants were asked to evaluate how these adjectives describe the character in the video in a scale with five steps. The middle choice was the default and it was instructed to be used if neither of the alternatives feels good or if the participant is unsure which one is better.

The questionnaire was made with a server side PHP script and the videos were embedded in the web page as Flash objects. 28 non-paid participants were recruited through social media. 8 of them were female and 20 were male.

An answer to our first research question can be found by examining a confusion matrix between the intended styles and the perceived styles as shown in figure 5. Each acted style has the ratings of videos by both actors except the neutral male and neutral female columns, which show how the ratings for *neutral* motions differ between the actors.

| Perceived style \ Acted style | weak | tired | afraid | sad | relaxed | angry | excited | happy | strong | neutral | neutral male | neutral female |
|---|---|---|---|---|---|---|---|---|---|---|---|---|
| masculine | ,4 | ,5 | ,2 | ,4 | ,5 | ,6 | ,3 | ,5 | ,3 | ,3 | ,5 | ,1 |
| feminine | ,2 | ,0 | ,5 | ,2 | ,3 | ,1 | ,5 | ,4 | ,5 | ,4 | ,0 | ,7 |
| confident | ,1 | ,3 | ,1 | ,2 | ,8 | 1,4 | 1,2 | 1,2 | 1,1 | ,5 | ,6 | ,4 |
| strong | ,1 | ,2 | ,1 | ,1 | ,5 | ,8 | ,6 | ,6 | ,6 | ,3 | ,3 | ,3 |
| happy | ,1 | ,0 | ,0 | ,0 | ,1 | ,3 | ,8 | ,3 | ,4 | ,2 | ,2 | ,1 |
| excited | ,1 | ,0 | ,2 | ,0 | ,1 | ,8 | 1,1 | ,6 | ,5 | ,1 | ,1 | ,2 |
| angry | ,1 | ,2 | ,1 | ,1 | ,1 | ,6 | ,2 | ,2 | ,2 | ,1 | ,1 | ,0 |
| relaxed | ,2 | ,4 | ,1 | ,4 | ,6 | ,4 | ,5 | ,5 | ,7 | ,6 | 1,0 | ,3 |
| sad | ,9 | ,6 | ,3 | ,7 | ,1 | ,0 | ,0 | ,0 | ,1 | ,1 | ,1 | ,1 |
| afraid | ,9 | ,2 | 1,3 | ,6 | ,1 | ,0 | ,0 | ,0 | ,1 | ,2 | ,2 | ,3 |
| tired | ,6 | 1,3 | ,3 | ,7 | ,4 | ,0 | ,1 | ,1 | ,1 | ,3 | ,5 | ,1 |
| weak | ,9 | ,7 | ,9 | ,6 | ,3 | ,1 | ,1 | ,0 | ,1 | ,3 | ,2 | ,4 |

**Fig. 5.** Confusion matrix between acted and perceived styles, showing on average how much each style was seen in each video on a scale from 0 to 2. Underlined scores tell how well an intended style was recognized. Strongest perceptions are on dark background.

| Perceived style \ Modified style | weak | tired | afraid | sad | relaxed | angry | excited | strong | female to masculine | female to feminine | male to feminine | energetic sadness |
|---|---|---|---|---|---|---|---|---|---|---|---|---|
| masculine | -,1 | ,0 | -,1 | ,0 | ,0 | ,4 | ,2 | 1,0 | ,0 | -,1 | -,1 | ,3 |
| feminine | ,1 | -,1 | ,1 | -,2 | ,0 | ,1 | ,1 | -,3 | -,4 | ,9 | ,2 | ,0 |
| confident | -,3 | -,4 | -,3 | -,4 | ,1 | ,7 | ,6 | ,9 | -,3 | ,1 | -,1 | ,2 |
| happy | -,1 | -,1 | -,1 | -,2 | ,0 | ,3 | ,3 | ,1 | ,0 | ,0 | ,1 | -,2 |
| strong | -,2 | -,2 | -,1 | -,2 | ,1 | ,5 | ,4 | 1,0 | -,2 | ,0 | -,1 | ,3 |
| excited | -,1 | -,1 | ,0 | -,1 | ,1 | ,5 | ,4 | ,3 | ,0 | ,0 | ,0 | ,1 |
| angry | ,0 | ,0 | ,0 | ,1 | ,0 | ,1 | ,1 | ,3 | ,1 | ,0 | ,0 | ,8 |
| relaxed | -,4 | -,5 | -,4 | -,5 | -,2 | ,1 | ,4 | -,3 | ,0 | ,0 | -,2 | -,8 |
| sad | ,3 | ,7 | ,0 | 1,3 | ,0 | -,1 | -,1 | -,1 | ,0 | -,1 | ,1 | 1,2 |
| afraid | ,3 | 1,0 | ,4 | ,4 | ,0 | -,2 | -,2 | -,1 | ,4 | -,1 | -,1 | ,1 |
| tired | ,4 | ,5 | ,3 | ,6 | -,1 | -,3 | -,2 | -,3 | ,0 | ,0 | ,4 | ,4 |
| weak | ,6 | 1,3 | ,3 | ,8 | -,1 | -,2 | -,2 | -,3 | ,1 | ,0 | ,2 | ,2 |

**Fig. 6.** Difference of scores between original and modified motions. Maximum possible change is 2. Positive changes higher than 0.25 are on white background and negative under -0.25 are on black background. Values for the intended styles are underlined.

The second research question calls for a comparison between ratings of the original *neutral* motions and the motions made by modifying them. The results are shown as differences of their scores in figure 6.

The third research question was about finding suitable characterizing dimensions to be rated when evaluating motions. We analysed how well the dimensions were chosen by estimating their common factors (using Matlab function *factoran*). Results in figure 8 show that the dimensions are not independent and some of them are effectively the same.

| | Modifications |
|---|---|
| A | very short motion paths |
| B | short motion paths |
| C | long motion paths |
| D | increased acceleration |
| E | constant speed |
| F | hands close to body |
| G | feet close to each other |
| H | head looking down |
| I | feet more apart |
| J | elbows broadly |

| Intended styles | |
|---|---|
| afraid | B, F, G |
| angry | C, D |
| energetic sadness | C, H |
| excited | C, D |
| feminine | F, G |
| masculine | I, J |
| relaxed | E |
| sad | B, H |
| strong | C, J |
| tired | A, H |
| weak | A, F, G |

**Fig. 7.** Intended styles and the modifications done to achieve them.

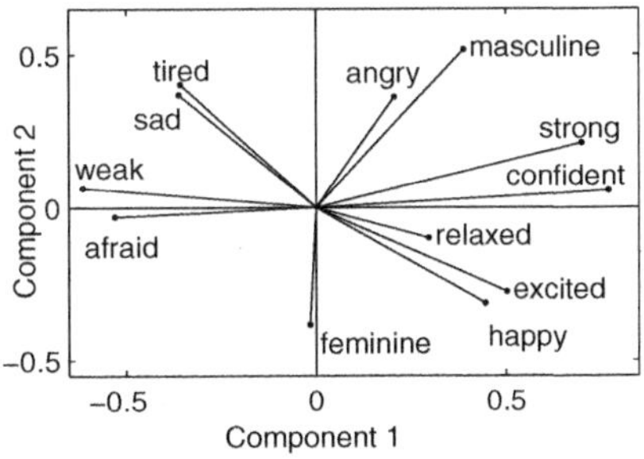


**Fig. 8.** Maximum likelihood estimate for common factors in the questionnaire. Loadings of the original dimensions are plotted into a two-dimensional model.

## 5 Discussion

The ratings of the acted videos in figure 5 tell that it is possible to see many styles from a motion that does not have hands or facial expressions. The styles are not seen one at a time, but rather a motion seems to fit a range of styles. This can be partly explained by close relations between the styles that are seen in figure 8, but it is also possible that motion alone does not separate all different styles and emotions as well as facial expressions do. Based on these findings, evaluation of motions requires multiple dimensions to be accurate and selecting more than one description should be allowed.

Figure 6 shows that the three modifications can change emotions and styles seen in motions. The effects of the modifications are not constrained to a single emotion or style. When we compare the intended effects and the perceived styles in figure 6, we can see that the *strong* and *sad* modifications worked well. A contributing factor could be that both modifications had postures that are easily identifiable. Modifications *weak*, *tired*, *afraid* and *excited*, created mainly with changes to motion paths, did add at least a little of the intended style, but the modifications *relaxed* and *angry* did not work as intended. *Anger* and *relaxedness* were hypothesized to be created with changes to the timings of the motions. It is possible that walking and knocking motions are not suitable material for the modification, but based on this data, the modification of timings has to be considered quite useless. A similar ineffectiveness of retiming motions has been noticed earlier when trying to change the emotional content of captured motions [12].

The modification *energetic sadness* in figure 6 created both *sadness* and *angriness*. The modification that was intended to create *sadness* did not create *angriness* and the only difference between the *sad* and the *energetic sad* modifications was in the length of motion paths. This suggests that the modifications do not have only one-to-one relations with emotions, but combinations of modifications can be used to create emotions that the modifications cannot produce separately. This also suggests that the effects of the modifications depend greatly on the styles and emotions of the input motion.

The evaluation shows that modifications to posture and motion paths are good tools for artists, but it does not reveal if the modifications can be used without a human checking the results. A systematic evaluation of different kinds of motions with all combinations of the modifications would be necessary for assessing the reliability of the modifications.

The dimensions in the questionnaire are not perfect as pairing two descriptions to one axis prevents those from being selected at the same time. A common factor analysis of the styles shown in figure 8 tells that there is redundancy in the descriptions we used. In this data set the pairs *tired-sad*, *weak-afraid*, *excited-happy* were closely related. We could simplify the questionnaire by removing one description from each pair without losing much information.

During the analysis two weaknesses were found from the questionnaire. One is related to calculating statistically meaningful variances, which is limited because we had only five steps in each dimension. The second weakness is that all descriptions cannot be used at the same time as one dimension joins two descriptions. A better solution could be to have dimensions that have continuous range instead of steps and descriptions that are in form 'happy - not happy'. However, this would increase the number of decisions a test participant has to do.

## 6 Conclusions and Future Work

We captured acted motions with different styles and emotions and then tried to produce similar stylistic effects with three algorithmic modifications applied to neutral motions. The motions were evaluated with a questionnaire to determine what styles and emotions are visible in them. This kind of evaluation was not done in any of the papers related to modifications to motion that we have found.

We found evaluating motions with a questionnaire to be a good tool for comparing motions. It was observed that many styles can be seen from one motion and that a single modification can affect many styles. This confirmed that comparison of motions is more meaningful, when examining several describing dimensions simultaneously, instead of only concentrating to one dimension. In this sense evaluating motions is different from evaluating facial expressions as forced choice of one description is not enough for motions. What are the best dimensions for evaluating emotions and styles in motions remains a question yet to be answered.

The results show that modifying posture allowed creating the *strong* and *sad* motions. Changing the length of the motion paths helped in creating *weakness*, *tiredness*, *fear* and *excitement*. Changing timings of the motions was not found to affect the content of the motions significantly. Adjusting timings might be helpful if different types of motions were studied.

When combining modifications, the effects on the style of the motion were not always the same as the sum of effects of the modifications separately. This suggests that modifying already emotional motions could reveal more about the modifications than modifying only *neutral* motions. Similar phenomena could also be present when interpolating emotional motions. Also, creating totally *neutral* motions by motion capture is hard as the physical appearance of actors always affects captured motions. In the end, bodily motions alone cannot express all emotions. Therefore, other methods such as facial expressions must also be used when making complete animations.

**Acknowledgments.** This work was partially funded by aivoAALTO project of Aalto University and by Academy of Finland, project Enactive Media (128132). Also, thanks to Timo Idnheimo for his help during the work.

## References

1. Menache, A.: Understanding Motion Capture for Computer Animation and Video Games, p. 238. Academic Press, New York (2000)
2. Amaya, K., Bruderlin, A., Calvert, T.: Emotion from motion. In: Proc. Graphics interface GI 1996, pp. 222–229. Canadian Information Processing Society (1996)
3. Hsu, E., Pulli, K., Popovic, J.: Style translation for human motion. In: Proc. SIGGRAPH 2005, ACM Transactions on Graphics, vol. 24(3), pp. 1082–1089 (2005)
4. Shapiro, A., Cao, Y., Faloutsos, P.: Style components. Proc. Graphics Interface GI'06, pp. 33-39. Canadian Information Processing Society. (2006)
5. Bruderlin, A., Williams, L.: Motion signal processing. Proc. SIGGRAPH 1995, ACM Transactions on Graphics 14(3), 97–104 (1995)
6. Heloir, A., Kipp, M., Gibet, S., Courty, N.: Evaluating Data-Driven Style Transformation for Gesturing Embodied Agents. In: Prendinger, H., Lester, J., Ishizuka, M. (eds.) IVA 2008. LNCS (LNAI), vol. 5208, pp. 215–222. Springer, Heidelberg (2008)
7. Hachimura, K., Takashina, K., Yoshimura, M.: Analysis and evaluation of dancing movement based on LMA. In: IEEE International Workshop on Robot and Human Interactive Communication, pp. 294–299 (2005)
8. Ruttkay, Z.: Cultural dialects of real and synthetic emotional facial expressions. AI & Society 24(3), 307–315 (2009)
9. Neff, M., Fiume, E.: From Performance Theory to Character Animation Tools. In: Klette, R., Metaxas, D., Rosenhahn, B. (eds.) Human Motion: Understanding, Modelling, Capture, and Animation, Springer, Heidelberg (2008)
10. Chi, D., Costa, M., Zhao, L., Badler, N.: The EMOTE model for effort and shape. In: Proc. SIGGRAPH 2000, pp. 173–182. ACM Press/Addison-Wesley Publishing Co., New York (2000)
11. Pollick, F., Paterson, H., Bruderlin, A., Sanford, A.: Perceiving affect from arm movement. Cognition 82(2) (2001)
12. Wallbott, H.: Bodily expression of emotion. European Journal of Social Psychology 28, 879–896 (1998)

# An Emotion Model for Virtual Agents with Evolvable Motivation

Zhen Liu, Yuan Hong, Qiong Liu, and Yan Jie Chai

Faculty of Information Science and Technology,
Ningbo University, Ningbo 315211, China
liuzhen@nbu.edu.cn

**Abstract.** Modeling emotion for virtual agents is an interesting topic in virtual reality; autonomous virtual agents with emotion can enhance the authenticity of a virtual environment. Motivation and personality are psychological parameters for a virtual agent, motivation is the direct cause to promote an agent's emotion and behaviors, and an emotion model for virtual agents should include motivations. A computational emotion model for virtual agents with evolvable motivation is presented. First, a virtual agent's architecture that integrates emotion and motivation is proposed. Second, a fuzzy inference based emotion model with the consideration of personality and motivation is set up, a motivation priority evolves by genetic algorithms. Finally, an experiment is realized to verify effectiveness of the model.

**Keywords:** Virtual agent, emotion model, motivation, cognitive.

## 1 Introduction

Modeling autonomous virtual agents is a challenging research field, early virtual agents had no autonomy, and designers used scripts or linear models to control the behaviors of virtual agents. In recent years, artificial intelligence is playing a very important role in the field [1]-[5]; a virtual agent has a built-in mental architecture with perception, emotion, personality and motivation. There are some famous works on emotion model for autonomous agents. Many emotion models are based on OCC model [6], Bartneck suggested that the OCC model can be simplified for applications, it also can be extended with a history function, an emotion interaction function and personality [7]. Sevin et al. presented a computational motivation model for behavior selection of virtual characters [8], the model did not include personality and emotion. Egges et al. used a matrix to model the personality for a virtual agent [9]. FLAME is a fuzzy inference system [10], which mapped the evaluation from events to emotional intensities, this model did not include personality parameters. Eisman presented an emotion model with personality for a virtual agent [11]. Gratch et al. presented the EMA emotion model by cognitive appraisal theories [12][13], the model includes domain-independent algorithms of cognitive appraisal, Mei Yii Lim et al. proposed the FAtiMA-PSI architecture to model autonomous agents, the model balances the

Z. Pan et al. (Eds.): Transactions on Edutainment VI, LNCS 6758, pp. 154–163, 2011.

physiological cognitive dimensions for creation of life-like autonomous agents [14]. Christian Becker-Asano presented the WASABI architecture to combine bodily emotion dynamics to simulate infant-like primary emotions as well as cognitively elaborated (more adults) secondary emotions [15].

In order to simulate the humanlike behaviors of virtual agents by the previous works, we try to design non-linear mechanism for emotions. We present a new architecture for virtual agents, the motivation priority of a virtual agent can evolve in the architecture (In Fig.1). In this paper, perception is mainly reflected in two aspects, the one aspect is that a virtual agent abstracts the impact of environmental stimuli to his own properties after interaction, the other is that the virtual agent uses memory module to extract the past evaluation of environmental stimuli. The memory module includes short-term memory (STM) (Global Database) and long-term memory (LTM). In reactive condition (such as dangerous condition), perception information is directly sent to emotion module. The appraisal module infers emotion intensities by fuzzy logic. Behavior module reflects feedback appraisal results, if a motivation need is stimulated, a behavior for the motivation need will be created. Action module is also called action library, and executes behavior codes. For example, walking in the environment, expressing emotion on the face, interacting with outer stimuli. The learning module uses genetic algorithms to evolve the priority sequence of a virtual agent's motivation.

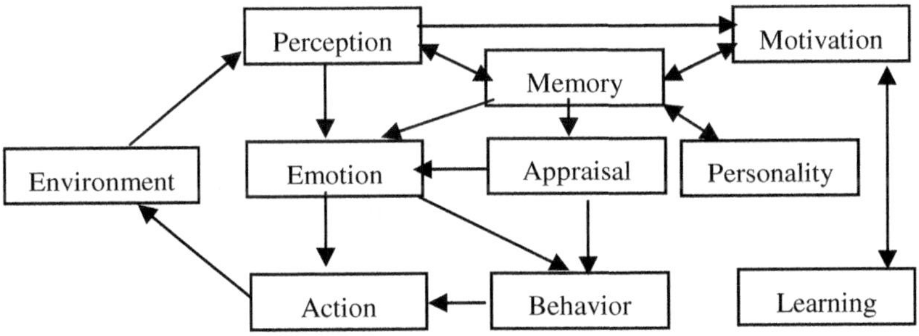


**Fig. 1.** The architecture of a virtual agent

## 2 Evolvable Motivation Priority

In this paper, motivation variables are divided into five categories by Maslow's theory [16]: thirsty need, hunger need, safety need, love need and curiosity need. There are some underlying motivations can be triggered simultaneously, one of the most important functions of selection system is the best suitable motivation. We decide to use genetic algorithms to determine the priority of a virtual agent's motivations by experience.

A potential motivation is $m_i$, $m_i \in \boldsymbol{M}$ ($m_1$, $m_2$... $m_i$ ... $m_n$), there are 0...$mg$ precedence relation for each motivation, the smaller the number is, the more urgent the priority is. Our goal is to determine the precedence relation of motivation elements in the motivation set dynamically. We propose our algorithm as followed:

(1) Coding: ***MP*** is a motivation's priority level set which represents the Genotype for the genetic algorithms, a motivation's priority level $mp \in \boldsymbol{MP} = \{mp_1, mp_2 ... mp_i ... mp_n\}$.

(2) Generating initial population: We know that a Genotype is *MP*, so we can generate a certain number of individuals to form a population; the size of population means the number of individuals of the population.

(3) Calculation of fitness: The fitness represents the degree of adaptation of an individual to the environment; in our work it means the adaptation of the precedence relation for the motivation set of an individual. We get this value by behaviors feedback that means if the result of the behaviors fits the initial target, the motivation set's current precedence relation gets a positive feedback; otherwise it gets a negative one. Let function $g(v_i)$ to be the way to get the final feedback, when there are 0...m feedbacks in the environment, then the function of total fitness $f(s)$ is calculated as followed:

$$f(s) = \sum_{i}^{0..m\,g} g(v_i) \tag{1}$$

(4) Selection: Pick the individual's Genotype with the lowest fitness $mp_{\min}$ from the population; we reset every bit of it using the corresponding elements from randomly picked the individual's Genotype among the others. So we can make sure the worst individual is eliminated which means the whole population is evolved.

(5) Crossover: For every individual of the population, we reset every bit of its Genotype using the corresponding elements from randomly picked individual among the others. So we can search the best answer among the solution set.

(6) Mutation: For every individual of the population, we reset every bit of its Genotype according to the probability. If we can get better Genotype from this process, it must be existed during the evolving process; otherwise it will be definitely eliminated over time.

Consequently, if the environment is stable, virtual agents will learn how to arrange their precedence relation for the motivation, and select the best appropriate from a long process of evolving in this way. In the long-tern memory database, there is a priority attribute in inclusion relation to store current various motivation priorities.

## 3 Emotion Model of Virtual Agents

Emotion derives from objects, agents and events. Precisely, emotion comes from the appraisal of these three components, and motivation variables are important parameters in the process. For example, when a virtual agent has hunger need, he will trigger a corresponding motivation to eat. Then we can judge whether the motivation intensity is big enough based on past experience first, if the motivation is generally satisfied, it will drive hope emotion, otherwise drive fear emotion or do not drive any emotion. After that if the agent may see an object, he can judge whether the object to satisfy the $MV_i$ hunger need based on past experience. If hunger need is completely satisfied, the agent will express love emotion, otherwise the agent will express hate emotion or do not produce any emotion. And finally, using of the object will yield a corresponding appraisal of hungry motivation. Being beneficial to ease hunger will result in a positive appraisal and produce joy emotion, or get a negative one and distress one.

Motivation variables represent inner needs, $MV_i$ is the motivation variable, $i\in[1, n]$, $n$ is the number of motivation variable. $IMV_i$ is the intensity of $MV_i$, $IMV_i \in [0, 1]$. If $IMV_i$=0, the current motivation need is completely satisfied.

In addition, agents in the previous content will be divided into ones with introverted or extroverted personality, and we use $pv$ to represent personality parameters, $pv\in v$ [0, 1], if $pv$=0, the agent is completely introverted.

Through the processing of physiological states and personality parameters, a cognitive appraisal includes subjective appraisal (an agent' appraisal) and objective appraisal (we can design a standard and different default values for virtual agents). Let $sub\_ap$ is subjective appraisal, and $obj\_ap$ is objective appraisal. When agents or objects in the range of agent's perception, we can get the following formula:

$$sub\_ap = obj\_ap \times (w_1 \times pv + w_2 \times IMV_i + w_3) \tag{2}$$

In the formula, we need to set three weights add up to 1 to control parameters for objective evaluation influence, because respectively considered personality and motivation parameters on the objective appraisal, the resulting of influence is subjective appraisal. When $w_1$ is 1, subjective appraisal is completely determined by personality. When $w_2$ is 1, subjective appraisal is entirely determined by motivation parameters. When $w_3$ is 1, subjective appraisal is completely determined by objective appraisal.

We regard the calculation above results as input of fuzzy inference system and the input values can be divided into three types fuzzy sets after fuzzification: low appraisal, medium appraisal and high apprasial.

We use fuzzy rulers to calculate emotion intensities, a set of fuzzy productive rulers are shown as follows:

IF Appraisal of AnticipateGood(event$_i$) is ***A***1 Then HopeEmotion is ***B***1
IF Appraisal of AnticipateBad(event$_i$) is ***A***2 Then FearEmotion is ***B***2
IF Appraisal of HappenGood(event$_i$) is ***A***3 Then JoyEmotion is ***B***3
IF Appraisal of HappenBad(event$_i$) is ***A***4 Then DistressEmotion is ***B***4
IF Appraisal of MeetGood(object$_i$) is ***A***5 Then LoveEmotion is ***B***5
IF Appraisal of MeetBad(object$_i$) is ***A***6 Then HateEmotion is ***B***6

***A***1 - ***A***6 are aimed at fuzzy sets of subjective assessment of different situations, ***B***1 - ***B***6 are fuzzy sets of intensity of different emotions. And event$_i$ represents a event, AnticipateGood (event$_i$) represents a expected evaluation before a good event happens, AnticipateBad (event$_i$) expresses a expected evaluation before a bad event happens, HappenGood (event$_i$) expresses a earning evaluation after a good event happens, HappenBad (event$_i$) means a profit and loss evaluation after a bad event happens, object$_i$ represents other virtual agents or objects, MeetGood (object$_i$) is an appraisal that one has seen the benefit of other agent or object, MeetBad (object$_i$) a appraisal that one has seen the adverse effect of other agent or object. "HopeEmotion is

***B*1" means that the membership function of hope emotion is affiliated to the ***B*1 fuzzy sets, the rest of meanings of emotional membership representation are similar.

***B*1 - ***B*6 fuzzy sets are also divided into three fuzzy subsets: low, medium and high. We suppose membership functions of three fuzzy subsets are the same as ones of subjective evaluation value respectively.

To get crisp data from the output fuzzy sets and regard as the corresponding emotion values, one of the most commonly methods we used is looking for the focus area to be occupied by fuzzy sets and its value of horizontal coordinate axis as an accurate output value. We assume the result obtained is $u_{B'}(y)$, and the gravity defuzzification method is listed in the form below:

$$I = \frac{\int_y u_{B'}(y) \cdot y dy}{\int_y u_{B'}(y) dy} \tag{3}$$

Formula (3) is the result of final value of emotional intensity corresponding to the input evaluation value, but the calculation is complex. This model we designed will be applied to the relatively high real-time environment, and therefore we can use it in the experiment of calculating the orthocenter of the output number of sampling points (that is the number of discrete values). In the case of not spending too much time, we adjust with sampling interval to provide required accuracy. This is the best compromise and the formula becomes as below:

$$I = \frac{\sum_{i=1}^{n} u_i y_i}{\sum_{i=1}^{n} u_i} \tag{4}$$

Emotion will not disappear immediately, they have a decay process. The emotion decay function is shown below:

$$e_t = e_{t-1} \cdot e^{-\sigma} \tag{5}$$

Where $e_t$ is the emotion intensity at *t*, $e_{t-1}$ is the emotion intensity at *t*-1 and $\sigma$ is decay factor.

## 4 Experiments and Result Analysis

We use Microsoft Directx9.0 SDK to program the demo system, in a 3D virtual museum, we design three different virtual agents, a man named Leon, a woman named Tina and a child named Tomi. Their personality parameters are 0, 0.5 and 1 respectively, the man is introverted and he can control his emotion, the child is extroverted.

If switching to tracking camera at this time, we can see motivation and emotion expression of a virtual agent in current time. The top-left corner shows priority, corresponding name and intensity of motivation, in which the square symbol represents the current state of motivation, red expresses it does not meet a trigger condition, yellow means to trigger a potential motivation and green means a motivation is triggered. In the demo system, a virtual agent can have six emotions, Bar charts of six current emotional states and mixed display of faces are as shown in Fig.2.

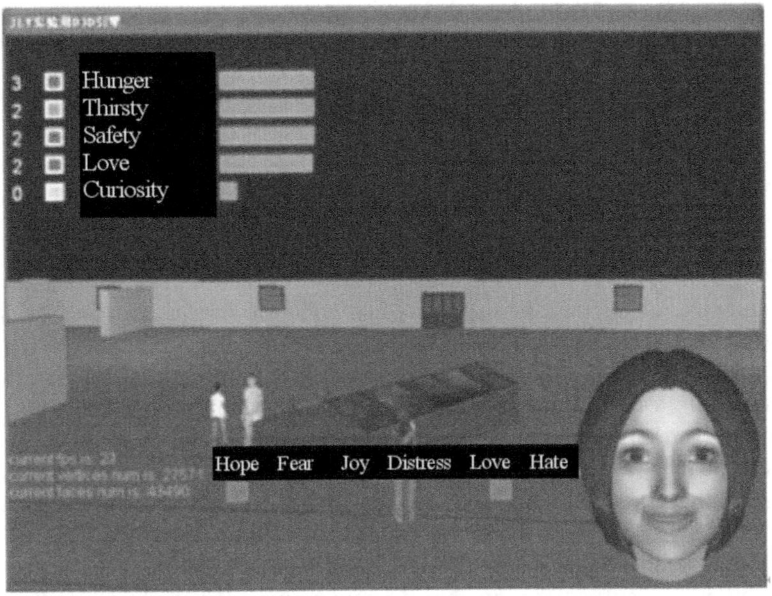


**Fig. 2.** Motivation and emotion state of a virtual agent

After running the program for a period of time, we record positive and negative emotion intensities once in a while in order to observe introverted and extroverted virtual agents, we want to test whether an extroverted agent is more emotional. We get curves as shown in Fig.3. We sample emotion intensities of the three agents respectively after a certain time of simulation, for the introverted agent such as Leon, emotion intensity change is not large; while the one of extroverted agent such as Tomi's values is obvious large, Tina's is between Leon's and Tomi's when they face the same scene. This result proves that the system is effective of combining personality in emotion model.

Since an agent's emotion comes from the appraisal of outside world which can be based on the event happened or the object seen. But this evaluation should not just happen, but get from interaction with the object in the past. In our system, the past interaction information for environmental objects are recorded in the long-term memory, when the long-term memory is loaded if necessary, a virtual agent still can behave emotion and make behaviors according to this memory. For example, when Tomi is thirsty, thirsty motivation is triggered and it can drive the behavior of looking for tea. When he finds a cup of tea on the table, there is no information of the tea in

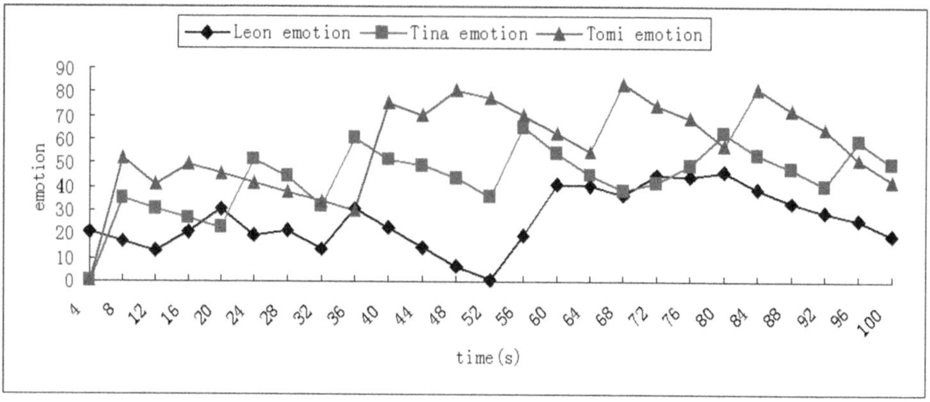


**Fig. 3.** The Different agents' emotion curves

memory, and there is no emotion for the tea at once. If he drinks the tea, and thirsty need is completely satisfied, he expresses love emotion for the tea, and the appraisal information for tea can be recorded in the long-term memory.

A motivation priority is not to unique. Take current scene for example, the agent originally wants to appreciate exhibits suddenly feels hungry and there will be two potential motivations: appreciating or looking for food. At this time, there will cause problems that most agents certainly choose to look for food but we cannot exclude some agents that like exhibits very much and forget hunger. To achieve such effect, we realize the codes of prior relation between motivations. We use genetic algorithm in this paper, using the past emotional feedback as evolutionary basis, and make positive emotion motivations to be triggered first, the virtual agent will act appropriate behaviors to current environment.

In order to illustrate the problem with the demo, we set initial gene sequences, which composed of 0-4 integer sequences as in Table 1.

**Table 1.** Initial genotype of priority sequence of motivation

| Name | Hunger | Thirsty | Safety | Love | Curiosity |
|---|---|---|---|---|---|
| Tomi | 0 | 0 | 4 | 3 | 4 |
| Tina | 3 | 2 | 2 | 2 | 0 |
| Leon | 2 | 3 | 0 | 2 | 4 |

**Table 2.** Evolution of priority sequence of motivation

| Name | Hunger | Thirsty | Safety | Love | Curiosity |
|---|---|---|---|---|---|
| Tomi | 0 | 3 | 0 | 3 | 4 |
| Tina | 3 | 2 | 1 | 2 | 4 |
| Leon | 2 | 3 | 0 | 2 | 5 |

Then, fires events are triggered in the scene and at this time only Leon triggers motivation meets safety demand, Tomi and Tina don't immediately trigger because their curiosity need priority is still greater than safety need. Therefore, they don't escape, but stay in site or are panic, they may run everywhere (when the physiology safety attribute of a virtual agent is below a certain value, except safety motivation, stunned or panic behaviors replace other behaviors). However, we use genetic algorithm for the fitness calculation. After a virtual agent successfully implements safety motivation, he will run out of the room, other virtual agents will gradually realize that safety motivation is prior to the other according to the evolution of whole population by genetic algorithm. In this experiment, because Leon's safety motivation is triggered, he will escape from the fireplace and express positive emotion. Leon'S sequence genotype of motivation of will be the optimal genotype, this can make the whole population genetic type evolve. The last population genotype is shown in Table 2. Finally, the safety demand of Tina and Tomi are successfully triggered, and they can run out of the fire scene. The specific experiment is shown in Fig.4.

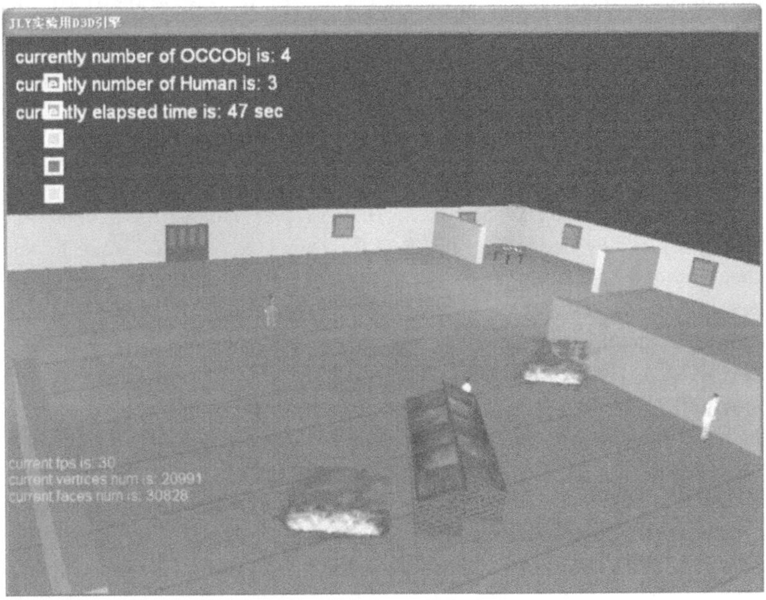


**Fig. 4.** Virtual agents successfully escape

## 5 Conclusion

Motivation variables are important parameters for a virtual agent, emotion models should include motivation variables. The current state of research on emotion models of virtual agents is reviewed, in previous researches, a virtual agent's motivation priority are usually viewed as static parameters. An evolvable method of motivation priorities for a virtual agent is set up, the priority sequences of an agent 's motivations are determined by genetic algorithm, the demo system shows that virtual agents can adapt to the environment better.

An emotion model for virtual agents is set up in this paper, the architecture integrates perception, emotion, motivation and personality together. The memory module can record the interaction information to an environment, and the memory information can also guide perception. A subjective appraisal method for other agents, objects and events is proposed with a formula, motivation variables and personality parameters are the part of the formula. Fuzzy productive rulers are constructed to inference emotion states, and the formula of emotion intensities is presented. A 3D demo system of virtual agents is realized, we use skeleton animation and facial animation (3D morphing method) to control an agent's actions, the result showed that the model is effective.

Our study also has some shortcomings. In the emotion model, we need to get appraisal value from the environment, how to determine the appropriate appraisal value is still a problem, we hope use machine learning method to solve the problem in the next work.

**Acknowledgments.** The work described in this paper was co-supported in part by the National Natural Science Foundation of China (Grant no: 60973099), the Natural Science Foundation of Zhejiang Province (grant no: Y1091158), the Natural Science Foundation of NingBo City (grant no: 2009A610088).

## References

1. Badler, N.I., Reich, B.D., Weber, B.L.: Towards personalities for animated agents with reactive and planning behaviors. In: Petta, P., Trappl, R. (eds.) Creating Personalities for Synthetic Actors. LNCS, vol. 1195, pp. 43–57. Springer, Heidelberg (1997)
2. Funge, J., Tu, X., Terzopoulos, D.: Cognitive Modeling: Knowledge, Reasoning and Planning for Intelligent Pedestrians. In: Proceedings of SIGGRAPH 1999, pp. 29–38 (1999)
3. Blumberg, B., Downie, M., Ivanov, Y., Berlin, M., Johnson, M., Tomlinson, B.: Integrated learning for interactive synthetic characters. In: Proceedings of SIGGRAPH 2002, pp. 417–426 (2002)
4. Pelachaud, C., Poggi, I.: Subtleties of facial expressions in embodied agents. Journal of Visualization and Computer Animation 13, 287–300 (2002)
5. Yungil, A., Picard, R.W.: Affective-cognitive learning and decision-making: a motivational reward framework for affective agents. In: Proceedings of the 1st International Conference on Affective Computing and Intelligent Interaction, pp. 22–24. Springer, Heidelberg (2005)
6. Ortony, A.: On making believable emotional agents believable. in R.P. Trapple(Eds) Emotions in humans and artifacts. pp.189-211, MIT Press, Cambridge (2003).
7. Bartneck, C.: Integrating the model of emotions in embodied characters. In: Proceedings of the workshop on Virtual Conversational Characters: Application, Methods, and Research Challenges (2002)
8. Sevin, E. de., Thalmann D.: A motivational Model of Action Selection for Virtual Humans. In Computer Graphics International (CGI), pp.540-543, IEEE Computer Society Press, New York (2004).

9. Egges, A., Kshirsagar, S., Magnenat-Thalmann, M.: Generic personality and emotion simulation for conversational agents. Computer Animation and Virtual Worlds 15(1), 1–13 (2004)
10. El-Nasr, M.S., Yen, J., Ioerger, T.R.: FLAME—Fuzzy Logic Adaptive Model of Emotions. Autonomous Agents and Multi-Agent Systems 3(3), 219–257 (2000)
11. Eisman, E.M., Lópeza, V., Castroa, J.L.: Controlling the emotional state of an embodied conversational agent with a dynamic probabilistic fuzzy rules based system. Expert Systems with Applications 36, 9698–9708 (2009)
12. Gratch, J., Marsella, S.: A Domain-independent framework for modeling emotion. Journal of Cognitive Systems Research 5(4), 269–306 (2004)
13. Stacy, C., Marsella, S., Gratch, J.: EMA: A process model of appraisal dynamics. Cognitive Systems Research 10, 70–90 (2009)
14. Yii, L.M., Aylett, R.: An Emergent Emotion Model for An Affective Mobile Guide with Attitude. Applied Artificial Intelligence Journal 23, 835–854 (2009)
15. Becker-Asano, C., Wachsmuth, I.: Affective computing with primary and secondary emotions in a virtual human. Auton Agent Multi-Agent System 20, 32–49 (2010)
16. Maslow, A.: Motivation and Personality. Harper, New York (1954)

# Sketch-Based Skeleton-Driven 2D Animation and Motion Capture

Junjun Pan and Jian J Zhang

National Centre for Computer Animation, Media School,
Bournemouth University, UK
{pjunjun,jzhang}@bournemouth.ac.uk

**Abstract.** We present a novel sketch-based 2D animation technique, which allows the user to produce 2D character animations efficiently. It consists of two parts, sketch-based skeleton-driven 2D animation production and 2D motion capture. The user inputs one image of the character and sketches the skeleton for each subsequent frame. The system deforms the character and creates animations automatically. To perform 2D shape deformation, a variable-length needle model is introduced to divide the deformation into two stages: skeleton driven deformation and nonlinear deformation in joint areas. It preserves the local geometric features and global area. Compared with existing approaches, it reduces the computation complexity and produces plausible results. Because our technique is skeleton-driven, the motion of character can be captured by tracking joints position and retargeted to a new character. This facilitates the reuse of motion characteristics contained in existing moving images, making the cartoon generation easy for artists and novices alike.

**Keywords:** sketch, skeleton, cartoon, 2D shape deformation, motion capture.

## 1 Introduction

Sketch-based animation has gained increasing popularity in the field of computer graphics due to its intuitiveness and importance as a useful tool for character modeling and animation. Many papers [1,2,3] have been published and several techniques have been developed into commercial software, e.g. [4]. With the help of sketch-based techniques, animators can translate their 2D drawings directly into 3D models. Instead of handling the detail step by step, the modeler/animator can visualize and evaluate the fast-prototyped models at an early stage, which can be further refined with other 3D tools to meet the practical needs. However, compared with the progress in 3D animation, 2D animation has not benefited as much from these advantages. Most professional cartoon studios still produce huge amounts of animation (key-frames and in-betweens) manually [5], which is a laborious and time-consuming process. The generation of key-frames and in-between frames are the two most important and labor intensive steps in 2D animation production. To best use the animators time, the key-frames are drawn by skillful *key-framers*, while the in-betweens by those who are less experienced and skillful, known as the *in-betweeners*. Although some software tools, e.g. Animo, Toon Boom [6], have been helpful in

Z. Pan et al. (Eds.): Transactions on Edutainment VI, LNCS 6758, pp. 164–181, 2011.

generating in-between frames, they often lack of 'personality' in comparison with those created by a human in-betweener. The software-generated in-betweens have to be tweaked by the animator to give back the 'personality' to the animation. In practice, many in-betweens remain created manually.

Motivated by the skeleton-driven 3D animation techniques and some recent progress in 2D deformations, e.g. [7], in this paper we present a new technique aiming to improving the degree of automation for the production of 2D animation without sacrificing the quality. Our method consists of two parts, Part 1: 2D animation sequence generation and Part 2: motion capture and retargeting. Part 1 can be used independently to create an animation sequence. If it is combined with Part 2, one can easily reuse the 'motion' of an existing animation sequence and apply it to a different character. The primary application of our technique is 2D animation production. But it is also applicable to interactive graphical systems where the user can deform a 2D shape directly by moving its skeleton. Since it is very simple to use, we anticipate that this method is not only of interest to professional cartoon production houses, but also to novices for creating 2D moving graphics.

The most important issue concerning Part 1 is to handle the complex shape deformation of characters both realistically and efficiently. For a character at a given orientation (for example, side view, front view or back view), we first generate its skeleton by analyzing the geometry of the boundary curve. Similar to a 3D character, the skeleton acts as the driving structure and controls the deformation of the character. To deform a character, we introduce the so called *variable-length needle model* and propose an algorithm called *skeleton driven + nonlinear least squares optimization*. The idea is to divide the 2D shape deformation into two components. The first is skeleton driven deformation, which is controlled purely by the corresponding segment of the character skeleton; and the other is nonlinear least squares optimization, which is to compute the deformation in the joint areas which are associated with the skeletal joints. Our observation suggests during animation most complex deformation occurs around the joint areas of a character. For the interest of computational efficiency, the skeleton driven deformation is treated simply as a linear transformation. Only the deformation in the joint areas is solved by nonlinear least squares optimization. To ensure realistic deformation, properties such as boundary features and local area preservation are maximized during animation. The property of global area preservation is also easily achieved by the *variable-length needle model*. Therefore once the first frame is given, the animator can easily create an animation sequence by drawing the skeleton for each subsequent key-frame. The system will produce the deformed character shape automatically, saving the animator from drawing the whole frame.

Although large amounts of video, cartoon and traditional 2D moving images exist, few effective approaches are available to make use of these abundant resources due to the special characteristics and principles of 2D animation [8,9]. The main objective of Part 2 is to patch this obvious gap. Because our cartoon production technique is skeleton-based, we can naturally borrow the idea of motion capture from 3D animation to capture the 'motion' of a 2D animation sequence. In 3D animation, the skeleton length of a 3D character is usually constant during animation. However, in a 2D case, changing feature lengths in the form of squash and stretch is one of the most powerful and expressive principles of animation [8]. In this paper we will demonstrate that with our method we can use the 2D skeleton to represent these important and expressive transformations.

Retargeting the captured motion to a different character has been extensively studied in 3D animation, e.g. [10]. We present a feature region based tracking method, commonly used in computer vision, to extract the motion of 2D objects in video or an image sequence. We apply a mixed optimization strategy coupled with template matching and Kalman prediction. Once the user has located all the joint regions of a character in the first frame, the system will track the motion of the joints automatically in the subsequent frames. The captured motion information is then retargeted to the predefined skeleton of a new 2D character to generate the deformation (animation). What to be noted is tracking is well studied in computer vision and our purpose here is not to develop a new tracking method. The novelty is to use this technique to capture 2D motion, which up to now remains an unsolved issue. To our knowledge, no effective 2D motion capture methods exist, which are good enough for 2D animation production.

There are three key contributions in this paper:

1. We present a sketch-based skeleton-driven 2D animation technique for cartoon characters. To produce a new key-frame, the user only needs to sketch the skeleton.
2. To handle 2D shape deformation, we have developed a *variable-length needle model* and introduced the *skeleton driven + nonlinear least squares optimization* algorithm. Compared with other approaches, it is more efficient and able to produce plausible deformation with squash-and-stretch effects.
3. We introduce a straightforward skeleton-based 2D motion capture method which can extract the motion from cartoon, video and rendered moving image sequences by tracking the motion of joints. Using both geometric and visual features, it prevents self-occlusion and feature disappearance in moving images.

The remainder of this paper is organized as follows: the related work is discussed in Section 2. Our sketch-based skeleton-driven 2D animation technique is described in Section 3, while in Section 4 we describe the motion capture method. Section 5 gives the experimental results and comparison with previous approaches. The limitations and possible improvements in future will be discussed in Section 6.

## 2 Related Work

There is a significant body of previous work concerning 2D character animation [7,11,12,13]. Here we only discuss the most relevant developments including 2D shape deformation and motion capture.

**2D shape deformation:** Most recent 2D deformation techniques are *control point* based. Although skeletons are incorporated into some commercial packages, the purpose is primarily to help pose a character, not to deform or animate a character [6]. Igarashi et al. [7] designed an "as-rigid-as-possible" animation system which allows the user to deform the shape of a 2D character by manipulating some control points.

To reduce the cost, the authors presented a two step deformation algorithm, which simplifies it into two linear least-squares minimization problems. As it only approximates the original problem, it can produce implausible results due to its linear feature. Weng et al. [13] presented a 2D shape deformation algorithm based on nonlinear least squares optimization. The authors used a non-quadratic energy function to represent this problem, which achieves more plausible deformation results. However, the iterative solution is computationally more costly. Schaefer et al. [14] proposed a 2D shape deformation algorithm based on linear moving least squares. It avoids input image triangulation and performs smooth deformation globally. They also extended this point-based deformation method to line segments. However, as the authors admitted, this method deforms the entire image with no regard to the topology of the object. This weakness limits its use in 2D character animation. Wang et al. [15] presented another 2D deformation technique based on the idea of rigid square matching. Instead of using triangular meshes, they use uniform quadrangular meshes as the control meshes. As the obtained deformation is quite rigid, it is not a perfect fit for soft objects and the global area is not preserved.

All above methods employ global optimization. One disadvantage of such global optimization is that the shape of all triangles needs re-computing even if a small pose change happens. This is computationally expensive and is not necessary in many cases. In our implementation, we divide the shape deformation into two components: skeleton driven deformation and nonlinear deformation of the joint areas. The former can be treated as a linear transformation and the latter is solved by nonlinear least squares optimization, but only for local regions. This local optimization scheme reduces the computation costs and can still achieve plausible deformation results.

**Motion capture and retargeting:** Most research on motion capture and retargeting focuses on 3D animation [10,16]. Many effective algorithms have been developed and benefited numerous applications including computer games and film special effects. In contrast, little has been done for 2D animation. Bregler et al. [17] presented a method to capture and retarget the non-rigid shape changes of a cartoon character using a combination of affine transformation and key-shape interpolation. It is effective in representing the qualitative characteristics (i.e. motion in this case). But it is difficult to be precise. Therefore, although it can be useful for cartoon retargeting, it is not easy for the animator to control the movement and deformation accurately. In contrast, a skeleton-driven approach gives the animator better control of the deformation during animation. Hornung et al. [18] presented a method to animate photos of 2D characters using 3D motion capture data. Given a single image of a character, they retarget the motion of a 3D skeleton to the character's 2D shape in image space. To generate realistic movement, they use "as-rigid-as-possible" deformation [7] and take projective shape distortion into account. In comparison, our method directly transfers the 2D motion data from an existing image sequence. We don't require 3D motion data. Also it does not need the user to manually specify the correspondence between 2D and 3D poses of a character. Sykora et al. [19] proposed an image registration method by combining locally optimal block matching with as-rigid-as-possible shape regularization. It can be used to motion capture a 2D object. However, the limitation is it cannot handle occlusion or large deformation.

2D animation can be regarded as a consistent image sequence. Our approach, which is influenced by several video based approaches [20,21,22], tracks the motion of the character's joints. However, since our system needs dealing with a variety of characters with different shape and topology, the model-based tracking methods are ineffective. We choose more general features: texture (colour) and geometry information (position, velocity) of the joints to extract the motion of a character. Comparing with the KLT tracker [20], not relying on good feature selection, our algorithm directly tracks the interested feature regions (joints) for each frame.

# 3 Sketch-Based Skeleton-Driven 2D Animation

Our technique consists of five steps. We use a popular cartoon figure, mm (Fig. 1a), to illustrate the technique.

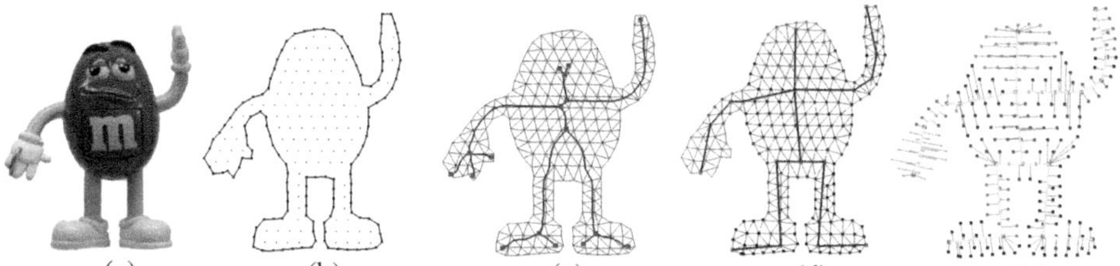

**Fig. 1.** Initial preprocessing before deformation. (a) Original template model, (b) Silhouette detection and discrete sampling, (c) Triangle mesh and curve skeleton, (d) Skeleton and decomposition, (e) The variable-length needle model.

## 3.1 Silhouette Detection and Triangulation

The user first imports a 2D character serving as the *original template model*, which can be represented by a BMP/JPEG image or vector graphics. The requirement is that the boundary of the object should be represented by a closed polygon. For BMP/JPEG images, we currently remove the background manually. Its silhouette is detected with the marching squares algorithm [23], forming a closed polygon. Distributing discrete points allows the polygon to be triangulated. Many triangulation algorithms exist. Here we adopt the Constrained Delaunay triangulation algorithm. The sampling density is adjustable at the user's will to form sparser or denser meshes depending on the requirements. To make sure a character shape is properly triangulated, we require the template model should be expanded or the limb occlusion is solved beforehand. This can be performed with image completion [24].

## 3.2 Skeletonization and Decomposition

The process of constructing a skeleton is called the *skeletonization*. The system first generates a *curve skeleton* of the character with the 2D thinning algorithm [25]. To produce an *animation skeleton*, the user locates the joints either on the curve skeleton or the mesh vertices. The curve skeleton of the example character is shown in Fig. 3c.

Some end points of the curve skeleton branches (red points in Fig. 3c) can be used as skeletal joints directly. After skeletonization, the system attaches every vertex to its nearest skeleton segment. This is called the *decomposition*, which classifies the vertices into different *regions*. Here we use a region growing algorithm described in [26]. The decomposition result for the example cartoon character is shown in Fig. 3d. In this figure, there are 16 skeleton segments, which have been colour-coded to represent the associated *vertex regions*.

Based on the classification of all the vertices, we now classify the triangles into two types, *interior triangles* and *joint triangles*. If the three vertices of a triangle are of the same color, i.e. they are all associated with one skeleton segment, the triangle is an interior triangle, otherwise the triangle is a joint triangle. Both types of triangles are shown in Fig. 1. We also sort the vertices into three categories, *silhouette vertices, interior vertices* and *joint vertices* illustrated in Fig. 2. Silhouette vertices form the contour of an object. Except for silhouette vertices, if all the neighbor triangles of a vertex are interior triangles, this vertex is an *interior vertex*; otherwise it is a *joint vertex*.

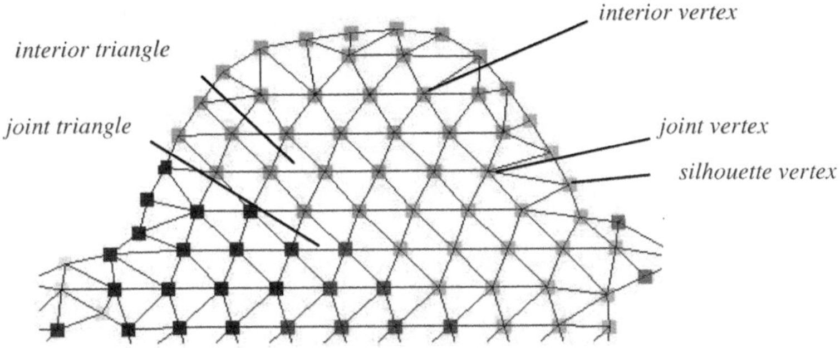


**Fig. 2.** Illustration of our definition of different types of vertices and triangles

## 3.3 Shape Deformation

Shape deformation is crucial to the quality of animation and is an essential step of our technique. The main objective for our algorithm design is both to minimize the boundary change, interior shape distortion and computational overheads. We deform a 2D character in two stages: skeleton driven deformation for each vertex region (Stage 1) and nonlinear deformation for the joint areas (Stage 2). For Stage 1, since the computation involves simple transformations, it incurs only a small overhead. Stage 2 minimizes implausible deformations. Although the computation is more complex, it involves only a small portion of the vertices.

### 3.3.1 Variable-Length Needle Model

Our Variable-Length needle model represents the geometry of the deformable object using a collection of variable-length needles. Each needle links a vertex to its attached skeleton segment. Each needle originates from the skeleton and extends outward in a fixed angle. The vertex is at the end point of a needle. The length of a needle is the Euclidean distance between the vertex and the corresponding skeleton segment. Fig. 1e illustrates the variable-length needles model.

### 3.3.2 Stage One: Skeleton Driven Deformation

In skeleton driven deformation, the geometry of all vertices is determined only by the position of the corresponding skeleton segment. Because the points are close to the skeletal segment, it is reasonable to regard the needles as being subject to the affine transformations of the skeleton segment during animation. Rotation and scaling are legitimate transformations here. During transformation, the length and direction of the needles relative to the skeleton segment are unchanged, leading to fast computation of the new coordinates of the mesh vertices.

Cartoon characters often exhibit significant squash-and-stretch deformations. An advantage of using our needle model is that the area enclosed by the boundary can be maintained by ensuring the change of the length of a needle to be reciprocal of the change of the linked skeletal segment length. Because the needles cover the character's surface, this simple method effectively preserves the global area of the character and express the squash-and-stretch effects. Fig. 3 demonstrates the effect of global area preservation. One skeletal segment is used to deform the bottle.

**Fig. 3.** Deformation with (middle) and without (right) global area preservation. The original object and variable-length needle model are shown on the left.

Fig. 4 illustrates the deformation process of a cartoon character. As can be seen in Fig. 4c, d, the deformation is realistic. However, the texture and contour curve in some joint areas are not sufficiently smooth, and some joint triangles even overlap. This suggests that to minimize shape distortion, we need to concentrate on the joint areas and ensure the deformation conforms to the original model. This forms the main part of Stage two.

### 3.3.3 Stage Two: Nonlinear Deformation in Joint Areas

We employ two geometric entities as constraints to prevent shape distortion: rotation and scale invariant (RSI) Laplacian coordinates [27] and edge lengths of the triangular mesh. The former preserves the local shape feature of the contour curve and the latter for local area preservation.

Let $(V, E)$ be the 2D graph of a character's mesh model, where $V$ and $E$ are the sets of vertices and edges respectively. $V$ can be divided into three subsets: $V_s$ which contains $k$ silhouette vertices, $V_p$ which contains $m$ joint vertices, and $V_q$ which contains $n-m-k$ interior vertices.

**a. RSI Laplacian coordinates**

As the ordinary Laplacian coordinates do not account for rotation and scaling of the curve, here we use rotation and scale invariant (RSI) Laplacian coordinates [27] to handle the deformation of the silhouettes. Given that we are mainly interested in the joint areas where visible distortions occur, we only need to constrain the silhouette vertices in the joint areas, denoted by $V_{s'}$. To preserve the local features of the contour curve, we need to minimize the following objective function:

$$\sum_{v_i \in V_{s'}} \| T(v_i) - T(\tilde{v}_i) \|^2 \tag{1}$$

where $T(v_i)$ stands for the RSI Laplacian coordinates of $v_i$ before deformation; $T(\tilde{v}_i)$ stands for the RSI Laplacian coordinates of $v_i$ after deformation.

**b. Edge lengths**

We use the following energy function to penalize edge length deviation for joint triangles:

$$\sum_{v_i, v_j \in V_p, (i,j) \in E} \| |v_i - v_j| - |\tilde{v}_i - \tilde{v}_j| \|^2 \tag{2}$$

$|v_i - v_j|$ is the edge length of $v_i v_j$ before deformation, and $|\tilde{v}_i - \tilde{v}_j|$ is the edge length of $v_i v_j$ after deformation.

Combining (2) and (3), our overall objective function can be rewritten in the following matrix form:

$$w_1 \| \mathbf{T}\mathbf{V}_{s'} - \mathbf{T}\tilde{\mathbf{V}}_{s'} \|^2 + w_2 \| \mathbf{H}\mathbf{V}_p - \mathbf{H}\tilde{\mathbf{V}}_p \|^2 \tag{3}$$

Assume the number of vertices in $V_{s'}$ is $k'$. $\mathbf{V}_{s'}$ represents the coordinates of these vertices. $\mathbf{H}$ is a $|E_p| \times m$ matrix, which is used to compute the edge vectors of joint triangles. The sum of weights: $w_1$ and $w_2$ are normalized to 1 and in our experiments we used equal weightings for both terms. However, the user can adjust the weighting to emphasize certain geometric properties.

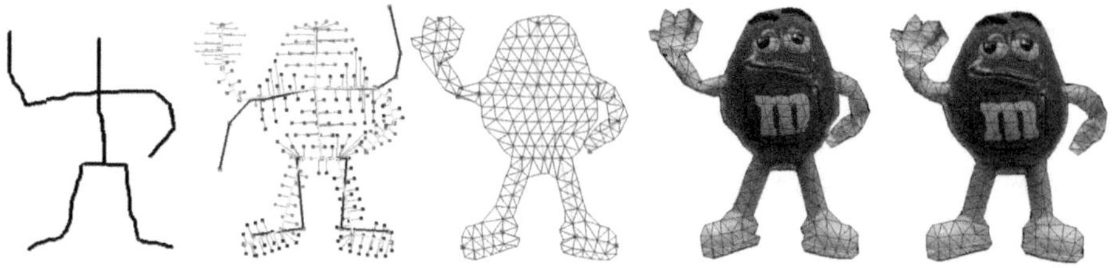

(a) (b) (c) (d) (e)

**Fig. 4.** Deformation process. (a) Sketched skeleton, (b) Deformed character displayed as a variable-length needle model. The blue lines represent the skeleton of the original template model before deformation, (c) Mesh and skeleton after the deformation of Stage one, (d) Character after the deformation of Stage one, (e) Character after the deformation of Stage two.

This is a non-linear function and to solve the optimization problem efficiently, we adopt the iterative Gauss-Newton method. The result is shown in Fig. 4e where both the silhouette and texture inside the object are smoothly deformed compared with the result of Stage one. For this particular example, the computation converges with 36 iterations. The number of iterations varies with many factors including the shape of model, the number of vertices and the magnitude of the deformation. In our experiment, the average number of iterations across all the examples is 35.

### 3.4 Depth Adjustment and Fine Tuning

Collision detection is a practical problem for the deformation of cartoon characters. When different parts of a character overlap, if the depths are not assigned properly, the overlapping parts may interpenetrate. Moreover, assigning static depth values for vertices [7] does not work in all possible situations. In our system, we allow dynamic depth adjustment through interaction. Upon the generation of a new deformed model, we monitor the mesh for self-intersection and set an appropriate depth order to the overlapping parts. When the user clicks any vertex in an overlapping part, all the vertices in this decomposed region will have the same depth value as the clicked one. Fig. 5a gives an example of depth adjustment.

Our system also allows the user to fine tune the local geometric details of the model in two ways: sketch curves and point dragging. The sketch curves are used to fine tune the silhouette of an object. Similar to the nearest neighbor method, we search the start and end points of the silhouette segment along the object contour (the shortest Euclidean distances from the start and end points respectively to the sketch curve). For each vertex on the silhouette segment of the variable-length needle model, we fix the angle between the needle and the skeleton segment, and change the length of the needle to move its end point to the new position on the sketch curve. An example is given in Fig. 5b where the profile of the right arm is altered with a sketch curve. Point dragging is more straightforward. The user picks and drags any vertex to reshape the character. It can be very useful to edit or generate detailed shape changes after the skeleton-driven deformation is complete, such as facial expressions. Fig. 5c shows two examples. The left one changes the face expression and the right one creates a hedgehog hair.

Fig. 5. Depth adjustment and fine tuning local geometric detail. (a) Deformed result before and after depth adjustment, (b) Sketch curve fine tuning, (c) Deformation through point dragging.

### 3.5 In-Betweening

In-between frames are generated by interpolating the deformation produced from the two stages discussed above, skeleton-driven deformation (stage 1) and non-linear deformation in the joint areas (stage 2). Many interpolation techniques can be used. In this Section, we explain how to generate the in-betweens given two key-frames. Suppose $f_{start}$, $f_{skeleton\text{-}driven}$ and $f_{end}$ represent the shape of the initial frame before deformation, the shape generated with the skeleton-driven deformation only and the shape of the end frame, respectively. The computation of each in-between frame $f(t)$ consists of two elements. The first describes the skeleton-driven deformation which is solved by spherical linear interpolation (slerp). The second element represents the non-linear deformation which can be computed by the linear interpolation of the geometry displacement between $f_{skeleton\text{-}driven}$ and $f_{end}$. The formula can be described as follows:

$$\underset{t\in[0,1]}{f(t)} = \text{slerp}[f_{start} \times (1-t) + f_{skeleton-driven} \times t] + (f_{end} - f_{skeleton-driven}) \times t \tag{4}$$

## 4 Motion Capture and Retargeting

Based on the method proposed above, we have also developed an effective algorithm to capture the motion of a 2D character. The basic idea is to track the joints using the well developed computer vision techniques. Once the first frame is identified from a moving image sequence, the curve skeleton is automatically extracted in the same way as was described earlier. Based on this curve skeleton, the animator marks the joints on the image. To capture the motion from the subsequent frames/images, the key step is to track the positions of the joints. Because we are concerned with 2D images/frames, it is reasonable to assume the texture of the joints unchanged between any two adjacent frames. Our design therefore is to track the joint positions using texture as the visual cue. It captures the motion of an *original character* and retargets it to the *target character*. To ensure it works correctly, the image sequences and the target character should satisfy the following preconditions:

1. The image sequence is consistent, i.e. the change between two adjacent frames is relatively small.
2. The target character has the same topology and a similar pose to that of the original character in the first frame.

3. The pose of the original character in the first frame is roughly expanded. There is no occlusion for all the joints.

What needs pointing out is that our motion capture method is not limited to cartoon sequences only. It can capture a cartoon sequence, a video and a rendered 3D animation image sequence (Fig. 12).

## 4.1 Tracking

For a given image sequence or video as input, the system first subtracts the background for each frame [28]. The user then locates all the joints by marking small rectangles on the original character to indicate the joint positions, using the automatically generated curve skeleton as a guide. Fig. 6a shows an *original character* to be tracked. The red rectangles represent the located joint regions. Tracking and connecting all the joint positions in these frames lead to the generation of the skeleton in the subsequent frames. To map the captured motion to a target character (Fig. 6b), we require the target character to have a similar topology and pose to those of the original character. Moving images of static objects can be relatively easy to track with color information alone. But it is not sufficient for articulated characters. This is because parts of a character may overlap from time to time where color information disappears. In order to solve this problem, in addition to the color feature as discussed, we also use the geometric feature. The geometric feature allows the joint positions to be predicted in the next frame by estimating the velocity of the joints.

(a) (b)

**Fig. 6.** Initial setup for motion capture. (a) Original character in the first frame and located joints, (b) Target character and its decomposition results.

Assume *n* joints to be tracked in each frame, the positions of the rectangle centres at frame *t* form a geometric feature vector $\mathbf{G}_t = [\mathbf{g}_{1t}, \mathbf{g}_{2t}, \ldots, \mathbf{g}_{mt}, \ldots \mathbf{g}_{nt}]^T = [(x_1, y_1)_t, (x_2, y_2)_t, \ldots, (x_m, y_m)_t, \ldots (x_n, y_n)_t]^T$ . For the visual feature, we use an *n* dimensional feature vector $\mathbf{C}_t = [\mathbf{c}_{1t}, \mathbf{c}_{2t}, \ldots, \mathbf{c}_{mt}, \ldots \mathbf{c}_{nt}]^T$ , where $\mathbf{c}_{mt}$ is the texture matrix of the *m*-th rectangle region. We track a joint (the centre of the corresponding rectangle) between adjacent frames by searching the closest match in the previous frame. Using the Bayes' rule with a uniform *a priori* distribution case, this process is equivalent to finding the maximum of $P(\mathbf{F}_t \mid \mathbf{\Theta})$, where $\mathbf{F}_t$ denotes a feature vector of the character at frame *t*. $\mathbf{\Theta}$ denotes the feature parameters corresponding to the tracked result at frame *t*-1. Here the whole feature space is divided into two sub-spaces: geometric and visual spaces as follows:

$$P(\mathbf{F}_t \mid \mathbf{\Theta}) = P_c(\mathbf{C}_t \mid \mathbf{\Theta}_c) P_g(\mathbf{G}_t \mid \mathbf{\Theta}_g) \tag{5}$$

where $P_c(\mathbf{C}_t \mid \mathbf{\Theta}_c)$ and $P_g(\mathbf{G}_t \mid \mathbf{\Theta}_g)$ are PDFs (probability density functions) corresponding to the visual and geometric features respectively. Maximizing $P(\mathbf{F}_t \mid \mathbf{\Theta})$ can be described as the following optimization problem, which is to minimize the sum of the Mahalanobis distances in the sub-spaces, i.e.

$$\min \sum_{m=1}^{n} D_{mt} \tag{6}$$

**s. t.** $D_{mt} = w_\alpha D_{c,mt} + w_\beta D_{g,mt}$, $D_{g,mt} = (x_{mt} - \overline{x}_{mt})^2 + (y_{mt} - \overline{y}_{mt})^2$

$$D_{c,mt} = w_r RedDiff(\mathbf{c}_{mt}) + w_g GreenDiff(\mathbf{c}_{mt}) + w_b BlueDiff(\mathbf{c}_{mt})$$

where $w_\alpha$ and $w_\beta$ are the weights used to normalize the corresponding distances. In our work, $w_\alpha$ is $1/(255)^2$ and $w_\beta$ is $(1/r)^2$. *r* is the radius of the search range. $D_{c,mt}$ represents the measuring distance in RGB space. $D_{g,mt}$ represents the distance between the centre of moving rectangle and the position of the predicted joint region centre.

The Kalman filter is widely used for tracking as a subject of computer vision. Since the interval between adjacent frames is small in our work, we treat it as a uniformly accelerated motion in a time interval and use the following prediction model to compute the centres of the joint regions $\mathbf{G}_t(\overline{x}_m, \overline{y}_m)$

$$\mathbf{G}_t(\overline{x}_m, \overline{y}_m) = \mathbf{G}_{t-1}(x_m, y_m) + \mathbf{V}_{m,t-1}T + \mathbf{A}_{m,t-1}T^2/2 \tag{7}$$
$$\mathbf{V}_{m,t-1} = [\mathbf{G}_{t-1}(x_m, y_m) - \mathbf{G}_{t-2}(x_m, y_m)]/T$$
$$\mathbf{A}_{m,t-1} = [\mathbf{V}_{t-1}(x_m, y_m) - \mathbf{V}_{t-2}(x_m, y_m)]/T$$

where $\mathbf{G}_{t-1}(x_m, y_m)$, $\mathbf{V}_{m,t-1}$, $\mathbf{A}_{m,t-1}$ are the tracked centre position, velocity and acceleration of the *m*-th joint at frame *t*-1. *T* is the interval between adjacent frames.

Fig. 7a illustrates the joint tracking result of the character in Fig. 6a. We select four tracked frames in an 18 frame image sequence. As can be seen from frames 6, 12, 18, the problem of self-occlusion is effectively solved with our position prediction algorithm.

**Fig. 7.** Tracking and retargeting. (a) Joint tracking for the original character, (b) Deformed target character.

This tracking method is not without limitations. Since the frame-by-frame tracking is inherently subject to error accumulation, the accuracy is limited to a small number of frames (around 30 in our experiments). One effective way to solve this problem is to divide a large image sequence into a number of segments which consist of fewer frames, and correct the tracking error for the first frame in each segment. Our system allows the user interactively adjust the tracking result at any frame when necessary.

### 4.2 Retargeting

To retarget a captured motion to the new character, we first produce a skeleton as described before. There is a lot of existing work on 3D animation, such as [10], which is directly applicable to our case. In this paper however, we only implemented a simple method to demonstrate the retargeting process. For a moving 2D character, a skeleton can have both linear (length) and angular (orientation) displacements, i.e. a skeleton segment can stretch / squash and rotate. The basic idea of our simple motion retargeting is to map the captured increments of both length and orientation angle of a skeletal segment, which can be computed by:

$$\Delta l_{m,t} = l_{m,t} / l_{m,t-1}, \Delta\alpha_{m,t} = \alpha_{m,t} - \alpha_{m,t-1} \tag{7}$$

where $l_{m,t}$ , $\alpha_{m,t}$ represent the length and orientation angle of the $m$-th skeleton segment at frame $t$. For the target model, the length $l'_{m,t}$ and orientation angle $\alpha'_{m,t}$ of the $m$-th skeleton segment at frame $t$ can be trivially computed by:

$$l'_{m,t} = l'_{m,t-1}\Delta l_{m,t}, \alpha'_{m,t} = \alpha'_{m,t-1} + \Delta\alpha_{m,t} \tag{8}$$

Fig. 7b illustrates the retargeting result for the target character in Fig. 6b.

## 5 Experiments and Evaluation

We design two experiments to comparatively study the computational complexity and visual performance of our deformation algorithm. The first is deforming a 2D flower model with our algorithm into four similar postures to those in [13]. The results are shown in Fig. 8. We test our algorithm on a 3.2GHz Pentium 4 workstation with 1GB memory. Table 1 gives the comparison results. Since our deformation algorithm does not perform nonlinear shape deformation for all triangles, it takes about a quarter of the time. This is especially significant when performing larger and more complex animations.

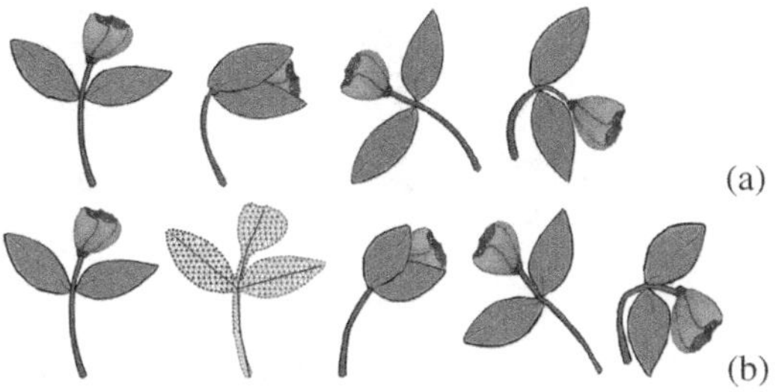


**Fig. 8.** Flower model deformed by our algorithm and [13]. (a) Deformation results with [13], (b) Deformation results with our algorithm (from left to right, original template, decomposition result and deformed figures).

**Table 1.** Comparison of data statistics and timing

| Cartoon model: Flower | Method in [13] | Our deformation algorithm |
|---|---|---|
| Boundary vertices | 114 | 123 |
| Interior vertices | 256 | 27 (Joint vertices) |
| Precomputing time | 22ms | 9ms |
| Iteration time | 0.589ms | 0.143ms |

The second experiment is to deform an elastic object both appeared in [7] and [15]. Two skeletal segments are used in our algorithm. Fig. 9 gives the results. As our method preserves the global area, comparing with the result in [7] and [15], it can express the squash-and-stretch effect of this elastic object naturally during deformation.

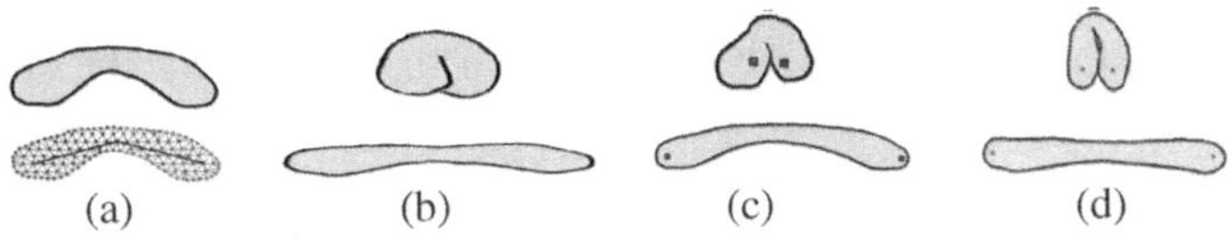


**Fig. 9.** Comparing our algorithm with the approaches in [7] and [15]. (a) Original object and decomposition result with skeleton, (b) Deformation result with our algorithm, (c) Deformation result in [7], (d) Deformation result in [15].

We also invited three animators to test our technique with two groups of experiments. The first was used to evaluate the visual quality and performance of animation production. The original characters were acquired from the Internet. Fig. 10 and the video give the results. The second group is to test our motion capture and retargeting method. There are two experiments. The first (Fig. 11) is to track the joints of a jumping cartoon man and retarget the motion to a new character. We treat the hat and the man as two objects, and track them separately. The second one (Fig. 12) is to track the joints of a 3D running horse (rendered as a 2D image sequence using Maya) and retarget it into a cartoon gazelle.

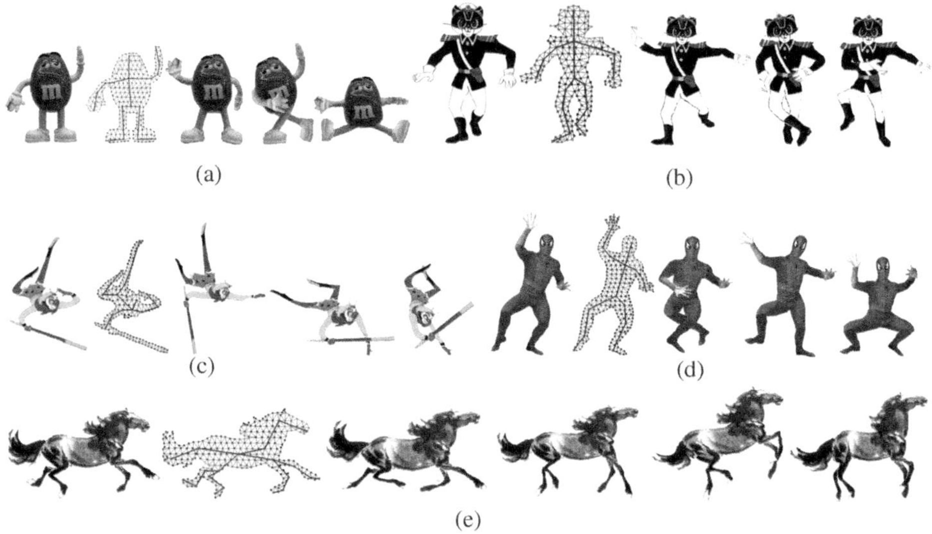


**Fig. 10.** Five groups of cartoon characters deformed by our algorithm. From left to right, original template model, decomposition results with skeleton, deformed figures. (a) mm, (b) Black cat sergeant, (c) Monkey king, (d) Spiderman, (e) Running horse.

The consensus from the animators showed that our method is more efficient than the current practice adopted in many commercial cartoon production houses, as sketching a skeleton is much faster than drawing a whole frame. In fact it is encouraging to see that our design is consistent with their animation practice. To create a key-frame, often the animator would first sketch a stick figure (i.e. the skeleton) and then overlay the body shape on top guided by the stick figure. This process is called the *deep structure*. Sketching the skeleton alone relieves them from some of the time-consuming tasks, i.e. to draw the whole character body. They also believe that our motion capture technique will make an animator's life much easier and have a positive impact on the cartoon production industry once a 2D motion database is established.

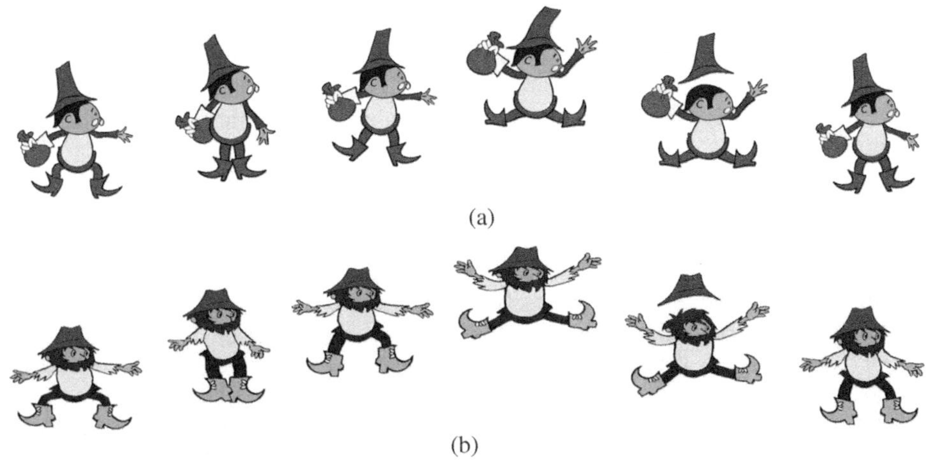


**Fig. 11.** Motion of a jumping cartoon man retargeted to a new character. (a) Original cartoon character, (b) Retargeted new character.

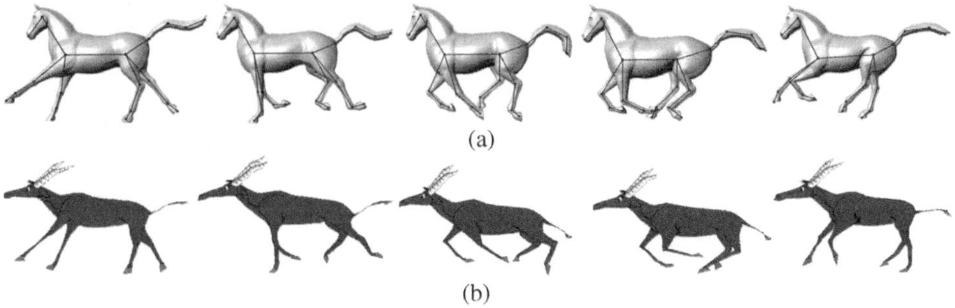


**Fig. 12.** Joint tracking of a running horse (a) and retargeting to a cartoon gazelle (b)

## 6 Discussion and Limitations

In this paper, we have presented a sketch-based skeleton-driven 2D animation technique using sketches as the primary inputting means both for the creation and the control of the animation artifacts. It consists of two main parts. The first is concerned with the fast production of 2D character animation by sketching only the skeletons. Comparing with the traditional cartoon production pipeline, drawing a skeleton is much faster than drawing a whole frame. This allows denser key-frames to be drawn by experienced animators. By reducing the interval between key-frames, in many cases the in-between frames can be produced mainly by software without compromising the realism, unlike the current practice where human in-betweeners are the main workforce, which is often expensive.

Given an original image of a character and the sketched skeleton sequence, our technique will generate a deformed character with different poses automatically. It is faster and less labour-intensive than the existing production practice. Our theoretical contribution in this aspect includes a variable-length needle model, which successfully preserves the global area of a character during animation, which is an essential property for squash-and-stretch effect in cartoon animation; and the skeleton driven + nonlinear least squares optimization algorithm, which is computationally economic.

The second part of our work is concerned with the development of a skeleton-based 2D motion capture technique. Once a skeleton is established in the first frame of a moving image sequence, we track all the joint positions from each subsequent image considering both geometric and visual features of the images. This 2D motion capture technique can be applied to various types of moving images, including 2D cartoon animation, videos and image sequences of rendered 3D animations.

Our research also reveals some limitations of the developed method. The first relates to the texture information of the template image. Because there is no 3D information of a 2D character, large pose change can result in loss of correct texture for subsequent frames. Although some research in matting, image completion and texture synthesis [18,24,29,30] has attempted to resolve this issue, it is still an open problem for all 2D deformation techniques. We plan to use image merging techniques to tackle it in the future. The second limitation is the error accumulation in tracking. Currently we correct the tracking error at the first frame of each sequence segment. We plan to use a more robust tracking approach in the future. The third place to improve is retargeting. Our current simple approach is only to demonstrate our motion capture method. It would be desirable to incorporate a 3D animation technique (e.g. [10]) to treat retargeting as a space-time optimization problem. The motion editing techniques developed for 3D motions are also relevant.

**Acknowledgments.** This research is in part supported by EPSRC grant EP/F030355/1.

## References

1. Davis, J., Chuang, E., Slesin, D.: A sketching interface for articulated figure animation. In: Proc. Eurographics/ SIGGRAPH Symposium on Computer Animation, pp. 320–328 (2003)
2. Thorne, M., Burke, D., Panne, M.: Motion Doodles: An interface for sketching character motion. In: SIGGRAPH 2004 Conference Proceedings, pp. 424–431 (2004)
3. Li, Y.: 3D Character Animation Synthesis From 2D Sketches. In: Proceedings of the 4th international Conference on Computer graphics and Interactive Techniques in Australasia and Southeast Asia, pp. 81–90 (2006)
4. Igarashi, T., Matsuoar, S., Tanaka, H.: Teddy: a sketching interface for 3D freeform design. In: Proceedings of ACM SIGGRAPH 1999, pp. 79–89 (1999)
5. Sykora, et al.: Sketching cartoons by example. In: Eurographics Workshop on Sketch-Based Interfaces and Modeling, pp. 27–34 (2005)
6. ToonBoom: `http://www.toonboom.com/products/digitalpro/eLearning/tipsTricks/2008`
7. Igarashi, T., Moscovich, T., Hughes, J.F.: As-rigid-as-possible shape manipulation. ACM Trans. Graphics 24(3), 1134–1141 (2005)

8. Williams, R.: The Animator's Survival Kit. Faber & Faber, London (2001)
9. Isaac, K.: Applying the 12 Principles to 3D Computer Animation. The Art of 3D Computer Animation and Effects (2003)
10. Gleicher, M.: Retargeting motion to new characters. In: Proceedings of ACM SIGGRAPH 1998, pp. 33–42 (1998)
11. Hsu, S.C., Lee, I.H.: Drawing and animation using skeletal strokes. In: Proceedings of ACM SIGGRAPH 1994, pp. 109–118 (1994)
12. Fekete, J., Bizouarn, E., Cournarie, E.: TicTacToon: A paperless system for professional 2D animation. In: ACM SIGGRAPH 96 Conference Proceedings, pp. 79–90. (1996)
13. Weng, Y., Xu, W., Wu, Y., Zhou, K., Guo, B.: 2D Shape Deformation Using Nonlinear Least Squares Optimization. The Visual Computer 22(9-11), 653–660 (2006)
14. Schaefer, S., Mcphail, T., Warren, J.: Image deformation using moving least squares. In: SIGGRAPH 2006 Conference Proceedings, pp. 255–262. (2006)
15. Wang, Y., Xu, K., Xiong, Y., Cheng, Z.: 2D shape deformation based on rigid square matching. Computer Animation and Virtual Worlds 19(3-4), 411–420 (2008)
16. Fayreau, L., Reveret, L., Depraz, C., Cani, M.P.: Animal gaits from video. In: Eurographics/SIGGRAPH Symposium on Computer Animation, pp. 277–286 (2004)
17. Bregler, C., Loeb, L., Erika, Chuang, E. Deshpande, H.: Turning to the masters: motion capturing cartoons. In: SIGGRAPH Conference Proceedings, pp 121–129. (2002)
18. Hornung, A., Dekkers, E., Kobbelt, L.: Character animation from 2D pictures and 3D motion data. ACM Trans. Graph. 26(1), 1–9 (2007)
19. Sykora, et al.: As-Rigid-As-Possible Image Registration for Hand-drawn Cartoon Animations. In: Proceedings of the 7th International Symposium on Non-Photorealistic Animation and Rendering, pp. 25–33 (2005)
20. Kong, Y., Rosenfield, A.: Digital topology: Introduction and survey. Comp. Vision, Graphics and Image Proc. 48(3), 357–393 (1989)
21. Drori, I., Cohen-or, D., Yeshurun, H.: Fragment-Basedimage completion. ACM Trans. Graph. 22(3), 303–312 (2003)
22. Cornea, D., Silver, D., Min, P.: Curve-skeleton properties, applications and algorithms. IEEE Transactions on Visualization and Computer Graphics 6(3), 81–91 (2006)
23. Shamir, A.: A Survey on Mesh Segmentation Techniques. Computer Graphics Forum 27(6), 1539–1556 (2008)
24. 27. Sorkine, O., Lipman, Y., Cohen-OR, D., Alexa, M., Rossl, C., Seidel, H. P.: Laplacian surface editing. In: Symposium on Geometry Processing, ACM SIGGRAPH/ Eurographics, pp. 179–188 (2004)
25. 28. Wang, J., Bhat, P., Colburn, A., Agrawala, M., Cohen, M.: Interactive Video Cutout. In: SIGGRAPH 2004 Conference Proceedings, pp. 124–131. (2004)
26. Li, Y., Gleicher, M., Xu, Y.Q., Shum, H.Y.: Stylizing motion with drawings. In: ACM SIGGRAPH/Eurographics Symposium on Computer Animation, pp. 111–122 (2003)
27. Eitz, M., Sorkine, O., Alexa, M.: Sketch Based Image Deformation. In: Proceedings of Vision, Modeling and Visualization, pp. 135–142 (2007)

# A Multi-layer Model for Face Aging Simulation

Yixiong Liang, Ying Xu, Lingbo Liu, Shenghui Liao, and Beiji Zou

School of Information Science and Engineering, Central South University
Changsha, Hunan 410083, China
{yxliang,lsh,bjzou}@mail.csu.edu.cn

**Abstract.** Face aging simulation is a very complex and challenging task and interests many researchers in the fields of psychology, computer graphics and computer vision due to its widely applications. In this paper, we propose a multi-layer coarse-to-fine face representation and aging simulation and animation algorithm. In the coarse layer, we build a global statistical appearance model for representation and faces are aged based on the learned age trajectory in the appearance space. In the mid layer, we learned a set of age specific coupled dictionaries and the faces are represented and aged via the sparse representation on the learned dictionary. At the fine layer, we sample a lot of patches of facial components and skin zones from images of each age group and use them as the dictionaries to simulate the aging effects of the facial components and wrinkles. We collect a database of 10, 050 Chinese passport-type images with different ages for the learning and aging simulation. Experimental results demonstrate the effectiveness of the proposed method.

**Keywords:** Aging simulation, Statistical appearance model, Age specific coupled dictionaries, Sparse representation.

## 1 Introduction

Aging is an inevitable process of human and it often causes the significant deformations in the appearance of a subject shown in a facial image. The capability to predict or synthesize an "aged" face image is an interesting task which may find many applications in our real life. Such applications include the development of age-invariant face recognition systems, prediction of the current appearance of missing persons, updating of passport/visa photographs, digital entertainment cosmetic surgery planning, age-adaptive human computer interaction, etc. Traditionally age progressed images are produced by forensic artists [5]. Recently, computer-based age-progression has attracted growing research interest from psychology [21], computer graphics [28,8,11,26], and lately computer vision [15,14,29,25,27,18,17,6,23,30,31].

Different from the appearance variations due to expression, pose, and illumination, it's very hard to build a geometric or statistical model to deal with the aging related facial variations due to its unique characteristics. First is that aging variations are *un-controllable*. It cannot be eliminated by the cooperation

Z. Pan et al. (Eds.): Transactions on Edutainment VI, LNCS 6758, pp. 182–192, 2011.

of subject and it is also often mixed with other variations (i.e. illumination, expression, etc.) during the process of imaging. In fact, collecting all facial images of different persons over a long time period is very difficult or even impossible. Second is that aging changes are *complex*. It occurs slowly over long period with both complex shape and texture variations. In different stages, the variations are manifested in different forms. From infancy to teen years, changes due to the aging effect are manifested in the form of nonlinear shape variations involving the changes in the underlying skeletal features toward the formation of the adult skull and face. While during the adulthood, the age-related changes involve the minor skeletal variations and large textural variations such as muscle relaxation, wrinkles growing and other skin artifacts emerging [27,5,14]. Third, the age progression is *diverse* and is specific to a given individual. It is effected by both innate factors and environmental factors such as heredity, gender, health, and lifestyle, and so on, which make the changes are seriously uncertain. These unique characteristics make the task of modeling age-related variations very challenging.

### 1.1 Previous Work

In the past several decades, there are many works aiming to simulate the aging effects on human faces. Here we only give a brief review on these techniques and see [27,6,14] and the reference therein for more details.

Early attempts mainly concerned on using coordinate transformations to model craniofacial growth [24,33]. Hutton et al. [12] constructed a shape model based on 3D facial meshes and defined age trajectories in the shape model space, which are used to simulate the aged images. Wang et al. [34] trained a set of support vector machines (SVMs) to predict the shape in the future. In a more recent approach, Ramanathan et al. [25] proposed a craniofacial growth model, in which psychophysical and anthropometric evidences on facial growth are considered. These methods mentioned above only consider the shape changes, and thus lack the validness of modeling texture variations. In order to capture the shape and texture changes at the same time, O'Toole et al. [22,21] proposed a caricature algorithm and applied it into 3D face model. Burt et al. [3] created facial prototypes for different age groups in both shape and texture and defined the differences between prototypes as aging transformations. Wang et al. [34] and Liang et al. [17] applied this prototype approach in shape subspace and texture subspace instead of the original image space, and Park et al. [23] further applied it to 3D face aging. The prototype-based methods often lack the capture of details such as wrinkles. Tidderman et al. [32] extended the prototype method by using the wavelet-based method to improve the texture of the facial prototypes. Attempts were also made for capturing typical aging details by anatomy skin model [35], wrinkle prototypes [2],details transferring [16] and merging [7].

Lanitis et al. [15] first attempted to build rigorous statistical approaches to age progression. They generated an active appearance model (AAM) [4] for parametric representation of faces and investigated aging functions which determine the relationship between the age and the model parameters. Scandrett et al. [9] defined both a person-specific and a global aging axis in the shape and texture subspace. In [14], the idea of reinforcing both person specific and global aging trends are further extended and the aging simulation is formulated as an similarity optimization problem. The methods based on parametric representation and age function are further applied to 3D face aging [28]. All these methods use parametric representation of the faces which discard high-frequency information and thus are only appropriate for modeling distinct age-related facial variations and major texture variations. In order to capture more texture variations, Jiang et al. [13] proposed a framework to simulate the aging process by means of super-resolution in tensor space. But their simulation results are not realistic enough. Suo et al. [31] presented a novel machine learning-based compositional and dynamic model for face aging, in which facial aging was modeled by means of a dynamic Markov process on the And-Or graph representation of faces.

### 1.2 Overview of Our Algorithm

In this paper, we adopt the coarse-to-fine strategy and propose a three-level model for facial representation and aging. A face image at age $t$ can be written as:

$$I_t = (I_{l,t}, I_{m,t}, I_{h,t}), \tag{1}$$

where the first layer $I_{l,t}$ is the low-resolution image in age group $t$, $I_{m,t}$ is the high-resolution one resulting from face hallucination [19] based on sparse representation [36] and $I_{h,t}$ is the facial components (eyebrows, eyes, mouths etc.) and wrinkles in different zones of the face. Based on this representation, we build a multi-layer aging model. For the first layer, the aging process is modeled by the learned age trajectories $g_s(t)$ and $g_t(t)$ in shape and texture space, respectively. For the second layer aging, we learned a set of coupled over-completed dictionaries of different age using K-SVD [1] and the aged face in this layer can be reconstructed by the sparse representation on the high-resolution dictionary of the corresponding age. In the last layer, we create a dictionary of different face components and wrinkles across different ages. The atoms of components and wrinkles dictionary are selected by shape and texture matching and then merged into the face image to simulate the aged one.

Our mainly contributions include: 1) A novel coarse-to-fine face representation, 2) a multi-layer aging model, especially the sparse representation based face hallucination aging model, and 3) a collection of 10,050 Chinese passport-type images with different ages on which the learning and simulating experiments are performed.

## 2 The Algorithm Details

In this section, we formulate the details of our algorithms about the coarse-to-fine representation and aging.

### 2.1 Layer 1: Global Appearance Representation and Aging

In the first layer, the global appearance is represented by two elementary components, namely shape and texture, as illustrated in Fig.1. The shape vector

$\mathbf{s}$ is represented by the coordinates of facial landmarks and then is aligned to the mean face shape through an iterative Procrustes Analysis [4]. The shape-independent texture vectors $\mathbf{t}$ can be captured by warping the face images to the mean shape using linear warping over the landmarks Delaunay triangulation. The $\mathbf{s}$ and $\mathbf{t}$ are further encoded in PCA which provides a highly effective means for modeling and transforming. Another merit of PCA encoding is that there are less parameters making the estimation of the global aging trajectory more feasible. An arbitrary face $\langle \mathbf{s}, \mathbf{t} \rangle$ is thus represented as:

$$\mathbf{s} = \bar{\mathbf{s}} + \mathbf{V}_s \theta_s, \qquad \mathbf{t} = \bar{\mathbf{t}} + \mathbf{V}_t \theta_t, \tag{2}$$

where $\langle \bar{\mathbf{s}}, \bar{\mathbf{t}} \rangle$ be the mean vectors, $\langle \mathbf{V}_s, \mathbf{V}_t \rangle$ be two sets of $q$ eigenvectors for shape and texture and $\langle \theta_s, \theta_t \rangle$ be the corresponding compact representation parameters.

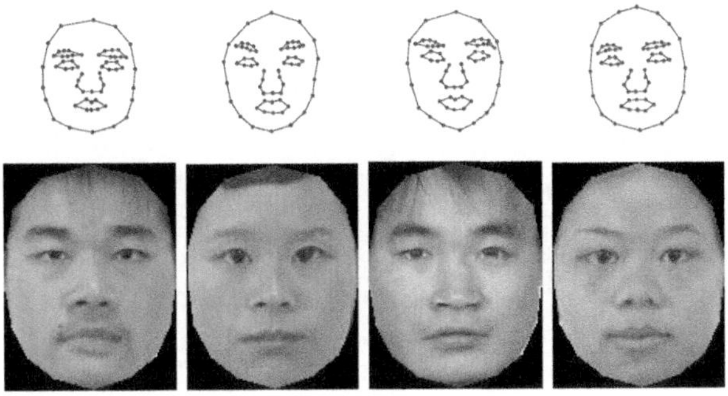

**Fig. 1.** The shape and shapeless-texture representation

Given a set of $n$ examples, $\langle \mathbf{s}_i, \mathbf{t}_i \rangle, (i = 1, \cdots, n)$, with their known age labels $age_i$, we can obtain their parameter representation $\langle \theta_{si}, \theta_{ti} \rangle$ and then construct the age trajectory in shape and texture space as the aging model. Since there is a difference in the timing and types of facial growth between men and women [15,12,9,17], we treat them respectively. Hence, in each model space, two age trajectories are defined, one for each gender. The path of the average age trajectory in the shape and texture space is estimated by using the kernel smoothing method:

$$\begin{aligned} \mathbf{g}_s(t) &= \frac{\sum_{i=1}^{n} w(age_i, t)\theta_{si}}{\sum_{i=1}^{n} w(age_i, t)}, \\ \mathbf{g}_t(t) &= \frac{\sum_{i=1}^{n} w(age_i, t)\theta_{ti}}{\sum_{i=1}^{n} w(age_i, t)}, \end{aligned} \tag{3}$$

where $t$ is the target age, $w(age_i, t)$ is the weighted function which stands for the contributions to target age from each age group. Here we choose Gaussian Kernel function

$$w(x, t) = \exp\{-\frac{\|x - t\|^2}{2\sigma^2}\}, \tag{4}$$

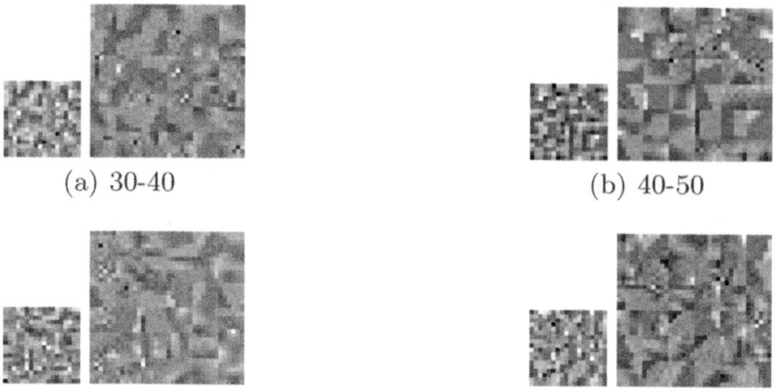

(a) 30-40 (b) 40-50 (c) 50-60 (d) 60-70

**Fig. 2.** Some atoms of the age specific coupled dictionary

where $\sigma$ is the width parameter of kernel which controls the radial scope of the function. In our experiments, the parameter $\sigma$ is the standard deviation of the input data.

Once the age trajectories have been established, for an arbitrary image $\langle \mathbf{s}, \mathbf{t} \rangle$ with age $t$, the aged shape and texture vectors at age $t^{'}$ can be generated by:

$$\begin{aligned} \mathbf{s}^{'} &= \bar{\mathbf{s}} + \mathbf{V}_s(\theta_s + \gamma_s(\mathbf{g}_s(t^{'}) - \mathbf{g}_s(t))), \\ \mathbf{t}^{'} &= \bar{\mathbf{t}} + \mathbf{V}_t(\theta_t + \gamma_t(\mathbf{g}_t(t^{'}) - \mathbf{g}_t(t))), \end{aligned} \tag{5}$$

where $\gamma_s, \gamma_t$ are the parameters to control the variations.

### 2.2 Layer 2: Sparse Representation and Face Hallucination Aging

As mentioned before, the above parametric representation and aging discards high-frequency information thus fails to capture the detailed variations due to aging. In the mid level of our model, we extend the sparse representation and face hallucination technique [36] to capture this variations as possible.

**Sparse Representation.** Considering an over-completed dictionary $\mathbf{D} \in \mathcal{R}^{d \times K}$ that contains $K(K > d)$ atoms and suppose a signal $\mathbf{x} \in \mathcal{R}^d$ can be represented as a sparse linear combination of these atoms. Then the signal $\mathbf{x}$ can be written as $\mathbf{x} \approx \mathbf{D}\alpha$, where $\alpha \in \mathcal{R}^K$ is a vector with very few nonzero entries, which is regarded as the sparse coefficients of signal $\mathbf{x}$. Finding the sparest representation leads to the following optimization problem

$$\min \|\alpha\|_0, \quad s.t. \;\; \|\mathbf{x} - \mathbf{D}\alpha\|_2 < \epsilon, \tag{6}$$

where $\|\cdot\|_0$ is the $l_0$ *quasi-norm* which counts the nonzero entries of a vector. It's a combinational optimization problem and thus it is a complicated NP-hard problem in general. Many numerical algorithms such as orthogonal matching pursuit (OMP) have been proposed to deal with this problem.

**Sparse Representation-Based Face Hallucination.** We assume that the low-resolution image is viewed as downsampled version of a high-resolution image. Given $N$ low-resolution image patch vectors $\{\mathbf{I}_l\}_i$ and the corresponding high-resolution ones $\{\mathbf{I}_h\}_i$, we obtain a new training set $\mathbf{X} = [\mathbf{x}_1, \cdots, \mathbf{x}_N]$ where $\mathbf{x}_i$ are obtained by concatenating the low-resolution and high-resolution vectors, namely $\mathbf{x}_i = [\mathbf{I}_{li}; \mathbf{I}_{hi}]$. We train a coupled over-completed dictionary $\mathbf{D} = [\mathbf{D}_l; \mathbf{D}_h]$ on $\mathbf{X}$ by solve the following optimization problem

$$\min_{\mathbf{D},\alpha_i} \sum_{i=1}^{N} \|\mathbf{x}_i - \mathbf{D}\alpha_i\|_2^2 + \lambda\|\alpha_i\|_0, \tag{7}$$

which can be solved by the K-SVD method [1], where $\lambda$ is the regularization coefficient. Given a new low-resolution patch $\mathbf{I}_l$, we can find a sparse representation with respect to $\mathbf{D}_l$ by using OMP such that

$$\mathbf{I}_l \approx \mathbf{D}_l\alpha_0, \tag{8}$$

and then the corresponding high-resolution patch can be reconstructed by

$$\mathbf{I}_h \approx \mathbf{D}_h\alpha_0. \tag{9}$$

**Face Hallucination Aging.** For each age group, we train a coupled dictionary to encode the detailed information of this age. Given a set of training images within each age range, we down-sample the images with factor 2 to obtain the low-resolution training set. Randomly sampling the original images and corresponding down-sampled images, we get more than 500, 00 patches respectively for each age range which are used to train the coupled dictionary. These age specific coupled dictionaries are deemed as the aging model. Some elements of the age specific coupled dictionaries are illustrated in Fig.2. Given an arbitrary image or the aged result from layer 1, we first downsample it and then find its sparse representation over the low-resolution dictionary of the target age using Eq. (8). Finally the corresponding aged image can be reconstructed by Eq. (9) using the same sparse representation coefficients on the corresponding high-resolution dictionary. The rational behind this is that the downsampling keep the identity while the hallucination with the age specific dictionary adding rich age-related (especially texture) information.

### 2.3 Layer 3: Facial Component and Wrinkles Aging

Although the proposed face hallucination aging can really capture some age-related details, we empirically observed that there are still some important information being ignored. Therefore we add the component and wrinkles aging layer to produce photorealistic aged faces. We divide the face skin into 6 zones (pouch_L, pouch_R, laugh_L, laugh_R, forehead, glabella) according to facial components (eyes, eyebrows, nose, mouth) [31]. Then for each age group, we also create a dictionary consisting of facial components and zone patches sampled from the training age specific images, as shown in Fig.3. The aging in this

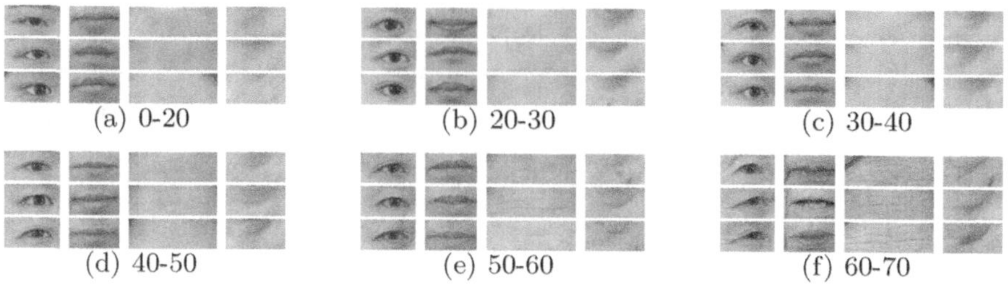

**Fig. 3.** Parts of the age specific components and zones dictionary

layer can be performed by merging or blending the appropriate element of the dictionary with the current component or zone.

As the aging variations of components include both geometry and photometry in general, we take advantage of both shape and texture information to find the most appropriate element. Local binary pattern (LBP) feature [20] and Hu moment invariants [10] are adopted to characterize the photometry and geometry information. We adopt the nearest neighbor search with the combination of histogram intersection distance and Euclidean distance of seven Hu moment invariants to find the most appropriate component element. For zone aging we only use the LBP feature for searching the most appropriate elements in the dictionary for blending.

### 2.4 Aging Animation

It's straightforward to scale our face aging method up to animation by interpolating and warping. Given a young face, we synthesize aged faces of different ages based on the proposed aging model. These aged faces are deemed as key frames, based on which we can generate a series of intermediate shapes and textures by both linear or nonlinear interpolating. The non-key frames are then obtained by warping the intermediate textures to the corresponding shapes.

## 3 Experiments: Aging Simulation and Evaluation

We collect a face database including 10,050 Chinese passport-type photos with different age range from 0 to 70 for our experiments. As the difference between actual age and appearance age is often about 3-5 years and there are less young people take part in the data collection, we divide the age range into six age groups: [0,20), [20,30), [30,40), [40,50), [50,60) and [60,70]. The shape information are represented by 61 landmarks which are annotated by hand or by AAM fitting [4]. We learned representation and aging models at each layer and performed face aging simulation using a number of young faces in the [0,20) age range. Some simulation results are shown in Fig.4.

The basic criterion to evaluate the aging synthesis lies in two aspects: identity invariant and the aging details. From Fig.4 one can see that our methods do produce realistic aged details. In order to evaluate the identity preservation,

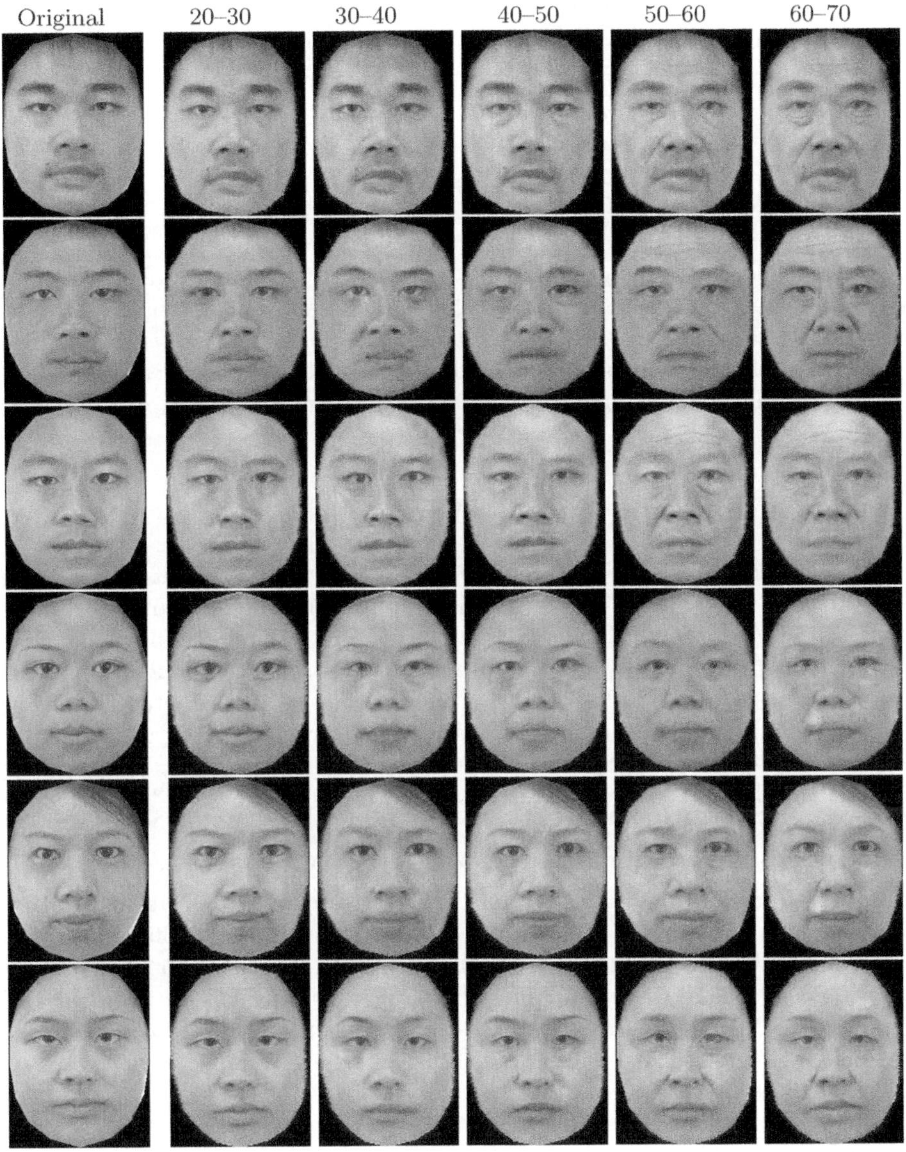


**Fig. 4.** The final aging simulation results

we conduct a face recognition experiment using the LBP feature and nearest neighbor classifier. The gallery set contains 25 young faces in $[0, 20)$ and the probe set consists of 125 aged faces. Each faces is divided into $12 \times 12$ patches and a 256-bins histogram is extracted from each patch. A face is finally represented by a $36,864$-bins histogram and matched by the nearest neighbor classifier using histogram intersection distance. The recognition results are listed in Table.1. For the first three age ranges, all the aged images can be corrected matched

**Table 1.** The recognition results

| Age Groups | Recognition Rate (%) |
|---|---|
| 20–30 | 100.00 |
| 30–40 | 100.00 |
| 40–50 | 100.00 |
| 50–60 | 92.00 |
| 60–70 | 92.00 |

to the corresponding young faces while for the latter two age ranges, two faces are mismatched to their young faces. This is reasonable since with increasing of the age, age progression method will make the appearance deformations more significant and thus increase dissimilarity. In a word, our proposed method can not only produce realistic aged details but also retain the identity of the subject well.

## 4 Conclusions and Future Work

We have presented a coarse-to-fine multi-layer face representation and aging model for age progression. The face images are first represented and aged in the statistical appearance space via age trajectory. The age-related subtle artifacts are further captured by the sparse representation-based face hallucination aging and components and wrinkles aging. Thus our method can capture both low-frequency shape and texture variations and high-frequency texture variations due to the aging. The experimental results demonstrate the effectiveness of the proposed method. In our ongoing research, we are working on the automatic person specific age estimation and trying to add richer features into the aging model such as the variant of hair, the person specific factors, etc.

**Acknowledgements.** This research is partially supported by National Natural Science Funds of China (No.60803024, No.60970098 and 60903136), Specialized Research Fund for the Doctoral Program of Higher Education (No.200805331107 and No.20090162110055), Fundamental Research Funds for the Central Universities (No.201021200062), Open Project Program of the State Key Lab of CAD&CG, Zhejiang University (No.A0911 and No.A1011).

## References

1. Aharon, M., Elad, M., Bruckstein, A.: K-SVD: An algorithm for designing over-complete dictionaries for sparse representation. IEEE Transactions on Signal Processing 54(11), 4311–4322
2. Boissieux, L., Kiss, G., Thalmann, N.M., Kalra, P.: Simulation of skin aging and wrinkles with cosmetics insight. In: proceedings of the EUROGRAPHICS Workshop, pp. 15–27 (2000)
3. Burt, D.M., Perrett, D.I.: Perception of age in adult caucasian male faces: Computer graphic manipulation of shape and color information. Proceedings of the Royal Society of London B 259, 137–143 (1995)

4. Cootes, T., Taylor, C.: Statistical models of appearance for computer vision. Technical Report, The University of Manchester School of Medicine (2004)
5. Dayan, N.: Skin aging handbook: An integrated approach to biochemistry and product development. Andrew William Press (2008)
6. Fu, Y., Guo, G., Huang, T.: Age synthesis and estimation via faces: A survey. IEEE Transactions on Pattern Analysis and Machine Intelligence 32(11), 1955–1976 (2010)
7. Fu, Y., Zheng, N.: M-face: An appearance-based photorealistic model for multiple facial attributes rendering. IEEE Transactions on Circuits and Systems for Video Technology 16(7), 830–842 (2006)
8. Golovinskiy, A., Matusik, W., Pfister, H., Rusinkiewicz, S., Funkhouser, T.: A statistical model for synthesis of detailed facial geometry. In: ACM SIGGRAPH, pp. 1025–1034 (2006)
9. Scandrett née Hill, C., Solomon, C., Gibson, S.: A person-specific, rigorous aging model of the human face. Pattern Recognition Letters 27(15), 1776–1787 (2006)
10. Hu, M.K.: Visual pattern recognition by moment invariants. IRE Transactions on Information Theory 8(2), 179–187 (2002)
11. Hubball, D., Chen, M., Grant, P.W.: Image-based aging using evolutionary computing. In: EUROGRAPHICS, Computer Graphics Forum, vol. 27, pp. 607–616 (2008)
12. Hutton, T.J., Buxton, B.F., Hammond, P., Potts, H.W.W.: Estimating average growth trajectories in shape-space using kernel smoothing. IEEE Transactions on Medical Imaging 22(6), 747–753 (2003)
13. Jiang, F.Y., Wang, Y.H.: Facial aging simulation based on super-resolution in tenson space. In: International Conference on Image Processing, pp. 1648–1651 (2008)
14. Lanitis, A.: Comparative evaluation of automatic age-progression methodologies. EURASIP Journal on Advances in Signal Processing 2008, 1–10 (2008)
15. Lanitis, A., Taylor, C.J., Cootes, T.F.: Toward automatic simulation of aging effects on face images. IEEE Transactions on Pattern Analysis and Machine Intelligence 24(4), 422–455
16. Lee, W.S., Wu, Y., Thalmann, N.M.: Cloneing and aging in a vr family. In: IEEE Conference on Virtual Reality, pp. 61–68 (1999)
17. Liang, Y.X., Li, C.R., Yue, H.Q., Luo, Y.Y.: Age simulation in young face images. In: International Conference on Bioinformatics and Biomedical Engineering, pp. 494–497 (2007)
18. Ling, H., Soatto, S., Ramanathan, N., Jacobs, D.W.: Study of face recognition as people age. In: IEEE 11th International Conference on Computer Vision, pp. 1–8 (2007)
19. Liu, C., Shum, H., Freeman, W.: Face hallucination: Theory and practice. International Journal of Computer Vision 75(1), 115–134 (2007)
20. Ojala, T., pietikainen, M., Maenpaa, T.: Multiresolution gray-scale and rotation invariant texture classification with local binary patterns. IEEE Transactions on Pattern Analysis and Machine Intelligence 24(7), 971–987 (2002)
21. O'Toole, Price, T., Vetter, T., Barlett, J.C., Blanz, V.: 3D shape and 2D surface textures of human faces: The role of averages in attractiveness and age. Image and Vision Computing 18(1), 9–19 (1999)
22. O'Toole, Vetter, T., Volz, H., Salter, E.: Three-dimensional caricatures of human heads: Distinctiveness and the perception of facial age. Perception 26, 719–732 (1997)
23. Park, U., Tong, Y., Jain, A.: Age-invariant face recognition. IEEE Transactions on Pattern Analysis and Machine Intelligence 32(5), 947–954 (2010)

24. Pittenger, J.B., Shaw, R.E., Mark, L.S.: Perceptual information for the age level of faces as a higher order invariant of growth. Journal of Experimental Psychology: Human Perception and Performance 5(3), 478–493 (1979)
25. Ramanathan, N., Chellappa, R., Biswas, S.: Modeling age progression in young faces. In: IEEE Conference on Computer Vision and Pattern Recognition, pp. 387–394 (2006)
26. Ramanathan, N., Chellappa, R., Biswas, S.: Modeling shape and textural variations in aging faces. In: 8th IEEE International Conference on Automatric Face and Gesture Recognition, pp. 1–8 (2008)
27. Ramanathan, N., Chellappa, R., Biswas, S.: Age progression in human faces: A survey. Journal of Visual Languages and Computing 15, 3349–3361 (2009)
28. Scherbaum, K., Sunkel, M., Seidel, H.P., Blanz, V.: Prediction of individual non-linear aging trajectories of faces. In: EUROGRAPHICS, Computer Graphics Forum, vol. 26 (2007)
29. Singh, R., Vatsa, M., Noore, A., Singh, S.K.: Age transformation for improving face recognition. In: Proceedings of the 2nd international conference on Pattern recognition and machine intelligence, pp. 576–583 (2007)
30. Suo, J.L., Min, F., Zhu, S.C., Shan, S.G., Chen, X.L.: A multi-resolution dynamic model for face aging simulation. In: IEEE Conference on Computer Vision and Pattern Recognition, pp. 1–8 (2007)
31. Suo, J.L., Zhu, S.C., Chen, X.L.: A compositional and dynamic model for face aging. IEEE Transactions on Pattern Analysis and Machine Intelligence 32, 358–401 (2010)
32. Tiddeman, B., Burt, D.M., Perrett, D.I.: Prototyping and transforming facial textures for perception research. IEEE Computer Graphics and Applications 21(5), 42–50 (2001)
33. Todd, J.T., Mark, L.S., Shaw, R.E., Pittenger, J.B.: The perception of human growth. Scientific American 242(2), 132–144 (1980)
34. Wang, J.N., Ling, C.J.: Artificial aging of faces by support vector machines. In: Advances in Artifical Intelligence, pp. 499–503 (2006)
35. Wu, Y., Kalra, P., Moccozet, L., Thalmann, N.: Simulating wrinkles and skin aging. The Visual Computer 15(4), 183–198 (1999)
36. Yang, J., Tang, H., Ma, Y., Huang, T.: Face hallucination via sparse coding. In: 15th IEEE International Conference on Image Processing, pp. 1264–1267. IEEE, New York (2008)

# Particle-Based Fracture Simulation on the GPU

Jiangfan Ning, Huaxun Xu, Liang Zeng, and Sikun Li

School of Computer Science, National University of Defense Technology,
410073 Changsha, Hunan, China
jiangfanning@gmail.com
xxhhxx@163.com
{liangzeng,lisikun}@263.net.cn

**Abstract.** In this paper, a particle-based framework is presented to simulate the fracture phenomenon in computer graphics field. First, the object is represented as discrete particles, and then we introduce the Extend Discrete Element Method (EDEM) simulation to describe the interactions between neighbouring particles based on the material mechanics analysis. To process the fracture, a reverse idea to traditional method is used to cooperate with auxiliary cone algorithm, which called anti-fracture mechanism. The physical computation is executed on the GPU with CUDA and a uniform grid data structure is used in order to search the neighbouring element effectively. Experiment results demonstrate the feasibility and effectiveness of our method.

**Keywords:** EDEM, fracture, anti-fracture mechanism, CUDA.

## 1 Introduction

With the rapid development of graphics hardware, people for virtual simulation, 3D games and movies in the visual effects made increasing demands. Fracture and explosion simulation results are directly affecting people's perception of the realism. To get complete and accurate simulation results, we must construct dynamic simulation model for object under impact according to different shapes and material properties, so as to simulate the complex physical process and get a good sense of reality. However, this method necessarily involves sophisticated and complex mesh model and needs to solve Partial Differential Equations. The large computational overhead, even using the current hardware, is still difficult to achieve real-time requirements for military simulation and 3D game.

In this paper, we present a real-time approach to simulate fracture caused by the collision between objects. Our approach is based on the particles. Firstly, we discretize the object into a series of particles, and then we use the Extend Discrete Element Method to simulate the interaction between the particles. To be different from the traditional fracture method, we presented a novel reverse thinking, named anti-fracture mechanism. It's based on the auxiliary cone algorithm which can easily determine the fracture area. Our algorithm has been implemented on the GPU using

Z. Pan et al. (Eds.): Transactions on Edutainment VI, LNCS 6758, pp. 193–205, 2011.

CUDA, the results show that our approach can simulate fracture phenomena much faster than the traditional mesh-based method or former meshless method on CPU [1].

To summarize, the major contributions of this paper are:

- Introduce the EDEM into fracture simulation for interaction between particle elements to describe the material properties.
- Present the auxiliary cone algorithm to determine the affected area by fracture.
- Present an anti-fracture mechanism to form debris after fracture.
- Use the uniform grid data structure for searching the neighbouring particles during the EDEM simulation.
- Prove the feasibility and effectiveness of implementing the particle-based fracture simulation algorithm on the GPU.

## 2 Related Work

There is a large number of excellent research works about fracture phenomenon in graphics. Basically, they can be divided into two categories: mesh-based simulation and meshless simulation. The former studies the real physical process of fracture, and then establishes the equations of motion to animate the process of fracture based on the mesh of the object. Taking account of avoiding the complex operation of topological changes for mesh, the latter uses meshless or particle-based methods to animate fracture phenomenon.

Mesh-based methods are discussed as follows. Terzopoulos [2] has done pioneering work to non-elastic deformation and fracture phenomenon in the field of computer graphics. He achieved a relatively simple fracture effect by introducing a simple fracturing mechanism of measuring the instantaneous deformation. Norton [3] used the spring-mass model to model the object that could be broken for the first time, and a fairly complete consideration of the collision detection between fragments was implemented to realize the ceramic teapot fracturing animation. O'Brien etc. [4] took the finite element model to analyze the stress and strain, and then took this as the fracture criterion. The simulation result is quite realistic while the complex finite element analysis has tremendous computational overhead, so his method couldn't be applied to the areas of real-time requirements. Parker etc. [5] inherited the research results of O'Brien and developed a new physical engine named DMM using simplified finite element analysis (FEA) calculation model, and this work has successfully been integrated into some popular game platforms. Bao etc. [6] also used FEA method, and his method is to discretize object into rigid form, and then solved the problem of rigid material fracture. However, this method also faces the problem of tremendous computational cost. Su etc. [7] expanded Bao's work by introducing the energy and momentum conservation with joining the collision center-based pre-process mechanism, reduced the computational cost of simulation greatly.

The main meshless simulation studies are listed as below: Desbrun and Cani [8] introduced meshless method into the graphics field first of all. They used a particle system coated with a smooth iso-surface for simulating soft inelastic material. Muller etc. [9] presented a method for modeling and simulating elastic, plastic, and melting volumetric objects based on the computation of the discrete displacement field using the Moving Least Squares procedure. And then they [10] presented a geometrically method to simulate deformable point-based objects. Pauly etc. [11] presented a meshless animation framework for elastic and plastic materials that fracture, using highly dynamic surface and volume sampling method. Guo and Qin [12] combined meshless method with modal analysis framework and provided real-time deformation of volumetric objects. Bell etc. [13] presented an effective method for granular material simulation based on particles using distinct element method (DEM).

There are also some noticeable researches working about physically-based simulation on GPU. Green [14] implemented a particle system on GPU with CUDA. Hirada [15] presented a rigid body simulation method using GPU. Georgii [16] explained how to implemente a spring-mass system with GPU. Weiguo Liu [17] used GPU to accelerate molecular dynamics simulations.

# 3 Modeling

In our system, the object is represented as particles, and then we model the interaction between particles using EDEM simulation. We are motivated in this choice by convenient implementation on the GPU and natural of ideal material structure.

## 3.1 Shape Representation

In our method, we model the object as a set of particles that are spheres of identical size, not polygons. Indeed, the polygons represent the shape more precisely than the particles, but the collision detections between polygons are very complex and heavy burden. And for complex shapes particles just have small number of data, compared to polygons which have large number of data even for simple shapes. Thus, it is much efficient to represent complicated shapes by particles. The particles can also represent object precisely if the number of particles is big enough in theory. In computer graphics, we are committed to the pursuit of visual effects, so we do not need to maintain a large number of particles as in material physical analysis.

Firstly, we discretize the space around the object by defining a 3D grid that encloses it, and then assign one particle for each voxel inside the object. By this way, we can represent the object shape as particles.

## 3.2 Extended Discrete Element Method

Distinct element method (DEM) is a discrete numerical method proposed by American scholar Cundall in 1971, and also known as discrete element method. In order to unify, we call it discrete element method in the following. In the discrete element method, because the object has been assumed to be a collection of discrete blocks, adjacent elements can either be contact or be separated. There are no deformation compatibility constraints between elements, so the elements only need to satisfy the equilibrium equation and constitutive equation. Meguro and Hakuno [18] presented Extended Discrete Element Method based on the DEM model to simulation the destruction and collapse of reinforced concrete. Their method could not only deal with the continuous conditions and constitutive relation before fracture, but also the fracture discontinuities problems after fracture of materials.

The general process of Discrete element method for solving problems is given as below: First, discretize the problem space for the discrete element cell array, and then connect the two neighbouring elements using reasonable connection based on the actual problems; as a basic variable, relative displacement between the elements is made up of the normal component and the tangential component, and they can be obtained from the relations of the force and relative displacement between the two neighbour elements; compute the resultant force on the element, according to Newton's second law of motion the acceleration of element can be obtained; and then we can get the velocity and displacement through its time integral. So far we could obtain the velocity, acceleration, angular velocity, linear displacement, rotation and any other physical quantities of all the elements.

### 3.3 EDEM Simulation

Generally, the simulated objects in DEM are discretized as polygonal blocks. The collision detection system for polygonal blocks is too complicated, so we use the EDEM method, which uses the spherical blocks instead of polygonal blocks. When the number of spherical blocks is big enough, we can get better approximate to the behaviour of simulated objects. And in our system, the object shape is represented by a series of particles, can be directly simulated by EDEM.

In our EDEM system, the motion of each element is decided by the resultant force and moment acted on them, expressed as translation and rotation around the centre block. Consider an element subject to changes of force $F$ resulting in motion, Newton's second law of motion can be expressed as:

$$\frac{\partial^2 u}{\partial t^2} = \frac{F}{m} \; . \tag{1}$$

where, $m$ is the mass of the element.

Using the central difference scheme to the left side of the above equation, we can obtain

$$\frac{\partial^2 u}{\partial t^2} = \frac{\dot{u}(t+\Delta t/2) - \dot{u}(t-\Delta t/2)}{\Delta t} \; . \tag{2}$$

Substituting the (1) and (2), we can get

$$\dot{u}(t+\Delta t/2) = \dot{u}(t-\Delta t/2) + \frac{F(t)}{m}\Delta t \; . \tag{3}$$

The velocity in half time step can be expressed as the displacement in the above equation:

$$u(t+\Delta t) = u(t) + \dot{u}(t+\Delta t/2)\Delta t \; . \tag{4}$$

The force is in dependence on displacement, so the calculation of force and displacement must be in the same time step simultaneously.

For element effected by multiple forces, the velocity equation is:

$$\dot{u}(t+\Delta t/2)=\dot{u}(t-\Delta t/2)+\frac{\sum F(t)}{m}\Delta t \ . \tag{5}$$

$$\dot{\theta}(t+\Delta t/2)=\dot{\theta}(t-\Delta t/2)+\frac{\sum M(t)}{I}\Delta t \ . \tag{6}$$

where $I$ is the moment of inertia of element, $M$ is the torque, $\dot{\theta}$ is angular velocity to the centroid.
Similarly, we can get the displacement and rotation equation:

$$u(t+\Delta t)=u(t)+\dot{u}(t+\Delta t/2)\Delta t \ . \tag{7}$$

$$\theta(t+\Delta t)=\theta(t)+\dot{\theta}(t+\Delta t/2)\Delta t \ . \tag{8}$$

The new location that every iteration produced will lead to new contact force. Resultant force and resultant moment produce line and angular acceleration, velocity and displacement may be obtained by integration throughout the time step increment, the loop will continue until the balance state or destruction state.

In the above equation of motion, $F$ is the resultant force of element in the system. The key to solve above kinematic equation is to establish force-displacement relationship of the element.

Considering two adjacent particle element, they are connected by the axial spring. In order to response to the impact of structural damping, we set a viscous damper in parallel with the spring. Fig.1 is the diagram to demonstrate the relation for the neighbouring elements.

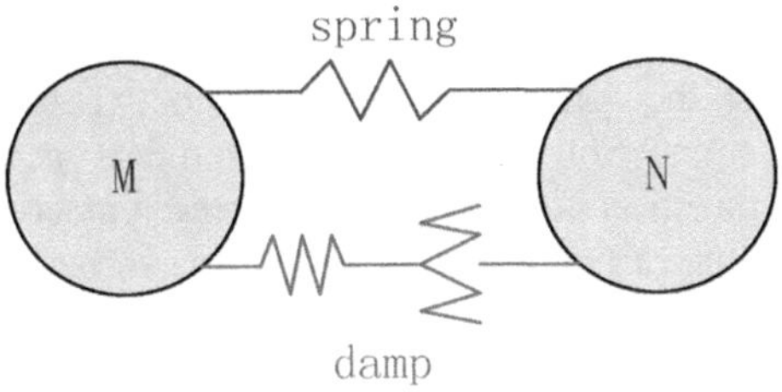


**Fig. 1.** The interaction force between neighbouring elements in EDEM

For each particle element,

$$F=\sum F_{spring}+\sum F_{damp}+mg \ . \tag{9}$$

$F_{spring}$ can be obtained by Hooke's law

$$F_{spring}=-k_{sping}\Delta x_{spring} \ . \tag{10}$$

In which, $k_{sping}$ is the spring constant, $\Delta x_{spring}$ is the change of relative position with respect to the initial state.

$F_{damp}$ is made up of the normal component and the tangential component, and the normal damp force is

$$F^n_{damp} = -k^n_{damp} \Delta x^n - \eta^n v^n \ . \tag{11}$$

While the tangential damp force is

$$F^t_{damp} = -\eta^t v^t \ . \tag{12}$$

Where, $\eta$ is damp constant, $v^n$ and $v^t$ are the normal and the tangential relative velocity of the two neighbouring particle elements respectively.

Elastic coefficient and damping coefficient are related to the material that composes the object, which can be set according to the actual.

Iteration time step also need to be set, if $\Delta t$ is not properly selected, we cannot get a stable solution. According to reference, we set

$$\Delta t \leq 2C\sqrt{m/k} \ . \tag{13}$$

Where, $C$ is constant and generally value of 0.1.

## 4 Anti-fracture Mechanism

The basic idea of fracture for traditional method is to build the grid model of the object first, and then create a logical connection between the grids, when the system is subject to external shocks; compute the connected relationship changes between the elements, and re-assess the connected relationship between elements. Set a threshold value to limit the connection between the elements according to the material constitutive. If the connection is destructed under the impact of the external force, it is deemed that there occurs a fracture phenomenon. In essence, this is a research method from the macro world to the micro world. Advantage of this method is that it is very intuitive and in line with people's perception of the law of natural phenomena. But this method requires well understanding of object's material properties and establishing accurate material physical model for the object. To get accurate simulation results it needs costly computing resources.

With contrast to this method, we propose a reverse fracture mechanism which from the micro to the macro. Our method is based on the idea of fuzzy clustering, which discretize objects into tiny particles in the area affected by impact firstly, then calculate the force, acceleration, velocity and position of each element. Estimate the connection between particles, re-compound some certain particles, and form the debris in macroscopic world. Finally, integrate the particle properties belonging to the same debris on the problem domain, and the motion law of the debris can be derived.

### 4.1 Auxiliary Cone Algorithm

A key of the fracturing algorithm is to determine the areas of cracks and fractures. Accurate simulation results require time-consuming physical computation, and this will lead to real-time demands are not met. Therefore, we present a new auxiliary cone algorithm:

For simplicity, we take a board hit by a ball for example to illustrate our idea. Taking a ball with certain mass into account, the faster the ball impacts the board, the more slowly the fragments and the debris fly faster, and the effected range should be smaller. Determine a distance as the tallness according to the velocity of the ball, and then take the initial position of the ball as the vertex of the cone. The greater impact velocity will result in greater distance and smaller cone vertex angle. So we can obtain the vertex angle and the highness of the cone.

Once the cone is generated, the bottom of the cone will form a circular area on the surface of the board. All particles in this area will obtain early speed and be separated. With the physical properties of the board and velocity of the ball, we can determine the radius of the crack area and fracture area.

According to the theory of fracture mechanics, cracks in samples under load can be divided into three types in accordance with its expansion in different forms: open-type crack, tear-type crack, and slide-type crack. These three kinds of cracks are also called the I, II, III type fracture type. I type crack is the most common type in everyday life, so the fracture criteria of this paper is mainly concerned with I type crack.

For I type crack, the stress intensity factor is

$$K_I = \lim_{r \to 0} \left[ \sqrt{2\pi r} \left( \sigma_y \right)_{\theta=0} \right] . \tag{14}$$

After computing the limit, $K_I = \sigma\sqrt{\pi a}$ , which, $\sigma$ is the average tensile stress, that related to physical properties of the material and the impact velocity of the ball; $a$ is equal to the half of the crack length.

The stress intensity factor reflects the stress field intensity near the crack tip. When the stress field intensity increases to a certain value, even if no more stress, cracks will expand rapidly which leads to the brittle fracture of material or structural damage. The limiting value $K$ is called the fracture toughness of the material, i.e. $K_{Ic}$. The fracture criterion of target object is

$$K_I \geq K_{Ic} . \tag{15}$$

Where, $K_{Ic}$ is the intrinsic properties of the material itself, so that $K_I = K_{Ic}$, obtained the largest allowed crack length is $a_c = \dfrac{K_{Ic}^2}{\pi\sigma^2}$ .

Suppose the ideal material for the rigid body, namely the complete isotropic brittle material, the maximum permissible crack length should be the radius of the fracturing area, then

$$fracture_{range} = a_c . \tag{16}$$

That is the radius of the cone bottom.

Let $v_m$ be the muzzle velocity of the ball, $\Delta t$ is the time step, then the tallness of the cone can be calculated:

$$h_{cone} = v_m \Delta t \ . \tag{17}$$

Have the radius of the cone bottom and the tallness, the auxiliary cone is determined.

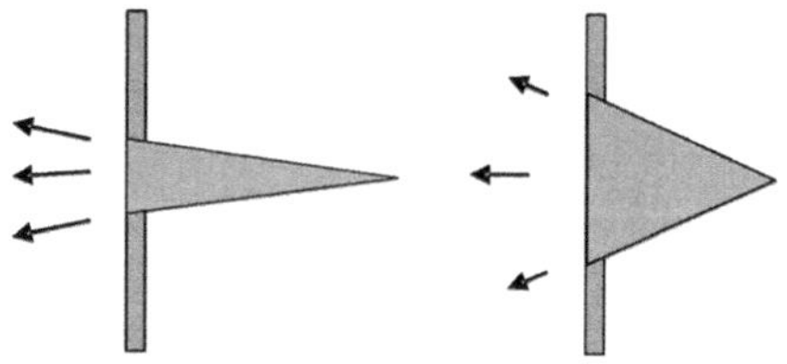

**Fig. 2.** Auxiliary cone algorithm

Fig.2 shows our idea.

### 4.2 Particle Elements Clustering

By now, we can obtain the object element and its corresponding particle velocity, position and other physical attributes during the simulation process. The following step is to cluster some certain particle elements in the domain space and reconstruct the debris that produced during the impact process.

Firstly, we define the two states between neighbouring elements:

- State1: Normal state. The equilibrium length of spring that connect the neighbouring elements is set to be $r_0$, according to the physical properties of the material itself, the maximum length that spring can be stretched or compressed is set to be $\Delta r$, so when the length of the spring (that is, the relative displacement between the particle elements) is ranged between $r_0 \pm \Delta r$, the connecting spring between the particle elements can work normally, we consider the connection between neighbouring particles as in normal state.
- State2: Discrete state. When the relative displacement between neighbouring particles is greater than $r_0 + \Delta r$, the spring no longer works, and with the relative distance increases, the force between particles gradually reduced to 0. Here we consider that the neighbouring elements as in discrete state.

In the simulation, the space is subdivided into uniform grid and the grid size is equal to the diameter of element. For each element, only search the adjoining 26 elements to perform the EDEM simulation. So the springs only exist between every element and its 26 adjoining elements. During each time step, estimate the state for every element. The elements in normal state are combined to form new big debris. With the elements in discrete state will be separated and form small debris or dust.

### 4.3 Debris and Motion

Based on above clustering method, the new forming elements will become the debris generated during simulation. After the collision detection and collision handling, they will be rendered in the rendering stage.

## 5 Data Structure and Algorithm Implementation on GPU

We implement our particle-based EDEM simulation system in CUDA using a uniform grid data structure presented by Simon Green [14]. We define a uniform grid to cover the computational domain. There are two benefits for uniform grid used in our EDEM simulations:

- The construction cost is very low.
- It is easy to access the memory for the voxel to a particle belongs.

The disadvantage is that the size of memory that is used for the grid may be large. But the latest GPU often has enough video memory, so the use of uniform grid is possible.

### 5.1 Data Structure

The key insight is to find the neighbouring particles of a given particle. A uniform grid could be the simplest spatial subdivision method. We subdivide the simulation space into a grid of uniformly size cells, and the cell size is the same to the size of the elements. Each particle is assigned to a certain grid cell according to its centre and then we store the particle index in the cell. The uniform grid data structure is generated in every time step. This method is so simple that it is possible to perform incremental updates on the GPU.

### 5.2 Implementation

We calculate the interaction between particles on GPU using the uniform grid above. Our GPU implementation algorithm is shown below:

```
  EDEM GPU Program
  1. Initialize the particle's status; set simulation
parameters;
  2. Load data into GPU device memory and launch the
kernel;
  3.   For all iteration steps do
  4.     Apply spring force, damp force and gravity force
to each particle;
  5.       Update velocity for each particle;
  6.       Update displacement for each particle;
  7.       Update each particle's position;
  8.       Do collision detection and collision response;
  9.        Compute new position for each particle;
  10.     End for
  11. Put statistics of each time step into the device
memory;
  12. Output and render
```

In practice, we use the atomic operation to construct the grid. Profiting from the awesome performance of modern GPU, multiple threads to update the same value in global memory simultaneously without conflicts is possible by atomic operation. We define two arrays in global memory: *gridNumbers* and *gridCells*. The *gridNumbers* stores the number of particles in each cell thus far and the initialized value is zero. The *gridCells* stores the particle indices for each cell, and has room for a certain maximum number of particles per cell.

Then we use the "*updateGrid*" kernel function to update the grid structure by which runs with one thread per particle. Perform calculation on each particle to decide which grid cell it is in. The *atomicAdd* function is used to atomically increment the cell counter with this location. By scattered global write, it then writes its index into the grid array at the correct position.

### 5.3 Rendering

As mentioned in section 3.1, our model is represented as a set of particles that are spheres of identical size. After the simulation, we render a triangle for each element in the EDEM.

The specific process is as follow:

```
  1. Calculate the center of mass for each triangle of
the object model.
  2. Store the offset of the vertex of triangle to the
center of mass.
  3. Put one particle at the center of mass.
  4. After EDEM simulation, calculate the new vertex
position based on the new position of center of mass and
the offset.
  5. Render triangles using the calculated new vertex
position.
```

## 6 Experiments and Results

We implement our algorithm on a GPU with nVidia GeForce 9800 graphics card (512MB) and a Intel(R) Core(TM)2 CPU with 1.87 GHz (2048MB RAM). The development environment is Visual C++.net 2008 and Microsoft Windows XP SP2.

### 6.1 Bunny

Fig.3 shows a bunny rabbit modeled with 16301 particles. Fig.3(a) illustrates how a bunny rabbit is represented by particles. Fig.3(b) demonstrates the fracture process of bunny by discrete particles. Fig.3(c) shows the rendering results. For the simulation in Fig.3(b), the performance is more than 60 and the rendering performance in Fig.3(c) is up to 40 fps. Fig.3(d) demonstrates the stresses created by forces acting on the interior cause the bunny to fracture and explode.

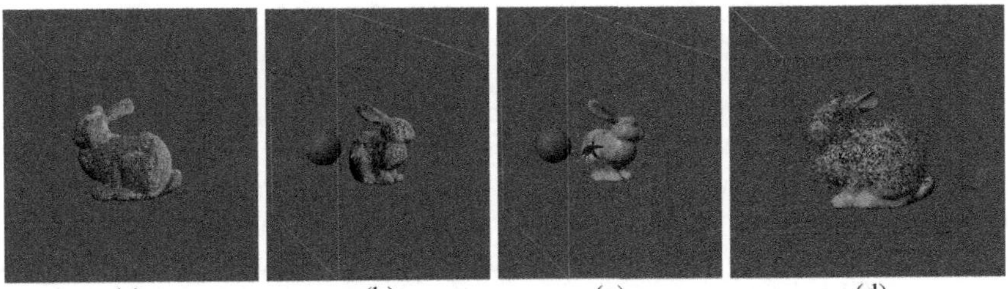

(a) (b) (c) (d)

**Fig. 3.** Fracture of bunny

## 6.2 Concrete Wall

In order to validate our algorithm and compare with the previous method, we simulate the fracture process of a concrete wall hit by a steel ball. Fig.4 is the simulation results comparisons chart, Fig.4(a)-Fig.4(b) is the result of literature [6], Fig.4(c)-Fig.4(d) is the result of literature [1] and Fig.4(e)-Fig.4(f) is our result. The literature [6] is based on finite element method and the efficiency is about 40 seconds/frame. The literature [1] used a particle-based method which is similar to us and the performance is up to 8.8 fps. Our concrete wall in Fig.4(e)-Fig.4(f) consists of about 3000 particles during simulation and the rendering performance of our system is more than 200 fps, while the effect of our realization is consistent with realistic. In Fig.4(a)-Fig.4(f), there is only one concrete wall, and in order to verify system performance we put four concrete walls side by side in Fig.4(g)-Fig.4(h). In this scene, we use about 12000 particles during simulation. Even so, the frame rate in Fig.4(g)-Fig.4(h) is still more than 30 fps. The experimental results show that our simulation framework is stable and efficient.

(a) (b) (c) (d)

(e) (f) (g) (h)

**Fig. 4.** Concrete wall fracture result comparison

## 7 Conclusion and Discussion

We implemented our particle-based fracture simulation algorithm on GPU based upon EDEM. The experiment results show that our approach is very feasible and effective. Because of the relative accurate physical model, the accuracy of our simulation is satisfactory and the result has a strong sense of reality. Profiting from the powerful computational capability of GPU, the simulation can meet the real-time requirement.

During our GPU implementation, we use the uniform grid data structure. However, for large computational problems, a uniform grid is obviously not the best choice. Generally, object does not distribute uniformly in the simulation domain. So there are many voxels containing no particles, this will lead to a waste of video memory. To solve this problem, we need to construct a more effective data structure. A hierarchical grid data structure may be a substituted choice.

**Acknowledgments.** This work is supported by the National Basic Research Program (No. 2009CB723803) and the National Science Foundation Program (No. 60873120) of China. We would like to thank the anonymous reviewers for their careful and valuable comments.

## References

1. Imagire, T., Johan, H., Nishita, T.: A Fast Method for Simulating Destruction and the Generated Dust and Debris. The Visual Computer 25, 719–727 (2009)
2. Terzopoulos, D., Fleischer, K.: Modeling Inelastic Deformation: Viscoelasticity, Plasticity, Fracture. In: Proceedings of Computer Graphics (SIGGRAPH 1988), pp. 269–278 (1988)
3. Norton, A., Turk, G., Bacon, B., Gerth, J., Sweeney, P.: Animation of Fracture by Physical Modeling. The Visual Computer 7(4), 210–219 (1991)
4. O'Brien, J., Hodgins, J.: Graphical Modeling and Animation of Brittle Fracture. In: Proceedings of the 26th Annual Conference on Computer Graphics and Interactive Techniques, pp. 137–146. ACM, New York (1999)
5. Eric, G., O'Brien, J.F.: Real-Time Deformation and Fracture in a Game Environment. In: Proceedings of the 2009 ACM SIGGRAPH / Eurographics Symposium on Computer Animation. ACM, New York (2009)
6. Bao, Z., Hong, J.M., Teran, J.: Fracturing Rigid Materials. IEEE Transactions on Visualization and Computer Graphics, 370–378 (2007)
7. Su, J., Schroeder, C., Fedkiw, R.: Energy Stability and Fracture for Frame Rate Rigid Body Simulations. In: Proceedings of the 2009 ACM SIGGRAPH / Eurographics Symposium on Computer Animation, pp.155–164. ACM, Louisiana (2009)
8. Desbrun, M., Cani, M.P.: Animating Soft Substances with Implicit Surfaces. In: Proceedings of SIGGRAPH 1995, pp. 287–290 (1995)
9. Muller, M., Keiser, R., Nealen, A.: Point-based Animation of Elastic, Plastic and Melting Objects. In: Proceedings of ACM Siggraph/Eurographics Symposium on Computer Animation, pp. 141–151. Eurographics Association, Grenoble (2004)
10. Muller, M., Heidelberger, B., Teschner, M.: Meshless Deformations Based on Shape Matching. ACM Trans. Graph. 24(3), 471–478 (2005)
11. Pauly, M., Keiser, R., Adams, B.: Meshless Animation of Fracturing Solids. ACM Trans. Graph. 24(3), 957–964 (2005)

12. Guo, X., Qin, H.: Real-time Meshless Deformation. Comp. Animat. Virt. World 16(3-4), 189–200 (2005)
13. Bell, N., Yu, Y., Mucha, P.: Particle-based Simulation of Granular Materials. In: Proceedings of the 2005 ACM SIGGRAPH/Eurographics Symposium on Computer Animation, pp. 77–86. ACM, New York (2005)
14. Green, S.: CUDA Particles. nVidia CUDA SDK Whitepaper (2008)
15. Harada, T.: The Grid: Real-time Rigid Body Simulation on GPUs. GPU Gem 3 (2008)
16. Georgii, J., Westermann, R.: Mass-spring System on the GPU. Simulation Modelling Practice and Theory 13, 693–702 (2005)
17. Liu, W., Schmidt, B., Voss, G., Muller-Wittig, W.: Accelerating Molecular Dynamics Simulations Using Graphics Processing Units with CUDA. Computer Physics Communications 179, 634–641 (2008)
18. Meguro, K., Hakuno, M.: Fracture Analyses of Concrete Structures by the Modified Distinct Element Method. Structural Eng./Earthquake Eng. JSCE 6, 283–294 (1989)

# Mining Subsidence Prediction Based on 3D Stratigraphic Model and Visualization

Ruisheng Jia, Yanjun Peng, and Hongmei Sun

College of Information Science and Engineering,
Shandong University of Science and Technology,Qingdao,China
jrs716@163.com, yjpeng@sdust.edu.cn, shm0221@163.com

**Abstract.** 3D phenomenon involved in mining subsidence was Classified, summarized and aggregated, established the hierarchical structure that describing the geologic phenomena and engineering phenomena of stratum structure. Proposed a 3D stratigraphic model that mixed Multi-DEM with Tetrahedral Network. The model uses Multi-DEM to build layered surface of the earth's surface and geology, and uses TEN to makeup inter layer geological mass. This is in favor of exactly expressing the surface information, and it is benefit to engineers and technicians to check the geological condition in the stratum, also it provides detailed geological mining conditions for the mining subsidence prediction research and accurately establishes prediction model. Engineering sample shows that the predicted results of the system is more close to the measured values.

**Keywords:** mining subsidence prediction; 3D stratigraphic model; DEMs-TEN model; 3D visualization.

## 1 Introduction

Coal which is the main energy in China plays an important role in the development of the national economy. However, coal mining resources causes a lot of problems such as leading to the movement and deformation of surface, destroying the buildings and other facilities on the surface, and bringing about the collapse and damage of land. The paper aims to build the 3D stratigraphic model and the visualization algorithm model which take into consideration the relevant geological mining conditions such as overburden strata structure and mining methods, and explore the approaches of combination of the 3D geological modeling and the subsidence prediction theory according to the 3D stratigraphic modeling and the visualization technology. So it provides analysis technology for the subtle study of movement and deformation of surface.Although many scholars in geography, mapping, compute science and other areas carried out a lot of studies on the theory and method of 3D GMS and made a lot of creative achievements,such as Simon W. Houlding [1],Dennis J. Burford [2], Cyril Galera [3],Hengxing Lan [4],Alex Smirnoff [5],Andrew Crooks [6],and so on. but this work is still in the theoretical research stage as a whole. So far, a whole 3D GMS hasn't been developed in the world. It makes the value of 3D original data in mining

Z. Pan et al. (Eds.): Transactions on Edutainment VI, LNCS 6758, pp. 206–215, 2011.

geology, petroleum geology, meteorology, ocean and many other fields not used fully and restricts severely the effective expression and visualization process of 3D space information. In addition, there are similar problems in the mining subsidence field. Therefore, it is very necessary to further study on the subject that GMS and the 3D visualization technology are used in mining subsidence prediction.

## 2 Mining Subsidence Prediction Model

The Random Medium Theory is brought in mining subsidence calculation by Polish scholar Lee's Wanny in the 1950s, and then developed into Probability Integral Method by Chinese academician Baochen Liu, Guohua Liao and so on, and be widely used in China's coal mining subsidence prediction area. This method takes the moving process of rock strata and surface caused by mining as a random process, and takes the rock strata as the particle body of random medium, the probability distribution model of the upper particle body movement caused by the particle body in the bottom fell out .

In Fig.1, shows prediction model of the arbitrary point's movement and deformation on the surface. The paper will take the model as the foundation to establish a 3D stratigraphic model that suitable for mining subsidence prediction. Suppose the calculation mining width of the mining alignment as $l_1$, the calculation mining width of the mining inclination as $l_2$, the sinking value $W_A$ of point $A$ will be the maximum subsidence value multiplied by volume that surrounded by the standard normal function curved surface of point $A$ and the mining area.

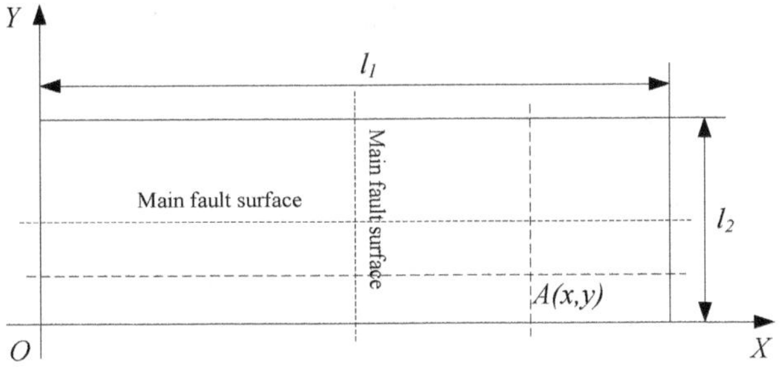


**Fig. 1.** Movement prediction of arbitrary point

Now take the lower left of the mining area as the coordinate origin, according to the sinking prediction formula on the limited mining main profile, the following kinds of formula founded:

(1) Sinking:

$$W(x,y)=W_{\max}\times\left\{\Phi\left(\frac{3x}{R_0}\right)-\Phi\left[\frac{3(x-l_1)}{R_0}\right]\right\}\times\left\{\Phi\left(\frac{3y}{R_0}\right)-\Phi\left[\frac{3(y-l_2)}{R_0}\right]\right\}=W_{\max}C_x\times C_y \tag{1}$$

(2) Inclination along the direction φ:

$$i(x,y,\phi)=\frac{\partial W(x,y)}{\partial \phi}=\frac{1}{W_{max}}\left[i^0(x)W^0(y)\cos\phi+W^0(x)i^0(y)\sin\phi\right] \quad (2)$$

(3) Curvature along the direction φ:

$$K(x,y,\phi)=\frac{\partial}{\partial \phi}i(x,y,\phi)=\frac{1}{W_{max}}\left[K^0(x)W^0(y)\cos^2\phi+W^0(x)K^0(y)\sin^2\phi+i^0(x)i^0(y)\sin 2\phi\right] \quad (3)$$

(4) Horizontal movement along the direction φ:

$$U(x,y,\phi)=bri(x,y,\phi)=\frac{1}{W_{max}}\left[U^0(x)W^0(y)\cos\phi+U^0(y)W^0(x)\sin\phi\right] \quad (4)$$

(5) Horizontal deformation along the direction φ:

$$\begin{aligned}\varepsilon(x,y,\phi)&=brK(x,y,\phi)\\&=\frac{1}{W_{max}}\left\{\varepsilon^0(x)W^0(y)\cos^2\phi+\varepsilon^0(y)W^0(x)\sin^2\phi+\left[U^0(x)i^0(y)+U^0(y)i^0(x)\right]\sin\phi\cos\phi\right\}\end{aligned} \quad (5)$$

The above model takes random medium theory as a foundation, and deduced a prediction model which takes the standard normal distribution as the sinking probability density function. The model calculates easily, and has definite geometrical and physical significance of this model's parameters; also it can do field measurement, and establish corresponding engineering calculation model for the development of 3D visualization system of mining subsidence prediction.

# 3 3D Stratigraphic Model

## 3.1 Modeling Process of 3D Stratum

Currently there are many technical methods for stratigraphic information detection, but the most direct and the most widely used method to obtain stratigraphic information is drilling method. According to the arrangement position of rock strata demarcation point in stratum borehole data, can determine the sequence of the stratum. And can treat the Multi-DEM by litho logy in cross-classification processing, thus can form 3D stratigraphic framework, which divided by elements of litho logy in 3D space. Also can introduce special body object (such as TEN objects and so on) to rich stratum content, last form complete meaning of 3D stratigraphic model.

The 3D stratigraphic model based on Multi-DEM is according to drill hole sampling points of subsidence prediction area, and establish DEM of the stratum boundary surface or the boundary surface of ore body and surrounding rock strata's from the earth's surface to underground in proper order, then form 3D stratigraphic model after separately suturing the DEM that adjacent and belong to the same stratum or ore body. In order to modeling, according to the stratum sequence, number the stratum that revealed by drill hole information within the research area, and the top layer is rock strata I, the following is rock strata II, rock strata III…, the modeling process is as follows:

(1) Borehole data pretreatment. Select some points in the research area to carry drilling sampling, due to the stratum existing wedge out phenomenon, so the rock strata's number in drill hole sampling is very different. As shown in Fig.2, according to the standard rock strata sequence, for the missing rock strata in some drill holes, we insert virtual layers which thickness is 0 in the drill hole, and after the pre-treatment making every drill hole have the same rock strata sequence and the same number of layers.

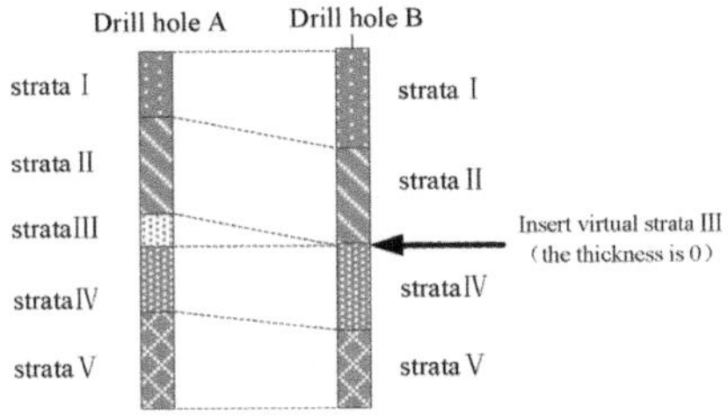


**Fig. 2.** Diagram of borehole data pre-processing

(2) Insert virtual drill hole in the four angular points of drill hole bounding box in the research area. Drill hole is mainly distributed inside in the research area, if the stratum modeling is carried by the original drill hole, will obtain an irregular 3D digital stratum, and this will be inconvenient to the following study of the stratum, therefore it needs outward expansion to form the bounding box. For this moment, need to insert virtual drill hole in the four angular points of the irregular 3D digital stratum bounding box.

(3) Build standard triangulation network of rock strata surface. According to the plane coordinate (x, y) of drill hole point for every rock strata surface, use plane Delaunay Triangulation Algorithm to build standard triangulation network of every rock strata surface, and use different colors or textures to express rock strata surface.

(4) Generate 3D stratigraphic framework model. Because of every drill hole has the same rock strata sequence, so start form the discrete points in the standard triangulation network of rock strata surface, and use the 3D constraint tetrahedron algorithm to build TEN from top to bottom. So this can establish the whole 3D digital stratum.

(5) The visualization of TEN. Use different colors or textures to express different attribute of rock strata.

### 3.2 The Mixed Data Model Based on Multi-DEM and TEN

The mixed data model based on Multi-DEM and TEN (the following called as DEMs-TEN model), DEMs consists of some adjacent triangles, so its basic geometrical element is triangle. TEN includes basic geometrical elements as follows: vertex, line segment (such as tetrahedron edge, triangle edge), triangle, tetrahedron and so on. Use object-oriented ideas, and abstract the stratum entity to the following four basic elements: vertex, line segment, triangle, tetrahedron and so on. In Fig.3, shows the DEMs-TEN model based on UML.

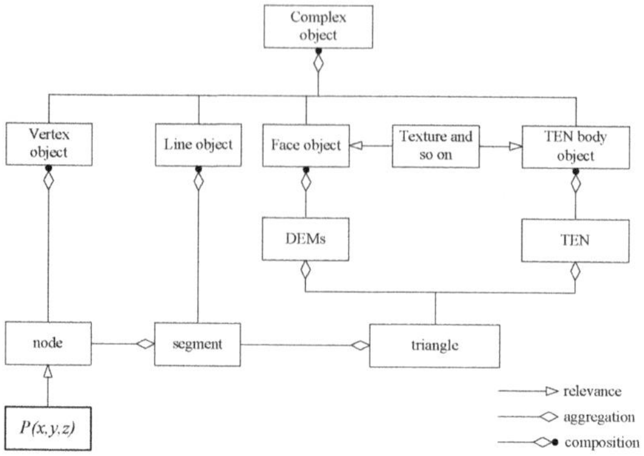


**Fig. 3.** DEMs-TEN hybrid model based on UML

From the stratum attribute perspective, drill hole is the line object that comprised by many line segments; adjacent triangles in the same layer face comprise a stratum surface object; under the restriction of the two neighbouring layers' surface, the TEN's Vexel that connected with each other comprises a whole geological object; the node can be used to describe a punctual object, that is the intersection between drill hole and rock strata surface; different space objects in certain space range can comprise a complex geological object. Fig.3 shows the corresponding relation between geometrical element and entity object.

### 3.3 Mixed Modeling Process and Related Algorithm of DEMs-TEN

In section 3.2, abstracted the borehole data to scattered point source information and designed the data structure of the scattered point source information, and on the base of this, provide reconstruction for the DEM of every stratum surface, then form the basic framework of 3D stratum. Using 3D constraint Delaunay TEN to create network on the adjacent stratum surface, and to reach the purpose of stitching the adjacent stratum surface, and then get the 3D model of the whole stratum.

Suppose the data set of one stratum surface's scattered points is $S_1=\{V_i \mid V_i \in R^3, i=1,2,3,\ldots\}$, its adjacent stratum surface's scattered points data set is $S_2=\{V_j \mid V_j \in R^3, j=1,2,3,\ldots\}$. Carry Delaunay triangulations on $S_1$ to form a triangle set, and use adjlink pointer $P$ to indicate the triangle set, and use the algorithm provided in literature[7,8] to achieve the Delaunay triangulation.

The following, will use recursion partition method to generate TEN of constraint surface. In order to describe conveniently, the paper designs data fields dissection algorithm *Partition_Subdivision()* and tetrahedral set generation algorithms *Create TEN()*. The algorithms are as follows:

Algorithm 1: TEN generation algorithms of constraint stratum surface *Partition_ Subdivision.*

Algorithm ideas: Make use of the splitting plane $\Omega$ which perpendicular to $X$ axis to divide the given data fields space into two approximately equal half-space $\Phi_1$ and $\Phi_2$, and divide the stratum surface triangle set $P$ into three parts: the triangle adjlink

$P_x$ which intersect $\Omega$, the triangle adjlink $P_l$ which in the left of $\Omega$, the triangle adjlink $P_r$ which in the right of $\Omega$; for the triangle in the $P_x$ ,can call the tetrahedral set constructed function *CreateTEN()* separately in half-space; if $P_l$ and $P_r$ is not null, recursive call *Partition_ Subdivision()* separately in the two half-space $\Phi_l$ and $\Phi_2$. The algorithm steps are as follows:

STEP 1: set the triangle storage adjlink pointer $P_x$,$P_l$,$P_r$ null;

STEP 2: use plane $\Omega$ to divide the point set into three point sets, separately is: $S_{2\text{-}0}\in\Omega$, $S_{2\text{-}1}\in\Phi_1$, $S_{2\text{-}2}\in\Phi_2$;

STEP 3: make the initial boundary triangles and the generated triangles in the process of new tetrahedron generation according to the different position that intersect $\Omega$, in the left of $\Omega$, in the right of $\Omega$, and make $P$ divide into three triangle adjlink sets, and separately assign to $P_x$, $P_l$, $P_r$;

STEP 4: call the tetrahedral set constructed function *CreateTEN ()* for every triangle $t$ in $P_x$; add the other triangles except the triangle $t$ of new generated tetrahedron to $P_x$, and update the value of the splitting plane$\Omega$;

STEP 5: if $P_l$ is not null, then recursive call the *Partition _ Subdivision(*$\Phi_l$,$P_l$*)*;

STEP 6: if $P_r$ is not null, then recursive call the *Partition _ Subdivision(*$\Phi_2$,$P_r$*)*;

Algorithm 2: the generation algorithms of tetrahedral set *CreateTEN ()*

In order to describe conveniently, appoint the data structure that the algorithm referred to as follows:

(1) the three vertexes' index *VertexID* of triangle that comprised TEN have counter clockwise arrangement;

(2) the four vertexes *ABCP* of TEN are arranged as follows: $\triangle ABC$ is one of TEN's faces, the $\triangle ABC$ has the counter clockwise arrangement from vertex $P$, $P$ is the vertex that the thumb pointed according to the right hand rule, then called $P$ is over the face where the $\triangle ABC$ is, or, called $P$ is under the face where the $\triangle ABC$ is, shown in Fig.4.

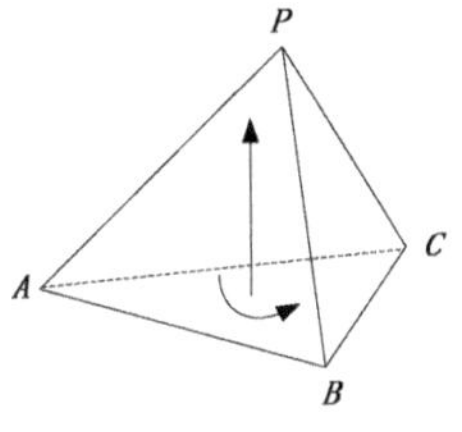


**Fig. 4.** Tetrahedron schematic diagram

Supposing $P(x, y, z)$ is a spatial arbitrary point, given the space coordinate of $\triangle ABC$ are respectively: $A(x_1, y_1, z_1)$, $B(x_2, y_2, z_2)$, $C(x_3, y_3, z_3)$, the space position relationship of point $P$ and $\triangle ABC$ is obtained by the formula (6) below:

$$V = \begin{vmatrix} x & y & z & 1 \\ x_1 & y_1 & z_1 & 1 \\ x_2 & y_2 & z_2 & 1 \\ x_3 & y_3 & z_3 & 1 \end{vmatrix} \qquad (6)$$

(1) If $V = 0$, said $P\ (x, y, z)$ is included in the face where the $\triangle ABC$ is.
(2) If $V = 0$, said $P\ (x, y, z)$ is above the face where the $\triangle ABC$ is.
(3) If $V = 0$, said $P\ (x, y, z)$ is below the plane where the $\triangle ABC$ is.

In order to construct a Delaunay tetrahedron on the basis of the given $\triangle ABC$, and the Delaunay tetrahedron has on overlap or cross with the current tetrahedral set and constraint surface triangle, the essence is to seek another vertex suited to $\triangle ABC$. If written $T\ (\triangle ABC,\ P)$ for the generated Delaunay tetrahedron, the vertex $P$ should meet the following conditions:

(1) $P$ is above the face of the $\triangle ABC$;

(2) The generated $T(\triangle ABC,P)$ is Delaunay tetrahedron, that is the external ball of $T(\triangle ABC,P)$ does not contain any other vertex; the algorithm to judge whether the other vertex $V$ in the external ball of $T(\triangle ABC,P)$ can refer to literature[9].

(3) While generating $T(\triangle ABC,P)$, recording the other vertex(set $O$ point) which in the same external spherical with this tetrahedron, record it in the linked list *Vertex_link*, after $T(\triangle ABC,P)$ successfully built, continue to look for the appropriate points in linked list *Vertex_link* for the new triangle to generate Delaunay tetrahedron, the generation process shown in Fig.5.

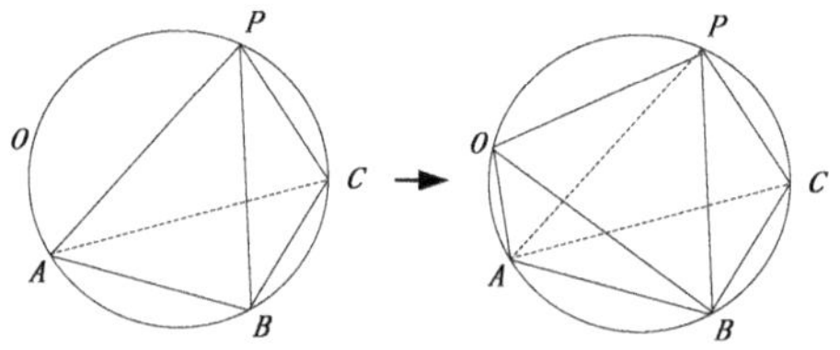


**Fig. 5.** New TEN generation process

## 4 Sample Analysis

Based on the ideas, *3D Subsidence* is developed which is used to predict mining subsidence and visualization. In order to analyze and validate the *3D Subsidence* system, the following method will be used to calculate mining Subsidence. That is: using the current probability integral method and *3D Subsidence* to calculate the mining subsidence respectively, then compare with the measured sinking value. A coal mine 3252 surface observation station is located up of the coal mine 3252 working face, the geologic structure of this place is complicated, the coal bed is mono clinal structure, the mean obliquity of the coal rake is 24 degrees, the coal bed is sandy shale and grey-white medium-grained sandstone, and the hardness is from 6 to 7.5 degrees, overlying rock strata is fine sandstone 11.8m, medium-grained sandstone 5m, sandstone 9.4m, sandy shale 27.2m, alluvium 15-20m; The parameter of the 3252 earth's surface observation station is in table 1, *3D Subsidence* system also uses the predicted parameter values in table 1.

**Table 1.** Parameter table of probability integration method

| parameter | value | unit |
|---|---|---|
| Mining coal rake mean obliquity $\alpha$ | 24 | $(^0)$ |
| Mining effects spread degree $\theta$ | 70 | $(^0)$ |
| Mining depth of the working face uphill $H_1$ | 103 | $(m)$ |
| Mining depth of the working face downhill $H_2$ | 42 | $(m)$ |
| Level projection length of the working face $l$ | 230 | $(m)$ |
| Level projection length of tilt direction of the working face $L$ | 123 | $(m)$ |
| Shifting distance of the inflexion besides open-off cut $S_1$ | -3.4 | $(m)$ |
| Shifting distance of inflexion besides stopping mining line $S_2$ | 1.9 | $(m)$ |
| ... | ... | ... |

Establish a rectangular coordinate system to take coordinate transformation for the point that has not compute. Take the crossover point $O'$ of left border and lower boundary of working face level projection as base point, $x'$-axis and $y'$-axis are parallel to uphill downhill of the coal rake. The coordinate of arbitrary point $A(x',y')$ can be obtained from the rectangular coordinate computing, the coordinate of the points that have not computed that need in the earth surface moving should be $A(x,y)$ after inflexion translation, then :

$$\begin{aligned} &l = l' + S_1 + S_2 \\ &x = x' + S_1 \\ &y = y' + H_1 ctg\theta + \frac{S_4}{\sin\theta}\sin(\alpha+\theta) \\ &L = L' + H_2 ctg\theta + \frac{S_3}{\sin\theta}\sin(\alpha+\theta) + H_1 ctg\theta + \frac{S_4}{\sin\theta}\sin(\alpha+\theta) \end{aligned} \tag{7}$$

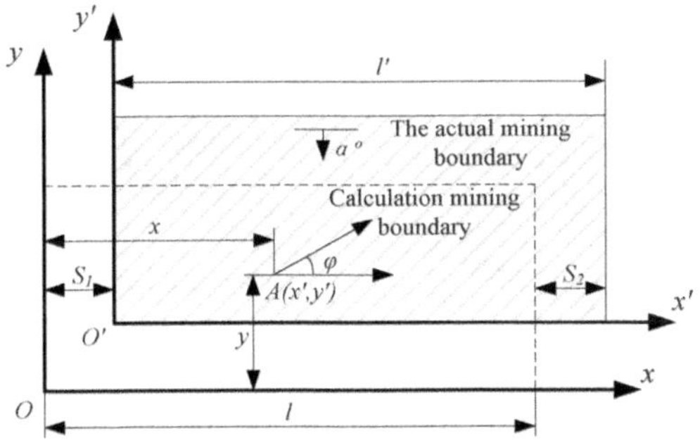


**Fig. 6.** Establishment and transformation of coordinate system

Compare the earth surface sinking value computed by probability integral and 3D Subsidence system with measured value obtained by observation station, and the comparison condition shows in Fig.7. $W_C$-measured observed value; $W_J$- the sinking value computed by probability integral; $W_M$- the sinking value computed by the system.

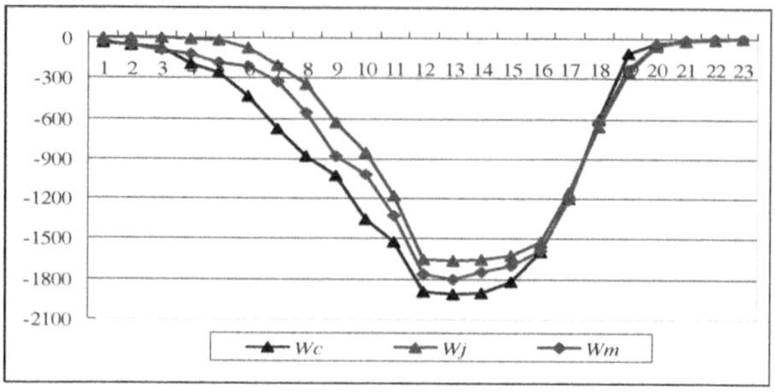


**Fig. 7.** Results comparison chart

It can be seen from Fig.7 that the prediction of the system owns more degree of accuracy and is more close to measured value. Because it considered the coal rake and overburden structure, what could be better to choose expected parameters, and it considered the distribution form of the coal rake in the 3D stratigraphic modeling, and fitting better with measured value.

The screen shot of the 3252 working face subsidence stratum modeling and 3D visualization simulation results by *3D Subsidence* system is shown in Fig.8, (a),(c) are 3D stratum effect drawing in different viewing angle,(b),(d) are the 3D stratum effect drawing with remote sensing corresponding (a),(c).

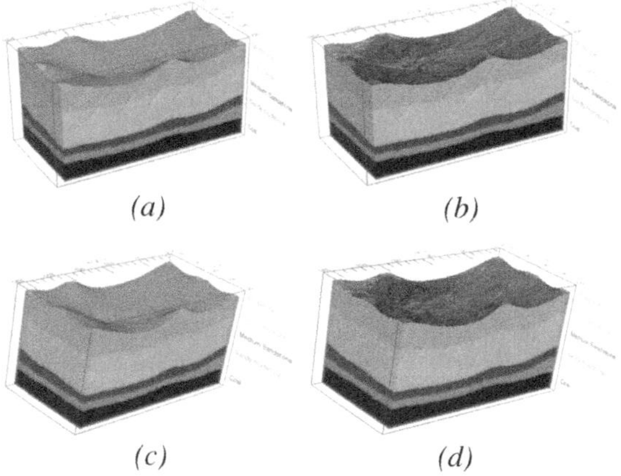


**Fig. 8.** Three-dimensional visualization of mining subsidence effect picture

## 5 Conclusions

(1) It takes 3D stratum model and mining subsidence prediction model together for the first time, then technical staff can obtain the mining subsidence prediction model that meet the actual engineering directly from 3D stratum modeling, and improve the accuracy of mining subsidence prediction by the reasonable expected parameter that chosen from the interactive modeling process. (2) We make a classification,

summarize, accumulation to the 3D geology phenomena by the object-oriented method, put forward Multi-DEMs and mixed tetrahedron grid 3D stratum model, the model uses multi-DEMs to structure the stratum's surface and layer geology surfaces, and uses TEN to structure inter layer geologic mass with the accurate express of face object. (3) It carry out the mining subsidence prediction 3D visualization system *3D Subsidence*. The system supports to the true 3D display of mining subsidence, meanwhile, it integrates 2D and 3D information together, further enriched and developed the methods and means of mining subsidence field.

**Acknowledgments.** This work was supported by a grant from the National High Technology Research and Development Program of China (863 Program) (No.2009-AA062704); Supported by Research and Development Program of Shandong Educational Commission (No.J09LG54).

## References

1. Houlding, S.W.: 3D Geoscience Modeling,Computer Techniques for Geological Characterization. Springer, Berlin (1994)
2. Burford, D.J., Ger, L., Blake, E.H., et al.: A seismic modelling environ-ment as a research and teaching tool for 3-D subsurface modelling. Int. J. of Applied Earth Observation and Geoinformation 2(2), 69–77 (2000)
3. Galera, C., Bennis, C., Moretti, I., et al.: Construction of coherent 3D geological blocks. Computers and Geo-Sciences 29(8), 971–984 (2003)
4. Hengxing Lan, C., Martin, D., Lim, C.H.: RockFall analyst: A GIS extension for 3D and spatially distributed rockfall hazard modeling. Computers and Geosciences 33(2), 262–279 (2007)
5. Smirnoff, A., Boisvert, E., Paradis, S.J.: Support vector machine for 3D modeling from sparse geological information of various origins. Computers and Geosciences 34(2), 127–143 (2008)
6. Crooks, A., Castle, C., Batty, M.: Key challenges in agent-based modeling for geospatial simulation. Computers, Environment and Urban Systems 32(6), 417–430 (2008)
7. Napieralski, J., Harbor, J., Li, Y.: Glacial geomorphology and geographic information systems. Earth-Science Reviews 85(1-2), 1–22 (2007)
8. Wu, Q., Xu, H.: An approach to computer modeling and visualization of geological faults in 3D. Computers & Geosciences 29(4), 507–513 (2003)
9. Zhang, H., Wen, Y., Liu, A., et al.: Basic of GIS algorithm. science press, Beijing (2006)

# Detail-Preserving Rendering of Free Surface Fluid with Lattice Boltzmann

Changbo Wang, Qiang Zhang, Zhuopeng Zhang, Peng Yang, and Zhengdong Xia

Software Engineering Insititute,
East China Normal University, 200062, Shanghai, China
cbwangcg@gmail.com

**Abstract.** Free surface flows represent a special case in the fluids simulation application. A highly effective method of modeling and rendering based on Lattice Boltzmann Model (LBM) to simulate the fluid with free surface is presented. Firstly, the LBM model with adaptive coarsening grids for free surface flows is adopted to model the fluid volume. And then a new method combined with the Marching Cubes and free surface algorithm is proposed to extract the fluid surface. Adaptive surface tension combining wave particles equation is used to show the details of fluid surface. After that, an external stack mechanism of moving obstacles is used to realize interacting calculation of fluid with environment. Finally, the hardware accelerating technology is successfully adopted to achieve realistic rendering of complex fluid scenes with different free surface, including flush flood, droplet, etc.

**Keywords:** Lattice Boltzmann Method; Fluid rendering; Free surface; Details.

## 1 Introduction

Recently physically based fluid simulation is a difficult research topic in computer graphics, which brings about many important applications in special effects, animation and games, virtual reality, etc. Free surface fluids represent a special case separated by gas and liquid, such as water droplet, flush flood, debris flow, etc. Such fluids with free surface are more difficult to simulate than these single flows with full space for their much more surface details and physical mechanism.

The Navier-Stokes (NS) equations have traditionally been used in fluid simulations. Instead of directly computing solutions for the discretized Navier-Stokes equations, the LBM method is a form of cellular automaton. It relaxes the incompressible criterion and thus does not require an additional step with an iterative method such as a multi-grid solver [1]. However, recent physically based fluid simulation works mostly focus on these fluids with small size and area. These can not show enough details of fluid surface, especially for these complex fluid interactions. Here, the key point is how to balance the contravention between more calculation amount and higher request of rendering quality. Although the GPU programming technology has been used for acceleration, it is not capable enough to render the complex free surface flows in interactive rates.

Z. Pan et al. (Eds.): Transactions on Edutainment VI, LNCS 6758, pp. 216–226, 2011.

This paper focuses on real-time rendering of complex free surface flows. We not only want to model the fluid extraction of free surface flows and their interactions, but also strive to show more details of flow surface.

The remainder of this paper is organized as follows: Section 2 briefly summarizes the work related to ours. Section 3 describes our free surface fluid based on Lattice Boltzmann with multi-scale grids, while Section 4 presents the extracting of fluid surface with details. Section 5 discusses the interaction between fluid and the environment. We present some results illustrating the use of our technique in Section 6, and conclude in Section 7.

## 2 Related Work

There are many research works in finding solutions to classical Navier-Stokes equations. However, considering that N-S equation is based on the hypothesis that the subject is of continuum and discrete solver and free surface fluid simulation are rather unsalable. In 1988, the first paper of lattice Boltzmann theory [2] discretizes the physical space into a lattice and the particles movement is measured using real number. In 2002, Wei et al [3] introduced lattice Boltzmann model into fluid simulation, including fire flame, and the smoke and gas in the air [4]. Further, it is used to simulate jellyfish in water [5], melting phenomena, heat mirage [6], and large-scale water surface [7]. Adopting LBM method, a solver can easily handle complex fluid boundaries and the obstacles [8], and LBM can also be used to simulate multiphase flow [9]. Considering the parallel characteristics of LBM method, GPU and cluster technologies can be used for the acceleration of the fluid simulation [10]. Conversional LBM model is based on regular cubic lattices while non-Cartesian lattices were also used for a better sampling [11] [12]. However, the above methods of LBM mostly simulate the space filled with fluid, and there are few performances for fluid with the gas-liquid separation features.

For the free surface fluid simulation, Tubbs [13] proposed shallow water equation, stacking up multiple 2D grids to get the final height of grid. In 2009, Liu et al [14] achieved shallow water equations on multiple grids. Irving et al. [15] also presented two and three dimensional coupling techniques to simulate large bodies of water.

The surface extraction of fluid is the key to the simulation of these free surface fluids. Enright et al. [16] further proposed Particle Level Set method to add more details for the free surface of water. Thurey et al. [17] used LBM free surface combined with level set method to calculate the curved water surface and simulate the thin body of water. Thurey et al. [18] further used the controlling particles to control the animation of water while preserving local details. In addition, SPH method based on particle systems and Lagrange method became popular recently [19] [20], which is easy to achieve with good performance of the details, while it is difficult to construct the surface and select smoothing kernel function.

Recently, the detail of fluid is heeded when simulating fluid. Yuksel et al. [21] introduced the concept of wave particles to track wave motion, which can simulate the fluid surface waves and their interactions with floating objects. Thurey et al. [22] efficiently simulated complex phenomena such as crown splash through triangle meshes based multi-scale surface tension. Brochu et al. [23] introduced an Eulerian liquid simulation framework based on the Voronoi diagram, which accurately captured the geometry and topology of the liquid surface. Zhu et al. [24] presented a new method to create and preserve the turbulent details in SPH fluid. However, it is still a challenging task to simulate different free surface fluids with more realistic surface details and high rendering speed at the same time.

# 3 Fluid Modeling on LBM with Multi-scale Grid

## 3.1 Free Surface Fluid on LBM Lattice

The main idea of LBM method is using simple rules of measuring micro particles movement to reflect macro fluid changes. The Bhatnagar-Gross-Krook (BGK) model with single-relaxation can be expressed:

$$f_{qi}(\mathbf{x}_i + \mathbf{e}_{qi}, t + \delta t) - f_{qi}(\mathbf{x}_i, t) = -\frac{1}{\tau}(f_{qi}(\mathbf{x}_i, t) - f_{qi}^{eq}(\rho, \mathbf{u})) \tag{1}$$

Where $f_{qi}^{eq}(\rho, \mathbf{u})$ is particle velocity and equilibrium distribution function, $\tau$ is relaxation time. In each discrete spatial grid points, density $\rho$ and speed $u$ can be expressed by a distribution function of a number of micro particles as follows:

$$\rho(x,t) = \sum_{i=0}^{b} f_i(x,t),\ u(x,t) = \frac{1}{\rho}\sum_{i=0}^{b} \vec{e}_i f_i(x,t) \tag{2}$$

This distribution function $f_i$ accounts for the number of particles along the direction, each discrete particle has $b$ directions of movement, just as shown in Fig 1.a. According to the conservation of energy, different initial conditions and boundary conditions of the recursive evolution for the distribution function can be derived.

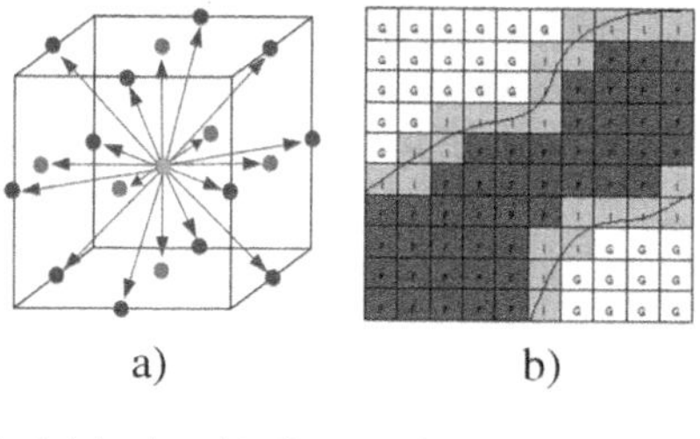

**Fig. 1.** a) A D3Q19 LBM Model lattice, b) Free surface grid tag (where G, F, I represent the grid full of gas, liquid-filled, and grid interface)

For free surface fluid, as the space discretized into grids, there exist fluid region and non-fluid region. Corresponding to the LBM model grid, it is divided into the gas and fluid grid, while the interspace of these two types of grids contains both liquid and gas. This intermediate grid state is the critical part in tracking fluid movement and we called it the grid interface. As is shown in Fig 1.b, G, F, I represent three types of grids, respectively. These states of the grid will be changed along with the fluid movement.

### 3.2 Grids Transfer and Updating

The movement of the fluid can be achieved by calculating the difference of the mass at each grid. Changes of the mass can be directly obtained by accumulating the inpouring distribution function from the adjacent lattice. Mass exchanged between liquid lattice and other lattice can be expressed as:

$$\Delta m_i(x,t+\Delta t)=(f_i(x+e_i,t)-f_i(x,t))\frac{(\varepsilon(x+e_i,t)+\varepsilon(x,t))}{2} \tag{3}$$

Where $f_i(x+e_i,t)$ is the fluid mass entering into grid from direction $i$ in the current time, $f_i(x,t)$ is the fluid mass leaving grid on this direction, $\varepsilon$ is the volume fraction ($\varepsilon = m/\rho$, $\rho$ is density of the fluid lattice). During the process of changing, we must ensure that the total mass is unchanged.

After the mass of all grids are updated, we need to update the lattice type if an interface grid is full or empty and thus it will be seen as liquid-filled or gas grid at next time step. The grid is full when the ε exceeds or equals to one, and empty when mass downs to zero. When the interface becomes full or empty during updating, the change of quality must be assigned to the adjacent grids.

If the mass of an empty interface grid becomes negative, it should be made up to zero by obtaining the mass of surrounding interface grids. While excessive mass of a full interface grid should be distributed to the surrounding interface grids.

### 3.3 Multi-scale Grids Construction

The local grids refinement scheme is firstly described in [25]. Adaptive coarsening algorithm locating fine grids at the area close to interface [26] can perform transferring between fine cells and coarse ones more accurately. However, when extracting the free surface, mass exchanging should be applied on the interface cells and those surrounding ones (shown in Fig 2.b). Since some interface cells are far away from viewer position with less visible details. So we develop the multi-scale grid algorithm only according to viewport information (Fig 2.c). That is to say, fine grids are near view point, and coarse girds are far away.

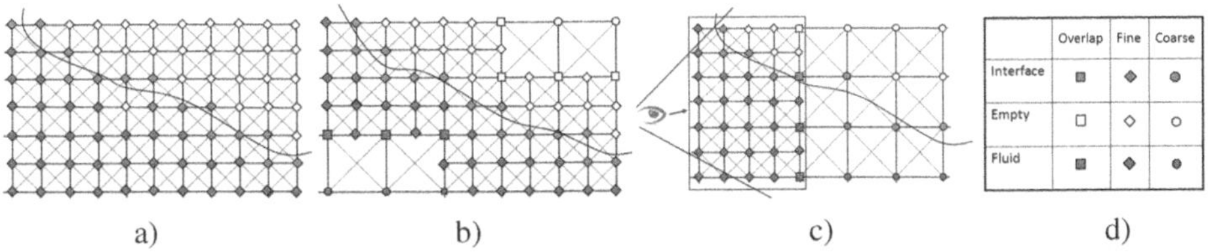


**Fig. 2.** Adaptive grids. a) Uniform grid. b) Fine grids surround interface cells as [26] described. c) Our adaptive coarsen algorithm, fine grid is the focus area that may be near the view point. d) It shows the marks of different grids.

To ensure the velocity and density consistency and continuity in different grids, the non-equilibrium parts of the distribution functions have to be rescaled. The stream, collision and cell updating on the fine grids performs twice as the coarse ones does once every step. The rescaling of distribution functions performed directly on overlapped different grids. When a neighbor cell of fine grid is absent due to that it is next to coarse grid, a fine grid (the neighbor) should be made up by spatial interpolating distribution functions of coarse grid.

Here, the external forces, such as the drop gravity, can change the velocity for uniform grids like: $\vec{u}^* = \vec{u} + \tau\vec{G}$, where $\vec{u}$ is the former velocity, and $u^*$ is the amended velocity, $\tau$ is relaxation time, and $\vec{G}$ is the gravity. However, for multi-scale grids, the affection is different for different positions, just as:

$$\vec{u}_f^* = \vec{u}_f + \tau_f \Delta x_f \vec{G}\ ,\ \vec{u}_c^* = \vec{u}_c + \tau_c \Delta x_c \vec{G} \tag{4}$$

Where $\vec{u}_f$、$\vec{u}_c$、$\tau_f$、$\tau_c$、$\Delta x_f$、$\Delta x_c$ is velocity, relaxation time and grid internal, respectively. Subscript f means fine grids, and $c$ for coarse grids.

# 4 Detail-Preserving Fluid Surface Extracting

## 4.1 Extracting Fluid Surface

The surface can be extracted by the Marching Cubes (MC) algorithm. However, the grid resolution of LBM is low, the rendered isosurfaces become angular due to too few MC voxels. Here we enrich the MC voxels near surface to show more details around fluid surface without increasing the number of girds.

We enrich one voxel into eight by adding point O, and calculate the volume fraction of it based on bilinear interpolation, and then perform the Marching Cubes method. Left of Fig.3 shows a possible ambiguity before enriching, where the isosurface may be different from two triangles (red triangles or green triangles) by the 8 original vertexes. However, after enriching, these vertexes will be compared among smaller rectangles, which make the isosurface become finer, just as shown in Fig 3.

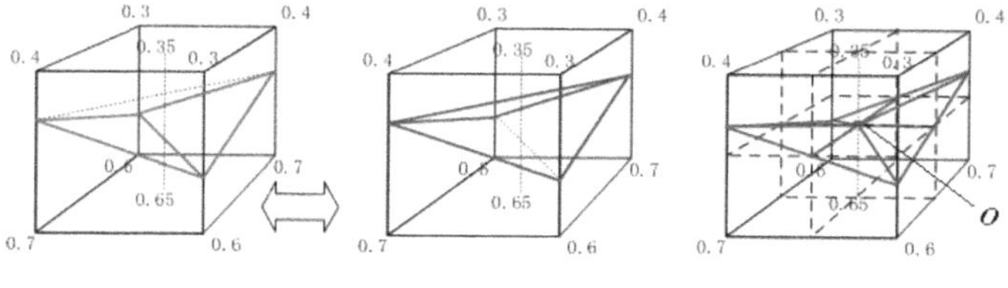

**Fig. 3.** Adaptive enriched voxels based on MC method

To get a continual surface between fine and coarse grids, the fluid volume fraction is interpolated at the boundary between coarse and fine grids to produce transitive grids. Then the MC algorithm can be applied on the interpolated and original volume fraction.

## 4.2 Detail-Preserving Based on Surface Tension

Detail-preserving is always necessary when the water interacts with environment, such as the splashing of droplets. Here, we address it with self-adaptive surface tension. In the LBM free surface model, when dealing the stream step between an "G" lattice and an "I" lattice, the formula is:

$$f_{\tilde{i}}(\vec{x},t+\Delta t)=(f_i^{(0)}(\vec{u},\rho)+f_{\tilde{i}}^{(0)}(\vec{u},\rho))\cdot\sigma-f_i(\vec{x},t) \tag{5}$$

Where $\sigma$ is influenced by the curvature of the surface. It is 1.0, when the surface tension is neglected. And $\sigma=1+\delta\kappa$, where $\delta$ is the coefficient of surface tension, and $\kappa$ is the mean curvature.

However, the number of surface mesh of vertexes is inconstant, which makes it hard to trace, and it is not fit for our lattice model. Here, we use the following method combining height map on LBM grids and oscillation equation to get more details.

Firstly, we establish a new height map on the surface. Just as shown in the box in Fig 4, mark the height of each vertex in initial surface F as $H_F(\mathbf{x},t)$ by the positions and the volume fractions of the "I" lattices, and get new height map $H_S(\mathbf{x},t)$ with the same dimension as $H_F(\mathbf{x},t)$ by smoothing with mean filter. Subtract the values of these two height maps and we can get

$$\Delta H(\mathbf{x},t)=H_F(\mathbf{x},t)-H_S(\mathbf{x},t)\,. \tag{6}$$

According to the moving rules for these small wave particles, we have the solution of the oscillation equation:

$$h(\mathbf{x},t)=\Delta H(\mathbf{x},t)\cos(\omega(\mathbf{x},t)t+\varphi_0(\mathbf{x},t))/2 \tag{7}$$

where, $\varphi_0$ in each vertex is set the same value, and $\omega$ is controlled by using the curvature and the horizontal velocity there. Thus we can get:

$$\Delta H^*(\mathbf{x},t)=\Delta H(\mathbf{x},t)/2+h(x,t) \tag{8}$$

Finally, add $\Delta H^*$ with $H_S$ and generate ultimate surface height, which is:

$$H^*_F(\mathbf{x},t)=H_S(\mathbf{x},t)+\Delta H^*(\mathbf{x},t) \tag{9}$$

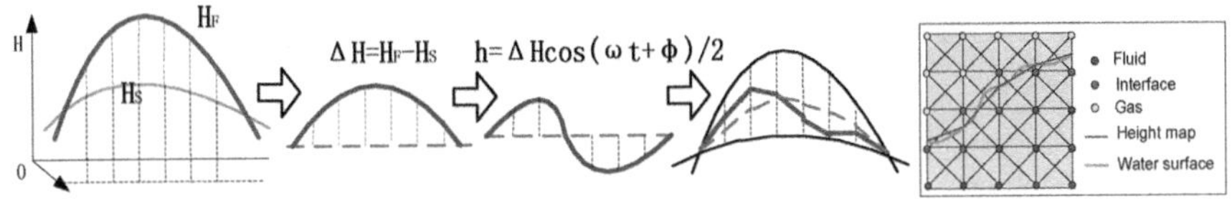


**Fig. 4.** The calculating process for surface tension with wave equation, top left is original gird F and S after smoothing. Bottom right is the oscillation equation according to grid, the bottom left one is ultimately generated grid.

## 5 Interaction of Fluid with Environment

Free surface flows often interact with the environments, such as the ripple, rain on the shallow water, dropped stone, ship on the river and so on. The interaction between fluid and environment must be considered when rendering free surface scenes. The interaction can be performed by marking these obstacles on lattices model.

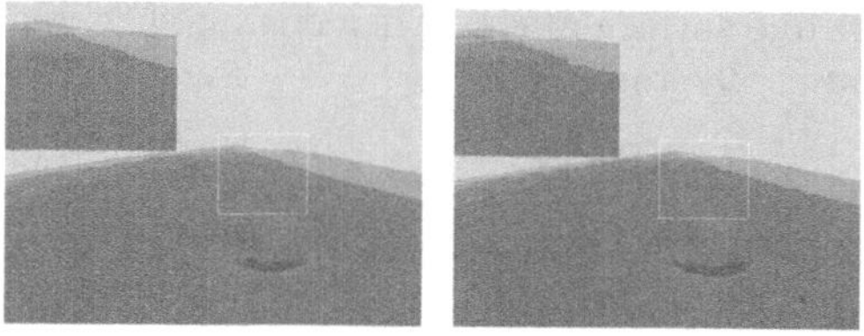

**Fig. 5.** Simulation of fluid surface detail. (left is the original smooth surface, and right shows more details as irregular waves by our method).

**Fig. 6.** A single drop falls into a pool of fluid

**Fig. 7.** A boat sails above a lake surface

**Fig. 8.** A stream of fluid fills up a Z-shaped domain

We need to mark the lattice of moving obstacles first. In general, the obstacles are surrounded by closed polygons, and the shape is never changed. Here, we introduced a new "MS" lattice for the fixed obstacle. When the simulation starts, the "MS" lattices are updated according to the geometric position of the moving obstacle. Then the corresponding sample points are taken, and the lattices contain these sample points can be marked as "MS".

When the stream step is taken between an “F” or ”I” lattice and an “MS” lattice, the bounce-back of density distribution function should be influenced by the velocity of the moving obstacle. For example, when the velocity of obstacle is pointing at the “F” or ”I” lattice, the density distribution going back $f_i(x,t+\Delta t)'$ should be larger than the original $f_{\bar{i}}(x,t)$, so that the lattice can gain a velocity, which is closed to that of the moving obstacle by change the density distribution.

When updating the “MS” lattices, an “F” or ”I” lattice is changed into an “MS” lattice, the mass just disappears; new mass appears as the density distributions become larger in the situation referred above. To ensure mass conservation, we need a process to remedy it. Before that we can make a judge whether there is a fluid lattice next to it, if there is, then make it an “I” lattice with suitable mass to ensure the conservation.

## 6 Implementation and Results

Using the principles above, we further calculate the evolution of free surface fluid and draw it using graphic hardware. GLSL shading language is used here to complete hardware calculation acceleration. The information of grids including distribute function, density, velocity, volume of fraction and grid type are dynamically updated by several fragment shaders and the water appearance shown by ray-casting algorithm.

Static obstacles in the scene intersect with the grids, and we mark intersection part as the solid part, which does not participate in the fluid evolution. While dynamic objects can interact with the water as section 5 described. To get a denser grid of water surface, the method described in 3.3 is used to generate the optimized grid.

Finally, with the Intel (R) Pentium (R) CPU 3.40GHz, memory 3GB, graphics card NVIDIA GeForce GTX 260 in the PC platform, we use OpenGL2.0 program produce the fluid rendering.

Fig 5 is our simulation results with more detail of surface. Fig 6 is a single drop falling into a pool of fluid and some drops feedback upwards. These splashes are realistic with grids of 80*80*80 and about 20 fps. Fig 7 is a boat sailing above a lake surface, the grids is 200*50*200, and our rendering speed achieves 0.8 fps. Fig 8 shows a stream of fluid fills up a Z-shaped domain, with grids of 100*100*100. From these results, we can see that our method is effective.

Table 1 lists the comparison of rendering capability for these models with different resolution and different shapes to render free surface scenes. Note every 2 row show the performance of different implement with an equal size of simulation field. Table 2 is the comparison among our method and the newly two fluids rendering methods. The grids remain 128*128*128. Bao et al. [9] described a method to simulate multi-phase fluid, but not consider the accelerate efficiency. Yan et al. [20] used SPH method to simulate fluids, but the processing of adjacent particles affects its rendering efficiency. Our method is based on LBM model and considers the surface detail, the local parallel arithmetic and data structures can be performed to achieve higher rendering efficiency.

**Table 1.** The comparison of capability of different LBM model for free surface rending

| Model Type | Grids Size | CPU/GPU | Render Speed |
|---|---|---|---|
| D2Q9 Model | 129*129 | CPU | 59 fps |
| D2Q9 Model | 33*65 coarse grid +65*129 fine grid | CPU | 39 fps |
| D3Q19 Model | 66*66*66 | CPU | 6 fps |
| D3Q19 Model | 33*33*33 coarse +33*33*33 fine grid | CPU | 20 fps |
| D3Q19 Model | 64*64*64 | CPU | 6.3 fps |
| D3Q19 Model | 64*64*64 | GPU | 20 fps |

**Table 2.** The comparison of capabilities between other methods and our method

| Method | Model | Parallel | Average speed |
|---|---|---|---|
| Bao2010[9] | Volume fraction | medium | - |
| Yan2009[20] | SPH | low | 5fps |
| Our method | LBM | high | 15fps |

## 7 Conclusion and Future Works

A new effective method based on LBM to simulate the fluid with free surface is presented here. The detail of fluid surface and rendering efficiency are both fully considered. Multi-resolution grids and adaptive enriched voxels algorithms are use to accelerate the modeling of free surface flow. Moving obstacle processing and detail-preserving based on surface tension are adopted to show more surface details and interaction between fluid and environment. Finally, we implement the real-time realistic rendering of large-scale fluid scenes with different free surface, including flush flood, droplet, etc.

Future works include: model fluid based on asymmetric adaptive lattice to achieve higher rendering performance, simulate more complex fluid with different Reynolds number and complex boundaries, and render the light effects among fluid for large-scale fluids scenes.

**Acknowledgments.** This paper was supported by Natural Science Foundation of China under Grant No. 61070128, 60603076. Shanghai Rising-Star Program (A type) under Grant No.08QA1402500, and Open Project of State Key Lab. of CAD&CG, Zhejiang University, China under Grant A1008 and the Fundamental Research Funds for the Central Universities.

## References

1. Causin, P., Miglio, E., Saleri, F.: Algebraic factorizations for 3D non-hydrostatic free surface flows. Computing and Visualization in Science 5(2), 85–94 (2002)
2. McNamara, G., Zanetti, G.: Use of the Boltzmann equation to simulate lattice gas automata. Physical Review Letters 61(20), 2332–2335 (1988)
3. Wei, X., Li, W., Mueller, K., Kaufman, A.: Simulating fire with texture splats. In: IEEE Visualization 2002, pp. 227–234. IEEE Computer Society, Los Alamitos (2002)

4. Wei, X., Li, W., Mueller, K., Kaufman, A.: The Lattice-Boltzmann method for gaseous phenomena. IEEE Trans. on Visualization and Computer Graphics 10(2), 164–176 (2004)
5. Qiu, F., Zhao, Y., Fan, Z., Wei, X., Lorenz, H., Wang, J., Yoakum-Stover, S., Kaufman, A., Mueller, K.: Accelerated dispersion simulation for urban security. In: IEEE Visualization 2004, pp. 553–560 (2004)
6. Zhao, Y.: Modeling Natural Phenomena with Lattice Boltzmann Method, Stony Brook University, Ph.d thesis (2006)
7. Geist, R., Corsi, C., Tessendorf, J., Westall, J.: Lattice-boltzmann water waves. In: Bebis, G., Boyle, R., Parvin, B., Koracin, D., Chung, R., Hammoud, R., Hussain, M., Kar-Han, T., Crawfis, R., Thalmann, D., Kao, D., Avila, L. (eds.) ISVC 2010. LNCS, vol. 6453, pp. 74–85. Springer, Heidelberg (2010)
8. Zhu, H., Bao, K., Liu, X.: Stable and efficient miscible liquid-liquid interactions. In: ACM symposium on Virtual reality software and technology, pp. 55–64. ACM Press, Newport Beach (2007)
9. Bao, K., Wu, X.L., Zhang, H., et al.: Volume Fraction Based Miscible and Immiscible Fluid Animation. Computer Animation and Virtual Worlds 21(3-4), 401–410 (2010)
10. Zhe, F., Qiu, F., Arie, E.K.: Zippy: A Framework for Computation and Visualization on a GPU Cluster. Comput. Graph. Forum 27(2), 341–350 (2008)
11. Alim, U.R., Alireza, E., Torsten, M.: The Lattice-Boltzmann method on Optimal Sampling Lattices. IEEE Trans. on Visualization and Computer Graphics Archive 15(4), 630–641 (2009)
12. Petkov, K., Qiu, F., Zhe, F., et al.: Efficient LBM Visual Simulation on Face-Centered Cubic Lattices. IEEE Trans. on Visualization and Computer Graphics 15(5), 802–814 (2009)
13. Kevin, R.T., Frank, T.C.: Multilayer shallow water flow using lattice Boltzmann method with high performance computing. Advances in Water Resources 32(12), 1767–1776 (2009)
14. Liu, H.F., Zhou, J.G., Burrows, R.: Multi-block lattice Boltzmann simulations of subcritical flow in open channel junctions. Computers & Fluids 38(6), 1108–1117 (2009)
15. Irving, G., Guendelman, E., Losasso, F., Fedkiw, R.: Efficient Simulation of Large Bodies of Water by Coupling Two and Three Dimensional Techniques. ACM Trans. Graph. 25, 805–811 (2006)
16. Enright, D., Marschner, S., Fedkiw, R.: Animation and rendering of complex water surfaces. ACM Transactions on Graphics 21(3), 736–744 (2002)
17. Thurey, N., Rude, U.: Free surface lattice-Boltzmann fluid simulations with and without level sets. In: Workshop on Vision, Modeling and Visualization, Stanford, California, USA, November 16-18, AkaGmbH, pp. 199–208 (2004)
18. Thurey, N., Iglberger, K., Rude, U.: Free Surface Flows with Moving and Deforming Objects for LBM. In: Proceedings of Vision, Modeling and Visualization 2006. IOS Press, Amsterdam (2006)
19. Muller, M., Charypar, D., Gross, M.: Particle-based fluid simulation for interactive application. In: Proceedings of ACM SIGGRAPH/Eurographics Symposium on Computer Animation, San Diego, California, pp. 154–159 (2003)
20. Yan, K., Wang, Z.Y., Wang, C.B., et al.: Real-time fluid simulation with adaptive SPH. Computer Animation and Virtual Worlds 20(2-3), 417–426 (2009)
21. Yuksel, C., House, D.H., Keyser, J.: Wave Particles. ACM Transactions on Graphics 26(3) (2007)
22. Thurey, N., Wojtan, C., Gross, M.: A Multiscale Approach to Mesh-based Surface Tension Flows. ACM Trans. Graph (SIGGRAPH 2010) 29(4), 1–10 (2010)

23. Brochu, T., Batty, C., Bridson, R.: Matching Fluid Simulation Elements to Surface Geometry and Topology. ACM Transactions on Graphics 29(4) (2010)
24. Zhu, B., Yang, X.B., Fan, Y.: Creating and Preserving Vortical Details in SPH Fluid. Computer. Graphics Forum 29(7), 2207–2214 (2010)
25. Filippova, H.D.: Grid Refinement for Lattice-BGK Models. J. Computational Physics 147(11), 219–228 (1998)
26. Thurey, N., Rude, U.: Stable free surface flows with the lattice Boltzmann method on adaptively coarsened grids. Computing and Visualization in Science 12(5), 247–263 (2007)

# A Human Action Recognition Algorithm Based on Semi-supervised Kmeans Clustering

Hejin Yuan and Cuiru Wang

Department of Computer, North China Electric Power University
071003 Baoding, China
{yhj_1977,Cr-wang}@163.com

**Abstract.** This paper proposes a new method of semi-supervised human action recognition. In our approach, the motion energy image(MEI) and motion history image(MHI) are firstly used as the feature representation of the human action. Then, the constrained semi-supervised kmeans clustering algorithm is utilized to predict the class label of unlabeled training example. Meanwhile the average motion energy and history images are calculated as the recognition model for each category action. The category of the observed action is determined according to the correlation coefficients between its feature images and the pre-established average templates. The experiments on Weizmann dataset demonstrate that our method is effective and the average recognition accuracy can reach above 90% even when only using very small number of labeled action sequences.

**Keywords:** human action recognition; semi-supervised learning; kmeans clustering.

## 1 Introduction

Recognition of human actions from video streams has many applications in visual surveillance, entertainment, user interfaces, sports and video annotation domains. As a challenging issue, in recently, there has been considerable work on this topic [1-3]. In [4], Yamato proposed a human action recognition method based on Hidden Markov Model (HMM). In his work, the human images are divided into equal meshes and the number of pixels in each mesh is used as the feature vector for action recognition. Though, HMM is appropriate for human action modeling, it needs a lot of training samples and the self-adaptive determination of its structure and parameters are still very difficult. In [5], Bobick and Davis put forward a human action recognition algorithm with two temporal templates, named motion energy image(MEI) and motion history image(MHI). Similar to ref. [5], Wang gave an action recognition algorithm with average motion energy and mean motion shape templates in [6]. In [7], Weinlan presented an action recognition approach using exemplar-based embedding. In this method, the motion sequences are represented with respect to a set of discriminative static key-pose exemplars and without modeling any temporal ordering. Though the effectiveness of these methods had been verified through many different experiments, they all need a lot of labeled examples to learn the recognition

Z. Pan et al. (Eds.): Transactions on Edutainment VI, LNCS 6758, pp. 227–236, 2011.

model. As we know, manually labeling much amount of human action sequences will be a time and labor consuming work. Moreover, the category of the action will change commonly with the variation of application environment and user requirements. So, the algorithms, which can achieve accurate classification with only a few labeled samples, are more favorable in practice. Since semi-supervised learning can combine the labeled and unlabeled data during in training to improve performance greatly. In this paper, we investigate the problems of semi-supervised learning application in human action recognition based on ref [5].

The rest of this paper is organized as follows. The details about the proposed method, such as human action representation based on motion energy image and motion history image, similarity measure between actions, unlabeled examples' category prediction based on constrained semi-supervised kmeans clustering and nearest neighbor based classification, is presented in section 2. In section 3, we evaluate our approach with well known Weizmann dataset before concluding in section 4.

## 2 Human Action Recognition Based on Semi-supervised Kmeans Clustering

The process flow of semi-supervised human action recognition method is shown in Fig.1. Its main steps include feature extraction, unlabeled data category prediction based on constrained semi-supervised kmeans clustering and action classification using nearest neighbor method.

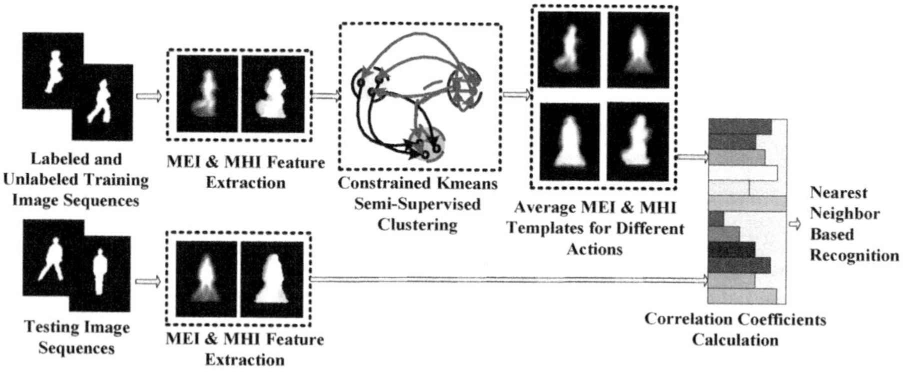


**Fig. 1.** Processing flow of action recognition based on semi-supervised kmean clustering

### 2.1 Human Action Representation

Many different methods have been proposed to represent human actions. These methods mainly can be classified into two categories: model-based and appearance-based. The appearance-based methods represent human action through lower level image features (such as silhouette, color) and motion information (such as speed, optical flow and trajectory). In model analysis, model parameters are obtained from the image sequences through reconstruction. Though the model-based representation can provide much more useful information, the reconstruction procedure is neither robust nor reliable for real images since there may be too many noisy in these images. So, appearance-based features are commonly used in action recognition since they can be easily and robustly extracted from video.

Here, we use the motion energy image(MEI) and motion history image(MHI) proposed in [5] as the representation of human action. MEI is the accumulation of binary image in each frame. Let $I(x, y, t)$ be an image sequence and $D(x, y, t)$ be a binary image sequence indicating regions of motion. The MEI $E_\tau(x, y, t)$ is defined as:

$$E_\tau(x, y, t) = \bigcup_{i=0}^{\tau-1} D(x, y, t-i) \tag{1}$$

Here, $\tau$ is the action duration time. The MEI of different actions of daria in Weizamman dataset [8] is shown in Fig.2 (a).

The MHI $H_\tau(x, y, t)$ is defines as:

$$H_\tau(x, y, t) = \begin{cases} \tau & \text{if } D(x, y, t) = 1 \\ \max(0, H_\tau(x, y, t-1) - 1) & \text{otherwise} \end{cases} \tag{2}$$

The MHI of different actions of daria in Weizamman dataset is shown in Fig. 2 (b).

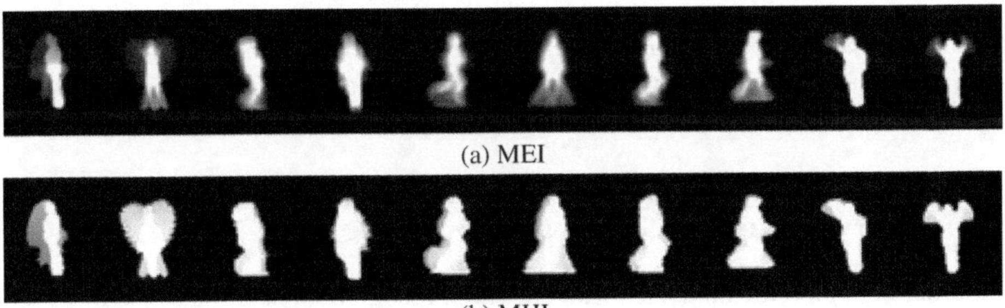

(a) MEI

(b) MHI

**Fig. 2.** MEI and MHI of daria in Weizmann dataset

Obviously, MEI shows the region and intensity of the actions in the image plane, while MHI reveals their temporal motion variation.

## 2.2 Similarity Measure between Human Actions

To measure the similarity between actions, we use correlation coefficient as follow:

$$Ce(x, y) = \frac{x \cdot y}{\|x\| \|y\|} \tag{3}$$

For the actions in Weizmann dataset, the pair wise similarity matrix of MEI and MHI is shown in Fig.3. In this figure, the color represents the similarity between different actions. And the brighter the color, the more similar between the actions. Here, these actions have been reordered according to their categories.

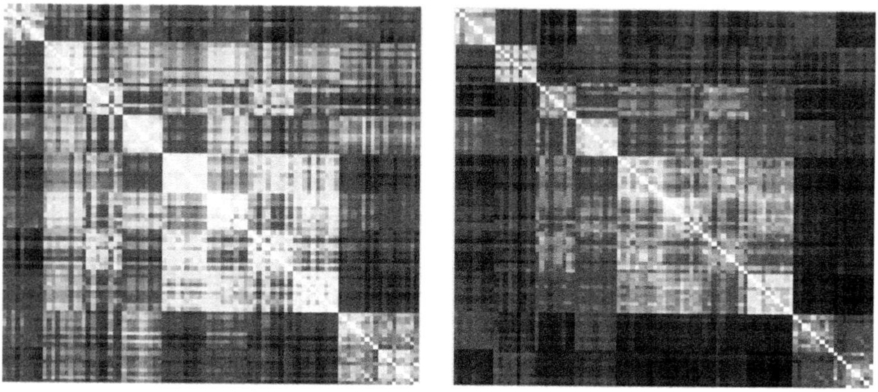

(a)MEI (b) MHI

**Fig. 3.** Correlation coefficient matrix between actions in Weizmann dataset

Obviously, our method can well distinguish out the actions since the coefficient between actions with same class label is much larger than others and the number of squares in the diagram is exactly equal to the number of action categories. Fig. 3 also indicates that MHI is more robust than MEI for human action recognition since it contains temporal information of actions.

### 2.3 Unlabeled Data Category Prediction Based on Constrained Semi-supervised Kmeans Clustering

In order to exploit the unlabeled data for action recognition, here the constrained semi-supervised kmeans clustering algorithm proposed in [9] is applied to predict their categories. In this algorithm, the labeled data is used as the seed to initialize the kmeans algorithm. And the cluster memberships of labeled data are kept unchanged during clustering. The category of unlabeled data is set identical to the labeled data in the same cluster.

The detailed steps of constrained semi-supervised kmeans algorithm are as follows [9]:

Input: Data set $X = \{x_1, x_2, ..., x_n\}$, number of clusters $K$, labeled data set $S = \bigcup_{l=1}^{K} S_l$

Output: Disjoint $K$ partitioning $\{X_l\}_{l=1}^{K}$ of $X$ such that the kmeans objective function is optimized.

Initialize:

$$\mu_h^0 = \frac{1}{|S_h|}\sum_{x \in S_h} x \text{, for } h = 1, 2, \ldots, K;$$

$t = 0$;

Repeat until convergence

a) For $x \in S$ ,if $x \in S_h$, assign $x$ to the cluster $h$; else assign $x$ to the cluster $h^* = \arg\max_h \frac{x \cdot \mu_h^{(t)}}{\|x\| \|\mu_h^{(t)}\|}$

b) $\mu_h^{(t+1)} = \frac{1}{|X_h^{(t+1)}|}\sum_{X_h^{(t+1)}} x$

c) $t = t + 1$

## 2.4 Action Recognition Based on Nearest Neighbor

With the predicted categories of unlabeled training examples, the average MEI and MHI for each category action is calculated as follows:

$$\overline{E}_\tau^j(x, y, t) = \frac{1}{\|X_j\|}\sum_{x_s \in X_j} E_\tau^s(x, y, t) \tag{4}$$

$$\overline{H}_\tau^j(x, y, t) = \frac{1}{\|X_j\|}\sum_{x_s \in X_j} H_\tau^s(x, y, t) \tag{5}$$

Here, $\overline{E}_\tau^j(x, y, t)$ and $\overline{H}_\tau^j(x, y, t)$ are the average MEI and MHI of the jth category action respectively. And $\|X_j\|$ is the number of actions in training set with class label $j$.

For the observed action $x$, MEI and MHI,denoted as $E_\tau^x$ and $H_\tau^x$, are firstly extracted using formula (1) and (2). Then the correlation coefficients to the average templates are calculated as follows:

$$Ce_x^j = \frac{E_\tau^x \cdot \overline{E}_\tau^j}{\|E_\tau^x\| \|\overline{E}_\tau^j\|} \tag{6}$$

$$Ch_x^j = \frac{H_\tau^x \cdot \overline{H}_\tau^j}{\|H_\tau^x\| \|\overline{H}_\tau^j\|} \tag{7}$$

The final category of the action $x$, determined by MEI and MHI, is respectively as follows according the nearest neighbor criteria:

$$h_E^*(x) = \arg\max_j Ce_x^j \quad h_H^*(x) = \arg\max_j Ch_x^j \tag{8}$$

## 3 Experiments and Analysis

### 3.1 Dataset

In order to evaluate the proposed algorithm, we use a publicly available dataset Weizmann[8], which is recently widely used in human action recognition algorithm evaluation. The dataset includes 10 natural actions: bending (bend), jumping jack (jack), jumping forward on two legs (jump), jumping in place on two legs (pjump), running (run), galloping-sideways (side), skipping (skip), walking (walk), waving one hand (wave1) and waving two hands (wave2), performed by 9 actors. The dataset in our experiments contains 10 actions and 93 videos. Among them, the actor named lena, has two run, skip and walk action videos. Silhouettes extracted from backgrounds and original image sequences are also provided in the dataset. In our experiments, all recognition rates were computed with the leave-one out cross validation. Details are as follows: 8 out of the 9 actors in the database are used as the training samples and the 9th is used for evaluation. This procedure is repeated for all 9 actors and the rates are averaged.

### 3.2 Processing

We directly use the silhouettes provided in the dataset for subsequent processing. The MEI and MHI were firstly calculated for each action, and the parameter $\tau$ is set as the frame number of the sequence. For each training set, randomly select some actions and set their class label as unknown. Then, the constrained semi-supervised kmeans algorithm is used to predict the category of unlabeled data. After this procedure, the average templates for each action are calculated. Fig. 4 shows the average MEI and MHI examples during processing.

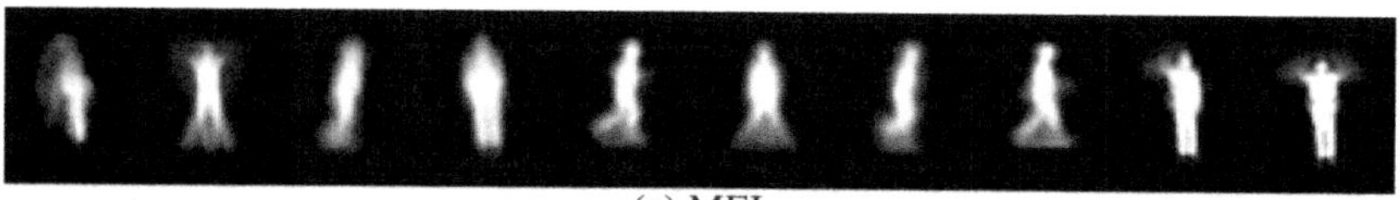

(a) MEI

(b) MHI

**Fig. 4.** Average MEI and MHI of different category actions

### 3.3 Analysis

The average recognition rates of our method for MEI and MHI are 95.70% and 93.55 when all the training examples are labeled. In comparison, the recognition rate of exemplar-based embedding method reported in [7] is 97.7% for 50 exemplars. The work of Ali et al. in [10] used a motion representation based on chaotic invariants and reported 92.6%, while Wang and Suter reported recognition rate of 97.78% with an approach that uses kernel-PCA for dimensional reduction and factorial conditional random fields to model motion dynamics in [11]. Table 1 summarizes action classification accuracies using different schemes on Weizmann dataset. So, the accuracy of our method is very close to those of state-of-art approaches. Comparing to the existed approaches, our method is much easier to be implemented and has less parameters to be adjusted.

**Table 1.** Action classification using different schemes

| Schemes | Accuracy (%) |
|---|---|
| Exemplar-based embedding in [7] | 97.70 |
| Chaotic invariants based motion representation in[10] | 92.60 |
| Kernel principal component analysis based feature extraction and factorial conditional random field based motion modeling in[11] | 97.78 |
| Hierarchical model in[12] | 72.80 |
| Space-Time shape models in[13] | 97.50 |
| Boosting EigenActions algorithm in [14] | 98.30 |
| MEI with correlation coefficients in our work | 95.70 |
| MHI with correlation coefficients in our work | 93.55 |

For each category action, we randomly select some sequence from training set and set their class labels as unknown. The average recognition rate vs. percent of labeled examples is shown in Fig.5. Here, the recognition rate is the average of 50 independent experiments. Obviously, the recognition rates rise gradually with the increase of percent of labeled examples. This result demonstrates that our approach is an effective semi-supervised human action recognition method. Its accuracy can reach above 80% even when the number of labeled data is very small (<=10%), and the accuracy of our algorithm can reach above 90% when half of the training examples are labeled.

To examine and analyze which action sequences are incorrectly classified, we specifically show the confusion matrixes in Fig. 6, where the percent of labeled data is 50%. From these two confuse matrixes, we can find the major classification error are caused by the three actions of “skip”, “jump” and “run”. This is because these three actions have both temporal and spatial similarities. Obviously, the misclassified actions, marked with gray in figure, are consistent to their indistinguishability as shown in Fig 3.

From Fig.6, we know the average recognition rate of MEI is slightly larger than MHI. This seems be some contradictory to Fig.3. This is because in Weizmann dataset, the MHI of “run” and “skip” are almost identical as shown in Fig.7. This can also be easily found through comparing Fig. 6 (a) and Fig. 6 (b). In Fig. 6, the average number of correct classified examples of action “skip” is 9.06 by MEI, while MHI is only 5.74.

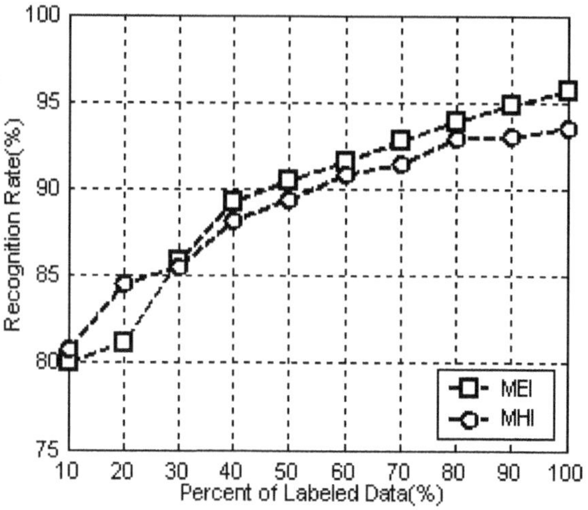


**Fig. 5.** Average recognition rates vs. percent of labeled data

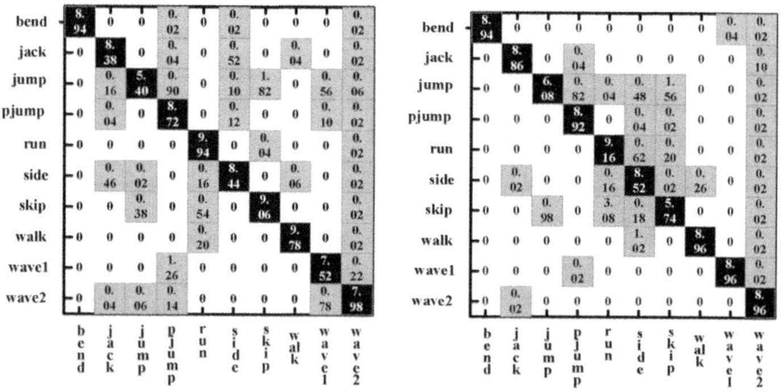


(a) MEI (b) MHI

**Fig. 6.** Confusion matrix with our method when the labeled training examples percent is 50%

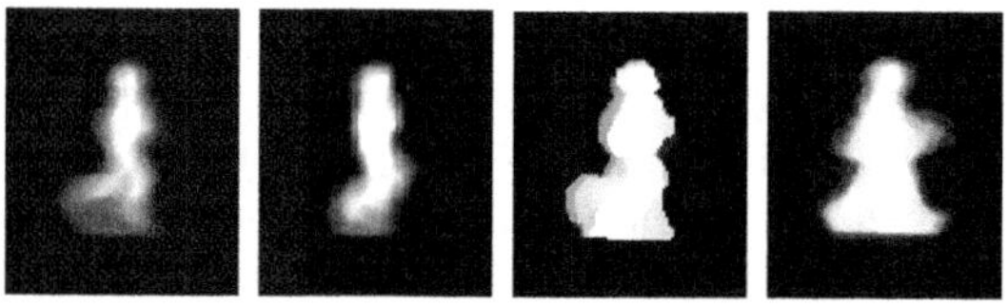

**Fig. 7.** MEI and MHI of action run and skip

### 3.4 Discussion

The main contribution of this paper is that the proposed method can correct classify human actions by only using very small number of labeled actions for training. And the feature extraction and action recognition methods are also very simple and have less parameter to be adjusted. However, much work still remains open: 1) although the results on Weizmann dataset are encouraging, evaluations on a larger and realistic database need to be investigated in order to be more conclusive; 2) the variation of camera orientation and zoom must be considered in practice. For Weizmann dataset, since the actions are captured from the side of the actors, MEI and MHI are effective feature representations for recognition. We think when the camera zooms changes, the actions, which can be distinguished by MEI and MHI are still distinguishable. Our method may still be effective. However, when the camera orientation changes, the actions, which originally can be distinguished by MEI and MHI, may become similar. In this condition, we need either choose other feature representations or use more than one camera. For example, using two cameras placed such that they have orthogonal views of subject. 3) Consideration of action semantics. In our method, we classify the human actions only by their visual information, without considering their semantics. So, our method may failure for some complex actions, such as grasping motions to high, medium and low positions. This action may lead to full MHI and MEI for the grasping arm. Hence, any motion of this arm could be viewed as a grasping motion even if it is not. For these complex actions recognition, the visual information may be inadequate; we also need context and background information for action understanding. And the simple pattern recognition may be not fully competent, that means we also need use some advanced artificial intelligence methods, such as rule-base reasoning, to understand such actions.

## 4 Conclusion

In this paper, a human action recognition algorithm based on constrained semi-superverised kmeans clustering is proposed. Compared to the exist methods, the main contribution of our approach is: it can achieve high accuracy recognition under the situation that only using very small number of labeled training data examples.

**Acknowledgments.** We would like to thank the anonymous reviewers for their valuable comments. The work was supported by "the Fundamental Research Funds for the Central Universities (10QG21)".

## References


1. Du, Y., Chen, F., Xu, W., et al.: A Survey On The Vision-based Human Motion Recognition. J. Acta Electrionica Sinica. 35, 377–387 (2007)
2. Gu, J., Ding, X., Wang, S.: A Survey of Activity Analysis Algorithms. Journal of Image and Graphics 14, 976–990 (2009)
3. Popple, R.: A Survey On Vision-based Human Action Recognition. J. Image and Vision Computing. 28, 976–990 (2010)
4. Yamato, J., Ohya, J., Ishii, K.: Recognizing Human Action In Time-sequential Images Using Hidden Markov Model. In: IEEE International Conference on Computer Vision and Pattern Recognition, pp. 379–385. IEEE Press, New York (1992)

5. Bobick, A.F., Davis, J.W.: The Recognition of Human Movement Using Temporal Templates. J. IEEE Trans. on Pattern Analysis and Machine Intelligence 25, 257–267 (2001)
6. Wang, L., Suter, D.: Informative Shape Representations for Human Action Recognition. In: International Conference on Pattern Recognition, pp. 1266–1269. IEEE Press, Hong Kong (2006)
7. Weinland, D., Boyer, E.: Action Recognition Using Exemplar-based Embedding. In: IEEE International Conference on Computer Vision and Pattern Recognition, pp. 1–7. IEEE Press, Anchorage (2008)
8. http://www.wisdom.weizmann.ac.il/~vision/SpaceTimeActions.html
9. Basu, S., Banerjee, A., Mooney, R.: Semi-supervised Clustering By Seeding. In: International Conference on Machine Learning, pp. 19–26. IEEE Press, Sydney (2002)
10. Ali, S., Basharat, A., Shah, M.: Chaotic Invariants for Human Action Recognition. In: International Conference on Computer Vision, pp. 1–8. IEEE Press, Janeiro (2007)
11. Wang, L., Sute, D.: Recognizing Human Activities from Silhouettes: Motion Subspace and Factorial Discriminative Graphical Mode. In: IEEE International Conference on Computer Vision and Pattern Recognition, pp. 1–7. IEEE Press, Minneapolis (2007)
12. Niebles, J.C., Li, F.F.: A Hierarchical Model of Shape and Appearance for Human Action Classification. In: IEEE Computer Society Conference on Computer Vision and Pattern Recognition, pp. 1–8. IEEE Press, Minneapolis (2007)
13. Gorelick, L., Blank, M., Shechtman, E., et al.: Actions as Space-time Shapes. J. IEEE Trans on Pattern Analysis and Machine Intelligence 29, 2247–2253 (2007)
14. Liu, C., Yuen, P.C.: Human Action Recognition Using Boosted Eigen Actions. J. Image and Vision Computing 28, 825–835 (2010)

# A New Region Growing Algorithm for Triangular Mesh Recovery from Scattered 3D Points

Chengjiang Long[1], Jianhui Zhao[1,*], Ravindra S. Goonetilleke[2], Shuping Xiong[3], Yihua Ding[1], Zhiyong Yuan[1], and Yuanyuan Zhang[1]

[1] Computer School, Wuhan University, Wuhan, Hubei, 430072, PR China
jianhuizhao@whu.edu.cn

[2] Dept. Industrial Engineering and Logistics Management, Hong Kong University of Science and Technology (HKUST), Hong Kong

[3] School of Design and Human Engineering, Ulsan National Institute of Science and Technology (UNIST), Ulsan, 689-798, Republic of Korea

**Abstract.** A novel region growing algorithm is proposed for triangular mesh recovery from scattered 3D points. In our method, the new principle is used to determine the seed triangle considering both maximum angle and minimum length; the open influence region is defined for the active edge under processing; positional element is added into the criterion to choose the most suitable active point; geometric integrity is maintained by analyzing different situations of the selected active point and their corresponding treatments. Our approach has been tested with various unorganized point clouds, and the experimental results proved its efficiency in both accuracy and speed. Compared with the existing similar techniques, our algorithm has the ability to recover triangular meshes while preserving better topological coherence with the original 3D points.

**Keywords:** surface recovery, triangular mesh, region growing, point cloud.

## 1 Introduction

Currently there are three typical approaches for surface reconstruction from scattered 3D points, and they are sculpting-based approach [1-3], implicit surface approach [4-6] and region growing approach [7-12]. The drawbacks of sculpting-based approach are its expensive computation and complex extraction. The limitation of implicit surface approach is that it only approximates rather than interpolates the scattered points, correspondingly it cannot guarantee the obtained surface passing through the original sample points. Different from the foregoing two approaches, region growing approach starts with a seed unit and then continues until all the points have been considered. Comparatively, the efficiency of this approach is very computationally high, thus has received more attentions.

The key technique of region growing approach lies in the selection of a point to form the new triangle with an active edge. In BPA algorithm [7], a sphere with user

[*] Corresponding author.

Z. Pan et al. (Eds.): Transactions on Edutainment VI, LNCS 6758, pp. 237–246, 2011.

specified radius pivots around an active edge until it contacts another point, and the contacted point is chosen to construct the new triangle. Petitjean presented their method based on regular interpolation [8], and the different properties are compared between the regular and irregular point sets. Huang [9] projected the K nearest points of each endpoint of an active edge onto the plane defined by the triangle adjacent to the active edge, and then a point is selected among the K points based on the minimal length criterion to form a new triangle. From a seed triangle, the algorithm of Lin grows a partially recovered triangular mesh by selecting a new point based on the intrinsic property of the point cloud, i.e. degree of sampling uniformity [10].

However, there are still four problems not well dealt with in region growing approach. (1) Determination of the seed triangle: the existing methods use specific principles to choose its three points, and a more comprehensive strategy needs to be defined to guarantee the quality of seed triangle and avoid possible awful effects on the subsequently generated triangles. (2) Determination of the influence region: closed region is often used to reduce the computing cost, but may cause poor performance on data with sharp and long edges. (3) Determination of the best active point: different with the seed triangle, the positional information in influence region should be considered in the evaluation criterion to select the most suitable active point. (4) Determination of the geometric integrity: geometric integrity has to be maintained in construction of new triangle, thus it is very important to analyze different situations of the selected active point in details and then treat with them respectively.

To solve the aforementioned problems, a novel region growing algorithm is proposed in this paper. Contributions of our method include: (1) points of seed triangle are determined with the principle considering both maximum angle and minimum length; (2) one open influence region instead of the closed region is defined for the active edge; (3) the criterion for active point selection also takes the positional element into account; (4) different situations of the active point and their corresponding treatments are analyzed in order to maintain the geometric integrity. The rest of our paper is organized as follows: related definitions and point cloud pre-processing are described in Section 2, the proposed new algorithm is presented in Section 3, experimental results are illustrated, compared and analyzed in Section 4, and then the conclusion is given in Section 5.

## 2 Definitions and Data Preprocess

### 2.1 Related Definitions

Following terms are defined for the proposed reconstruction algorithm:

(1) Active edge: each newly reconstructed edge prior to processing;
(2) Influence region: the region of searching for a new point to form a new triangle with an active edge, which may or may not contain a new point;
(3) Inner edge: the edge with 2 adjacent faces;
(4) Fixed point: a point from the point cloud whose incident edges are all inner edges;
(5) Bounded edge: an edge whose influence region contains only fixed points, i.e. the edge has only one face adjacent to it;

(6) Fixed edge: the edge whose adjacent triangles have been determined completely, thus both inner edge and bounded edge are fixed edges;
(7) Active point: the point with no edges or an active edge incident to it.

### 2.2 Preprocessing of Point Cloud

In region growing based surface recovery, searching for the best active point is very time consuming. For the unorganized $n$ scattered 3D points, the time complexity of global search on the entire point cloud is $O(n^2)$. The best active point can only lie in the neighbor region of the related active edge, i.e. the local regions of its two vertexes. Therefore, to avoid the global search, the preprocessing techniques are applied to determine the local region of each scattered point, i.e. its K nearest neighbors [13]. Based on our experiments, parameter K is assigned with a value which varies from 20 to 50.

## 3 Our Algorithm

### 3.1 Determination of the Seed Triangle

For region growing approach, quality of the reconstructed triangular mesh can be improved with a better seed triangle, and it is determined in our approach as follows:

Step 1. Search for the point $P$ whose z-value is the maximum in the point cloud;
Step 2. Search for the point $Q$ that is the nearest to $P$ and forms a line between them;
Step 3. Search for the third point $R$ ;

For point $R^*$ from $N_P^K$ (K nearest neighbors of $P$ ) or $N_Q^K$ (K nearest neighbors of $Q$ ), its energy value can be evaluated by the following functions:

$$E_s(R^*) = \mathrm{E}_L(R^*) \bullet \mathrm{E}_A(R^*) \tag{1}$$

$$\mathrm{E}_L(R^*) = d_{PQ}^2 + d_{PR^*}^2 + d_{QR^*}^2 \tag{2}$$

$$\mathrm{E}_A(R^*) = ctg\angle PR^*Q \tag{3}$$

where $d_{PQ}$ , $d_{PR^*}$ and $d_{QR^*}$ are the lengths of segment $PQ$ , $PR^*$ and $QR^*$ respectively, while $\angle PR^*Q$ is the angle between $PR^*$ and $QR^*$ . Therefore, considering the principle of both "minimum length" [14] and "maximum angle" [15], point $R$ is determined by

$$R = \min_{R^* \in (N_P^K \cup N_Q^K)} (E_s(R^*)) \tag{4}$$

Step 4. Take $\Delta PQR$ as the seed triangle.

Thereafter, normal vector of the seed triangle is adjusted to be outward as the base for the other triangles to be produced. If the inner product of the normal vector of the seed triangle and the constant vector (0, 0, 1) is positive, it points outward; otherwise the direction of the normal vector is reversed. Once outward normal vector of the seed triangle is determined, normal vectors of the subsequently generated triangles can be adjusted to be outward in the same way.

### 3.2 Influence Region for Active Edge

To maintain the topological consistency, a suitable active point for the active edge should be in front of the existing triangle, i.e. not all the active points satisfy with the necessary geometric constraints. As illustrated in Fig. 1, a new defined open influence region instead of the usually used close region is determined in our method to help filter the active points.

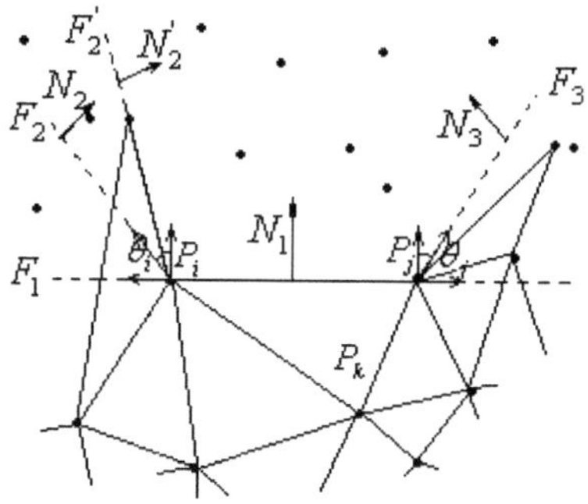

**Fig. 1.** The open influence region

The open influence region is determined with three faces, $F_1$, $F_2$ and $F_3$, and angle $\theta_i$, $\theta_j$ are used to control the influence region. Suppose $N_{ij}$ is the normal vector of triangle $\Delta P_i P_j P_k$, each face of the region can be represented by one point in the face and the normal vector of the face as

$$F_1(P_i, N_1 = norm(N_{ij} \times P_i P_j)) \tag{5}$$

$$F_2(P_i, N_2 = norm((N_1 + tg\theta_i \bullet norm(P_j P_i)) \times N_{ij}) \tag{6}$$

$$F_3(P_j, N_3 = norm(N_{ij} \times (N_1 + tg\theta_j \bullet norm(P_i P_j))) \tag{7}$$

To maintain the geometrical integrity of the reconstructed triangular mesh, the intersection between the triangle to be generated and the existing triangles should be null or the existing active edges. Thus, among the edges incident to point $P_i$ ($P_j$), if there are some edges lying in the same side of face $F_2$ ($F_3$) with the edge $P_i P_j$, face $F_2$ ($F_3$) should be renewed. As shown in Fig. 1, face $F_2$ is changed in this case to be

$$F_2^{'}(P_i, N_2 = norm(P_i P_h \times N_{ij})) \tag{8}$$

### 3.3 Select the Most Suitable Active Point

There are some active points in the influence region of the active edge, one of them should be selected and used to construct a new triangle with the active edge in each step of the region growing method. Often used criteria to select the most suitable active point are minimum length or maximum angle. Besides them, the positional information is also considered in our algorithm to obtain better triangles.

Similar with selection of the third vertex of the seed triangle, the best active point is selected from K neighbors of two vertexes ( $N_{P_i}^K$ and $N_{P_j}^K$ ) of the active edge, and the difference is that the candidates are further filtered by the influence region. Suppose the set of active points in the influence region of active edge $P_iP_j$ is $Inf(P_iP_j)$, the most suitable active point only needs to be chosen from the point set of $(N_{P_i}^K \cup N_{P_j}^K) \cap Inf(P_iP_j)$.

It is possible to avoid more sharp triangles if the selected active point is not too close to any of the three faces of the open influence region, so positional element of the candidate point is also taken into account. Suppose $O$ is the geometric centre of $(N_{P_i}^K \cup N_{P_j}^K) \cap Inf(P_iP_j)$, the active point $P_{g^*}$ can be evaluated by the following functions:

$$\xi(P_{g^*}) = \mathrm{E}_L(P_{g^*}) \bullet \mathrm{E}_A(P_{g^*}) + \mathrm{E}_{Inf}(P_{g^*}) \tag{9}$$

$$\mathrm{E}_L(P_{g^*}) = \| P_i - P_j \|^2 + \| P_i - P_{g^*} \|^2 + \| P_j - P_{g^*} \|^2 \tag{10}$$

$$\mathrm{E}_A(P_{g^*}) = ctg\angle P_i P_{g^*} P_j \tag{11}$$

$$\mathrm{E}_{Inf}(P_{g^*}) = \eta \| P_{g^*} - O \| \tag{12}$$

where $\eta$ is the adjusting parameter. Its value usually varies with different 3D scattered point cloud. Thus the best active point $P_g$ is determined by

$$P_g = \min_{P_{g^*} \in (N_{P_i}^K \cup N_{P_j}^K) \cap \mathrm{Inf}(P_iP_j)} (\xi(P_{g^*})) \tag{13}$$

### 3.4 Constraints of Geometric Integrity

After the best active point is selected, it can be used to construct a new triangle with the active edge. However, generation of the new triangle may bring a sequence of effects, e.g. producing the other triangles, changing the status of some related edges or points. Therefore, this step is very important for the region growing approach. In our method, different situations of the active point are considered, and they are divided into ten situations as shown in Fig. 2 ( $P_g$ is the selected active point, $P_i$, $P_j$, $P_m$, $P_n$, $P_{m1}$, $P_{m2}$, $P_{m3}$, $P_{n1}$, $P_{n2}$, $P_{n3}$ are the points connected to $P_g$ ).

For the above ten situations, the corresponding treatments are different but their principle is similar. First, add the newly generated triangles (one, two or three) to the list of triangles, label the active edge just processed as fixed edge and then remove it from the active edge list. Second, check each newly generated edge: if the edge is active, add it into the active edge list and label it as active edge, otherwise label it as fixed edge. Third, check the states of the directly connected edges and points; change the state label if it has been converted from active to fixed while the edges should be removed from the active edge list if their states were converted from active to fixed.

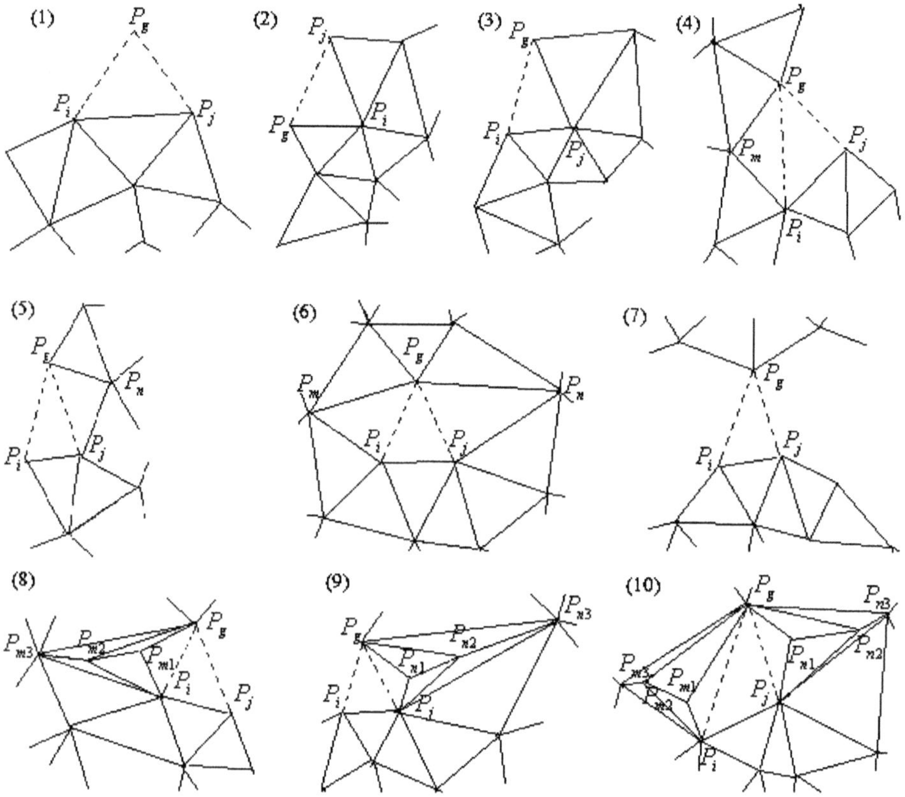

**Fig. 2.** Different situations of the active point

### 3.5 Description of the Algorithm

The pseudo-code for our recovery algorithm is described as follows:

```
Our recovery algorithm [in-file, out-file]
Input: in-file is the point cloud file.
Output: out-file is the triangle list file.
```

```
   (/*APList: Active point list*/)
   (/*AEList: Active edge list*/)
   (/*TList: triangle list*/)
1. read in the point cloud from in-file and store them in
   APList.
2. Search K neighbors for each point.
3. determine the seed triangle, add the triangle in TList and
   add 3 edges in AEList
4. while (AElist is not empty) do
5.    determine influence region for one edge from AEList.
6.    if no active point in the influence region
         set the edge as boundary edge, update AEList, and then
         return 4.
7.    end if
8.    select the best point from active points in the influence
     region considering Eq. 13. add the newly generated
     triangles in TList.
9.    check and update APlist and AEList according to the
      contrain of geometric integrity.
10.  end while
11.  write out TList into out-file.
12. return.
```

## 4 Experimental Results

Our algorithm has been tested by experiments on a PC with Intel(R) Core(TM) i3 CPU, 2.27GHz, 1.92GB RAM. As shown in Fig. 3, seven sets of scanned 3D point cloud (1st row) including Bonze, Eight, Fandisk, Hand, Manequin, Rockeram and ThreePeaks are used as the experimental data, and the numbers of points in them are 32570, 776, 11984, 39231, 11703, 10043 and 1907 respectively. The recovered triangular meshes of the 7 models (2nd row) show that the proposed algorithm can generate surfaces with good quality from scattered 3D points.

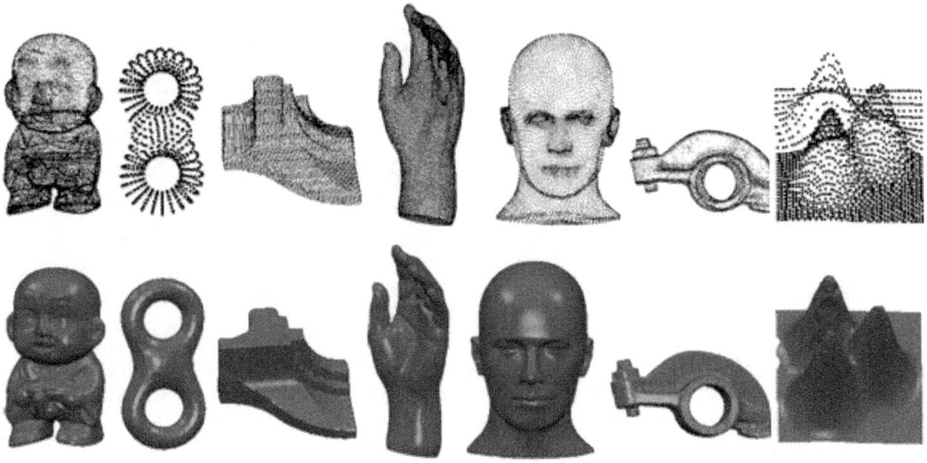

**Fig. 3.** Triangular mesh recovery from 7 point clouds

To illustrate the performance of our method for more complicated point clouds, three data, i.e. Buster with sharp edges, Dino with long tails, Frog with bottom holes are tested, as shown in Fig. 4. It can be found that fine details are preserved in the recovered surface.

Ref. [10] is also a region growing based approach for triangular mesh recovery, so it is implemented and compared with our algorithm in both speed and accuracy. Computational cost of 7 point clouds in Fig. 3 are listed in Table 1, where K is the number of nearest neighbors, KNN is the time spent on searching for K neighbors, Ref1 and Ref2 are spent time from Ref. [10] for surface recovery without and with KNN, Our1 and Our2 are spent time from our algorithm without and with KNN. It can be found that our approach has better performance in time complexity.

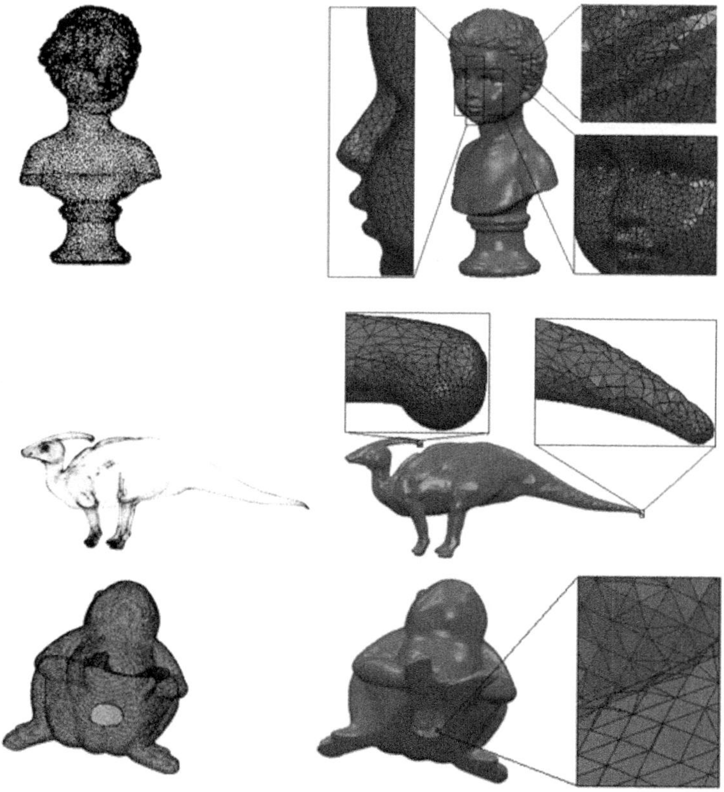

**Fig. 4.** Reconstructed results with enlarged details

Two sets of 3D scattered point clouds are selected to compare the quality of reconstructed surface, as shown in Fig. 5. The original point clouds are presented in the first row; the reconstructed surfaces from Ref. [10] are displayed in the second row, while the reconstructed triangular meshes from our algorithm are displayed in the third row. For point cloud on the left, result from Ref. [10] ignores many details on the border, but result from our method recovers the boundary shape much better. For point cloud on the right, result from Ref. [10] can only generate a rough approximation of the hole in the 3D point cloud, but result from our method has reconstructed the hole with much higher precision. It can be proved that our proposed approach has the ability to produce the triangular meshes with good quality from scattered 3D points while preserving the topological coherence from the original point cloud.

**Table 1.** Comparison of computational expense (Unit: second)

| Name | Vertices | K | KNN | Ref1 | Our1 | Ref2 | Our2 |
|---|---|---|---|---|---|---|---|
| Bonze | 32570 | 25 | 1.25 | 2.921 | 1.468 | 4.171 | 2.718 |
| Eight | 776 | 28 | 0.093 | 0.094 | 0.047 | 0.187 | 0.14 |
| Fandisk | 11984 | 30 | 0.5 | 1.297 | 0.64 | 1.797 | 1.14 |
| Hand | 39231 | 30 | 1.562 | 3.703 | 2.062 | 5.265 | 4.624 |
| Manequin | 11703 | 35 | 0.578 | 1.453 | 0.672 | 2.031 | 1.25 |
| Rockeram | 10043 | 35 | 0.546 | 1.203 | 0.563 | 1.749 | 1.109 |
| ThreePeaks | 1907 | 25 | 0.125 | 0.156 | 0.078 | 0.281 | 0.203 |

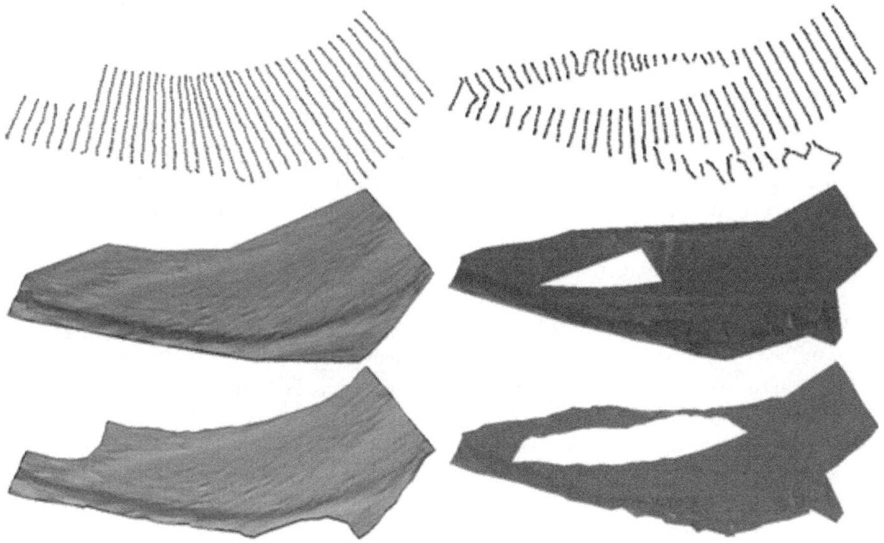

**Fig. 5.** Comparison of surface quality

## 5 Conclusion

A novel region growing based algorithm is presented in this paper for triangular surface reconstruction from unorganized 3D points. For the four key problems, i.e. determinations of seed triangle, influence region, the best active point, and the geometric integrity, related new techniques are proposed to deal with them.

Our method can recover a triangular mesh from the scattered 3D point cloud with good quality. Compared with the existing similar techniques, our algorithm can perform better in both accuracy and speed. Currently, the method is tested with more point clouds, and will be compared with the other approaches for triangular mesh reconstruction except for the ones of region growing type.

**Acknowledgments.** The work was supported by National Basic Research Program of China (973 Program, No. 2011CB707904), National Natural Science Foundation of China (No. 60603079, No. 61070079, No. 71001066), Research Grants Council of Hong Kong (No. 613008), Shanghai Pujiang Program (No. PJ[2009]00861), PhD Programs Foundation from The Ministry of Education of China (No. 20100073120046).

## References

1. Kuo, C.-C., Yau, H.-T.: Reconstruction of virtual parts from unorganized scanned data for automated dimensional inspection. J. Comput Inf. Sci. Eng. Trans. ASME 3(1), 76–86 (2003)
2. Kolingerova, I., Zalik, B.: Reconstructing domain boundaries within a given set of points using Delaunay triangulation. Computers & Geosciences 32(9), 1310–1319 (2006)
3. Wang, D., Hassan, O., Morgan, K., Weatherill, N.: Efficient surface reconstruction from contours based on two-dimensional delaunay triangulation. International Journal for Numerical Methods in Engineering 65(5), 734–751 (2006)
4. Hoppe, H., DeRose, T., Duchampy, T., McDonaldz, J., Stuetzlez, W.: Surface reconstruction from unorganized points. In: Proceedings of SIGGRAPH 1992, pp. 71–78 (1992)
5. Carr, J.-C., Beatson, R.-K., Cherrie, J.-B., Mitchell, T.-J., Fright, W.-R., McCallum, B.-C.: Reconstruction and representation of 3D objects with radial basis functions. In: Proceedings of SIGGRAPH 2001, pp. 67–76 (2001)
6. Schreiner, J., Scheiclegger, C.-E., Silva, C.-T.: High-quality extraction of Isosurfaces from regular and irregular grids. Visualization and Computer Graphics 12(5), 1205–1212 (2006)
7. Bernardini, F., Mittleman, J., Rushmeier, H., Silva, C., Taubin, G.: The ball pivoting algorithm for surface reconstruction. IEEE Trans. Vis. Comput. Graph. 5(4), 349–359 (1999)
8. Petitjean, S., Boyer, E.: Regular and non-regular point sets: properties and reconstruction. Comput. Geom. Theory 19, 101–126 (2001)
9. Huang, J., Menq, C.-H.: Combinatorial manifold mesh reconstruction and optimization from unorganized points with arbitrary topology. Comput-Aided Design 34(2), 149–165 (2002)
10. Lin, H., Tai, C., Wang, G.: A mesh reconstruction algorithm driven by an intrinsic property of a point cloud. Computer Aided Design 36(1), 1–9 (2004)
11. DoRego, R.-L., Araujo, A.-F., De, L.-N., Fernando, B.: Growing self-organizing maps for surface reconstruction from unstructured point clouds. In: IEEE International Conference on Neural Networks, pp. 1900–1905 (2007)
12. Lv, H., Wang, Y.: A heuristic approach to reconstruct triangle mesh from unorganized point cloud. In: The 6th International Conference on Fuzzy Systems and Knowledge Discovery, pp. 87–91 (2009)
13. Jagan, S., Hanan, S., Amitabh, V.: A fast all nearest neighbor algorithm for applications involving large point-clouds. Computers & Graphics 31, 157–174 (2007)
14. Boissonant, J.-D., Cazals, F.: Smooth surface reconstruction via natural neighbor interpolation of distance functions. In: Proceedings of 16th Annual Symposium On Computational Geometry (SCG 2000), Hong Kong, pp. 223–232 (2000)
15. Cheng, W., Sorguc, A.-G., Shinoda, J., Hagiwara, I.: MOAA and topology judgment for mesh construction. American Society of Mechanical Engineers 482, 227–238 (2004)

# Detecting Moving Targets from Traffic Video Based on the Dynamic Background Model

Bin Shao[1,2], Yunliang Jiang[1,2], and Qing Shen[1]

[1] School of Information and Engineering, Huzhou Teachers College, Huzhou, 313000, China
[2] State Key Laboratory of CAD&CG, Zhejiang University, Hangzhou, 310027, China
shaobin@hutc.zj.cn

**Abstract.** An efficient method to detect the moving target in traffic video based on the dynamic background model is proposed in this paper, after analyzing existing methods for target detection. The model of target detection is given firstly, then a rough set weighted classification method for video image is presented. Based on the video classifications, the background model is established on the historical data. The background judgment and moving object detection for video are done with this model and then the background model is updated with the current video. The experimental results show that this method can adapt the diversification of background and has high adaptability and precision. The processing speed can meet the requirement of real time detection.

**Keywords:** image processing;rough set weighted classification;transportation monitoring;dynamic background mode.

## 1 Introduction

With the development of modern transportation, the research and application of Intelligent Transportation System (ITS) draw more and more attention. How to separate the moving object from complex backgrounds is a crucial step. A wrong moving object detection will cause transportation monitoring to be invalid. Generally Moving target detection methods are classified to being background subtraction, adjacent frame difference method, background model and optical flow based method. The background subtraction method is the method of detecting the target with the difference between the current frame picture and the known background image [1]. The adjacent frame difference method is the method of detecting the target with differential of the current frame image and the adjacent frame image [2]. For the background model method, establish a specific model to simulate background image, determine whether object pixel or background pixel by comparing the pixel value of current frame image with background model, thus the target is detected [3]. It can be regarded as a kind of background subtraction. The optical flow based method is a method for detecting moving targets by the change of optical flow fields in image sequences [4]. Targets can be detected ideally with all the above theories. However, in the practice, the moving target detection becomes complex because of various

Z. Pan et al. (Eds.): Transactions on Edutainment VI, LNCS 6758, pp. 247–255, 2011.

external conditions. The complexity is shown in the illumination change, the interference, block, hole problem, shadow problem, the missing of target and so on.

Dynamic background model belongs to the background model method. Firstly original video images are preprocessed, including image de-noising, image enhancement, image restoration and so on and are classified according to rough set classification method. Then on the basis of video image preprocessing, deal with original video images with machine learning, establishing pixel distribution model of each kind of video images. Lastly, after machine learning, deal with real-time video images. Thus self-learning function is realized. The process is shown as Fig.1.

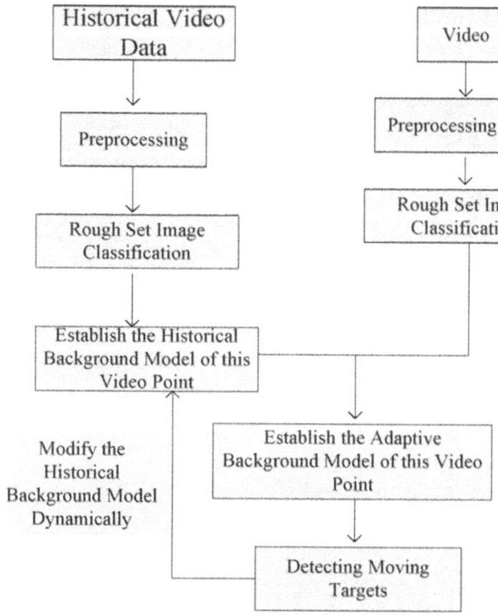


**Fig. 1.** Detecting moving targets from traffic video based on the dynamic background model

In the detection model shown as Fig.1, video images are classified according to rough set classification method and dynamic background model is established. These are the key of detecting moving objects successfully. The background varies with time, if it isn't classified, when gradual change accumulates to a certain degree, it will lead to qualitative change. If there is no obvious discrepancy between day and night, but because the illumination is different, day and night should belong to different background classifications respectively. Rough set is a good tool for classifying the uncertainty.

# 2 Video Image Classification Based on Rough Set

## 2.1 Probabilistic Rough Set Models

A knowledge representation system is expressed by a 4-tuple S=<U, A, V, f> [6], where $U = \{x_1, x_2, \ldots, x_n\}$ is a non-empty finite set called the universe; $A=C\cup D$

is the union of condition attribute set and decision attribute set; $V = \bigcup_{a \in A} V_a$, $V_a$ is the domain of attribute $\alpha$; $f : U \times A \to V$ is information function, the value of every object $x_i$ in the designated U, namely $\forall a \in A, x \in U, f(x,a) \in V_a$. The equivalence relation R formed by attributes or attribute sets partitions the universe into equivalence classes. In rough set theory, equivalence class is also called basic concept or knowledge granule and is basic cell of knowledge. Let $[x]_R$ denote the equivalence class of R, containing x. For object subset $X \subseteq U$ and relation R, if R consists of the union of equivalence classes generated by R, X is definable for R, otherwise X is not-definable. The not-definable set is also called rough set. In Pawlak rough set model, rough set is defined by a pair of accurate sets called the R-lower and the R-upper approximation, respectively, and defined as follows:

$$\underline{R}(X) = \bigcup\{Y \in U/R | Y \subseteq X\}$$
$$\overline{R}(X) = \bigcup\{Y \in U/R | Y \cap X \neq \varnothing\} \quad (1)$$

The lower approximation is the greatest definable set included in X, and the upper approximation is the least definable set containing.

The above formula is based on completion of available information, ignoring incompletion and distortion of available information, so this is powerless in extracting rules of the inconsistent decision table. Probabilistic rough set is used to describe uncertain information system [7]. The triplet $A_P$ = （U， R， P） is called a probabilistic approximation space, where U is the universe, and P（X|Y） denote the conditional probability of an object X being in state Y given. Let $0 \leq \beta < \alpha \leq 1$, for any $X \subseteq U$, the probabilistic lower and upper approximations of X about the probabilistic approximation space $A_P$ = （U， R， P） with parameter α and β are defined respectively as follows.

$$\underline{R}_\alpha(X) = \{x \in U | P(X|[x] \geq \alpha\}$$
$$\overline{R}_\beta(X) = \{x \in U | P(X|[x] > \beta\} \quad (2)$$

If $\alpha = 1$, $\beta = 0$, this model is the standard rough set model.

The difference set of lower and upper approximation sets is defined as the boundary of the set X and it can not be exactly described according to the existing knowledge. Rough set theory can quantify these uncertain information. The probabilistic rough set allows some equivalence classes to be partitioned into the positive region or the negative region when the conditional probability is between 0 and 1 in standard rough set, so the boundary in probabilistic rough set is less than it in standard rough set. It is shown that the application of probabilistic rough set is more widespread than it of standard rough set.

Let $F=\{X_1, X_2, \ldots, X_n\}$ be a class of U, and the class is independent of knowledge R. It maybe the decision given by realm experts. The subset X=(i=1, 2, …, n) is the class of classification F, then the lower approximation and upper approximation of F are defined by :

$$\underline{R}F=\{\underline{R}X_1,\underline{R}X_2,\ldots,\underline{R}X_n\}$$
$$\overline{R}F=\{\overline{R}X_1,\overline{R}X_2,\ldots,\overline{R}X_n\} \tag{3}$$

where the definitions of $\underline{R}X_i$ of $\underline{R}X_i$ are given in the formula (1). The lower and upper approximations of the classification in probabilistic rough set can be defined by:

$$\underline{R}_{\alpha}F=\{\underline{R}_{\alpha}X_1,\underline{R}_{\alpha}X_2,\ldots,\underline{R}_{\alpha}X_n\}$$
$$\overline{R}_{\beta}F=\{\overline{R}_{\beta}X_1,\overline{R}_{\beta}X_2,\ldots,\overline{R}_{\beta}X_n\} \tag{4}$$

where the definitions of $\underline{R}_{\alpha}X_i$ and $\overline{R}_{\beta}X_i$ are given in the formula (2).

### 2.2 Image Classification Based on Probabilistic Rough Set

In the probabilistic rough set model, the importance of each attribute to the decision attribute is described by information entropy and the classified decision information is introduced to attribute importance weights. The sample set is partitioned into equivalence class of $U=\{X_1, X_2, \ldots\ldots, X_n\}$ according to the class number. R is the equivalence relation formed in the light of different features. Based on precision rough set model, the lower and upper approximation sets about the parameter α and βin probabilistic approximation space $A_P=(U, R, P)$ are defined by:

$$\underline{R}_{\alpha}U=\{\underline{R}_{\alpha}X_1,\underline{R}_{\alpha}X_2,\ldots,\underline{R}_{\alpha}X_n\}$$
$$\overline{R}_{\beta}U=\{\overline{R}_{\beta}X_1,\overline{R}_{\beta}X_2,\ldots,\overline{R}_{\beta}X_n\} \tag{5}$$

$\underline{R}_{\alpha}X_i$ and $\overline{R}_{\beta}X_i$ denote the lower and upper approximation sets of a set $X_k$ about parameter α and β in probabilistic approximation space $A_P$, respectively. $\underline{R}_{\alpha}U$ and $\overline{R}_{\beta}U$ describe the sets that the equivalence classes of equivalence relation R partitioning U affirmatively or possibly included in the equivalence classes of decision attribute partitioning U, respectively. The uncertain degree partitioned by this relation is measured with information entropy, defined by:

$$H(R)=-\sum_{i=1}^{n}P(X_i)\log P(X_i) \tag{6}$$

If S is another equivalence relation, let $S=\{Y_1, Y_2,\ldots, Y_n\}$, the conditional entropy of S when the knowledge R is known is defined by:

$$H(S \mid R) = -\sum_{i=1}^{n} P(X_i) \sum_{j=1}^{m} K \tag{7}$$

$$K = P(Y_j \mid X_i) \log P(Y_j \mid X_i)$$

The mutual information of the knowledge S and R is defined by:

$$I(R:S) = H(S) - H(S \mid R) \tag{8}$$

The information entropy measures the probability that the equivalence class of relation R partitioning the universe is exactly classified into the equivalence class decision attribute partitioning. Or it measures the information consistency that the relation formed by relation R and decision attribute partitions the universe. Intuitively, the high consistency, the larger the contribution of the attribute to classification will be and the more important the feature is. It can be seen that the mutual information I（R : S) measured the consistency of the attribute forming relation R with classification.

According to the decision attribute feature set S of the traffic video expert, the classified decision attribute is introduced to feature weights. The consistency of the feature partition with decision partition is computed by this kind of classification formula. This reflects the importance of the feature to classification. Video images can be classified according to the importance.

The nature of classifying video images is a kind of coarse classification. The coarse classification is simple and fast, so the image with color distribution features is a good method for coarse classification. The distinguishable chromatic aberration in the traditional RGB color model is nonlinear, so HSV color model is adopted here. This conversion needs consuming some computing resources, but the whole processing time is within the allowable range. So the distribution of historical video according to HSV image is taken as classified feature. The algorithm is as follows in more detail.

Step1: domain experts classify historical video into n classifications and give the typical video of each classification. Compute the HSV means of each frame of historical video, and give the initial value of parameter $\alpha$ and $\beta$.

Step 2: computer the lower and upper approximation sets under certain parameters $\alpha$ and $\beta$ according to formula (5). Thus each historical video image can be classified into the n classifications given by domain experts.

Step 3: according to the formula (8), analyze the classified historical video and experts give that the entropy between each kind of typical video images reaches the consistency or not. If it doesn't reach, the values of parameter $\alpha$ and $\beta$ need to be revised and go to step 2.

Step 4: classify the immediate video images with the revised parameters $\alpha$ and $\beta$ according to the formula (5).

The rough set method for video classification proposed in this paper is analyzed in the following example and the superiority of the new method is verified.

# 3 Background Automatic Model

Based on the rough set classification, the background model of each monitoring point is established. The immediate video images recognize moving objects according to each background model.

## 3.1 Establishment of Model

The background is gradually changed and the difference of the same classification is little within a certain time, so each pixel can be considered to satisfy the normal distribution $N(\mu,\sigma^2)$ and each pixel is independent, that is

$$p(x_{ij}) = \frac{1}{\sqrt{2\pi\sigma}} e^{-(x-\mu)^2/2\sigma^2} \tag{9}$$

Use historical images to establish models, give the maximum likelihood estimates. Each pixel satisfies the normal distribution $N(\mu,\sigma^2)$, and the historical pixel values $X_1, X_2, \ldots\ldots, X_n$ are samples. The likelihood function is designed as follows.

$$L = \prod_{i=1}^{n} \frac{1}{\sqrt{2\pi\sigma}} e^{-\frac{1}{2\sigma^2}(x_i-\mu)^2} = (\frac{1}{2\pi\sigma^2})^{\frac{n}{2}} e^{-\frac{1}{2\sigma^2}\sum_{i=1}^{n}(x_i-\mu)^2} \tag{10}$$

$$\ln L = -\frac{n}{2}\ln(2\pi) - \frac{n}{2}\ln\sigma^2 - \frac{1}{2\sigma^2}\sum_{i=1}^{n}(x_i-\mu)^2 \tag{11}$$

The likelihood equation is

$$\begin{aligned} \frac{\partial \ln L}{\partial \mu} &= \frac{1}{\sigma^2}\sum_{i=1}^{n}(x_i-\mu) = 0 \\ \frac{\partial \ln L}{\partial \sigma^2} &= \frac{1}{2\sigma^4}\sum_{i=1}^{n}(x_i-\mu)^2 - \frac{n}{2\sigma^2} = 0 \end{aligned} \tag{12}$$

The estimators of $\mu$ and $\sigma^2$ gotten by formula (14) are:

$$\begin{aligned} \hat{\mu} &= \frac{1}{n}\sum_{i=1}^{n} X_i \\ \hat{\sigma^2} &= \frac{1}{n}\sum_{i=1}^{n}(X_i-\mu)^2 \end{aligned} \tag{13}$$

For the original data of monitoring points, HSV background models of each pixel are established according to formula (13).

### 3.2 Jugement and Update of Background

After establishing background model according to the historical data, the new frame can be fitted. First judge the background. For the pixels of the new frame, if their HSV values are all among $[\mu-\sigma,\mu+\sigma]$, they are considered to be the background, otherwise they are judged to be moving objects.

After detecting the background, update the background model for the pixels judged to be the background. If $\mu$ and $\sigma^2$ are recalculated, the workload is large. We think that the weights of the current frame in the moving background should be relatively large, so suppose the update rate $\beta$ to compute:

$$\begin{aligned} \mu' &= (1-\beta)\mu + \beta X \\ (\sigma^2)' &= \min(\sigma^2, (1-\alpha)\sigma^2 + \beta(X-\mu)^2) \end{aligned} \quad (14)$$

$\mu'$ and $(\sigma^2)'$ are the mean and variance respectively after updating. $\mu$ and $\sigma^2$ are the mean and variance before updating. X is the pixel value of the new frame.

It can be seen that the updating of a background model has correlation with the current frame (including the historical image data) and is related to the current frame. So the background model can maintain stability in this classification.

## 4 Experimental Result and Analysis

We dealt with an image in Intel C2D E4600 PC. The resolution of the image is 460*345. Classify the historical image coarsely, and establish the background model according to formula (13), then process the real-time video image. Judge the background and update it according to formula (14). The historical video in the experiment is a detecting point on the data between October, 2006 and September, 2007. the real-time video is the detecting point on the data at October 16, 2007. The probabilistic parameter $\alpha$ is 0.75, $\beta$ is 0.35 and the background updating rate $\gamma$ is 0.3. The results are shown as Fig.2 and Fig. 3. Fig.2 is the original image and Fig.3 and the result.

From the original image, it can be found that the illumination of Fig.2(2) and Fig.2(b)is different from that of Fig.2(c) and Fig.2(d). Fig.2(2) and Fig.2(b) are brighter than Fig.2(c) and Fig.2(d), and there is a mountain shadow at the right road in Fig.2(2) and Fig.2(b). These are all the gradual change of the background. They can be recognized correctly with the method. The moving objects including falling leaves and flying birds can be detected. In the subsequent pattern recognition, the influence of small moving objects can be removed and only recognize the car.

The classification and modeling of historical video images are time-consuming. Processing one year video of a monitoring point needs 20 hours, however after modeling, processing one second real-time video needs about $0.3*10^{-2}$ seconds and the accuracy of recognizing moving objects is about 94.4%. The real-time, accurate and effective processing can be realized.

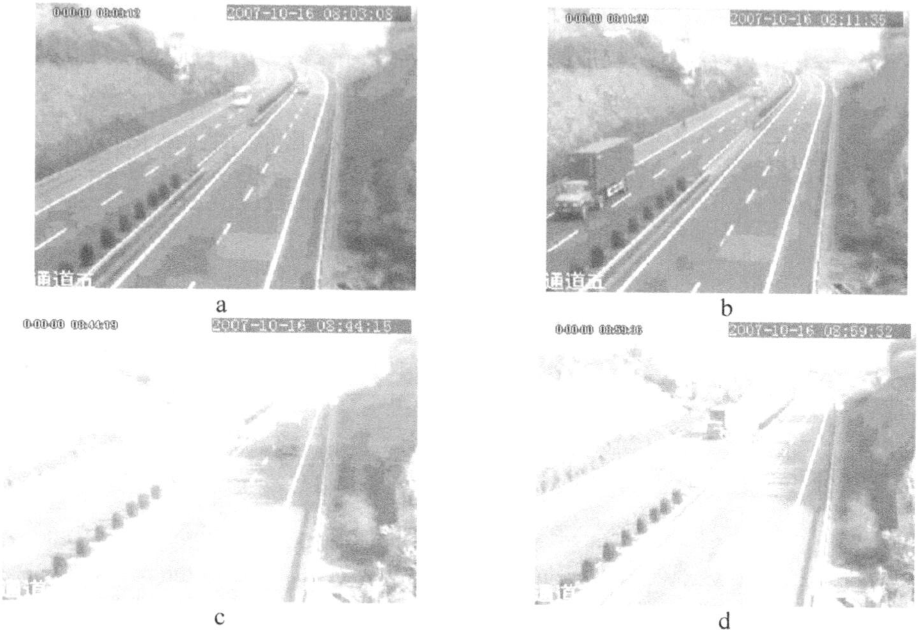


**Fig. 2.** The original video images

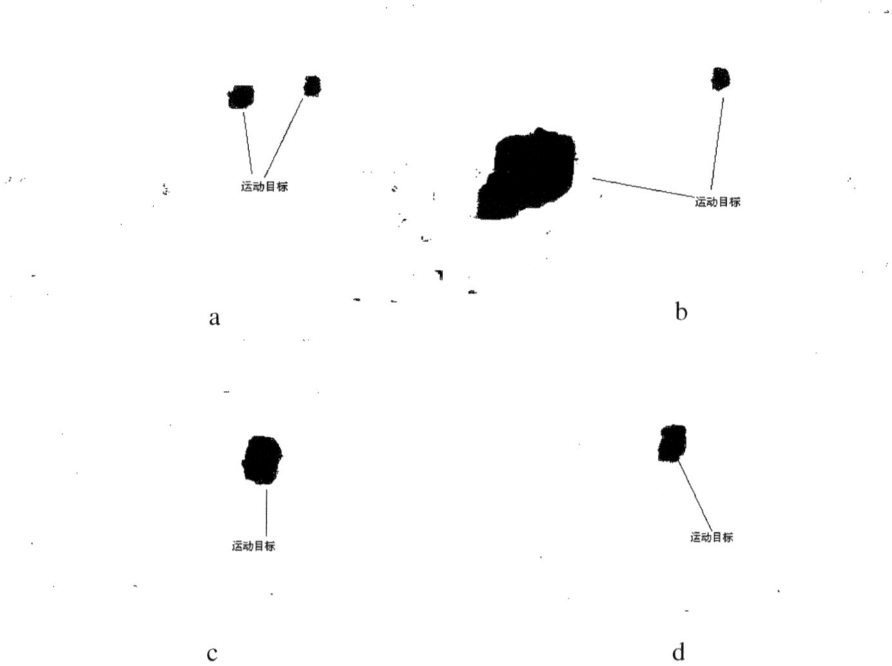


**Fig. 3.** The processed video image

## 5 Conclusions

The accurate and effective detecting can be realized with the method for detecting moving targets from traffic video based on the dynamic background model. The further research of ITS can be based on this. The following work is the feature extraction and tracking of moving targets. This can be applied to traffic management and replace the monitoring ways based on hardware such as vehicles' monitor.

## References

1. Foresti, G.L.: Object recognition and tracking for remote video surveillance. IEEE Transactions on Circuits and Systems for Video Technology 9(7), 1045–1062 (1999)
2. Stringa, E., Regazzoni, C.S.: Real-time video-shot detection for scene surveillance applications. IEEE Transactions on Image Processing 9(1), 69–79 (2000)
3. Stauffer, C., Crimson, W.: Learning patterns of activity using real-time tracking. IEEE Trans. Pattern Analysis and Machine Intelligence 22(8), 747–757 (2000)
4. Enkelmann, W.: Investigation of Multigrid Algorithms for the Estimation of Optical Flow Fields in Image Sequences. Computer Vision, Graphics and Image Processing 43, 150–177 (1998)
5. Kreucher, C., Kastella, K., Hero, A.O.: Multi-Target Tracking Using the Joint Multi-Target Probability Density. IEEE Transactions on Aerospace and Electronic Systems 41(4), 1396–1414 (2005)
6. Wenxiu, Z., et al.: Rough Set Theory and Method, pp. 17–25. Science publisher, Beijing (2001)
7. Yao, Y.Y.: Relational interpretations of neighborhood operators and rough set approximation. Information Sciences: An international Journal 111, 239–259 (1998)
8. Tsai, L.-W., Hsieh, J.-W., Fan, K.-C.: Vehicle detection using normalized color and edge map. In: IEEE International Conference on Image Processing (ICIP 2005), September 11–14 2005, vol. 2, pp. 598–601 (2005)
9. Jacques, J.C.S., Jung, C.R., Musse, S.R.: Background Subtraction and Shadow Detection in Grayscale Video Sequences Computer Graphics and Image Processing. In: 18th Brazilian Symposium on SIBGRAPI 2005, pp. 189–196 (2005)
10. Beynon, M.: Reducts within the variable precision rough sets model: A further investigation. European Journal of Operational Research 134, 592–605 (2001)
11. Youtian, D., Feng, C., Wenli, X.: Region-based moving shadow detection approach. Journal of Tsinghua University (Science and Technology) 1, 141–144 (2006)

# Real-Time Implementation for Weighted-Least-Squares-Based Edge-Preserving Decomposition and Its Applications

Qingfeng Li[1] and Hanli Zhao[2,*]

[1] College of Electron & Information Engineering, Ningbo University of Technology, Ningbo 315016, China
[2] College of Physics & Electronic Information Engineering, Wenzhou University, Wenzhou 325035, China
hanlizhao@gmail.com

**Abstract.** This paper presents a GPU-based implementation for constructing edge-preserving multiscale image decompositions. An input image is decomposed into a piecewise smooth base layer and multiple detail layers. The base layer captures large scale variations in the image, while the detail layers contain the small scale details. The detail layers are progressively obtained with the edge-preserving weighted least squares optimizations. The improvement of performance is achieved by introducing a Jacobi-like GPU solver, which converges to the right solution much faster than the standard Jacobi iterator. Note that the whole pipeline design is highly parallel, enabling a real-time implementation. Several experimental examples on edge-preserving tonal adjustment and image abstraction are shown to demonstrate the feasibility of the proposed method.

**Keywords:** Edge-preserving smoothing, detail enhancement, image abstraction, Jacobi, GPU.

## 1 Introduction

Edge-preserving image smoothing techniques play an important role in computer graphics community and image processing field. In computational photography, images are often decomposed into a piecewise smooth base layer and one more detail layers [3]. The base layer contains the larger scale variations in intensity obtained by an edge-preserving smoothing operator to the original image, while the detail layer is the difference between the original image and the base layer. As a result, the base image preserves the low-frequency structural information in the original image and the detail layer captures the high-frequency features.

The bilateral filter proposed by Tomasi and Manduchi [12] is one of the most commonly used edge-preserving smoothing techniques. The filter takes into consideration not only the spatial distance between pixels but also their range difference in intensity. Higher intensity difference leads to lower filtering weight, which

* Corresponding author

Z. Pan et al. (Eds.): Transactions on Edutainment VI, LNCS 6758, pp. 256–263, 2011.

**Fig. 1.** User interface of our interactive tonal adjustment

prevents the excessive smoothing of edge information effectively. However, in order to support stronger capability of smoothing, it is not enough to increase the spatial weight only and we must increase the range weight as well. Therefore, the edge information may be overly blurred when increasing the smoothing power.

In order to address the defect of the bilateral filtering, Farbman et al. [3] introduce a new image smoothing approach based on the weighted least squares optimization framework. The new operator is particularly well suited for progressive coarsening of images and for extraction of detail at various spatial scales. The solution to the weighted least squares is a linear system, requiring roughly 3.5 seconds per megapixel on a 2.2 GHz Intel Core 2 Duo CPU. Consequently, the optimization-based filter only process static images, which limits its application.

In this paper, we presents a new GPU-based implementation for constructing edge-preserving multiscale image decompositions (see Fig. 1). In particular, the improvement of performance is achieved by adopting a Jacobi-like GPU solver, which converges to the right solution much faster than the standard Jacobi iterator. Our method enables a real-time processing of online images and videos benefiting from the highly parallel pipeline design.

The rest of the paper is organized as follows. Section 2 briefly reviews some of previous work. Section 3 describe our approach in detail, while experimental results and applications are presented in Section 4. Finally, we conclude the paper in the last section.

## 2 Related Work

Several edge-preserving smoothing operators have been developed over the last decade. Anisotropic diffusion is a boundary finding intra-region smoothing method and is a gradual, time-dependent evolution of an image towards a piecewise-constant approximation. Tumblin and Turk [13] introduce a low curvature image simplifier (LCIS) inspired by anisotropic diffusion [10] and pioneered their use in tone mapping. However, the original diffusion scheme tends to over-sharpen edges.

Despite the recent improvements to anisotropic diffusion in the image processing context, most of applications employ the bilateral filter [12] as their non-linear smoothing filter. The filtered result in each pixel is a weighted mean of its neighbors, where the weights decrease both with spatial distance and with difference in range. In recent years, many approximate algorithms have been proposed in order to accelerate the filtering time. Chen et al. [2] introduce a new GPU-based bilateral grid to parallelize and linearize the computation in real time. The bilateral grid is a three-dimensional array combining the two-dimensional spatial domain with a one-dimensional range dimension. However, the bilateral filter trade off its smoothing capability with its edge-preserving capability. As the scale of the extracted detail features increases, the bilateral filter would blur over more edges.

Recently, Farbman et al. [3] introduce an alternative edge-preserving smoothing approach based on the weighted least squares optimization framework. The new operator is particularly well suited for constructing multiscale edge-preserving decompositions that progressively capture detail layers at a variety of scales. They use the multiresolution preconditioned conjugate gradient solver [11] to implement the optimization on the CPU. Unfortunately, the efficiency of 3.5 seconds per megapixel is reported in their paper. Therefore, their approach cannot achieve real-time performance and the user parameters must be prepared beforehand. Once the filtering result is not satisfactory, it must be restarted from scratch.

Several GPU-based systems have been proposed to allow the processing of online images or videos. For instance, Zhao et al. [16] extract the coherent lines using hardware-supported Direct3D shaders and achieve real-time flow-based video abstraction. NVIDIA's compute unified device architecture (CUDA) [9] enables more flexible control on the GPU and exposes many new hardware features for data-parallel computation. Our new algorithm is based on Farbman et al.'s weighted least squares optimization while real-time visual feedback is achieved.

## 3 Algorithm

Our goal is to develop a real-time edge-preserving image decomposition algorithm. In this section, we begin with the introduction of the weighted least squares and then present the acceleration scheme in detail.

### 3.1 Weighted Least Squares

For a given image $I$, the goal of edge-preserving smoothing is to produce a new image $F$, which, on the one hand, is as smooth as possible everywhere except the pixels with significant gradients in $I$, and at the same time, is as close as possible to $I$. The two possibly contradictory goals may be compromised as the minimization of an energy function [3]:

$$E(F) = \sum_p \left\{ (F_p - I_p)^2 + \lambda \left( a_{xp}(I)(\frac{\partial F}{\partial x})_p^2 + a_{yp}(I)(\frac{\partial F}{\partial y})_p^2 \right) \right\} \quad (1)$$

where $p$ is the two-dimensional location of a pixel in the image. The first term minimizes the range distance between $I$ and $F$, whereas the second term tries to minimize the partial derivatives of $I$. $\lambda$ is the coefficient for balancing between the two terms, while the spatial smoothness weights $a_x$ and $a_y$ are dependent on $I$.

The energy function $E(F)$ in Equation (1) can be rewritten using the matrix notation as the following:

$$E(F) = (F - I)^T(F - I) + \lambda(F^T D_x^T A_x D_x F + F^T D_y^T A_y D_y F) \quad (2)$$

where $D_x$ and $D_y$ are matrices of discrete partial differentiation operators in $x$ and $y$ directions respectively, and, $A_x$ and $A_y$ are diagonal matrices with each element containing the spatial smoothness weights $a_x$ and $a_y$ at $p$.

The smoothness weights are defined as the same manner in [6]:

$$a_{xp}(I) = (|L_x(I)|^\alpha + \epsilon)^{-1} \quad (3)$$

$$a_{yp}(I) = (|L_y(I)|^\alpha + \epsilon)^{-1} \quad (4)$$

Here $L(I)$ is the log-luminance of the input image $I$, and therefore, $L_x$ and $L_y$ are partial derivatives of the log-luminance. The exponent $\alpha$ is a parameter controlling the sensitivity to the gradient of $I$, while $\epsilon \leq 0.0001$ denotes a small constant for preventing division by zero.

Using the standard finite differences for the spatial derivatives, the minimization problem $\min\{E(F)\}$ is obtained by solving the linear system:

$$\mathbf{M}F = I \quad (5)$$

Here the matrix $\mathbf{M}$ is defined as:

$$\mathbf{M}_{ij} = \begin{cases} -\lambda(|L_i(I) - L_j(I)|^\alpha + \epsilon)^{-1} & j \in N_4(i); \\ 1 - \sum_{k \in N_4(i)} \mathbf{M}_{ik} & j = i; \\ 0 & \text{otherwise.} \end{cases} \quad (6)$$

For a color image, we first convert RGB color space to $l\alpha\beta$ color space [15] and apply the weighted least squares optimization on the luminance channel only, and then convert $l\alpha\beta$ color space back to RGB color space for final output.

### 3.2 Jacobi-Like Iterative Solver

From Equation (6), we can see that $\mathbf{M}$ is a symmetric positive definite sparse matrix. Thus Equation (5) can be solved iteratively using some efficient linear system solver.

Farbman et al. employ the preconditioned conjugate gradients (PCG) to solve Equation (5). In addition, their solver utilizes a multigrid-like approach [5,7] to speed the solution. A series of matrices $\mathbf{M}^0, \mathbf{M}^1, ..., \mathbf{M}^n$ are computed by progressively coarsening the image $I$. The resultant solution is obtained by progressively solving the PCG iterations at coarser level and then upsampling the intermediate solution to the finer level. Although such CPU-based implementation is highly optimized, it requires roughly 3.5 seconds per megapixel on a 2.2 GHz Intel Core 2 Duo CPU. Buatois et al. [1] describe a GPU implementation of a general PCG solver and report speedups by a factor of 3.2. However, the interactivity is also limited to low image resolutions with this GPU-based solver. Moreover, the convergence of PCG strongly depends on the choice of preconditioner.

Perhaps the simplest way to solve the linear equation is to use Jacobi iterations. However, this basic approach converges quite slowly and takes more than 20,000 iterations for a modest $512 \times 512$ pixel image. In this paper, we employ a fast Jacobi-like GPU solver, which is first introduced by Jeschke et al. [8]. Jeschke et al. present the new Jacobi-like Laplacian solver for real-time diffusion curve rendering and seamless image cloning but do not address the performance issue in edge-preserving image decomposition described in this paper. Now, let us describe why the Jacobi-like solver converges to the right solution much faster than the traditional Jacobi solvers.

For simplicity, assume $I$ and $F$ are one-dimensional images, and $\mathbf{M}$ is a Laplacian operator in the linear system Equation (5). Clearly, the converged solution is always linear. In the standard Jacobi solver, $N$ is the 1-pixel neighborhood. The interesting point is that $\mathbf{M}$ remains irreducibly diagonally dominant no matter where the off-diagonal elements are placed. Therefore, we can generalize $N$ to be the $h$-pixel neighborhood. If $F$ is the solution of the standard system and we run a single Jacobi iteration on the new system, any non boundary pixel $F_i$ will be $(F_{i-h} + F_{i+h})/2$ during the iteration. Since all three pixels lie on the same line by construction, the new solution is equal to $F_i$. As the result, the modified linear system has the same solution as the standard solver.

The direct two-dimensional extension is to use circular neighborhood. However, it is too slow for practice. So Jeschke et al. suggest reducing the number of neighbor pixels to only four in axis-aligned directions. To reduce artifacts similar to mach banding, we should successively shrink $h$ during the iteration. In our implementation, we enable users to specify the appropriate neighborhood size $h$ and then shrink it linearly in each step. As demonstrated in the paper [8], a few iterations (e.g., 8) are enough to approximate the right solution. Since each Jacobi-like step is highly parallel, the linear system solver can be implemented efficiently on the GPU. Jeschke et al. employ Microsoft HLSL to implement the solver, whereas we adopt NVIDIA CUDA instead. The main reason is that CUDA is an easy-to-code C-like programming language and avoids the rasterization for the image. In addition, we use Microsoft Direct3D 10 environment for rendering the resultant image.

## 4 Applications and Results

We have tested our GPU algorithm on a PC with an NVIDIA GeForce GTX 280 GPU with 1GB of graphics memory. Our system achieves 42 frames per second and 19 frames per second for smoothing a $1024 \times 1024$ pixel image with 20 and 50 Jacobi-like iterations, respectively. The reported timings include the color space conversion, the linear system construction and solution, and the result rendering. Contrarily, the solution to the weighted least squares requires roughly 3.5 seconds per megapixel on a 2.2 GHz Intel Core 2 Duo CPU. Obviously, our GPU-based algorithm is several times faster than Farbman et al's CPU-based approach. Such speedup enables use a real-time online image and video processing. Although Buatois et al. have implemented a GPU-based general PCG solver and reported 3-5 times faster than the CPU-based algorithm, the Jacobi-like linear solver employs larger step to achieve much faster convergence.

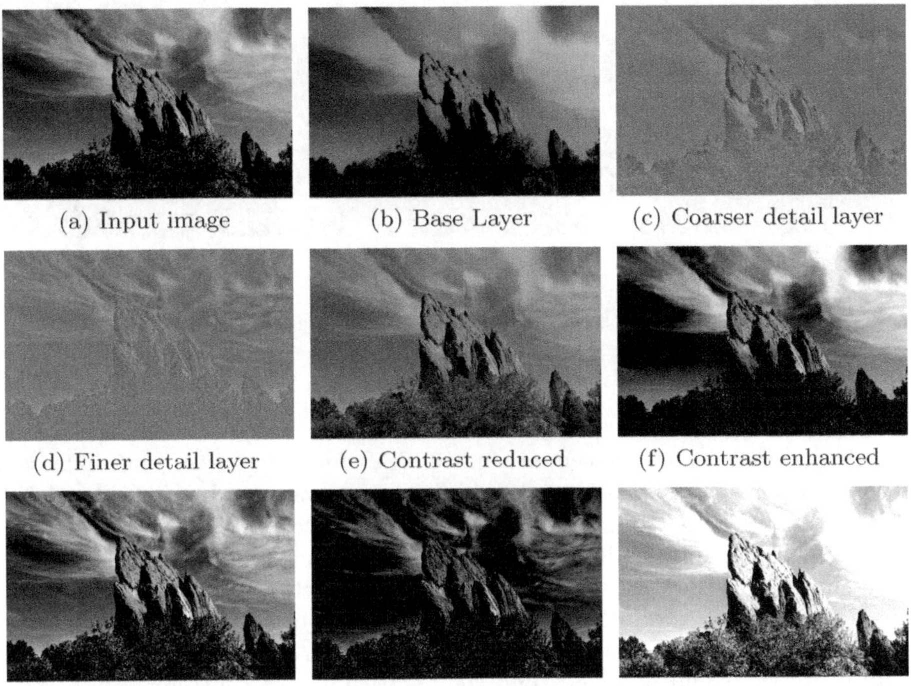

(a) Input image (b) Base Layer (c) Coarser detail layer
(d) Finer detail layer (e) Contrast reduced (f) Contrast enhanced
(g) Detail enhanced (h) Exposure decreased (i) Exposure increased

**Fig. 2.** Our tool interactively adjust the tonal values in the input image

We have designed an interactive multiscale tonal adjustment tool. We employ the proposed edge-preserving smoothing algorithm to progressively construct a three-level decomposition: a coarse base layer $b$ and two detail layers $d_1$, $d_2$. The result of the tonal adjustment at each pixel $p$ is:

$$I' = m + S(e \cdot b - m, t_0) + S(d_1, t_1) + S(d_2, t_2) \qquad (7)$$

where $m$ denotes the mean of the intensity range (0.5 for the normalized image), $e$ is the exposure of the base layer, $t_0$, $t_1$, and $t_2$ control the contrast of the three layers respectively, and $S$ is a simple linear function. Therefore, $t_1$ and $t_2$ can be used to smooth the image or to exaggerate the details at different scales. We show a variety of results in Fig. 2.

We have also implemented a real-time video abstraction system using our GPU-based edge-preserving smoothing filter. We use Zhao et al.'s coherent line extraction algorithm [16] to emphasize the high-contrast area and the edge-preserving smoothing filter to smooth the low-contrast pixels in images. In addition, Winnemöller et al.'s [14] luminance quantization algorithm is applied to improve the frame-to-frame coherence in videos. An example of the abstraction effect is shown in Fig. 3.

(a) Smoothed Tulip (b) Abstracted result (c) More coherent lines

**Fig. 3.** Abstraction effect for Tulip image in Fig. 1

## 5 Conclusions

In this paper, we have presented a novel real-time edge-preserving multiscale decomposition algorithm using a Jacobi-like linear system solver. The Jacobi-like GPU solver converges to the right solution much faster than the standard Jacobi iterator, which gains significant speedup of performance. Experimental results have shown that our proposed approach runs much faster than the state-of-the-art algorithm. Additionally, the applications on multiscale tonal adjustment and video abstraction demonstrate the feasibility of the proposed algorithm. In the future, we would like to extend the algorithm to various image processing techniques related to edge-preserving smoothing.

**Acknowledgments.** This work was supported by the Zhejiang Provincial Natural Science Foundation of China (Grant No. Y1110004), the Scientific Research Fund of Zhejiang Provincial Education Department, China (Grant No. Y201010070), the Science and Technology Plan Program of Wenzhou, China (Grant No. H20100088), and the Open Project Program of State Key Lab of CAD&CG, Zhejiang University, China (Grant No. A1117).

## References


1. Buatois, L., Caumon, G., Lévy, B.: Concurrent number cruncher: An efficient sparse linear solver on the GPU. In: Perrott, R., Chapman, B.M., Subhlok, J., de Mello, R.F., Yang, L.T. (eds.) HPCC 2007. LNCS, vol. 4782, pp. 358–371. Springer, Heidelberg (2007)
2. Chen, J., Paris, S., Durand, F.: Real-Time Edge-Aware Image Processing with the Bilateral Grid. ACM Transactions on Graphics, 26(3), Article 103 (2007)
3. Farbman, Z., Fattal, R., Lischinski, D., Szeliski, R.: Edge-Preserving Decompositions for Multi-scale Tone and Detail Manipulation. Proc. of ACM SIGGRAPH '08, ACM, article 67 (2008)
4. Fattal, R., Agrawala, M., Rusinkiewicz, S.: Multiscale Shape and Detail Enhancement from Multi-light Image Collections, Proc. of ACM SIGGRAPH '07, ACM, article 51 (2007)
5. Goodnight, N., Woolley, C., Lewn, G., Luebke, D., Humphreys, G.: A Multigrid Solver for Boundary Value Problems using Programmable Graphics Hardware. In: Proc. of EUROGRAPHICS/SIGGRAPH Workshop on Graphics Hardware 2003, pp. 102–111. EUROGRAPHICS Association (2003)
6. Lischinski, D., Farbman, Z., Uytendaele, M., Szeliski, R.: Interactive Local Adjustment of Tonal Values. ACM Transactions on Graphics 25(3), 646–653 (2006)
7. Ian, J.B., Farmer, I., Grinspun, E., Schroeder, P.: Sparse Matrix Solvers on the GPU: Conjugate Gradients and Multigrid. In: Proc. of ACM SIGGRAPH 2003, pp. 917–924. ACM, New York (2003)
8. Jeschke, S., Cline, D., Wonka, P.: A GPU Laplacian Solver for Diffusion Curves and Poisson Image Editing. In: Proc. of ACM SIGGRAPH Asia 2009, pp. 1–8. ACM, New York (2009)
9. NVIDIA Corp.: CUDA Programming Guid for CUDA Toolkit 3.0 (2010), `http://developer.nvidia.com/object/gpucomputing.html`
10. Perona, P., Malik, J.: Scale-Space and Edge Detection using Anisotropic Diffusion. IEEE Transactions on Pattern Analysis and Machine Intelligence 12(7), 629–639 (1990)
11. Press, W.H., Teukolsky, S.A., Vetterling, W.T., Flannery, B.P.: Numerical Recipies in C: the Art of Scientific Computing, pp. 871–888. Cambridge University Press, New York (1992)
12. Tomasi, C., Manduchi, R.: Bilateral Filtering for Gray and Color Images. In: Proc. of IEEE International Conference on Computer Vision (ICCV 1998), pp. 839–846 (1998)
13. Tumblin, J., Turk, G.: LCIS: A Boundary Hierarchy for Detail-Preserving Contrast Reduction. In: Proc. ACM SIGGRAPH 1999, pp. 83–90. ACM, New York (1999)
14. Winnemöller, H., Olsen, S., Gooch, B.: Real-Time Video Abstraction. ACM Transactions on Graphics 25(3), 1221–1226 (2006)
15. Wyszecki, G., Stiles, W.: Color Science: Concepts and Methods, Quantitative Data and Formulae. Wiley, New York (1982)
16. Zhao, H., Jin, X., Shen, J., Mao, X., Feng, J.: Real-time Feature-Aware Video Abstraction. The Visual Computer 24(7-9), 727–734 (2008)

# Author Index

GPSR Compliance

*The European Union's (EU) General Product Safety Regulation (GPSR) is a set of rules that requires consumer products to be safe and our obligations to ensure this.*

*If you have any concerns about our products, you can contact us on ProductSafety@springernature.com*

In case Publisher is established outside the EU, the EU authorized representative is:

Springer Nature Customer Service Center GmbH
Europaplatz 3
69115 Heidelberg, Germany

**Batch number: 10844619**

Printed by Printforce, the Netherlands